KING ZOG

SELF-MADE MONARCH OF ALBANIA

JASON TOMES

SUTTON PUBLISHING

First published in the United Kingdom in 2003 by
Sutton Publishing Limited

This paperback edition first published in 2007 by
Sutton Publishing, an imprint of NPI Media Group Limited
Cirencester Road · Chalford · Stroud · Gloucestershire · GL6 8PE

British Library Cataloguing in Publication Data
A catalogue record for this book is available from the British Library.

ISBN 978-0-7509-4439-7

Typeset in New Baskerville.
Typesetting and origination by
NPI Media Group Limited.
Printed and bound in England.

Contents

Ex-King Zog 1939–61

Preface

King Zog I of the Albanians was the most unusual European monarch of the twentieth century – a man entirely without royal connections who founded his own kingdom in 1928. Contemporaries hardly knew what to think. Their epithets for him range far and wide: 'the last ruler of romance'; 'a despotic brigand'; 'an appalling gangster'; 'a picturesque sub-monarch'; 'the modern Napoleon'; 'Mussolini's lackey'; 'perhaps the finest patriot of them all'; 'a small-size, indolent oriental potentate'; 'a reader of Shakespeare and a fine fighting man'; 'an *homme de salon* of first-rate intelligence'; 'an ignorant mountaineer'; 'ultimately an erratic and treacherous barbarian'; 'not at all an unpleasant character'; 'a Balkan product *par excellence*'; 'the ludicrous Zog'; 'Saviour of the Nation'; 'the father of his country'; 'frankly a cad'.

Certainly, in the eyes of foreigners, the sudden advent of this self-proclaimed king added to the mysteriousness of a land known chiefly for mountains, revolts, and blood feuds. However much the King desired to be identified with order and progress, his name was more often linked to cut-throat political intrigue. He confessed: 'My life is an adventure story.'[1]

His miniature court in Tirana briefly caught the imagination of the Western world in the 1930s, before Fascist Italy drove him into exile and postwar Stalinists kept him there. The communists then minimised the place in national history of a man who, by any objective standard, must rank as one of its foremost figures. For five decades, Albania was a closed country, synonymous with rigid Marxism–Leninism, but, as elsewhere in eastern Europe, the ending of the cold war has disclosed continuities with the pre-war past that totalitarianism concealed.

An editorial in *The Times* once referred to 'the bizarre King Zog adding a touch of unreality' to Albanian history.[2] This book should make him seem rather more real. And less bizarre? Like all of us, Zog was the product of a unique time and place. People who live in secure, stable countries, with well-defined frontiers and a tradition of government, are invited to set aside some of their assumptions about modern European monarchy.

ACKNOWLEDGEMENTS

The author wishes to thank all who have assisted him, especially: Chris Collins, Bejtullah Destani, Jason George, Christina Petsoulas, and Michael Thornhill for reading all or part of the manuscript; the late Teri Cooper, Roderick Bailey, Georges Doumergue, Rainer Egger, and John Umfreville for information; the Centre for Albanian Studies and Westrow Cooper for help with illustrations; and Robert Peberdy, Philip Waller, and Martin and Susan Tomes for their encouragement.

A NOTE ON ALBANIAN PRONUNCIATION

c	is pronounced	'ts' (as in 'bits')
ç		'ch' (as in 'church')
dh		'th' (as in 'these')
ë		'e' (as in 'term')
gj		'g' (as in 'region')
j		'y' (as in 'yet')
q		between 'ky' (as in 'stockyard') and 'ch' (as in 'church')
x		'dz' (as in 'adze')
xh		'j' (as in 'joke')
y		'u' (as in 'tune')

A NOTE ON MONEY

The Albanian gold franc was a gold-based currency. The exchange rate was fixed in 1925 at £1 = 25.2215 gold francs (= \$4.86). After Sterling went off the gold standard in 1931, the exchange rate fluctuated around £1 = 15 gold francs.

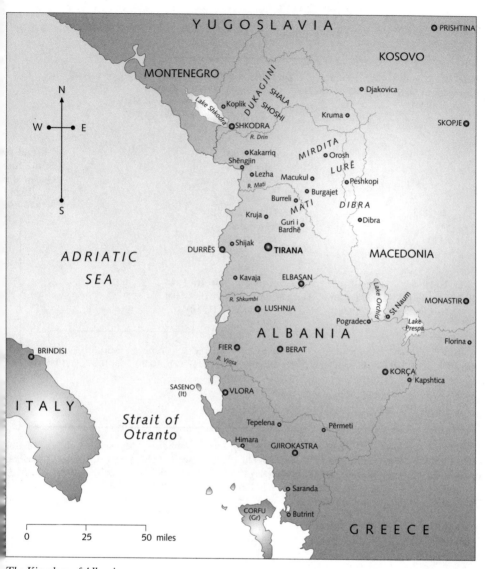

The Kingdom of Albania

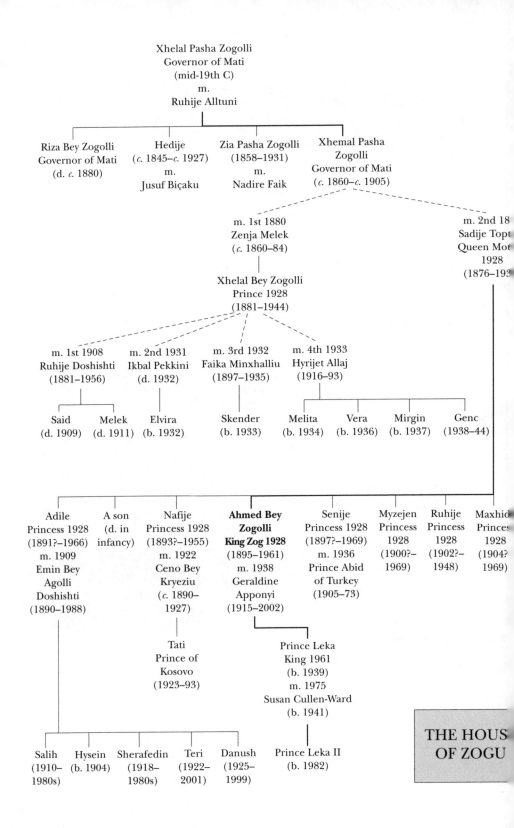

Xhelal Pasha Zogolli
Governor of Mati
(mid-19th C)
m.
Ruhije Alltuni

Riza Bey Zogolli
Governor of Mati
(d. c. 1880)

Hedije
(c. 1845–c. 1927)
m.
Jusuf Biçaku

Zia Pasha Zogolli
(1858–1931)
m.
Nadire Faik

Xhemal Pasha
Zogolli
Governor of Mati
(c. 1860–c. 1905)

m. 1st 1880
Zenja Melek
(c. 1860–84)

m. 2nd 18
Sadije Topt
Queen Mot
1928
(1876–193

Xhelal Bey Zogolli
Prince 1928
(1881–1944)

m. 1st 1908
Ruhije Doshishti
(1881–1956)

m. 2nd 1931
Ikbal Pekkini
(d. 1932)

m. 3rd 1932
Faika Minxhalliu
(1897–1935)

m. 4th 1933
Hyrijet Allaj
(1916–93)

Said
(d. 1909)

Melek
(d. 1911)

Elvira
(b. 1932)

Skender
(b. 1933)

Melita
(b. 1934)

Vera
(b. 1936)

Mirgin
(b. 1937)

Genc
(1938–44)

Adile
Princess 1928
(1891?–1966)
m. 1909
Emin Bey
Agolli
Doshishti
(1890–1988)

A son
(d. in
infancy)

Nafije
Princess 1928
(1893?–1955)
m. 1922
Ceno Bey
Kryeziu
(c. 1890–
1927)

Ahmed Bey
Zogolli
King Zog 1928
(1895–1961)
m. 1938
Geraldine
Apponyi
(1915–2002)

Senije
Princess 1928
(1897?–1969)
m. 1936
Prince Abid
of Turkey
(1905–73)

Myzejen
Princess
1928
(1900?–
1969)

Ruhije
Princess
1928
(1902?–
1948)

Maxhid
Princes
1928
(1904?–
1969)

Tati
Prince of
Kosovo
(1923–93)

Prince Leka
King 1961
(b. 1939)
m. 1975
Susan Cullen-Ward
(b. 1941)

Salih
(1910–
1980s)

Hysein
(b. 1904)

Sherafedin
(1918–
1980s)

Teri
(1922–
2001)

Danush
(1925–
1999)

Prince Leka II
(b. 1982)

THE HOUS
OF ZOGU

CHAPTER ONE

Prologue: An Audience

The most ignored country in Europe – that was Albania. By the 1930s, ferries were crossing daily from the heel of Italy and an Adria-Aero-Lloyd five-seater flew into Tirana airport three times a week, but the services were under-used and could not have run without subsidies. Here in the smallest of the Balkan states, foreigners remained so scarce as to be automatic celebrities. A respectable Englishman, Frenchman, or American who expressed a plausible interest in the country might find it comparatively easy to obtain an audience with its politician-king. There was even a story that Zog, when bored, would ring up hotels on the off-chance of finding a foreigner to fill an odd half-hour. His palace stood less than five minutes away and a common language could often be found. This King was not a cosmopolitan, but he spoke fluent Turkish, good German, and conversational French. English was not on offer; he refused to waste his time on a language of which only ten per cent followed the grammar.

A sentry with a gleaming 'Z' on his kepi escorted visitors through the red-brick gateway of the royal compound south-east of the central square. A secretary, Sotir Martini perhaps, or dapper aide-de-camp Zef Sereqi, would appear in the driveway with some tips on protocol. Then it was up a dozen steps into a square two-storey villa of yellow stucco, which had been built for a Turkish merchant before the war.

Led into a showy little reception salon, with gilded mirrors and Venetian chandeliers, the visitor saw the equerry peer around a curtain before drawing it back to expose a pair of glass doors. A brown-haired man instantly came into view, sitting alone at the far end of a long, well-lit room, sparsely furnished in the modern style with green zigzag-patterned wallpaper. The King appeared small and almost insignificant between the massive mahogany desk before him and the life-size portrait on the wall behind. The desktop was uncluttered and highly polished. The painting showed a stern middle-aged woman of no very regal appearance.

The visitor entered and stifled a cough. There was always a fog of cigarette smoke and rarely a window open. He bowed three times (as instructed) and advanced with careful steps. The unwary had occasionally come to grief in the archipelago of decorative rugs strewn across the shining floor. As he neared the desk, his eyes would be drawn to the most extravagant feature in view: the King's moustache. Though far from big, it was normally waxed and curled into neat little points.

The temptation to stare had to be resisted as the King rose smoothly and uttered a few words of greeting in a low clear voice. His height was an inch or two over six feet, his bearing erect, and his figure slender and narrow-hipped. He was sure to be immaculately turned out: a grey double-breasted pin-stripe suit from Savile Row, a white shirt from Sulka of Paris, gleaming shoes handmade in Italy. A calm smile accompanied his firm handshake, and the visitor took a seat.

'A cigarette?'

With a languid gesture, the King offered a selection of brands from boxes on his desk. He invariably took one himself (begging leave of any non-smoker), and, as lighter and cigarette-holder momentarily engaged him, the visitor might scan the royal countenance. It was a long pale pinkish face, not Mediterranean in complexion, tapering from a slightly broad brow to a narrow chin. The forehead was high, and would have been higher but for long strands of hair combed over from the left. Then, strange to say, the chin was weaker than it looked in official photographs. More distinguished was the long straight nose, which in profile merged with the forehead in one continuous line. Exceptionally sloping eyebrows imposed a lugubrious long-suffering expression which was sympathetic and mildly comical. The visitor began to ask himself if this genteel 38-year-old could really be the ruthless mountain chieftain who had scattered his rivals and founded a kingdom.

Zog sat back in his chair and smiled again slowly, as if letting his visitor into a secret known only to himself. Despite the air of tiredness about him, the grey-blue eyes were alert. 'Fire away with your indiscreet questions,' he laughed, before proceeding to give impeccably discreet answers.

Why did he transform Albania from a republic to a monarchy a few years ago?

'There was but one reason. The change was made in accordance with the spirit and wish of the Albanian people whose political foundation had ever been its division into chieftainships or baronies, each of which recognised a supreme chief over itself'.[1] His tone of voice sounded unexpectedly juvenile; a kind of adolescent reserve dispelled any earlier suggestion of a lounge-lizard. 'The only difference it has made to me,' he added with a droll grimace, 'is that instead of working seven or eight hours a day, I now work eighteen and I carry the responsibility of the whole State. I am only a single workman doing my job. That is all kingship means to me.'[2]

The King would surely not deny that Albania had very serious economic problems. How could so poor a nation afford a royal family?

This objection was gently waved aside. 'Financially, a king will not cost the country a penny more than a president.' Both of them required a palace. Both had to be guarded. With yet another smile – tinged with an irrelevant hint of romantic melancholy – Zog referred to the gorgeous white and gold uniform popularly associated with him. That was bought before he took the throne: 'When I was President, I had to dress the part, but the poorest Albanian has a sense of royalty, and now that I am their King it is not necessary to emphasise it in any way.'[3]

In some subtle manner, he seemed to be appealing for approval, even for intimacy. He affected a confidential tone at variance with the impersonal content of his answers, and he kept his eyes squarely on his guest, oblivious to the gaggle of aides peering through the glass doors.

It was generally a great mistake to think of monarchy as a luxury, he continued. 'In adopting the regime most congenial to the country, Albania is guaranteed greater internal stability, which in turn will assure greater foreign support.' A Balkan republic had simply been an anomaly. Of course, the King of the Albanians laid no claim to Divine Right. He was a constitutional monarch who realised that his power came from the people.

Did that imply a free and democratic regime?

Zog was about to shake his head in assent, when he recalled that foreigners had the confusing habit of nodding their heads when they meant yes and shaking them when they meant no. He forced himself to nod. 'As King of my people, I shall have no interest as to which political party obtains the upper hand by constitutional methods. This will help educate the people along democratic lines, as in the United States, and will insure greater freedom for all.'[4]

Were there political parties in Albania?

Not at present in a formal sense, he confessed. For the moment, the King of the Albanians had still to be the leader and teacher of his people. Genuine political development takes time. 'One cannot teach a child of five in the same way that one would a young man who has come of age. Only as the fight against illiteracy goes on can the powers and responsibilities of the people's elected representatives be increased.'[5] Good progress had been made in education, he pointed out. Not long ago, there were only two thousand children in school. Today the figure was nearer sixty thousand.

When would Albanian women gain equal political rights?

'The high status of women is one of the greatest factors in the strength of a State,' declared Zog with emphasis. 'I think I shall feel the greatest mission of my life accomplished when the status and culture of women in Albania is raised, first to that which obtains in the other Balkan States and then to that held by women in the Western world.'[6] Political rights were only one part of that process. 'I want to educate the women but also to teach them to be good mothers and house-managers. I want Albanian women to be good women like her.' He turned in his chair and made the slightest of bows to the portrait hanging on the wall behind him – the only picture in the room in fact. 'She is my mother,' he explained with feeling, and paused for an instant to collect his thoughts and light another cigarette.[7] Polygamy and infant betrothal had already been abolished and soon the veil would be too. 'It will be a long process, because we have a great deal of prejudice to get over, and before it is accomplished, the vote for women will come.'[8] Female suffrage was new to even the most advanced societies, remember.

'We are centuries behind the rest of Europe in civilisation,' remarked the King with a frown.[9] Anyone could see that most of his subjects were ignorant and backward. It was not their fault. Turkish rule up until 1912 had preserved in them the sentiments, morals, and farming methods of the Middle Ages. If the visitor travelled in the mountains, he would be shocked by some of the poorest living conditions in Europe. 'I feel very ashamed of it sometimes,' he sighed. 'Our only excuse is that we cannot do everything at once.'[10] Five hundred years of stagnation had somehow to be reversed. 'It is my determination to civilise my people and make them as far as possible adopt Western habits and customs.'[11] The blood feud might still prevail in parts of the kingdom, alas, but law and order had recently made great strides. The King drily observed that he was himself the object of dozens of feuds – and not one had yet succeeded.

At some point in the interview, Zog was likely to put down his cigarette and bend forward slightly with a reflective look in his eyes. Laying his delicate white hands on the desktop, he spoke softly and very earnestly: 'I will remain ever true to the interests of Albania and to the welfare of her people, even if it demands the sacrifice of my life. If these words belie my acts, then all I have done so far for my country is a sham.'[12]

Anybody still not won over to Zog by this stage probably never would be. Either way, the courteous visitor wished him well in his mission. Minister of the Interior at twenty-four, Prime Minister at twenty-seven, President at twenty-nine, King at thirty-two – he had clearly worked hard to consolidate the Albanian nation.

The gratified sovereign would then compliment the visitor on his perspicacity. Foreign governments were sadly not always so quick to appreciate the value of his labours. Albania was a small country, about half as big again as Wales or the state of New Jersey: 210 miles long and less than 90 wide. But Zog insisted that its position at the entrance of the Adriatic Sea gave it great strategic importance. 'Albania's independence is essential to the peace of Europe,' he asserted.[13] It should be a permanent neutral state like Switzerland. Could not the comparison be taken further? It was his hope that fine new roads and hotels would one day turn his 'Cinderella' land into a top tourist destination, offering both Alpine ski-slopes and Mediterranean sands.[14]

In conclusion, Zog thanked his visitor most politely for taking the trouble to explore Albania. 'Come back if you can in a few years, and see what vast changes will have taken place.'[15] He expressed his own desire to travel abroad as soon as his country was placed on a firm foundation. If the visitor were British, he might add that a trip to the Scottish Highlands was his priority, as there appeared to be a strong resemblance between the Highland clansman and the Albanian. Then he looked on benignly as his new friend retreated backwards with an effort to avoid skidding on the rugs and kicking the gigantic spittoons near the door. The audience was over.

People usually left feeling happy. They said that here at least was a monarch to whom it was possible to speak with full frankness. Zog was at his best *tête-à-tête*. He had a knack of making his visitors think that he agreed with their sentiments entirely. This was often all that was needed to convince them that Albania possessed a ruler of exceptional wisdom and intelligence. Even those who realised that the King tailored his answers to suit their opinions granted that he must be clever to do it so well. And he flirted fascinatingly, distracting all but the sharpest interviewers from the fact that this technique betokened caution rather than confidence. No one met King Zog and still took him for a joke, but nearly everyone was struck by his incongruity. 'Rather like a smaller edition of our Mr Eden,' observed one British visitor. 'An Oxford don who has seen service in the army,' suggested another.[16] 'He *was* really tall, dark, handsome and intelligent,' exclaimed a press photographer. 'It was just like covering an ordinary film star.'[17]

Albania had been reckoned ungovernable until this slight, graceful, and rather pathetic figure established himself. He was reputed to be a warrior-king, but he gave no impression of force. Could it be true that he once had seven horses shot under him in battle? That he arranged the murder of his brother-in-law? That he drew a gun and fired back at assassins outside the Vienna opera house?

Effete urbanity and suave evasive words were only one side of King Zog I of the Albanians, alias Ahmed Zogu, alias Ahmed Bey Zogolli. One afternoon the King and his retinue were driving along the mountain road to Durrës. They had earlier stopped for a picnic lunch at which wine was served. The chauffeur had imbibed freely. Consequently the car was veering erratically from side to side, its wheels several times slipping on the edge of the precipice. Terrified courtiers begged the King to change driver, but Zog saw no need for that. Instead he took out his revolver, put it to the neck of the chauffeur, and said, 'Now drive slowly or I shall kill you.'[18] The chauffeur sobered up instantly and completed the journey with the utmost care. He knew the other side of King Zog.

CHAPTER TWO

The Star of Mati

'Thus from obscurity, a guiding star rose from out of Mati which was to extend its rays of erudition and calmness over an entire nation.'[1] This authorised version of the life-story was certainly true in one respect: by the standards of monarchy in the twentieth century, the background of King Zog was obscure. How could it be otherwise? Conventional monarchs are born to celebrity; he declared himself royal as an adult, and no one had chronicled his youth for posterity. Nor did anyone rush to do so on his attaining national fame aged twenty-four. Ninety per cent illiteracy was a decisive factor here. The number of Albanian printing presses did increase during his reign, but they operated under his supervision – and the approved line was not subtle. A sketch of his life published in Tirana in 1937 aimed to acquaint readers with 'the rare virtues which our adored King possesses' by showing 'the characteristics of his great soul in their true historic forms'.[2] Meanwhile, David Maitland-Makgill-Crichton, a would-be independent biographer, faced first obstruction from the palace and then such intrusive 'assistance' that he abandoned the project. Over-inquisitive interviewers were easily deflected: 'I don't consider it good form to talk about myself. Let us talk about something more important – perhaps my country.'[3]

This monopoly on information was doubtless advantageous for a king who rose from the people, but his fall from power in 1939 did not release a flood of revelations. When others took control of Albania, it was a brave (or foolish) citizen who spoke of the old regime at all except in stock derogatory phrases. Freedom of speech had to wait another fifty years.

These constraints make contemporary foreign sources the more important, yet they are often unreliable. Albanian news filtered out through Rome, Belgrade, or Athens, acquiring a political bias in the process. To wilful misrepresentation was added much innocent confusion, as Albanian spelling was irregular, and various equivalents were used for local names. Korça, Korcë, Korcha, Kortcha, Korytsa, Koritza, Coritza, and Corizza were all one town in southern Albania (not to be muddled with Konitza). Dates of birth and death were arguable in a land without civil registration. Albanians of different faiths used different calendars. Numbers themselves could be inexact where 'five' was sometimes used to mean a few and 'a hundred' meant a lot.

Even in the inter-war years, diplomats complained of events in Tirana being obscured by 'a regular Albanian fog'.[4] That fog was much thicker over the northern mountains at the turn of the century. There facts blurred into legend with amazing speed, and the happenings of three generations back could be as uncertain as ancient history. Zog was a contemporary of Edward VIII, Duke of Windsor, but at times it can seem as if closer parallels might be found with the boyhood of Charlemagne. In a thousand years, Albania had probably experienced less change than anywhere else in Europe. Turkish conquest in the later Middle Ages had detached all Balkan peoples from the European mainstream. The Renaissance, Reformation, and Enlightenment touched them only indirectly if at all. They spoke of 'Europe' as something remote.

The isolation of Albania had been especially severe. Sheer geographical inaccessibility separated much of the country from the rest of the Balkan Peninsula. Between the Montenegrin massif and the Pindus mountains lay a relentless succession of high and jagged ranges divided by narrow river valleys. A few towns near the sea, like Shkodra, Durrës, and Vlora, appeared on maps under their Italian names of Scutari, Durazzo, and Valona, but it was rare for any foreigner to pass beyond the marshy coastal plain. Most of the landscape was as wild as on the day it was created, with towering scarps and scree-choked gulleys, and snow-capped peaks which sent narrow streams hurtling down over rocky beds. A highway might be a crumbling ledge 9 inches wide above a drop of 1,000 feet. The lonely peaks and virgin forests did attract the occasional brave romantic in the nineteenth century, but two hard facts discouraged regular contact: the majority of Albanians had neither goods to sell nor money to buy; and they were said to be exceptionally fierce.

Travellers who did penetrate as far as the plain of Mati yet found relief from the starker northern highlands. Mati, named after its river, was one of the broadest, longest, and most populous mountain valleys. Squat stone towers, square and white, dotted the green landscape, about a quarter-of-a-mile apart. Each was home to an extended family of anything up to fifty. Animals and poultry occupied the ground floor and the people lived above. Women and men were segregated in all but the poorest households, and only the female quarters had windows of any size. There was no agglomerated village in Mati, no road, no shop, and no school.

Men in white fezzes and embroidered jackets squatted on the ground outside their homes and conversed in high-pitched voices, telling riddles and gambling with bullets for stakes. Each had to hand his most precious possession: a Mauser or Martini rifle, or else an ancient flintlock, its butt elaborately chased with silver. Wealth hereabouts was computed in guns. Now and then, one of the men would stand, hitch up his sagging white felt trousers, and patrol the perimeter of the house, keeping his eyes on the mountainous horizon: the Baza range to the west, Dejë to the east, Martenesh further south. The outside world knew such warriors only by repute. A Turk given to sudden rages was said to possess 'an Albanian temper'. A stubborn Greek was 'an Albanian-head'. An Italian who feigned stupidity 'played the Albanian'. It was scarcely reassuring that the mountaineers proverbially protested: 'The devil is not so wicked as people believe, neither is the Albanian.'[5]

While the fighting men of Mati stood guard, the women ground maize and cooked over an open fire. Their long black bell-shaped skirts were made of heavy homespun wool. Necklaces of old silver coins clinked against their metal-plated belts, six inches wide and studded with nails. The maize bread would be eaten with white cheese and green peppers and washed down with salted goats' milk. Other women periodically trudged up to the house laden with water from the river, brushwood from the forest, and fresh bracken for bedding. In this land, a polite greeting to a lady was 'Strength to your arms!', for Albanian clansmen scorned to be burdened by anything but a weapon.

In the distance, towards the east of the plain, was a gentle isolated hill, well-covered with mulberry and chestnut trees. On its crest stood a solid rectangular building with two small wings facing into a courtyard. This was Castle Burgajet, citadel of the chieftain of Mati. Although not vast, it was the biggest house for miles and the only one with glazed windows. The interior was even more distinctive. Most Albanians sat cross-legged on rugs in bare white-washed rooms, but to step inside the castle living-room was to enter the nineteenth century in all its fussiness. Fancy furnishings, imported from Austria, had recently become the hallmark of wealth. Salon chairs, draperies, table-lamps, and bric-a-brac, such as survived the pack-horse trail, transformed old stone chambers into lodgings fit for a modern-day chief.

It was here in the women's rooms at Burgajet that nineteen-year-old Sadije Zogolli (*née* Toptani) gave birth to a son on 8 October 1895. Naturally, the boy, called Ahmed Muhtar, was cause for profound rejoicing. Albanian women were not proud of their beauty but of the number and merit of their sons. Though no one could know it at the time, Sadije would have to concentrate on quality rather than quantity. Her first boy had died in infancy a couple of years earlier. Her six other children were destined to be girls. She raised them all with a fine combination of iron discipline and affectionate care. 'Only donkeys get slapped,' she would say; 'children you talk to, to show them their mistake.'[6] Ahmed, only son of a Muslim mother, was inevitably the centre of attention. Reputedly, he had been born with a caul, considered a sign of future greatness. 'Happy are the people,' exclaimed his father, 'for this son of mine will bring them great happiness.'[7] Xhemal Zogolli Pasha had been Hereditary Governor of Mati since the murder of his half-brother, Riza Bey, ten or fifteen years earlier. By restoring order and unity, he won the respect of the clan and, now in his thirties, this sharp-featured man with melancholy eyes was conscious of his duty to perpetuate a fabled family history.

Old songs related how the Zogolli had come to preside in Mati over four hundred years ago, shortly after the Turks first conquered Albania. A warrior from a village called Zogaj chanced to be crossing the valley at the time of a Turkish outrage. Gazi Bey, an Ottoman official set on humiliating the families of Mati, ordered that their unmarried daughters must come and dance naked before him. Horrified at this, the young man from Zogaj inspired the Mati to fight for their honour. The evil Gazi Bey was slain, and a grateful chief rewarded the stranger with the hand of his daughter in marriage. An alternative story, sometimes repeated by foreigners, concerns a putative German duke (i.e. *Herzog*), who settled in Mati after the crusades, dropping the *Her* and keeping the *Zog*. This sounds like journalistic invention. By contrast, the man from Zogaj followed Albanian custom when he used his village as a surname. The form Zogolli incorporated a corruption of the Turkish suffix *-oglu*, meaning 'son of'.

Zog the Great (as he became known) was most likely a Roman Catholic on his arrival in the valley. Either he or his successor converted to Islam in order to appease the Turks, for, by the time of his grandson, Zog the Small, the head of the family was recognised as Hereditary Governor of Mati. This expedient change of faith was not at all exceptional. 'Where the sword is, there lies religion', states an Albanian proverb. The Ottomans imposed a poll tax on Christians and especially persecuted Catholics. In course of time, nearly three-quarters of Albanians had opted to become Muslims. Most were Sunni, like the Turks, but a minority belonged to the heterodox Bektashi sect. Islam was strongest in the central regions. In the south, the Greek Orthodox Church kept Christianity alive. The far north (outside Shkodra) stayed nominally Roman Catholic, because all it ever saw of the Turks was an occasional punitive raid.

Religion was seldom a cause of conflict in itself. Islam and Christianity alike sat lightly on peasants steeped in pagan lore. Crucifixes and verses from the Koran were used like amulets and spells, and it was not unknown for people to go to the mosque on Friday and the church on Sunday. In Mati, there were a few hodjas to be seen, in black robes and turbans, but women went about unveiled, and the mosques looked just like the houses. The religious tolerance (or laxity) of the average Albanian exasperated zealots of all faiths.

King Zog liked to emphasise that adherence to Islam had not turned his ancestors into Ottoman puppets. Far from it, they had always fought to defend their privileges and avoid paying taxes. Back in 1633, Sultan Murad IV had taken the head of Abdullah Bey Zogolli for raising a revolt against him. (At least, that is how Zogists presented it – others believed that Abdullah's crime was plundering of lowland towns, but rebellion and brigandage could be difficult to distinguish.) In the 1850s, Ahmed's grandfather, Xhelal Zogolli Pasha, had striven to win more autonomy for Mati. The Turks interned him in Istanbul for intriguing with foreign powers after he appealed to the Emperor of Austria.

It was nevertheless on the maternal side that King Zog could claim his most illustrious forebear. Connections between leading families were intricate and no two accounts of the detail are the same, but Sadije traced her ancestry back to a woman named Mamica of Kruja. She was the sister of Gjergj Kastrioti Skanderbeg, who may himself have come from the region of Mati. There was no more famous name in Albanian history.

Born Gjergj Kastrioti around 1405, the legendary patriot was taken as a tribute child to be reared as a Muslim and trained for the Ottoman army. He covered himself with glory fighting for the Turks, and to his Islamic name Iskandar was added the honorific title *bey* (or *beg*). The Sultan appointed him Governor of Kruja, but in 1443 he mutinied, reverted to Catholicism, and declared himself ruler of Albania. Allied with Hungarians and Venetians, Skanderbeg resisted the Turks for twenty-five years, and his victories against tremendous odds won him an enduring place in European history. But, as so often with a military genius, his legacy proved unsustainable. Skanderbeg died of fever in 1468, and independence was lost within a decade, despite the efforts of his heirs. This did not deter later Albanian patriots from regarding this quarter-century of conflict as the golden age of the nation. King Zog would one day have his people believe that the spirit of Skanderbeg lived again in him.

Since the fifteenth century, the Turks had managed to uphold a tenuous and uneven suzerainty over Albania. The south was more firmly under the yoke. Feudal lords called beys owned big estates and enhanced their fortunes by collecting taxes for the Turkish authorities. Many a southern peasant was held in virtual serfdom, yet there were also towns and some small-scale commerce. The north remained tribal and undeveloped, and its chieftains paid only lip-service to the Sultan.

Mati was on the northern edge of central Albania, on the margin of effective Turkish oversight, and consequently somewhere between the two social systems. Its people were Sunni Muslims led by bey landowners yet they kept many elements of tribal organisation. Though the valley was home to maybe forty thousand people, power in Mati was exercised by five established families (Celaj, Olomani, Bogshixh, Sknjeri, and Zogolli), since society took the form of a strict hierarchy. Every settlement, district, and clan recognised the authority of a designated head whose rule was near-absolute. Below the chieftain came the elders, below the elders were masters of households, and at the base of the pyramid each husband controlled his wife and children (with the right to kill them in certain situations).

Thus Xhemal Zogolli Pasha, father of King Zog, governed his Mati followers as an autocrat – and yet not as a tyrant. At each level, Albanians accepted subordination to their superior on the understanding that he would exercise his authority in line with the unwritten law. In most districts, this oral code of custom was known as the Canon of Lek Dukagjini or the Law of Lek. Lek Dukagjini, a contemporary of Skanderbeg, was the hero-chieftain supposed to be its author. In reality, the Canon had evolved over centuries with many local variations, and the version followed in Mati was usually attributed to Skanderbeg himself. Rooted in ancient moral notions of honour and shame, the Canon provided a thousand rulings on almost every aspect of life from accidental parricide to haircutting. Leaders like Zogolli Pasha expounded this law and settled disputes on the basis of precedent.

It follows that in the local context – and that was the one which mattered most – Ahmed Zogolli was born into a ruling family and brought up at the centre of power. One of his first memories, indeed, was of creeping into the gallery of the hall at Burgajet to listen to his father in conclave with the elders. A pale child with a serious countenance, he expressed himself with unnerving maturity. Bored by the fairy-tales told in the women's quarters, from the age of three, Ahmed was already accompanying his father on tours of inspection, perched up before him on the horse. He watched Xhemal resolving quarrels and learnt to help his father by recounting things he overheard which people had thought him too young to understand. Grazing rights, boundary stones, and sheep-stealing were typical concerns. The chieftain punished lesser offences by confiscating a cow or burning down a house. However, when the crime was grave or raised questions of honour, the obligation lay with individuals and families to exact the retribution that justice demanded. In most foreign books about Albania, the Canon of Lek means one thing only: the blood feud.

No people in the Balkans was more attached to feuding. On hearing that a man was dead, the normal inquiry in the highlands was not 'What did he die of?' but 'Who killed him?'[8] In certain valleys, feuds accounted for a quarter of male deaths, as even fairly trivial offences (to foreign eyes) might demand blood, and each man in the offender's family became a legitimate target. It was not unknown for twenty to die before honour was satisfied.

This was one reason why men lingered around the homestead and left distant work to women. Although revenge might be taken for the killing of a mother, sister, wife, or daughter, females themselves were free from the obligations and dangers of a feud. It was quite acceptable to shoot an unsuspecting man in the back if his family were 'at blood', but the Canon precluded an attack on his womenfolk. Similarly, a man escorting a woman need have no fear. A multiplicity of rules governed feuding, dictated not so much by chivalry as by self-preservation. People so given to bloodshed needed to define safe circumstances, or life would have been impossible.

The shortcomings of the Canon grew even more apparent when disputes arose between men of different clans. On each side, the chief might summon a formal assembly by sending a man around his district beating on a drum. The elders then gathered in the open air at the customary place in order of precedence. If they judged their own man to be the injured party, and mediation failed, the ensuing feud might become localised war. A man could not ignore a summons to arms if he wished to keep his good name.

The chief led his warriors in battle, but it paid him to be a diplomat as well as a judge and general. Clans sometimes agreed to limit fighting to specific seasons of the year or times of the day, or their chieftain could negotiate a *besa* (an oath of peace whose contravention incurred extreme dishonour). A besa permitted erstwhile foes to unite against a common enemy and also provided opportunities to affiance infants and the yet unborn, as men did not marry within their clan. The Mati usually picked their wives from the neighbouring Muslims of Dibra and Lurë, giving a cow or four or five sheep in exchange.

As the son of a local ruler, Ahmed Zogolli steeped himself from an early age in the delicate business of the blood feud and besa. Authentic Albanian politics knew no higher form. The State was an unfamiliar concept. The Turks periodically extorted tax, but there was nothing at all to show for it. In public matters great and small, military and civil, ordinary people looked no further than their chief or their bey. Only a handful of rich magnates from the south – beys with second homes in Istanbul – really felt part of the Ottoman Empire.

Thus Albania was not a single political community or even a clearly defined geographical area. There were Albanians, about one-and-a-half million of them, living in the Ottoman provinces of Shkodra, Janina, Kosovo, and Monastir. They called themselves *Shqiperi* in the (probably fanciful) belief that this word meant 'Sons of the Eagle'. Centuries of living in isolated communities produced marked regional differences, and there was one notable ethnic divide. Albanians north of the River Shkumbi tended to be tall, fair, and dour, and they were known as Ghegs. The Mati were of this type. Southern Albanians, or Tosks, were stereotypically short, dark, and animated. Language did unite them, for Gheg and Tosk dialects were basically similar, yet Albanian had only just started to be reduced to writing for everyday purposes, and the literary pioneers were at odds. Some used Latin letters and some Greek, while others wrote in Arabic script (as used for Turkish until 1928). The Ottoman authorities did not want Albanian written at all: schools were forbidden to teach it.

Thus it was easy for the rest of the world to overlook the Albanians, given that the Ottoman Empire categorised subjects by religion only. Muslim Albanians were labelled Turks and Orthodox Albanians assumed to be Greeks. At the Congress of Berlin (1878), Bismarck insisted: 'There is no Albanian nationality.'[9] Partisans of Serbia and Bulgaria emphasised that Albanians volunteered to fight on the Turkish side in Balkan wars. What sort of oppressed nationality assisted its oppressors?

Albanians believed themselves to be the aborigines of the Balkans, beside whom all other Europeans were newcomers. Their ancestors do appear to have occupied the same mountain valleys throughout recorded history. They were sometimes identified with the semi-mythical Pelasgians (mentioned by Homer) or the ancient Illyrians. Whatever their origins, Albanians had never paid much heed to those who successively claimed to rule over them: Greeks, Romans, Byzantines, Normans, Serbs, Bulgars, Venetians, and then Turks. In places where the state meant nothing, who cared if the state were foreign?

One invasion, however, may have made more of an impression on the Albanian collective memory. The influx of Slavs into the Balkans in the sixth century had been less a military conquest than a mass migration from across the Danube. The precursors of the Albanians found themselves beleaguered in the highlands of the west, where they fought hard to keep such land as remained to them. A millennium later, Albanians still found the idea of being conquered by Slavs particularly objectionable. Some went so far as to say that Albanian and Slav were like cat and dog, if only in reaction to the growing national assertiveness of their Slav neighbours. If Turks would help defend them from Serbs and Montenegrins, Albanians were ready to acknowledge Turkish overlordship.

Such reasoning helps to explain why Albania was apparently unmoved by the tide of Balkan nationalism. The nineteenth century had transformed south-eastern Europe with the creation of Greece, Serbia, Romania, and Bulgaria as modern states, but the majority of Albanians seemed as content (or discontent) with Turkish rule in 1900 as they had been a hundred years earlier. The handful of brave intellectuals who wanted to teach in the Albanian language were clearly cultural nationalists, yet even they eschewed early independence, knowing that the fall of the Ottoman Empire would probably entail their 'liberation' by Slavs.

When Ahmed Zogolli was an infant, therefore, no one could have imagined that he would grow up to be King of Albania. Very few people could have envisaged a Kingdom of Albania at all.

13

CHAPTER THREE

Young Ahmed

Though a throne was not in prospect, the auspicious Ahmed might have been born heir to a chieftainship. He was not quite, for his mother was the second wife of Xhemal Pasha. Zenja, the late first wife, had given him a son fourteen years before. This boy, Xhelal, did not seem very bright, but he had a good chance of succeeding his father – until his step-mother intervened.

The women of the Toptani family had a reputation for assertiveness, and Sadije was no exception. Small and spirited, and essentially warm-hearted, she could yet appear formidable even when young. Dark eyes with a slant and projecting cheek-bones gave her a slightly Mongolian look. Her book-learning was fairly meagre – she attended a Turkish finishing school before marrying at fifteen – but her mental sharpness was evident. She saw to it that Xhelal was excluded from tribal councils. He did not seem to mind. Nor apparently did his father. Primogeniture was never an absolute rule: Xhemal himself had been chosen as chief in preference to an elder brother.

The matter came to a head sooner rather than later. Xhemal Zogolli Pasha died of natural causes before reaching the age of fifty. He may have been as young as forty, for the date of his death is peculiarly obscure even by local standards. Estimates range from 1901 right up to 1911, though 1904 and 1908 are the more common and plausible suggestions. As an adult, Zog chose not to clarify the age at which he was orphaned, and Zogist literature heavily emphasised the influence of Sadije, who 'made our King what he is today, for she gave him character, and manliness and a good deal of high aspirations'.[1] She also crucially secured his future by convincing the elders of Mati that her stepson was unfit to be chieftain. Xhelal was portrayed as a hopeless idler with a fondness for the bottle. The Mati, she argued, had much better wait for Ahmed to come of age, and, in the meantime, she would lead them herself. The Canon of Lek allowed widows and single women to assume masculine status in special cases. Equal to the task, Sadije was latterly glorified as a matriarch who led her warriors on horseback. Possibly she really did fight sword in hand, although it may be noted that legendary Albanian heroes were often credited with Amazonian mothers.

Ahmed himself went away from the valley around this time – *circa* 1906 – in order to be educated. From the age of five, he had been taught at home in the company of a few local boys. He latterly recalled spending his lessons learning Turkish and his playtimes pretending to fight the Turks. His classmates took their studies no further, but a youth of his standing normally received some formal schooling, and Sadije was a great believer in its value. It is therefore curious that King Zog was never entirely clear about which schools he attended, and downright unclear about when. Information is so uniformly sketchy as to raise the suspicion that he wanted people to think that he had more formal education than was really the case. The claim that he managed to complete two years' study in the space of each school year only confirms his sensitivity on this point.

Ahmed was enrolled for a time at a Turkish cadet school at Monastir (modern Bitolj), a busy carpet-making town about eighty miles from Mati with a very mixed population. Almost every ethnic group in the southern Balkans (except the Albanians) had cultural institutions there, established with an eye to future territorial claims, and even a young boy cannot have remained unaffected in this forcing-house of rival nationalisms.

Then – though it might have been before – he experienced a far greater change of environment. It was perhaps not completely voluntary. Though the notorious child levy imposed on Christian families under Ottoman rule had died out back in the seventeenth century, the Turks still sometimes took intelligent boys away from powerful families. The practice supplied the Sultan with hostages against rebellion and turned potential dissidents into a faithful administrative élite. The boys were given a first-class Turkish education and directed into government service.

After Xhemal Zogolli Pasha died, the Turkish authorities anticipated instability in Mati. The story goes that they told Sadije to send her only son to Istanbul. She had mixed feelings as she watched him set off on horseback. Ahmed was her pride and joy, but it was not wholly fanciful to think that he could rise to be Grand Vizier. Over five centuries, thirty Albanians had done so. There was also the glorious example of Skanderbeg (a precedent which probably colours the tale, even if it did not inspire it). Two trusted servants with rifles accompanied him through notoriously anarchic Macedonia.

It was a far cry from Mati, or even Monastir, to the teeming streets of a great city. Over a million people lived in Istanbul, including a hundred thousand foreigners. There were many splendid palaces and nearly four hundred mosques. There were also railway stations, theatres, libraries, department stores, trams, steamships, gas-lamps, and telegraphs. There might have been electric light and telephones too, had the Sultan not banned them as tools of conspiracy. Ahmed was impressed but not overawed. In him, the adaptability of a child was combined with an uncommon degree of self-containment. He moved into a couple of rented rooms and set about exploring the metropolis. In fact, Istanbul was at least two cities. South of the Golden Horn lay Stamboul, the city of Muslims, tradition, and the poor. Its maze of narrow streets, its bazaars and minarets had not changed much since the later Middle Ages, and here Ahmed could observe a society much more strictly Islamic than Mati and far more old-fashioned than Monastir.

To cross the Galata Bridge was to enter another world. Pera (nowadays Beyoglu) was the most cosmopolitan city in the Empire – in some ways, it seemed almost outside it. The diverse humanity common to seaports thronged the quayside, while just inland, in the district of Galata, lived Greeks, Jews, Armenians, Tatars, Persians, Arabs, and dozens of other nationalities – prostitutes, pimps, and drunkards, according to pious Stamboul Muslims. Then, up the hill, reached by a steep stepped-street or an underground funicular railway, Pera proper was the city of Christians, bright lights, and the *nouveaux riches*. Ahmed saw western Europeans for the first time in significant numbers. Alighting from the Orient Express, they drove to their hotels on the Grand Rue de Pera and visited their embassies, music halls, and cafés, radiating faith in their own superiority.

An Albanian schoolboy could experience little of the privileged life of Pera, but its prosperity and power made an impression. The northern side of the Galata Bridge was the one which Ahmed found more attractive. Thin, with a deceptively modest demeanour, he soon fancied himself the perfect young gentleman. He never went out without his fez, kept his shoes polished, and pressed his trousers under the mattress every night. Western-style clothing was now his everyday attire (if it had not been before) and only seldom did he ever appear in Albanian costume. Indeed, Mati clansmen would later laugh at his inability to tie his *opinga*, the native goatskin footwear.

That said, his classmates would have been even more amused, and not a little scornful, if he had turned up for lessons in tribal garb. It is generally believed that Sadije secured him a place at the Imperial Lycée of Galata Saray. This was a prestigious fee-paying state school, established by French educationalists in 1869, with the most progressive curriculum in the Empire. The Galata Saray provided generations of bureaucrats, diplomats, and writers for Turkey – and also a king for Albania? The Lycée (still thriving) does count Zog among its famous old boys, as the absence of his name from surviving records proves only that he never *completed* a course there.

Surrounded by scions of the metropolitan élite, sons of Turkish ministers, Phanariote Greeks, and Armenians, Ahmed may at this stage have developed his protective shell of reserve. He must have grown aware that his background in Mati struck people as unsophisticated. Mature for his age, he excelled in many of his studies. Some sources say that he preferred subjects relevant to a military career. Others cite history and languages (Turkish, Arabic, Persian, and French) as his main interests. He developed an abiding fascination with the life of Napoleon Bonaparte. When reading of the solitary young Corsican at L'École Militaire, he could perhaps be forgiven for drawing parallels with himself. His precocity did not endear him to his teachers; he was the sort of boy who always had an answer and liked to point out mistakes.

Even so, one has to wonder how much credence can be given to one of King Zog's reminiscences. While in Istanbul, as son of the Governor of Mati, he had to appear before his sovereign. This was Abdul Hamid II, known to Christian Europe as the 'Red Sultan' of Bulgarian horrors and Armenian massacres. On stepping into the presence, it was customary to bow deeply, touch chest, lips, and forehead, and say, 'Master, thy word is law.' Ahmed simply bowed his head and looked the Sultan straight in the eye. Amused rather than offended, the old autocrat engaged him in conversation and was so impressed by his replies that he appointed him equerry to one of his younger sons. 'No,' answered Ahmed proudly, 'I shall never in my whole life be an adjutant to another.'[2] This kind of tale went down well with some Albanians. Another anecdote found in Zogist propaganda has Abdul Hamid awarding Ahmed the Osmani order. He tossed the precious collar about as if it were a toy: 'With this thing or without it, I shall always be myself!'[3]

The impertinent youth is supposed to have annoyed the Sultan so much that, as a punishment, he was denied all contact with his family, which meant that he could not receive his remittance from Sadije. Ahmed survived on credit until evicted from his lodgings. Then, unwilling to give up his studies, he found shelter with the Albanian palace guards. Undernourished, without a piastre to his name, he collapsed in the street that winter. Fortunately, a kind doctor took him home and nursed him through pneumonia. On his recovery, he persuaded four Albanian soldiers to go with him to an outlying Zogolli estate, which had been sending no money either to Sadije or himself. The uncle who collected the rents maintained that he was saving them till Ahmed came of age. The fourteen-year-old put his hand on his pistol and refused to leave without his due.

'You would really shoot your uncle?'

'Yes,' he replied and returned to the city with enough money to clear his debts and buy a house.[4] (True or not, this incident belonged in the King's own repertoire of stories.)

While in Istanbul, Ahmed made his first political speech to an audience of his schoolfellows. Debates were common among the students, and the Young Turk Revolution of July 1908 galvanized those with any interest in politics, as prisons were thrown open, women tore off their veils, and banners extolled 'Liberty, Equality, Fraternity, Justice'. A new parliament was elected (including Albanian deputies) with the aim of radical reform. When the Sultan obstructed it, he was swept aside. Zogolli, with his head full of Napoleonic France, shared in the euphoria. Everything that he had learnt convinced him of the merits of modernisation, and even his countrymen back home assumed that change could only be for the better. Like them, he did not appreciate that 'Union and Progress' (as defined by Young Turks) would be far from congenial to Albanians.

The new regime set out to revive the Ottoman Empire by imposing uniformity. Turkish law, regular taxation, military service, and the Arabic alphabet would be enforced from Baghdad to Shkodra. Faced with the threat of effective Ottoman rule, the Albanians predictably revolted, demanding the right to remain a law unto themselves. Every spring, four years running, a major clan or region rebelled and suffered violent reprisals (including Mati in 1909). It was not until 1911, however, that the Albanians scented success, as the Italo-Turkish War weakened their opponents.

Despite his sympathy for some Young Turk ideas, Ahmed never doubted where his loyalties lay. He had kept himself informed of events, not from the newspapers (which were censored), but from speaking to Albanians newly arrived in the city. In late 1911 or 1912, he abandoned his studies, slipped away to Salonika, and met up with a cousin at school there. Together they made for Mati to play their part in the imminent historic developments. Recalling this reunion with his mother over twenty years later, King Zog came close to tears. In a few days, he ceased to be a schoolboy and became a chieftain. Ahmed Bey Zogolli, in his native valley, passed for a man of the world at sixteen. Battle-scarred warriors bowed before him and elders deferred to his learning. But there was only one place where he could really prove his worth: on the field of battle. When the northern clans launched a fresh revolt in April 1912, it swept the land as never before and Mati joined in the fight. This time the Albanians were victorious. The Turks, tired of conflict, conceded autonomy. Ahmed had fought in no more than a skirmish, but, if he wanted to see serious action, he had not long to wait. The First Balkan War broke out on 8 October 1912, his seventeenth birthday. The Balkan League of Montenegro, Serbia, Greece, and Bulgaria turned on the Ottoman Empire with the goal of driving the Turks from Europe once and for all.

Most Albanians reacted to this with a dramatic turn about face. They had just been fighting the Turks themselves to block unwelcome reforms. Now they had to fight 'liberation' by Greeks and Slavs. Serbia was demanding access to the sea, which could only mean part of Albania.

Greece said that the south was 'Northern Epirus' and claimed all its Christians as Greeks. King Nicholas of Montenegro swore that Shkodra was the sacred burial place of his forefathers. Under simultaneous attack from north, south, and east, Albanians could scarcely stay neutral. Zogolli sent a request to the Prefect of Dibra for arms and ammunition. In return, he rallied Mati in defence of the Ottoman Empire.

With a besa suspending feuds, two thousand warriors massed at Burgajet, where they instantly quarrelled over which district should lead the march. When rivals for the honour resorted to gunfire, Zogolli faced his first test. He strode out in full Turkish uniform and leapt on his black horse: 'Down with your guns! I give the orders here. Lurë shall be the vanguard.'[5] Without waiting to see the response, he spurred his steed and rode forward – and the fighters fell in behind him. In front walked two men who sang of past battles. Next came a stalwart with the crescent flag. Rank and file followed on foot, firing in the air for joy.

Most stories of Zogolli's military exploits derive from the 'rhapsodies' of the oral tradition. These long poems, chanted to rhythmic accompaniment, typically first catalogued the ancestry of the warriors before describing the outward march, the decisive encounters, and the return with the spoils. Retelling enhanced glorious feats; setbacks tended to be forgotten. There is every sign that Zogolli showed sufficient bravery to give the minstrels something to rhapsodize.

In this campaign, the Mati first went north to confront the Montenegrin invaders. Battle was joined at a place called Kakarriq between Shkodra and its port of Shëngjin (known to foreigners as San Giovanni di Medua). The rhapsodies tell that 'Ahmed the Hawk' cut his way through two whole armies and had several horses shot under him. The casualty rate was grievous: over eighty warriors killed in a day. Worse still, news arrived that Mati itself was in danger. The Serbs, having already conquered Kosovo, were now striking west towards the Adriatic. Abandoning Shëngjin, Zogolli marched his men back thirty miles to defend families, homes, and livestock. The mood at Burgajet was grave, as superior enemy forces threatened to breach the passes. 'Take heart. They will not,' Zogolli asserted.[6] Then, by a supernatural act of will, he reputedly sowed such confusion in the minds of the Serbs that two whole regiments wiped each other out. The Mati valley was saved.

The wider war told a different story: everywhere the Turks were in need of miracles but more were not forthcoming. Macedonia fell to the Greeks and Serbs. The Bulgarians threatened Istanbul. The Montenegrins were besieging Shkodra and Serbian forces merely bypassed Mati in their haste to reach the sea. Leading Albanians faced up to the fact that Turkey-in-Europe was a sinking ship and asked themselves how they might escape. A congress of chiefs and beys assembled at Vlora on 28 November 1912.

In the afternoon, an elderly magnate, named Ismail Kemal Vlora, stepped out onto a balcony to unfurl the red and black banner of Skanderbeg and proclaim the independence of Albania.

Zogolli agreed that it was worth the gamble. 'Our country,' he said, 'has on one side the shining vision of liberty; on the other it is menaced by the tremendous danger of a partition and new slavery. We hope that international justice will not abandon us.'[7] That his signature does not appear on the declaration of independence is simply a result of his reaching Vlora too late for the ceremony. Arriving there at all was an achievement for northerners. To evade the Serbs, Zogolli and his cousin Dervish Biçaku had taken a roundabout route, crossing occupied territory at night. Ismail Kemal supposedly exclaimed: 'My son, your place is here among us, for the first man who dared to take up arms against the Turks for the cause of Albania's independence was your own kinsman and grandfather.'[8]

Zogolli lodged with Ismail's nephew, Ekrem Bey Vlora, who afterwards recalled, 'Like any young scion of an Albanian noble family, he was self-confident, silent, reserved, proud, and shy in company . . . But nothing led me to suspect that he would climb the ladder to the highest position in the land.' This verdict is unsurprising. In terms of the Ottoman establishment, the beys of Vlora were grandees while the beys of Mati were backwoodsmen – 'without means', by the standards of Ekrem Bey, 'I would almost say poor!'[9]

The Vlora congress sat for a week and elected a Provisional Government with Ismail Kemal as President. Desperate appeals went out for international recognition, before communications were cut by a Greek naval blockade.

The Albanian nationality had won a few friends since the Congress of Berlin. British sympathisers like Aubrey Herbert and Edith Durham – the first a young Conservative MP, the second an intrepid traveller – assisted an Albanian delegation to lobby the London Conference, where representatives of the six Great Powers were trying to contain the Balkan War. More importantly, Austria–Hungary and Italy now espoused Albanian independence for reasons of their own. The former was anxious to keep Serbia landlocked. The latter preferred to see small weak states on the far side of the Adriatic. Russia, however, backed the claims of the Balkan League. It was not inconceivable that the struggle for Shkodra might spark a general European war.

On the ground in Albania, the independence declaration did not impress the Greeks and Slavs, who captured even central towns like Berat and Elbasan. Zogolli confessed to his clansmen, 'Given the dispersal of forces and the lack of liaison between different parts of our country, there is nothing to be done except to guard our passes and repel any invasion attempt from whichever side it comes.'[10] Albanians pinned their hopes on the London Conference.

On 20 December 1912, the Great Powers agreed to create an Albanian principality to serve as a neutral buffer state between Serbia and the sea. The Russians concurred with reluctance. They were not yet ready to fight for the sake of their Balkan clients, but they did insist that Serbia retain most of Kosovo, regardless of its generally Albanian population. In order to keep the peace between Russia and Austria–Hungary, the borders of Albania would be drawn so small that half of all Albanians were outside them.

The warring parties did not lay down their arms and accept the Treaty of London till May 1913. By then, the Turks had been so soundly beaten that there was no longer any question of their retaining nominal suzerainty over Albania. The principality would have full independence (assuming that the Balkan League actually withdrew). Thus was born the state of Albania: 'an illegitimate child of Austrian diplomacy with Italy figuring as the midwife'.[11] It was nearly to die in infancy.

CHAPTER FOUR

Prince Wilhelm's
Loyal Subject

What the new state needed was peace and stability. What it experienced was quite the opposite. To forge a nation in a land with few nationalists was never going to be easy, and the timing could hardly have been worse. The very mention of 1913 suggests Europe on the edge of the precipice, though for Albania the war of 1914–18 is subsumed in a longer period of strife, commencing with rebellions against the Turks and lasting into the 1920s.

In the midst of this confusion, Ahmed Zogolli embarked on his political career – with a series of paramilitary adventures, as small-scale civil war appeared to be the ordinary business of Albanian politics. One month he would risk his life; the next he might rest at Burgajet with little to do but read and smoke. The anarchical condition of his homeland – and of Europe indeed – in his formative years bred in him a distinctive blend of fatalism and opportunism. King Zog was to show a firm grasp of the truth that in politics nothing is final. What looked impossible today might become easy tomorrow. He developed a habit of saying that everything was ultimately in the hands of inscrutable fate. His actions yet suggest a belief that the scope for manipulation in the meantime was infinite.

There did not seem to be much finality about the Treaty of London in 1913: a second Balkan war briefly flared in the summer, and Serbian, Greek, and Montenegrin troops stayed in Albania. In the absence of proper maps, disputes about frontiers could easily be rendered interminable. The Greeks wanted all of the area that they called Epirus and Albanians called Chameria. The Serbs were determined not to relinquish land between Djakovica and Dibra.

Dibra was the clan district just east of Mati. The proposed Albano-Serbian border cut it in two. When Dibra rose against the Serbs in September, Zogolli lent assistance, but, by the time his men were engaged, Serb regulars had arrived in force. Mati could only help cover the evacuation of Dibra town. The Serbs ravaged seventeen villages in reprisal. Phineas Kennedy, an aid worker who witnessed a parley of chiefs at Burgajet, described Zogolli as 'a reader of Shakespeare and a fine fighting man'. To offers to evacuate one of the wounded, Ahmed responded, 'No, I cannot spare the men. He has got to recover or die.'[1] Mati and Dibra then retaliated by raiding almost as far as Skopje.

Ten months after independence, sporadic guerrilla activity remained the best that Albania could manage in terms of defence. A self-governing nation needs a government: one government. In 1913, Albania had two, neither effective, with no accepted head of state to choose between them. The Great Powers had dubbed the new land a principality. Who should be prince? No chief or bey had a strong claim to supremacy by virtue of power or tradition. Hence the Conference of Ambassadors barred native aspirants as too divisive and searched for an eligible outsider. It was not easy: Austria–Hungary rejected anybody favoured by Russia and vice versa. A couple of Ottoman princes came forward, but they were unacceptable to all but the Russians (who probably wanted Albania to fail). Prince Moritz of Schaumberg-Lippe, the Count of Turin, and the Duke of Urach were canvassed in vain. No one really seemed eager for the crown.

In the meantime, the Provisional Government at Vlora acted as a stopgap, but there was little unity of purpose. Its members attached themselves to competing candidacies, backed by different foreign powers, in an attempt to guarantee their influence in the future. President Ismail Kemal was unenthusiastic about a foreign prince. Much worse, a new contender for power had emerged in the shape of a fifty-year-old soldier called Essad Pasha Toptani. In a country fond of villains and heroes, it is hard to believe that anybody famous was quite as black (or as white) as he is painted, but few dispute this man's status as an archetypal traitor. Head of a major landowning family in central Albania, Essad saw himself as a fledgling president or prince. Ismail Kemal was in receipt of Austro-Hungarian subsidies, so Essad offered his services to the Slavs (though Serbia and Montenegro wanted any Albanian state to be as small as possible). He plotted to murder his commanding officer at Shkodra in April 1913, allegedly sold the town to the Montenegrins, and marched south to Durrës, where he set up his own Central Albanian Republic.

Zogolli was a distant cousin of Essad Toptani, not that such links necessarily counted for much. Among leading families of the same religion almost everybody was related somehow, and Albanians often disregarded kinship on the maternal side.*

Although Zogolli had reason to amplify their enmity in retrospect, it required no more than slight exaggeration to cast Essad Pasha in the role of wicked uncle: with his curly black moustache, he plainly looked the

---

* Contrary to what is often stated, Essad was not Ahmed's maternal uncle. Sadije Zogolli came from the separate Pisha branch of the Toptani family.

part. When Essad entertained Zogolli for a week in Tirana in the autumn of 1913, he promised him riches if Mati would support his cause. Ahmed would not repudiate the Vlora regime. 'He will do well in our country,' growled the Pasha, 'and push us all aside if we don't shorten his legs at the right time.'[2]

Unfortunately for Albania, Essad's lust for power and lack of scruple were exceptional only in degree, for he epitomised an approach to politics characteristic of his class and generation. These men had prospered amidst the anarchy and corruption of the decadent Ottoman Empire, where brigand-like Gheg chieftains were not alone in 'prizing honour above honesty, gold more than both and power beyond them all'.[3] Turkified beys, superficially more civilised, had worked a system where officials bought their posts and extracted what money they could from them, where anyone with sufficient power could be his own judge and policeman. In other Balkan countries, when the Christians won independence, the worst of the beys fled with the retreating Turkish army, but in Albania they stayed in place. National independence signified to them the abolition of any vestige of authority over themselves.

The background of Zogolli was not dissimilar, but he was better educated than some beys and chieftains and far younger than most. Numerous beys had spent a few years in the capital in their youth. They remembered the Istanbul of Abdul Hamid II, who had seemed to embody the Ottoman malaise. Zogolli knew the city of the Young Turks, where at least the talk was of progress.

The rival regimes at Vlora and Durrës conspired against each other throughout the year, obliging the Conference of Ambassadors to assume a more active part in setting up the new nation. At the behest of the Great Powers, the Balkan League ostensibly withdrew its troops. From January to March 1914, the government of Albania was entrusted to an International Commission of Control.

A Head of State had been named by now. Prince Wilhelm of Wied was a 37-year-old army officer from a tiny state on the Rhine. His candidature was the fancy of his overwhelming aunt, the poetess Queen Elisabeth of Romania (pen name: Carmen Sylva). In the absence of an alternative, no Great Power could object to her inoffensive protégé, who landed at Durrës on 7 March 1914 with Princess Sophie, two young children, a suite of five, a piano, a rocking-horse, and a pair of guard-dogs. Essad Pasha greeted the couple, having submitted to the International Commission grudgingly. Within ten days, Toptani was Minister of War and the Interior in the new (nominally unified) Government.

Wilhelm was ignorant of local ways. When he helped his wife from a carriage and let her walk in front of him, Albanians took him for a henpecked weakling. He failed to impress the beys and chieftains, on whose unlikely co-operation his future was certain to depend. Ismail Kemal, Essad Pasha, and Prenk Bib Doda (supreme chieftain of the Roman Catholic clans) remained locked in fierce competition, encouraged and subsidised by their foreign patrons. Without experience, reliant on his interpreters, Prince Wilhelm of Albania was not unconscientious so much as utterly bewildered. His effective authority extended no further than the outskirts of the capital, and probably not even that far.

To this hotbed of intrigue came Ahmed Bey Zogolli in early May to swear allegiance to the sovereign. Other local potentates did the same, but the chieftain of Mati sought more than a ritual exchange of greetings. He urged Wilhelm to make haste in widening his circle of advisers and convening a national assembly. Zogist sources tell that the Prince was so impressed that he begged him to join the Government. Before leaving Durrës for home, Zogolli was arrested on trumped-up charges by order of the Minister of the Interior. The intervention of Prince Wilhelm secured his release, but Ahmed and Essad now knew where they stood.

By the end of the month, even the Prince could not fail to see the treachery surrounding him. Toptani was implicated in a Muslim uprising which threatened Durrës itself. When he refused to accept dismissal, Wilhelm set up two field guns in his palace garden and bombarded the ministerial residence next door till a white sheet fluttered from the bedroom window. Even then, Essad did not give up. Exiled to Rome, he persuaded the Italians that the Prince was an Austrian agent and thus obtained funds for the insurrection. The Muslims of central Albania were led to believe that a Protestant monarch endangered their religion.

Zogolli had a strong suspicion of what inspired the Islamic revolt. After consulting Prenk Bib Doda, he published a manifesto that called on Albanians to rally to the Prince who offered peace and progress. His disappointment came quickly. Having marched his 800 warriors as far as Kruja in June, less than halfway to Durrës, he found his countrymen indifferent. An attempt to co-ordinate an assault with Prenk on a rebel base at Shijak came to nothing. After a meeting of elders, the Mati decided to go home. Many of them had never really understood why their chief wanted to fight fellow Muslims with whom they were not at blood.

Thus Zogolli's political debut was a failure. He latterly put this down to a simple shortage of war *matériel.* Others have suggested that, like Prenk Bib Doda, he was not sincere in his loyalty to Prince Wilhelm. They imply that the future King Zog never wanted another royal house in Albania, but it is hardly valid to project his ambitions to kingship as far back as 1914. No Albanian chieftain felt unquestioning devotion to the crown. Zogolli gave Wilhelm more backing than most did, and, for this, he may or may not have been paid with Austrian gold. Either way, when he found himself isolated, self-interest dictated a prompt withdrawal. Albanian leaders might talk about fighting to the last man, but (mercifully) they very rarely did.

He was right to conclude that the House of Wied, for the moment at least, was a hopeless cause. The onset of European war deprived the Prince of financial subsidies. Bottled up in Durrës by rebel forces, he told his subjects on 3 September 1914: 'it is more useful if for some time I go to the west.'[4] He left two days later and never came back. Prince Wilhelm became the butt of much derision. He might in fairness have made a good monarch in a land more amenable to government. By all accounts, he was good-natured and honest, yet a ruler of Albania required other qualities – as Zog was later to demonstrate.

CHAPTER FIVE

Powers and Puppets

Albania was technically neutral throughout the First World War. This did not save it from being overrun by seven different foreign armies: Serbs, Montenegrins, Italians, Greeks, and French on the Allied side, and Austro-Hungarians and Bulgarians from the Central Powers. Some engaged in looting and terror; others, freer with their gold, found locals fairly co-operative. No occupation authority exerted much control outside the towns. First came the Greeks, who had never really left 'Northern Epirus'. Next Italy occupied Vlora and claimed it as strategic compensation for the Austrian invasion of Serbia.

These incursions were in the south. Of more direct concern to Zogolli was the swift return to Durrës of Essad Toptani, back with his old Balkan League patrons and again proclaiming himself President. However, the Muslim rebels who had driven out Prince Wilhelm shunned him in favour of reunion with Turkey and asked a son of Abdul Hamid to fill the vacant throne. This was wholly unacceptable to Essad's Serbian backers, as Turkey soon joined the Central Powers. Hence the latest configuration of Albanian civil strife pitted Essadists against Turcophils.

Zogolli gave some support to the Turkish party in late 1914. On the face of it, this ill became a self-styled hero of Albanian nationalism, and he later tried to explain his conduct by arguing that he 'could not fight both factions at the same time'.[1] He did hold aloof at Burgajet to a considerable extent, and, in general, it would be naive to draw a clear division between true patriots and mere adventurers in the history of Albanian nationalism. The men who worked for independence also sought personal power.

By December 1914, the Turcophils had won the upper hand in central Albania. Toptani was surrounded on the Durrës peninsula, just like Prince Wilhelm four months earlier. Unlike the Prince, however, Essad did not flee, but presented himself to the world as a beleaguered friend of the Allies. Lest Turkey gain Albania as a base, Serbian troops invaded in 1915, defeated the Muslims, and stayed to prop up Essad and his puppet regime. Zogolli came under pressure to recognise this Durrës Government but resisted and asserted that Mati would tolerate Serbian occupation if its traditional freedom to govern itself were respected. In a letter of September 1915, he cautioned Nikola Pašić, the Serbian Prime Minister, that Essad Toptani was an unreliable egoist heading a 'government of illiterates'; if the Serbs were wise, they would drop him at once.[2] Was Zogolli offering himself to Pašić as an alternative? It appears that Essad heard about the letter, for he promptly added to his demands: not only must Mati submit to his authority as President, but its chief must go into exile. Zogolli rejected the ultimatum.

To understand the gravity of the crisis, it is necessary to note two additional facts. First, the Essadists were armed with machine-guns, supplied to them by the Serbs. Second, the post of President of the Supreme Court in Essad's administration was held by Xhelal Bey Zogolli, half-brother of Ahmed. His judicial abilities were non-existent, but his political value was plain. Essad was intending to split the Mati, depose their chieftain, and install Xhelal as a compliant successor.

Ahmed prepared for the Essadist attack with a thoroughness unusual in Albanian warfare. He divided his men into small groups with precise orders to skirmish and retreat in a given direction. In this way, the main confrontation would take place at Macukul, a strong defensive position to the north of the valley, where he built up his stores and ordered the digging of trenches, a novel exercise for Albanian fighters. The plan worked very well. After capturing several hamlets with ease, the Essadists suddenly came under fire from concealed positions on the hillside. Time after time, the attackers were repulsed, and the Mati would often have charged in pursuit, had Zogolli not restrained them. He adhered to his defensive strategy and waited for the wider war to bring his salvation.

On 6 October 1915, Austria–Hungary renewed its invasion of Serbia with German support and Bulgaria joined in. The Serbs could no longer afford to consolidate control in Albania; Essad had to withdraw from Mati. Within six weeks, indeed, the entire Serbian army was retreating through Albania.

The collapse of Serbia transformed the political situation. Now those beys who had eschewed the Serbs (or seemed to have done so) would come to the fore. Once the advance guard of the Austro-Hungarian XIX Corps occupied Shkodra on 23 January, they called on the locals to help expel the Slavs. Zogolli told his followers that their moment had come. They could not hope to resist the new invaders, but if they set up a skeleton administration before the Austrians arrived, they could present themselves as a government and try to negotiate for autonomy. To achieve this they had only weeks or even days. Starving remnants of the Serbian army were still fighting rearguard actions as they concentrated near the coast to await evacuation. Austrian patrols meanwhile fanned out from Shkodra, working south along the lowlands. The Bulgarians pressed forward from Macedonia, but conditions were terrible in the highlands. Snowdrifts blocked passes and obscured footpaths when Zogolli led his clansmen out to claim central Albania. His first objective was Kruja, a natural fortress on the edge of the massif, but, as the Mati neared the town, a scout reported that the Austrians were already in the citadel. Descending to Tirana, 15 miles away, Zogolli again discovered that the Austrian advance guard had pre-empted him. Where next?

Durrës was still in Allied hands, as one of the ports from which the Serbs were being ferried out under cover of an Italian expeditionary force. When President Essad also left on board an Italian warship on 24 February 1916, not even the pretence of a government remained on Albanian soil. The vacuum was instantly filled: with slaughtered pack animals littering the streets and the air still acrid from burning stores, Zogolli strode into the derelict villa on the Durrës waterfront that had briefly served as a palace and hoisted the national flag in the name of Prince Wilhelm. Basing his actions on those of Ismail Kemal in 1912, he then formed a Committee of Initiative, with a couple of former cabinet ministers (from 1914) and himself in the chair. Before they could do anything, however, they were obliged to move on by the massing of Austrian troops on the heights above the town. Zogolli set off up the Shkumbi valley to Elbasan, but too late: the Bulgarian First Army was already in possession. That said, the garrison was small, and the Bulgarians saw a chance to boost their influence *vis-à-vis* the Austrians by acquiring some local clients. Once convinced of his anti-Serb credentials, they let Zogolli nominate the civil administration of the town.

Having at last secured a base, he despatched token forces to the other towns of the south central region – Lushnja, Fier, and Berat – and then sent out envoys with an invitation to the chiefs and beys of all Albania and Kosovo:

Elbasan, 3rd March 1916
We have the honour to inform you that it has been decided that on the 18th March 1916 a National Congress will be held, in this city, to consider the present situation of our country and take the necessary measures to safeguard its vital interests. We beg you to send two duly accredited delegates.[3]

This congress, he hoped, would establish a government and appeal to Prince Wilhelm to return to his principality. The emphasis on an absentee Prince made sense: Wilhelm was a German, and Germany the ally of Austria–Hungary and Bulgaria. Might not Albania then be accepted as an autonomous confederate of the Central Powers? Zogolli greeted the Austrians as liberators, voicing confidence that they would grant to Albania a 'frontier line in accordance with the principle of nationality'.[4]

All this presented a dilemma to the occupation authorities. Ahmed Bey Zogolli was known to the Austrian consulate in Shkodra. Since Essad

Pasha was a client of Serbia, his foes were reckoned potential allies of Austria–Hungary. The consul had even supplied ammunition to Mati for use against the Essadists in 1915. Zogolli had ignored Austrian appeals for support, however, and his recent perambulations incurred disapproval. What had Austria–Hungary to gain from establishing an Albanian client state while the war was still under way? It would merely complicate matters.

The immediate problem for the Austrians was how to prevent Zogolli's national congress. Their ingenious solution: a reported outbreak of cholera at Elbasan. Quarantine orders and road-blocks made the meeting impossible. Then the occupation authority banned all political assemblies for the duration of the war. Zogolli had been stymied. Vague promises of future independence were the most that Austria–Hungary would offer. 'Words are not sufficient,' he complained, 'I want facts.'[5]

CHAPTER SIX

Colonel Zogolli

Ahmed Bey Zogolli retired to Mati in disgust, but his foray in the first months of 1916 had brought him to the forefront of national affairs. Desiring their occupation of Albania to be as cheap and untroubled as possible, the Central Powers decided to send envoys after him. Prince Ludwig Windischgraetz wrote:

> We reached his castle by night. It was built into the rock and constructed of massive blocks of stone, quite in mediaeval style. The castle had two forecourts, which were lit with torches; there about a hundred Albanians were camped round the open fire, in military equipment, bristling with arms. It was romantic and weird. We had to climb a wooden staircase, and then await the mighty Achmed Bey Zogolaj by a stone balustrade. We pictured him as fierce and martial as his warriors in the courtyard, but we were conducted further, and arrived in a carpeted boudoir. It might have been the abode of a *demi-mondaine*. Then a slight young man in a smoking suit came in and spoke to us very pleasantly in French. It was Achmed Bey Zogolaj. Black coffee was handed round; the Bulgarian Colonel negotiated with him first, offered him 40,000 levas, and went to bed. I had 50,000 levas handed to the powerful Prince, on which he promised to help Austria–Hungary.[1]

Zogolli was given the rank of colonel in the Austrian army and paid ostensibly to recruit Albanians to fight against Italy.

Awareness of the part played by Austro-Hungarian diplomacy in securing independence in 1912 led many educated Albanians to view the Habsburg Empire with a measure of favour. To them, the Austrians were progressive westerners – and they were not Slavs. With Serbs and Greeks on the Allied side, Albanian sympathy for the Central Powers was unsurprising. In later years, it was nevertheless a cause of some slight embarrassment to Zog that he had voluntarily served an occupying power. His compatriots knew that it was, literally, the business of Gheg chiefs to fight for money and advantage. Foreigners were less understanding, and he could not explain his patriotic motive without revealing that he had desired the Allies to lose the war. Favourable testimony came from August Kral, Austrian governor of northern

Albania. Asked about Zogolli as a collaborator, he said that the future King had displayed a fanatical belief in Albanian independence: 'No means were negligible to achieve this purpose. He was appointed an Austrian Colonel at the age of twenty-one. And I think he conceived this as a sacrifice he made for his country.'[2]

The Austrians initially sent Zogolli on an official tour of the Dalmatian coast and occupied Montenegro. He went in the hope of meeting high-ranking persons with whom he might discuss self-government for Albania. In fact, he was shown around fortresses, naval bases, and airfields. Undaunted, on his return to Shkodra, he once more raised the issue of autonomy, telling the Austrian commander, General Ignaz von Trollmann, that there seemed to be a small misunderstanding between them: Albania was not part of the Habsburg Empire. 'When you realize that,' he was heard to say, 'then you can rely upon my help.'[3]

Zogist sources relate such episodes with a heavy-handedness which proclaims that they protest too much:

> Many tried to convince him that it was useless to resist, that it was not a shame to serve Austria, even as a tool. But Zogu had nobler sentiments and higher aspirations. He would readily have given his life if such an act meant the independence of his country. The arguments that his friends used failed to convince him; for he could not reason; he could not see. The love of country was now his master; and love is to be blind.[4]

The official biography says little about the remainder of 1916; it is clear from independent sources that he spent these months in Austrian service. Archival evidence is slight: his colonelcy seems to have been a courtesy title that never reached the army list. He did don Austro-Hungarian uniform, but the troops under his command were primarily his own Mati warriors.

The Austrians had started recruiting Albanian irregulars almost as soon as they arrived in Shkodra, and there was a good deal of small-scale military activity further south during 1916. To consolidate the front line, Austrian troops occupied Fier and Berat, and the Bulgarians drove the Greeks from Korça. Then, to contain them, an Italian expedition advanced inland from Saranda with the aim of meeting the French moving west from Salonika. In the words of one admirer, Zogolli the legendary guerrilla became 'a provocative spur in the Allies' side, a will o' the wisp, an enigma, a romance'.[5]

This assessment may well be as fanciful as it sounds. Not until the Second World War did it suit King Zog openly to admit that he fought the Italians during the First. Hagiographers had put it about in the interim that he was something of a military genius. Over fourteen years, 1911 to 1925, he must have gained enough experience of Albanian warfare to feel at home in this world of scouts and skirmishes, random fire and ricochets:

> . . . the clatter of men and mules as they stumbled and kicked against the stones and rocks of the path, the clanking of equipment and the creaking of the saddles on the mules, the rattle of a man's rifle as it carelessly hit an overhanging rock or branch, and his muttered oath . . . the smell, usually a mixture of human and mule sweat, blended with garlic, and the reek of locally grown tobacco.[6]

It did him no harm that the clansmen knew the King as a man who could aim a rifle, scramble down a rockface, ford a river, and stage an ambush. That said, such skills were commonplace. Anti-Zogists derided the notion that he had been anything special as a fighter, and the officers of the XIX Corps reached a similar conclusion. In four months, Zogolli went from being a political nuisance in Austrian eyes to a military disaster. General von Trollmann at first placed all Albanian irregulars, some five thousand men, under the leadership of Leon Ghilardi, a Croat freebooter who had eked out a living in Albania – most recently in the pay of Ahmed Bey Zogolli, who now refused point blank to serve under his social inferior. So Trollmann removed Ghilardi and put Zogolli in charge of the skirmish front along the Vjosa River between the Austrian and Italian occupation zones.

'The results came to light almost instantaneously,' recalled Austrian officer Georg Veith:

> The Albanian youth had not in the slightest the brutal authority of his predecessor, control of the bands of fighters slipped right out of his hands, the wildest indiscipline broke out . . . it ultimately turned to mutiny and treachery, necessitating the summary shooting of a number of officers and men and the disbanding of part of the formation. The maintenance of the Vjosa line was thereby endangered in the highest degree.[7]

Colonel Veith described Zogolli as 'very ambitious but militarily quite incapable'. In fairness, the likely root of the problem was the failure of the Austrians to foresee that assorted clan levies would not obey the orders of a single local chief. Trollmann did learn this lesson. After the fiasco on the Vjosa front in May and June 1916, irregulars were recruited only as individuals to serve in a militia with Bosnian Muslim officers. All the same, King Zog could count himself lucky that the official Austrian war history omitted to mention the latter-day fame of one 'Ahmed Bei Mati', under whom the Albanian volunteers 'quickly went to the dogs'.[8]

The Austrian military would not trust Zogolli with further missions of any importance. Underemployed, however, he gave the political department increasing grounds for concern. Predictably, the explanation current in the 1930s was yet another illustration of his exemplary patriotism. After initially permitting Albanian irregulars to use their own flag, the Austrians then decreed that they must fly the Habsburg colours. Three bold Albanian officers refused and were shot for insubordination. When Zogolli heard of this, he had three Austrians put to death in reprisal. 'And they paid us in our own money,' Kral supposedly exclaimed. 'Only that the Albanians have showed us that they are more manly than we. They gave our men an honourable burial while we dumped theirs in a ditch.'[9] This story ends with the Austrians ready to reinstate Skanderbeg's banner but not to pardon Zogolli.

Another explanation sounds more likely. The Bulgarians, who still occupied an area around Elbasan, were toying with the idea of persuading Albanian nationalists to abandon their clamour for the restoration of Prince Wilhelm and to call instead for Prince Kyril, younger son of King Ferdinand of Bulgaria. Zogolli was an obvious man to approach with such a scheme. He passed part of the year in Elbasan, and, by the autumn, the Austrians felt that his attachment to the Bulgarians was unduly close. Having failed to manage this troublesome chief by the usual bribes and promises, August Kral determined to put a stop to his intrigues.

In late January 1917, Zogolli was invited to Vienna with a ceremonial delegation to offer Albania's compliments to the new Habsburg monarch. The formal side of the trip went well enough; the Emperor Karl granted them an audience, and the 'Lord of Mati' was awarded the Commander's Cross of the Order of Franz Josef I. Then, on the final day, as he was about to leave his hotel, an Austrian officer knocked on the door. As Zogolli remembered it, the position was baldly stated: 'I have come to tell you, Sir, that the Austrian Imperial Government thinks it necessary that you remain in Vienna as your presence in Albania impedes the interests of Austria in the country.'[10] Any attempt to leave the city would be treated as desertion.

In this unorthodox fashion, Zogolli embarked on what can be seen as the final stage of his disrupted education. The trickery rankled, but he seemed to accept that, while the Austrians ruled two-thirds of Albania, little could be achieved for the national cause without their co-operation. Safe in the knowledge that his mother would guard his status at home, the frustrated 21-year-old could perceive the compensations of exile in a European metropolis. True, the city was not at its best in 1917. The

Viennese considered it a dismal time of horsemeat, power cuts, and ersatz coffee. The Albanian saw things with different eyes.

During the twentieth century, many a poor country with a traditional society developed a westernised élite. In Albania, the process was only just beginning. A small number of emigrants, mostly Tosks, had returned home comparatively wealthy after work abroad, but their impact had been very local. The town of Korça was known for such people. Most had toiled in menial jobs in the USA or Italy without much chance to acquire western notions. In any case, the beys were hostile to their influence. A few beys had 'been to Europe' too, but Albania gained nothing from its richest men throwing money about in Parisian night-spots.

King Zog always professed to have made the very best use of his years in Vienna, following a daily timetable of library work and physical exercise. Engrossed in the study of western culture, he lived by the maxims written in his notebook:

1. Never remain without work.
2. Use your leisure to increase your culture.
3. Always base yourself upon facts, not upon imagination.
4. Earn before you spend.
5. Never spend more than you earn.
6. Never act or speak when you are angry.
7. If they speak badly of you, act in a way that will make people disbelieve what they have heard.
8. A person can never harm his character if the things he undertakes to do are worthwhile, beneficial and moral.[11]

The only passion he admitted to indulging was an insatiable one for history, and his subsequent command of German might be proof of his diligence. It nevertheless seems likely that a rich young man without any obligations found time to sample the social life of Vienna at war. In spite of the curfews and dubious Hungarian champagne, nightclubs stayed crowded. Where else could King Zog have acquired his 'sublime' tango technique? High military rank conferred a certain standing and a splendid light blue uniform. A sleek Albanian with a waxed moustache must have cut an exotic figure, especially when he tinted his hair with henna. He might have strolled with the smart set in Kärntnerstrasse. Then there were theatres, opera, the Prater, cabarets, cafés, and *chambres séparées*. There was also the Imperial Museum, where he went to draw inspiration from two particular exhibits: the helmet and broadsword of Skanderbeg. The helmet was topped with chamois' horns. The sword was said to have slain three thousand Turks.

Even before he went to Vienna, Zogolli conceived of himself as a reformer. Now his sense of superiority was bolstered by the idea that he was a European as well as an Albanian. He knew that his homeland could not survive as an ethnographical museum piece. Like other Balkan peoples, Albanians should repudiate the Ottoman period and catch up with the rest of Europe. Many educated young men already thought this way, but Ahmed was not a schoolmaster from Korça; he was a powerful Gheg chieftain.

Zogists later claimed that it was this second sojourn abroad which had made their King so 'liberal' and 'democratic'. Probably he did pick up something about superficial western constitutional forms. Some date his monarchical aspirations to this time. He was alone with the leisure to indulge his imagination; his historical reading included biographies of great men and kings. The Habsburg example was directly before him. Photographs of the Emperor Karl showed a young man not unlike himself wearing the ancient Magyar crown and brandishing the sword of St Stephen. King Zog related afterwards how, standing before the museum display case, he had dreamt of placing Skanderbeg's helmet on his head.

Though journalists liked to speculate about Austria–Hungary as the germ of the Kingdom of Albania, its influence could easily be exaggerated. After all, he was still in Vienna to witness the downfall of the Habsburg monarchy in November 1918. The Austrian occupation of Albania came to an end at the same time. Elbasan, Durrës, Tirana, and Shkodra fell one after another to the French or Italians, raising fresh possibilities for the national cause and also significant perils.

Zogolli left Austria in 1919. During two years 'in Europe', he had gained a keener admiration for western civilisation and a renewed sense of mission, along with fluency in German and a penchant for Austro-Hungarian women.

CHAPTER SEVEN

Minister of the Interior

The end of the First World War held the promise of a new dawn for many European nationalities. President Wilson came to the Paris Peace Conference to enshrine the principle of self-determination and build an international system in which small nations could flourish. Poles, Hungarians, Czechs and Slovaks, Lithuanians, Latvians, Estonians, and Finns regained independence after centuries. Some Albanian nationalists were as idealistic as any, but, with Serbia and Greece on the winning side, Albania could easily end up a loser, whatever Woodrow Wilson might say.

Several rival bands of Albanians went to Paris to lobby for the national cause, with Aubrey Herbert and Miss Durham lending assistance. Essad Toptani was also there, having spent the last two years with Allied forces at Salonika. The pasha seemed open to offers from any foreign Power in need of a client. European statesmen wondered if an independent Albania had been a mistake. Austria–Hungary had demanded it; Austria–Hungary was now no more. Experts argued that warring tribesmen needed supervision. France looked after the Riffs and Berbers. Britain policed the Indian frontier. Who should govern the Albanians?

The situation within Albania also gave meagre encouragement to the nationalists, yet where there was uncertainty, there might also be potential. Zogolli itched to return and give a lead. What the country needed, he believed, was the kind of direct endeavour that he had attempted in 1916. With the Austrians gone, Albanians should try to reassert their rights before other foreign troops became entrenched. The French, in control of Korça and Shkodra, seemed too friendly with expansionist Greeks and Serbs, and an even more serious threat came from over the Adriatic.

The Italians had entered the war in 1915 with the aim of self-aggrandizement, and the Allies had promised them a slice of Albanian territory. The total partition of Albania between Italy, Greece, and Serbia had even been agreed in a treaty. Three years later, however, a slice was not enough for the Italians – not if it meant the Serbs getting hold of a slice as well. The union of Serbia with Croatia and Slovenia disturbed Italian strategists, who worried that the Slavs were getting too powerful. There was no respite for Albania from the rivalries of foreign Powers: once Austria–Hungary and Russia ceased their contest, Yugoslavia and Italy took over. Their antagonism initially focused on disputed areas of their new common frontier, like Trieste and Fiume, but strategic competition soon spread southwards. From the heel of Italy to Albania is a mere 50 miles. The Italians knew that, if they held both shores, their navy could close the Straits of Otranto in 2 hours, ensuring full protection for the eastern shore of Italy and control of maritime access to Yugoslavia. At the armistice, Italian troops held every Albanian coastal town from Saranda to Shëngjin. They seemed in no hurry to leave.

When Ahmed Zogolli, a known Albanian nationalist heading home, crossed from Austria to Italy in early 1919, he found his progress hindered by bureaucratic delays. The Italians were not satisfied with his travel documents, and he heard that civilian passage between Bari and Durrës was impossible due to emergency restrictions. His pro-Austrian (so anti-Italian) record counted against him. Zogolli passed a couple of months kicking his heels in Rome, where the River Tiber divulged its secrets to him – or so he later said. Beside the ruins of the forum, he pondered on 'the greatest incarnation of political man'.[1] Caesar became his third historical idol after Skanderbeg and Napoleon.

On reaching Albania, he rallied the Mati for the customary opening gambit: occupying the nearest town. Kruja was not a major centre, but it possessed symbolic value as Skanderbeg's historic stronghold. Having announced his presence, Zogolli sought allies among the beys and chiefs. At first this was not easy. The bulk of Albanian notables favoured a Provisional Government recently set up at Durrës under Italian sponsorship. Its elderly leader, Turhan Përmeti, was basically a tool of Rome, but the Italians won over many Albanians with pledges to defend the integrity of the country. (Their aim to make it a satellite state was not so widely publicised). Then news came from Paris at the end of the year that the Peace Conference was considering a partition after all. This transformed local opinion at a stroke: if the Italians were too weak to exclude the Serbs, why collaborate with them?

The initiative passed to those who were not in league with Italy. Zogolli joined in calling a new national congress to meet at Lushnja on 21 January 1920. Confusion about the place and date, likely sown by Italian agents, meant such poor attendance on the opening day that the congress had to adjourn. Undeterred, one week later, fifty Albanian leaders approved the Declaration of Lushnja – in effect a second independence proclamation. They repudiated the Durrës puppet regime, rejected any protectorate, and vowed to fight for full sovereignty. 'We cannot permit our enemies to penetrate our territories like a house without a master,' said Zogolli. 'To their rifles and their cannons we shall oppose the fortresses of our bodies.'[2]

The congress reminded the Great Powers that they had already recognised Albanian statehood back in 1913. Given the outcome of the war, however, it seemed unwise to recall a German prince to the throne. Instead a Council of Regency was created with four native Regents (a Sunni, Bektashi, Orthodox, and Roman Catholic). The congress then, on its final day, 31 January 1920, elected a Provisional Government. The Premier, Suleiman Delvina, was a former Ottoman bureaucrat who owed his post to inoffensiveness. This heightened the importance of the Interior Minister: Ahmed Zogolli, at twenty-four the youngest man in the Cabinet.

The appointment made sense. To achieve national unity, the Provisional Government would have to win over the Gheg clans, who would not be receptive to a Tosk bey or a Hellenised townsman but might listen to the chief of Mati. 'The decisions of the Congress must be enforced and without loss of time,' he pronounced. 'I am marching upon the capital; those who wish to remain may do so.'[3]

The troops of the Lushnja Government – the armed retainers of its leaders – moved north, straight through a couple of roadblocks, where Italian troops were too startled (and outnumbered) to stop them. Halting briefly at Kavaja, Zogolli turned down an appeal from the Durrës Government for talks. There seemed no need for compromise when his forces could occupy a village less than five miles from Durrës without opposition. He shrank from pushing on to the port, however, lest the Italian garrison intervene.

On 12 February, the erstwhile Lushnja Government moved to Tirana, a small town 25 miles inland, and proclaimed it the provisional capital. Power fast ebbed away from the Italian-backed authorities as individuals switched allegiance. Ten days settled the matter. The Durrës regime disbanded and offered its resources to the three-week old Provisional Government. This gave a particular boost to Zogolli, who took control of the Albanian gendarmerie: a paramilitary force created by Dutch officers in Prince Wilhelm's day and revived by wartime occupiers. It was hardly cohesive or disciplined, but on paper it signified 3,000 men. By placing cronies on the payroll, Zogolli could use the gendarmerie to supplement his Mati fighters.

As Minister of the Interior in 1920, his primary job was to assert the authority of the Provisional Government by setting up prefectures and gendarmerie posts across the country. This could sometimes entail skirmishing with raiding parties and rebellious clans. Albania was awash with abandoned war *matériel*. There were also the ordinary rigours of travel. Tracks scaled cliffs where a mule could stumble. In marshes, horses sank belly-deep in mud. It was spring, moreover, when dried-up streams turned into fast-flowing rivers: crossing them was a regular ordeal with so few bridges left intact. Nights were spent in the homes of local men of rank. Albanian hospitality guaranteed a feast and a mattress, and, while the bread was baked and the sheep killed and boiled, Zogolli had three or four hours in which to expound the merits of the Tirana Government. Morsels of cheese, onion, and cucumber sustained the guests until the big meal. Most Gheg households were thoroughly traditional. Men sat cross-legged around a low circular table and ate with their fingers from communal bowls. After they had belched appreciation, the room would be cleared to make space for them to sleep.

At all times, Zogolli retained his dignity, attired in a Norfolk jacket and breeches, with his height enhanced by a high-crowned white fez. (This he would shortly set aside in favour of western headgear except when attending specifically Muslim functions. All his hats were worn with a hint of vanity: the fez was perfectly perpendicular, the peaked cap rakishly angled.) His face still had a callow look, despite a receding hairline, but his youthfulness rarely showed itself in high spirits. Stoical about discomfort and visibly exhilarated by danger, like many Albanians, Ahmed yet exercised strict self-control. While his eyes might brighten and his movements grow more rapid, his mode of utterance remained cautious and terse. The ideal chieftain kept his composure and never showed anger real or feigned; he fused ferocious pride with an even temper. Though the outward forms of discipline found in regular armies were virtually unknown to Albanians, it came naturally to Zogolli to give orders in a quiet but definite tone that ruled out further discussion. That said, he acknowledged that his men were experts at guerrilla fighting. 'They ought to be good at it', he added, 'for they have been doing nothing else for centuries.'[4]

In late February, Zogolli led his warriors north with the aim of securing Shkodra, Albania's largest town. An inter-allied occupation force was soon to be withdrawn, and rumour suggested that Serbian troops (maybe with French connivance) were going to move into the vacuum. This was what Zogolli aimed to prevent. To French or British eyes, his Mati fighters were indistinguishable from clansmen coming to market, so he surreptitiously packed the town with followers. On 12 March, the Allies marched out after formally transferring control to the town council. Next morning, the council swore allegiance to Tirana, the Mati having proclaimed their presence. Serbia was denied an easy conquest.

Because of the World War, the exact frontiers of Albania had never been finalised. The basic 1913 settlement satisfied nobody. Expansionists in Belgrade published maps showing all of northern Albania within a Greater South Slav kingdom resembling the Serb empire of the fourteenth century. Their apologists claimed that the Albanians were too anarchic to form a proper state. On the other side, Albanian nationalists wanted self-determination for 700,000 kinsmen in Kosovo. The Yugoslav authorities, admitting to 300,000, reoccupied the territory regardless and set about its forcible 'pacification'. Muslim Kosovars bitterly resented the rule of a Christian Serb minority. Their leaders organised the illegal Kosovo Committee to inspire resistance and agitate for Albanian unification. Its military wing, the *kaçak* (outlaw) movement, was fighting a guerrilla war. The Serbs pursued the kaçaks into Albania proper, and violence ravaged the region.

From March 1920, Zogolli was the main representative of the Tirana Government in the north. Though the Roman Catholic Regent and the Justice Minister were also based in Shkodra, it was Ahmed Bey who did most to co-ordinate its defence. Even Henry Baerlein, a commentator of fanatically anti-Albanian outlook, admitted the patriotism of this 'slender, pale, aloof young man, frock-coated, and so plunged in thought that he passed like a shadow through the bowing ranks of his retainers'.[5]

While Zogolli tried to stabilise the northern frontier, his colleagues came close to losing the very heart of the country to a revolt by adherents of Essad Pasha Toptani (probably funded by Serbia or Italy). After repulsing an Essadist attack on Burgajet on 7 April, the Interior Minister decreed draconian penalties for subversion. Even so, by the summer, the Government had been reduced to offering Essad a Cabinet seat. Then came sensational news from Paris: a student had shot him dead. Zogolli appealed for unity. Speculation that he had helped plan the murder only enhanced his reputation. The assassin, Avni Rustemi, bizarrely acquitted by a French court, returned to his homeland a hero.

The elimination of Essad coincided with another major turn of events. During May 1920, Italy had withdrawn its troops from Durrës and Shëngjin to concentrate on the defence of Vlora, the port near the Straits of Otranto. On 9 June, a surprise attack by 3,000 Albanians overran their outlying positions and forced them back into the town. Zogolli hurried south to add his clansmen to the fray. The Tirana Government denied responsibility for what was supposedly a spontaneous uprising (sooner than risk a declaration of war), but its Interior Minister played a secret role in supplying the guerrillas. With 30,000 Italians in Vlora, a long hard siege looked likely. Great was Albanian joy then, when on 2 August 1920, Italy agreed to evacuate its army within a month. Among the reasons for retreat were malaria and dysentery in Vlora itself, ministerial changes in Rome, and strikes and mutinies all across Italy. Albanians attributed it to their own efforts, though, and the Battle of Vlora was later hailed as the turning-point of the liberation struggle.

Zogolli could not pause to savour the victory. In the north and east, the Serbs were again on the offensive. Mati and Dibra counter-attacked on 13 August, and Zogolli thrashed a band of Montenegrins at Koplik four days later, but the Serbs then regrouped and invaded in earnest, devastating villages along the Drin valley with mortars, hand-grenades, and kerosene. They even raided Mati. Sadije and her daughters fled from Burgajet, which was looted and gutted by fire. Many a Gheg chieftain would have sworn eternal vengeance. This one took a more pragmatic view.

Quite when Zogolli assumed a definite stance on Kosovo is hard to ascertain, but it seems that sometime in 1920 he came to a secret understanding with the Serbs. His sister's fiancé from Kosovo, Ceno Bey Kryeziu, had sometimes acted as an intermediary between Mati and Belgrade since 1919, when Zogolli had asked for arms to use against Italy. Any deal was strictly personal. The Kosovo Committee branded talk of compromise with Yugoslavia as treason. It can still be argued that compromise was prudent. Zogolli accepted that Albania had neither the military might nor the diplomatic sway to pursue its claim to Kosovo with success in the near future. What the nation urgently needed was peace. His subsequent behaviour is consistent with the supposition that he tried to get the Serbs to withdraw from Albania by promising to restrain the Kosovar guerrillas. Reluctance to embrace the cause of irredentism was to be significant for his career.

Castle Burgajet remained a ruin. Later asked why he did not restore his ancestral home, King Zog piously replied, 'It is more important to build up my country.'[6] He in fact erected a villetta in Tyrolean style near Qafë e Shtamës, south of Mati, but he paid it only short visits. He no longer wished to be seen so much in a local context. He was rather a leader of the Albanian nation – which at length made a step towards international recognition when admitted to the League of Nations in January 1921.

Diplomatic progress had been made possible by the revision of Italian ambitions. Having failed to grab Albania themselves, the Italians concentrated on depriving Greece and Yugoslavia of territorial gains. Italy did manage to annex the isle of Saseno (or Sazan), however, 5 miles off Vlora, as a naval base, yet the absence of fresh water limited its value. The Conference of Ambassadors made one later concession to Italian wishes on 9 November 1921 with what became known as the Paris Declaration:

> If Albania should at any time find it impossible to maintain intact her territorial integrity, she shall be free to address a request to the League of Nations for foreign assistance. The Governments of the British Empire, France, Italy, and Japan decide that, in the above-mentioned event, they will instruct their representatives on the Council of the League of Nations to recommend that the restoration of the territorial frontiers of Albania should be entrusted to Italy.[7]

This weak provisional protectorate allowed the Italians to boast that they had secured a foot in the door, but most Albanians did not care too much. More important to them was the fact that the occupiers were finally gone.

As a fighting Minister of the Interior, Zogolli had helped recover Shkodra, hold back the Serbs, disperse the Essadists, and expel the Italians in the space of six hectic months. He was seen to be an exceptionally energetic chief. For just that reason, as the Albanian Government became more established, his own position was called into question. Since March, the Prime Minister had allowed him a free hand in security matters, and Zogolli used his powers to the full as a roving plenipotentiary. Other ministers started to complain that he acted without consultation and even usurped their functions. Some colleagues also despised his attitude to Kosovo and pressed for his replacement.

Sensing a conspiracy, Zogolli brought the issue to a head in October 1920. He published an order forbidding prefects and sub-prefects from corresponding with Government ministers except via the Interior Ministry. His opponents declared this proof of his autocratic tendencies. When Delvina, the premier, refused to dismiss him and even indicated that he shared his views on peace with the Serbs, the Cabinet split irreparably. On 14 November, the Provisional Government resigned, leaving Zogolli to declare that it had 'brought the dignity of the nation to the point where it stood 500 years ago during the time of Skanderbeg'.[8]

Southern magnates formed a new ministry headed by Ilias Bey Vrioni. There was no place for Zogolli.

CHAPTER EIGHT

His First Coup

In theory, the focus of political life from late 1920 was the Parliament House in Tirana. Formerly an officers' club, it was fitted out with desks and resembled a whitewashed schoolroom. The deputies who sat there were a mixed crowd, with the plainest contrast between those who aspired to a western (*alla Franka*) lifestyle and those who held to authentic Albanian ways. Educated townsmen tried to appear as European as possible. A few were as smart as Zogolli; English suits were highly prized. Others looked rather shabby in western-style jackets run up by local tailors; they often came from the south, where the white kilt of the Tosks was going out of fashion. Traditional costume remained daily garb for many Gheg chieftains, with the occasional substitution of bowler hats for skull caps. Conservative beys retained the frock-coat and fez of the Ottoman functionary.

The parliamentary deputies were even more divided in their loyalties than in their dress. Formal party allegiance was not a very important factor. The two main groups initially promised prosperity and reform in almost identical terms. Reactionary beys soon came to the fore in the Progressive Party, however, leaving most westernisers in the Popular Party. Still the situation was extremely fluid. Ethnicity, religion, region, and clan signified more than party labels, but even these factors were not supreme. Personalities and self-interest appeared to be paramount.

Centuries of Ottoman corruption had taught Albanians that political office meant wealth, and deputies were not fastidious about the methods employed to obtain it. Even under the Law of Lek, chieftains routinely took bribes, and thieving from another clan was hardly considered a crime at all. Given that principles and consistency could obstruct personal advancement, politicians rarely bothered with even a semblance of them. The deputies owed their election to clan or regional loyalties, and the spoils of office boosted local prestige, so what mattered was being on the winning side. Parliamentarism was at best a veneer – and more often a transparent varnish – on the politics of power.

Loyal opposition was not much in evidence. The Government had only to announce its appointments and disgruntled men began plotting to oust it, some through a sort of freemasonry known as 'the Clique'. This shadowy organisation, dating back to Ottoman times, would exert a significant if unfathomable influence over the next four years. Intrigue merged into criminal conspiracies. Everyone in politics carried a gun, and leading figures employed gangs of bodyguards drawn in relays from their districts. French journalists had a saying: *Pays balkanique, pays volcanique.* The culture of insurgency was such in Albania that no call for revolt went entirely unheeded. Mountain valleys provided reservoirs of fighters to whom national government meant little more than the presumptuous 'men of Tirana'. They respected their chieftain as a rightful ruler; all else was foreign tyranny. It was easy for frustrated politicians to rouse them to rebellion with appeals to loyalty, promises of plunder, or stories of slights to their honour. Greek, Serb, and Italian agents readily assisted, with money up front. Sedition and treason, conscious or unconscious, were basic facts of political life.

It has sometimes been said that where there is anarchy, the wicked come to rule. Albania in the early 1920s was undoubtedly anarchic. Ahmed Bey Zogolli became its supremo, and later Zogist propaganda glossed over the details of these critical years. The impression was given that natural selection or divine providence had inevitably raised the most capable person to the leadership. Revolutionary exiles correspondingly dwelt on the events of 1920–25 with the aim of showing that the Albanian monarchy was rooted in opportunism, treachery, and bloodshed. Even Zogists could not deny that their man made a great many enemies. Perhaps the rival explanations of his rise to power are not wholly incompatible.

For most of 1921, however, Zogolli was obliged to bide his time. The absurdly misnamed Progressive Party, which supported the Vrioni Government, won a chaotic general election in which a system of indirect voting provided ample scope for fraud and almost guaranteed that every prefecture elected its chiefs and beys. As a deputy, Zogolli joined the opposition Popular Party (and also the Clique which virtually ran it). Though prominent, he was never well enough integrated to be called a party leader. The Popular Party primarily attracted Christians, townsmen, and merchants, so a Muslim landowner excited suspicion. In so far as a political spectrum existed, Zogolli stood on its liberal wing. His rhetoric was reformist – 'We must raise from the ruins our nation worm-eaten by age-old slavery'[1] – but parliamentary debates were of scant account compared with events outside.

The international position of Albania remained parlous. The question of its frontiers lodged at the bottom of the peace settlement agenda, and raiding continued unabated. In southern Albania (or northern Epirus), Greek irregulars put Muslims to flight in order to show how Greek it all was to compilers of population statistics. In the north-east, refugees streamed out of Kosovo: the Red Cross estimated that up to ten thousand of them had died of exposure, starvation, or disease in 1920. The Yugoslav Government evicted ethnic Albanians to make way for Serb colonisation, and Kosovar beys ended up in Tirana, demanding retaliation. Members of the Kosovo Committee, such as Hassan Prishtina and Bajram Curri, impugned the patriotism of anyone who failed to endorse their call for all-out war.

A bad situation grew even worse in July 1921. The Mirdita clans announced their secession from the rest of Albania. Roman Catholic by faith, the old-fashioned Mirdites were notorious for resisting all outside authority. Even so, a Republic of Mirdita sounded incongruous; this was really a fresh attempt by the Serbs to detach northern territory. The old chieftain of Mirdita, Prenk Bib Doda, died in a feud in 1920, leaving no clear successor. The Yugoslavs then gave arms and money to one of the claimants, Gjon Marka Gjoni, who let them issue an independence declaration in his name. Gjoni justified this step to his people by claiming that the 'Turks' in Tirana were going to ban Catholicism.

Thus hostilities between Albania and Yugoslavia flared up once more. To many Albanians the obvious riposte was a full-scale uprising in Kosovo. Others agreed with Zogolli that this entailed too great a risk. The division of opinion cut across party lines, and the Government dithered helplessly while the Serbs intervened in support of their Mirdite clients. In October 1921, the raiders came within thirty miles of Tirana. At this, Vrioni resigned the premiership, and it was only with difficulty that an emergency coalition (called the Sacred Union) could be formed behind his successor, Pandeli Evangjeli.

Zogolli played a lone hand in the feverish politicking that surrounded the change of Government. First, he expressed support for the Sacred Union. Then, once it had taken office, he attacked it and threatened to form a new opposition party. To win him back (and secure the services of his Mati fighters), Evangjeli offered him, on 4 November, the joint military command of the northern district. He was to lead the fight against Mirdita and the Serbs in conjunction with Bajram Curri. The chieftain of Mati knew the character of the Mirdites. They were almost traditional foes. In 1877, indeed, Mati had actually joined with the Turks to 'subdue' the Catholic clans. Many of his warriors even now were eager for pillage and pig-burning, but Zogolli preferred restraint. He let Curri engage the Mirdites first amid the wooded hills.

Resistance was surprisingly muted, thanks to belated action by the Allied Powers, who had finally lost patience with Serbian expansionism. The Conference of Ambassadors officially recognised the Albanian Government on 9 November and instructed Yugoslavia to withdraw to the pre-war frontier or face sanctions. This reaffirmation of the 1913 borders disappointed the Kosovars, but Zogolli accepted it as the basis for peace.

On 28 November, he offered the Mirdites liberal terms: no reprisals, if they ended their revolt. With Yugoslav support fast fading away, Gjon Marka Gjoni chose to flee, leaving the elders to reach a deal with the Tirana Government – or at least with Ahmed Bey Zogolli, who may have promised to exempt them from taxation.

To pacify Mirdita appeared a notable achievement, especially to ordinary Albanians who knew nothing about the angry diplomatic protests which Lloyd George had been sending to Belgrade. Zogolli and Curri both increased their prestige, but this only heightened the power struggle between their respective associates in Tirana, which the Prime Minister, Evangjeli, was too weak to contain. He protested vigorously when two of the Regents – in blank defiance of constitutional propriety – began to interfere with his powers of appointment to the advantage of the anti-Zogolli faction. For his pains, he awakened on 6 December 1921 to find armed men in his bedroom, who 'persuaded' him to resign. Twenty-four hours of turmoil ensued, as rival gangs of bodyguards took to the streets. Then one of the renegade Regents swore in Hassan Bey Prishtina, leader of the Kosovars, as Prime Minister.

Zogolli was still at Orosh in Mirdita when he learnt of the *coup d'état*. A telegram notified him of his instant dismissal and gave sole command of the Albanian forces to Bajram Curri, who was away at the frontier, pursuing the Serbs. 'Fate is a blind raging bull that often tramples us under foot,' Zogolli later commented, 'but just sometimes it stands before us in a favourable position. Clever and capable is the man who sees his moment, takes the bull by the horns, and masters it.'[2] Calling his clansmen together, he told them what had happened. He no longer had an official status, but his personal authority was as great as ever.

After a forced march of sixty hours via Mati, replacing the tired and sick *en route*, Zogolli led his warriors into Tirana on 14 December 1921. They numbered around 1,200, enough to occupy strategic points. There was in fact no fighting, as the Prishtina Ministry had already collapsed. Once in physical control, Zogolli simply awaited the next scheduled sitting of parliament. He went to his usual place in the chamber on 22 December as if nothing had occurred. It fell to others to make the speeches. A series of resolutions replaced the Regents with four likely to be more compliant. Then a technical quibble was invoked to unseat five deputies from Dibra who were absent (including Prishtina). Two days later, a new Government took office. The figurehead Prime Minister was Xhafer Bey Ypi, a landowner from Korça of limited intelligence. The Interior Minister was Ahmed Zogolli.

International reaction was favourable. The disintegration of the Albanian Government, less than a month after diplomatic recognition, had threatened to reopen the Adriatic question at the very time when it was supposed to be coming to a close. The young chief from Mati had shown himself to be decisive. He might impose some sort of order. As the first foreign legations opened their doors, diplomats awarded him the benefit of the doubt. The British Minister, Harry Eyres, reported that Ahmed Bey was 'the moving spirit of the Cabinet' and 'a natural leader of men. But there is no reason whatever to believe the assertions of his foes that he is aiming at supreme power in Albania.'[3]

CHAPTER NINE

Surviving

The Interior Ministry in Tirana in 1922 was a shabby office adjoining the mud-brick local prison, but Zogolli understood the potential of this Cabinet post. First, he issued warrants for the arrest of his opponents, charged with breaching the constitution. Though they had long since escaped to the mountains, indictments served to keep them there. Then he resumed the work of expanding the gendarmerie and linking command posts by telegraph. Far more controversially, he also began disarming civilians. Albania would never know peace, he argued, until the number of guns in private possession was greatly reduced. This sounded very reasonable to foreign diplomats. It outraged many Albanians – at first. Most calmed down when they saw that priority went to confiscating weapons in accessible places associated with Zogolli's foes.

Some liberals regretted his use of Mati clansmen to regain power. Such democrats were a tiny urban minority, without armed followers. Zogolli sympathized with their wish for westernisation and would have liked their backing, but he considered that these people, though highly politicised, were not substantial politicians. The chieftains and beys were the men who mattered. He accepted that government could not function without support or acquiescence from a preponderance of them.

The Cabinet looked uninspiring (most of the ministers were former Ottoman officials), and the position of Zogolli within it was more delicate than outsiders supposed. As creator of the new Government, he remained by far its most important member, but he was isolated. To this isolation, paradoxically, he owed much of his importance. In essence, this was a ministry of the Clique – or rather what was left of it after the split over Kosovo. The Clique members most anxious to fight the Serbs had broken away in support of Prishtina and Curri. The residue was mostly from the south, as the Tosks, living farther from Kosovo, tended to feel less hostility to Yugoslavia. As that comparative rarity, a 'Serbophil' Gheg, Zogolli was therefore pivotal. In order to form a Government with any claim to be national, the Tosk beys needed a prominent northerner. Much manoeuvring in Cabinet and Parliament in 1922 and 1923 therefore boiled down to this: was the Clique using Zogolli as a token Gheg, or was Zogolli using the Clique as a springboard to personal power?

The immediate threat to the Government came from north of the River Mati. There the exiled Kosovars and their kaçak bands refused to be conciliated. They had a genuine cause, and it was also the case that Italian agents encouraged their struggle (to weaken Yugoslavia), so it could be hard to distinguish the most zealous nationalists from traitors in Italian pay.

Zogolli tried to depict Hassan Bey Prishtina as one of the latter. He viewed him as a rival – with good reason, as Prishtina lacked neither experience nor education. His surname was actually Berisha, but Albanians invariably called him Prishtina after the town which he had represented in the Young Turk Parliament. There his eloquent denunciations of Ottoman brutality placed him in the front rank of educated nationalists, and much wider fame followed when he led the successful revolt against the Turks in the spring of 1912. A fluent French-speaker, Hassan Bey then served Prince Wilhelm as Postmaster General and raised volunteers for Austria–Hungary during the war. Where he differed from Zogolli was in his uncompromising hatred of the Serbs. Expelled from Kosovo in 1918, he went to Rome and made contact with other anti-Yugoslav groups – separatist Croats, Macedonians, and Montenegrins – in the hope of staging a general uprising against Belgrade.

Bajram Curri was a more straightforward fighting man. About sixty years old and illiterate, he had first turned rebel in the 1890s, since when his prestige as a guerrilla had grown until it stood second to none. Hoping to win him over, Zogolli overlooked their differences and made him Inspector-General of the Frontier, but the effort was futile. Curri mutinied in early March 1922 and led his kaçaks against Shkodra. They were soon contained, but not before the revolt had spread. Zogolli insisted that Italian spies were at work, undermining Albania to justify a protectorate, yet there was really little sign of central direction. Various warlords joined in a backlash by the Kosovar irredentists.

On hearing that Halid Lleshi and Elez Jusufi of Dibra were moving, the Government ordered its remaining fighters to the south and east. By chance, however, Jusufi's band slipped down an unguarded road to Kruja, joined forces with other rebels and approached Tirana unexpectedly from the north, occupying part of the capital on 11 March. The stage being set for a showdown, the Government packed their bags and fled.

Ahmed Zogolli was the sole exception (apart from a minister who hid under a bed at the American hospital). He had not seized power in December only to surrender it in March. Relying on Mati warriors, he barricaded himself inside the Interior Ministry and sent his henchman 'Osman the Terrible' (who wore five gun-belts) to conduct sorties in the streets. There were repeated exchanges of gunfire, yet the kaçaks seemed to be holding back. Were they waiting for reinforcements? Were there divisions in the enemy camp? Zogolli needed to know.

He telephoned the British minister at Durrës and begged him to come and see him. Harry Eyres was a widower in his sixty-sixth year, who had passed his entire working life in British consular service in the Ottoman empire. A visitor to the legation remarked of him, 'Here was England as she used to be . . . the great Power *sans pareil*, whose word was her bond, who was a law unto herself, whose many eccentricities were her pride.'[1] Eyres devoted much of his time to swimming, duck-shooting, and auction bridge, but he was not the kind of diplomat to wait for instructions. He tied a Union Jack to the bonnet of his car and drove to Tirana. 'The position seemed fairly desperate,' he recalled, 'and Ahmed Bey was plainly at the end of his tether. They explained to me the state of affairs and left me to do what I chose.'[2] He opted to go to the rebel quarter and demand in the name of England to speak to Elez Jusufi. The old chief emerged and listened while Eyres urged withdrawal in the national interest. He asked for time to consult the elders. Next day at four o'clock, however, shooting resumed and carried on all night, so Eyres intervened again. Jusufi now denied complicity in any wider revolt and said that he was angered by the government's failure to pay his men for guarding the frontier. Eventually he accompanied Eyres to the Interior Ministry, swore a besa of peace with Zogolli, and marched his clan out in good order, saying that it had all been a matter of honour.

The critical phase of the rebellion was past, but, just as Eyres prepared to go home, news arrived of an outbreak at Shijak on the road between Tirana and Durrës. The challenger this time was Hamid Bey Toptani, a relative of Essad Pasha. Zogolli did not hesitate. Leading his thousand clansmen in person that night, he cleared the hills near Tirana, defeated Toptani in a skirmish at Kashar, and occupied Shijak at dawn, after fighting for 6 hours and marching 20 miles. This utterly demoralised the rebels, who dispersed as quickly as they had formed. The American writer, Rose Wilder Lane, witnessed the return of the victor:

Picture of Ahmet, riding back from Durazzo. Riding the tired bay horse, at the head of his Mati men. Riding through a crowd which silently parted to let him pass. Rifle and revolver, knives and cartridge belt, gone. The grey business suit cleaned and pressed. A white face, and darkness under the eyes, and eyes that see straight to the end of things. Soft tramping of feet in rawhide *opanji* behind him, and the Mati men in dingy black-braided trousers and coloured sashes and Skanderbeg jackets, rifles all angled above their kerchiefed heads, pouring down the narrow street. Then lumbering behind them, dust filmed and mud splashed, the empty automobile of the Albanian government, gone forty miles to Durazzo to fetch Ahmet and come back empty because he would ride at the head of his men.[3]

The balance sheet of the revolt and subsequent reprisals was 70 dead, 300 arrested, and hundreds of houses burnt. To suppress Kosovar propaganda, the Government outlawed songs that criticised neighbouring countries or politicians. One side only of the story could be rhapsodised:

> Ahmet, the Son of the Mountain Eagle!
> His wings spread out and cover us,
> The shadow of his wings is over us,
> His claws are terrible to his foes.
> Ahmet Bey, the Beautiful! O! O! Ahmet Bey!
> The men of Dibra came with their rifles,
> Elez Jusufi, the chief of the Dibra,
> The Toptani family, curse of Albania,
> Hamid Toptani, with nine hundred soldiers,
> Nine hundred soldiers armed by Italians,
> Came from Durrës to murder Albania.
> Elez Jusufi goes back to Dibra,
> Besa of peace he has given to Ahmet.
> Hamid Toptani flees through the mountains,
> Cursed be the trees that give him hiding . . .
> Five thousand napoleons, fine of Durrës,
> Five thousand napoleons, fine of Tirana,
> Five villages burned. Let the market place tell
> Names of the men who were hanged there at dawn.[4]

Five secondary leaders were indeed hanged, though Prishtina and Curri escaped once more to the disputed frontier districts.

Eyres reported that Zogolli was the hero of the crisis. He was equally appreciative. Had he not always said that the British were the finest people in the world? Harry Eyres was henceforth a confidant. It is too much to say that this allowed him to run Albanian foreign policy (as jealous Italians alleged), but his influence was certainly exceptional. During long conversations in Turkish, often alone over dinner, Zogolli sought his advice not only on the etiquette of diplomacy, but on the whole range of policy, domestic as well as foreign. In time, Eyres did not wait to be asked. He judged that peace in the Adriatic was best served by assisting the most promising Albanian leader to stay in power. Zogolli told how the British Minister was 'constantly at his hand, helping him in his difficult work by drawing his attention to the misdeeds of this or that Prefect'.[5]

Experience had taught Albanians to view most great powers with hostility. Italy had tried to annex the country. France was too friendly with Yugoslavia. Russia had long been a Pan-Slavist foe. There was yet widespread faith in

British disinterestedness. Lots of people knew of Edith Durham, and the Dowager Countess of Carnarvon (Aubrey Herbert's mother) ran a charity for Kosovar refugees. Heartened by these few enthusiasts, Albanians failed to see that British disinterestedness was generally synonymous with lack of concern. Some Englishmen had barely heard of the place: did the inhabitants have white hair and pink eyes? The foreign office did not wholly approve of the extent to which Eyres interfered (without knowing the half of it), but no one matched his local knowledge. He stayed in Durrës another four years, a good friend to Zogolli.

After the failed rebellion, the Ypi Ministry continued as before, though Zogolli was forever intervening with colleagues to suppress undiplomatic despatches and overrule bad decisions. This inevitably antagonised the Clique, whose obvious Tosk bias increasingly irked him. This problem went to the heart of current Albanian politics. If the Government were to control the country, it needed to conciliate the Gheg chiefs of the north. To keep his majority in Parliament, however, Zogolli had to favour Tosk beys from the south. His dilemma became acute when the chamber met in the autumn after seven months in recess. Even if the Clique did not abandon him, he warned the British Legation, he might have to resign in order to preserve his influence among the Ghegs. Since he alone held the regime together, he wondered whether he should take matters into his own hands, 'make a clean sweep' of the current leaders, disregard Parliament, and appeal to the chiefs for direct support. 'Government would be carried on provisionally on a practically feudal basis.'[6]

Caution prevailed. Zogolli made no attempt to overthrow the parliamentary system in December 1922, yet he did take a step in the direction of one-man-rule by assuming the premiership himself (while keeping the interior portfolio). This was a gamble, since it made his position more exposed. There had been much to be said for having an expendable puppet prime minister. On the other hand, as Head of Government, he could better deal with the chieftains on a personal basis (the form of politics they understood).

His elevation jarred on senior beys; to yield precedence to a 27-year-old was galling. In his first speech as Prime Minister on 2 December, he appealed to more progressive opinion by promising to strengthen democracy, construct new roads, expand trade, combat malaria, and even run a budget surplus. The present Government would 'realise all patriotic sentiments,' he declared, 'especially our idea of building upon an occidental State with western civilisation.'[7] To symbolise his belief in reform, he had started to sign his name differently. Out went the suffix *-olli* and with it the honorific *Bey*. Both were relics of Ottoman times. Though popular usage was slow to change, the prime minister was formally Ahmed Zogu. It was one measure of westernisation achievable without money.

CHAPTER TEN

Zogu, PM

Every Albanian Government faced a fundamental difficulty: how was it to pay for an army, a police force, a civil service, schools, hospitals, roads, and economic development when it was in a state of intractable financial insolvency? The tax system inherited from the Turks was outrageously inefficient and unfair. While the tithe and cattle tax drove impoverished peasants deeper into debt, income tax stood at no more than 6 per cent even for the highest earners, most of whom bribed the tax inspector. Only about a quarter of taxable income was ever declared.

Westernisers kept talking about obtaining a major loan from the League of Nations to improve communications and set up modern industries. With this in view, the Government had appealed to the League as early as May 1922 to send a financial adviser, but when he at length arrived, the Dutchman Jan Hunger predictably decided that Albania was uncreditworthy. Drastic spending cuts and tax reform were his prescription. Zogu rejected this as politically impossible, frankly doubting that the beys and chieftains would tolerate any Government which set out seriously to tax them.

Rebuffed by the League, he then tried approaching foreign banks and governments directly. But who would lend money to such a fragile regime? Only people with ulterior motives. Yugoslavia offered small sums – if loans were secured with border territory. That too was politically impossible. The idea of high tariffs as a source of revenue crossed his mind, but Italy (which dominated external trade) implacably opposed their imposition.

The Government could scarcely afford to do anything except cling to office, which itself meant spending peace money to keep the clans in order. Zogu enrolled chiefs as reserve colonels and paid for the notional military services of their men. Each month bands of Gheg warriors descended on Tirana to collect their gold and renew their besa with the Prime Minister. Putting on a show of hospitality, he would first greet the chief with an embrace and approach of the lips to each cheek (right, then left), and then ply him with coffee, tobacco, and raki, the local spirit. Frequent toasts ('*Gëzuar!*') punctuated polite enquiries about family and clan, till the chieftain pledged his loyalty and pocketed his 'pay'. The system was cheaper than suppressing revolts but it required a steady flow of funds.

This heightened the importance of his one remaining option: the sale of commercial concessions to foreigners. The Government repeatedly touted rights to engage in forestry, mining, tobacco growing, and even archaeology, despite local conditions tending to deter respectable businessmen. Zogu had himself been known to quote the Turkish proverb, 'You shouldn't be sure of keeping your head in Turkey, your wife in Romania, or your property in Albania.'[1] The only concession which excited real interest was the right to prospect for oil. The Italians had detected traces of it during the war, and, as early as 1921, the Albanians signed a preliminary agreement with D'Arcy Exploration, a subsidiary of the Anglo-Persian Oil Company (forerunner of BP). Though inclined to the British firm for political reasons, Zogu did not let his lack of commercial know-how deter him from attempting to secure better terms by encouraging alternative bids. To Captain Edward Shearme of Anglo-Persian Oil, he came across as 'ambitious, quite uneducated, clever, and absolutely fearless'.[2] A fuller picture of the young premier comes from Rose Wilder Lane:

> He sits in a gilded *Louis Seize* chair, under a painted Turkish ceiling. Half a hundred rifles, museum pieces he has chosen from the long mule trains of rifles brought down to Tirana as the mountain tribes are disarmed, are stacked behind his chair. A box telephone on the wall, an English grammar on the table, a Mati man lying on the threshold of the door. Ahmet saying: 'Albania needs men, trained men. What am I, with power in my hands that I cannot use because I am ignorant? I do not know Europe, America. Tirana needs factories, Tirana needs industries. The people are starving and ragged: they walk with bare feet over the earth that covers their fortunes.[3]

By spring 1923, Zogu was ready to close the deal. The Anglo-Persian Oil Company would acquire prospecting rights over 200,000 hectares and pay Albania a 13.5 per cent royalty on output. Happy with the terms, he failed to foresee how his dalliance with other oil firms would rebound on him. Thinking that Anglo-Persian would have claimed all the promising sites, they refused to bid for any other fields and determined to destroy the agreement. Since the British Government owned a controlling stake in Anglo-Persian, France and Italy lodged diplomatic protests, and the agents of Standard Oil returned on a US navy destroyer. Once more Zogu feared that his Government would fall. The concession required ratification by Parliament, but, while Standard Oil lobbyists were so open-handed and Italian ones so menacing, deputies could not be trusted to pass the Bill even on a confidence vote. He therefore resorted to delay while distracted by other problems.

Under the guidance of Harry Eyres, Zogu had been striving (sometimes against his instincts) to stabilise Albania's foreign relations. Profoundly suspicious of Italy and Yugoslavia and not at all sure about Greece, he initially aimed at strict neutrality verging on isolationism, but in the feverish climate of Adriatic politics his every action came under scrutiny. Did he incline to Rome or Belgrade? Eyres told how 'Ahmed Bey almost with tears in his eyes implored me to believe that the Government was neither Serbophil nor Italophil but purely Albanophil'.[4]

Naturally, Kosovar irredentists called him the cat's paw of Yugoslavia – an accusation which he dismissed as patently absurd, given that relations with the Serbs remained so bad. 'Today they dominate half the Albanian nation and territory,' he acknowledged grimly. Nationalist anger was perfectly justified. But what could in fact be done for Kosovo? He had to seek peace with Yugoslavia, regardless of his feelings, since kaçak violence was more likely to wreck the Albanian state than to redeem the lost province. 'I do not fear the Serbs at all,' he protested, 'but Albanian bands understand only pillage, theft, and assassination.'[5]

Cartographers from an international boundary commission were gradually mapping the frontiers prior to their final demarcation. The average speed of pack ponies never exceeded 2mph in the mountains, and work stopped in winter. Diplomatic headway was no more swift, as contested areas came before the Conference of Ambassadors, where France normally endorsed what Zogu called 'the marvellous ethnographical statements' of the Serbs. Did not Albania have an equal right to protection? 'We can only look to England to help us and though your country is desirous of shaking us off into the hands of the League of Nations we still cling to her skirts and implore her aid.'[6] From 1922 until 1926, Zogu was prone to wishful thinking about Britain. Oil aside, he said that the leading naval power could not be indifferent to the fate of a coastal nation – but the Adriatic was a backwater, as far as the British Empire was concerned. Perhaps he feigned a simple-minded faith in British interventionism in order to stimulate British sympathy.

In response to his piteous accounts of frontier troubles, Eyres repeatedly recommended closer relations with Italy as the obvious counter-balance to pressure from the Serbs. Zogu showed reluctance. The Battle of Vlora had imbued young patriots with exaggerated contempt for Italians; any move to conciliate Italy would further damage his nationalist credentials. Moreover, he believed that Italian agents continued to finance his fiercest opponents, the hardline Kosovars, in order to sharpen conflict with Yugoslavia. 'The Italians desire a government which will purely and simply install them in Albania,' he remarked, 'and unfortunately for our country there are people who are at their disposal.'[7]

Among them Zogu counted the Franciscan friars. Traditionally a conduit of news to remote Roman Catholic clans, they sometimes acted as (partly unwitting) agents of Italian policy. The Greeks and the Serbs put Orthodox priests to similar use. As the non-national organisation of religion had historically been one of the gravest obstacles to Albanian nationhood, Zogu encouraged the creation of an autonomous Albanian Orthodox Church in 1922 (though it took another fifteen years to wring acceptance of its autocephalous status from the Ecumenical Patriarch). Meanwhile, the Vatican took umbrage at a new law requiring all active clergy to be native Albanians. Not that the Muslim faith escaped reform. A congress in Tirana in 1923 declared Albanian Islam independent of the caliphate. Asked if his regime was Muslim and willing to work in close accord with Turkey, Zogu replied that secular Albania intended to progress on occidental lines.

This aversion to renewed Turkish patronage might have endeared him to the Greeks, but, here again, continuing border raids ruled out genuine co-operation. When Greece enhanced its ethnic claim to disputed regions by deporting Muslim Albanians to Turkey, Albanian opinion was outraged. The Greeks, for their part, disliked Zogu's attitude to the most dramatic event in the Adriatic in 1923: the Italian attack on Corfu in retaliation for the murder of three Italian members of the boundary commission working on the Greek-Albanian frontier. As the first example of Fascism in action in international affairs, the Corfu Incident provoked loud protests, but not from Albania, where many felt that Greece was getting its comeuppance. If one pro-Italian source can be believed, Zogu said he was delighted to see Italy strong. A debilitated Italy might consent to partition Albania with Greece and Yugoslavia; an arrogant Italy would never allow Albanian territory to fall to its rivals. Long anti-Italian though he had been, 'I expect now to look to her again as the trump card to play in the game of preserving the integrity of my country.'[8]

It was almost inevitable that Albanian policy would turn into a deliberate balancing act, the usual recourse of a nation too weak to defend itself. Once he thought in these terms, Zogu treated the Serbs and Italians to the same brand of two-faced charm that he used to play bey against bey.

Independent Albania had experienced an unprecedented eighteen months of relative peace and stability by autumn 1923. Within his narrower remit as Interior Minister, Zogu could claim success. At the same time, as Premier, he had failed to solve either of his basic problems: state finances worsened by the month, and his relations with the Clique grew ever more strained.

Annual revenue was 15 million gold francs while expenditure topped 24 million, so far as anyone could tell. Reliable accounts did not exist and large sums frequently vanished as a result of ministers drawing on the Treasury for unbudgeted secret services (presumably informers). The worst offender was Zogu himself. As official salaries fell five or six months in arrears, he feared losing influence over the chiefs, army, and gendarmerie.

He had also managed to alienate several members of his Cabinet by recruiting a team of foreign advisers. There were seven of them, one for each ministry, and they hailed from seven different lands: Meissner Pasha (Public Works) was the German engineer who had laid the Hedjaz railway for the Turks; Colonel Stirling (Interior) was a former British governor of Jaffa; Baron Menzinger (Justice) set up the courts in Libya after the Italian conquest; General von Myrdacz (War) had served in the Austrian army in Albania. Only Martin, a French educationalist, went home within a week. The others set about reform of their departments, but ministers did not like surveillance by Zogu's nominees. The first resignation came in September, when the War Minister, Ismail Tatzati, went into opposition.

The parliamentary situation was already precarious. For months, Zogu vacillated over when to press the oil concession to a vote – to the intense exasperation of the Anglo-Persian Oil Company. Albanians looked on their oil as an economic panacea, but so long as the rival firms (British, American, Italian, and French) greased the deputies' palms with equal munificence, it was difficult to see how a majority could ever be assembled to ratify any specific concession. Zogu made every effort to settle the matter during the autumn session, but the Clique failed to whip members into line, and only about a quarter of the deputies personally supported him. To survive a confidence vote, he had to postpone the oil concession yet again and make a series of contradictory promises and unrealistic spending pledges.

Failure to ratify the Anglo-Persian contract was a serious blow to Zogu, who had been absolutely banking on it. Disenchanted with Albanian parliamentarism, he invited Harry Eyres to dinner and talked into the early hours about the utter inadequacy of a constitution so at odds with reality:

> He pointed out that Albania was not at present being governed according to institutions which were native to the country and developed according to the political sense of the people, but they were doing what they could with a system borrowed from other lands. He himself, he said, owed little or none of his authority to the fact that he was Prime Minister; his position as hereditary Chief of Mati was the greater of the two. I asked if he referred to the fact that he always had at his disposal a considerable body of armed men, and he said it was not merely that but the mere name of his family.[9]

According to Zogu, the authority which Albanians instinctively respected was that of the chiefs and heads of great families. The Mirdites stayed loyal to Gjoni, their exiled chief, even though he was a drunken failure. Conversely, Evangjeli, who was not of high family, had been illegally ousted from the premiership, and most people could not have cared less. The chief of Mati thought it would be better 'to conduct the government of the country through those persons of his own class through whom it had been conducted for centuries'.

> Albania, he continued, fell into three divisions so far as government was concerned. In the North and in the mountains generally it might easily be ruled according to some form or other of the feudal system. In Central Albania, the people were amenable to authority generally, and where they were not they could be swayed by playing on their religious ideas; but so far as the South was concerned it was not easy to find a principle that would always hold good.[10]

This was because the old ruling families of southern Albania had been massacred by the Turks in 1830. The Ottoman clients who replaced them had never won popular respect, and now in the Tosk towns there were 'young apostles of democracy', who, having spent some time in the USA, would never agree to the kind of hereditary Upper Chamber which he wanted to put in place.

The returned emigrants formed part of a wider problem: the best educated and the most powerful were not the same people. 'A great deal of his difficulties in the North has arisen from the fact that Prefects and Sub-Prefects had been appointed to posts who were quite unfitted for them.' They were 'small people from the South who could read and write and had a smattering of legal knowledge but who were quite incapable of governing'. Where he could, he preferred to appoint established local leaders; 'They signed their names where necessary with a seal and continued to rule their districts as those had been ruled for generations.'[11] Needless to say, this practice found no favour among ambitious young Tosks. Zogu hoped to train the sons of each influential family to become literate administrators.

In the meantime, Albania needed a constitution conducive to effective government. It cannot be pretended, however, that Zogu worried about legal technicalities. With the futile parliamentary session of September 1923, he had clearly reached an impasse. His priorities were to ditch the Clique before it ditched him, secure a submissive chamber, and ratify the vital oil concession. After a few weeks, he took the plunge and called a general election. Any semblance of political stability immediately vanished.

CHAPTER ELEVEN

Down and Out

The poll conducted in December 1923 turned out to be the last genuinely contested general election in Albania for nearly seventy years. Its key issue was ostensibly constitutional reform (for the Parliament would double as a Constituent Assembly), but in reality the question of Zogu's own leadership overshadowed all else. Critics alleged that any constitution designed by him would perpetuate his rule. He let it be known that, once the system of government was settled, he intended to leave politics for a time to study languages in London or Paris. Nobody believed him.

His manifesto, published on 16 November, promised a new constitution based on 'all those political principles which are found in the freest countries', and called for 'a party of ideas whose discipline will be soldierly' to 'effect the great reforms and the drastic economies which are needed if the life of Albania is not to flicker out'.[1] Eyres thought that his catchwords would 'appeal to the type of petty attorney turned politician which has proved an obstacle to him in the last Parliament. To the great mass of the people they will mean nothing at all, while the name of Ahmed means a good deal.'[2] That was true, but his name meant very different things to different people. Frustrated Kosovars, jealous beys, and disenchanted liberals were intent on his downfall. More insidiously, cabinet colleagues in the Clique knew that an organised Zogist Party would spell the end of their influence, so they turned against him too.

Given the static nature of bey politics, it may appear odd that anyone could expect the new Parliament to differ much from the old. A few seats changing hands, however, might be enough to make office-hungry deputies flock to the winning side. Moreover, an election meant chances for bribery and intimidation. Here Zogu expected to have the edge. He was suddenly in funds after selling a forest in Mati to an Italian timber company for 300,000 lire. Eyres, on looking into the transaction, discovered the woods to be inaccessible and commercially unviable. The Italian secret service hedged its bets by subsidising the opposition too.

Even more important was control of the electoral machinery. The prefects who organised polling (and the gendarmes who policed it) were answerable to the Interior Ministry headed by Zogu. His calling the vote of his own volition only stoked distrust. Anti-Zogists demanded his resignation as Interior Minister to restore public confidence in the fairness of the system. When he refused it, many concluded that he had to be stopped *before* polling day. Thus the dissolution of Parliament began a precipitous breakdown of public order.

Anti-Zogist officers in the armed forces ignored commands from Zogu. Gossip swept Tirana that Colonel Tatzati was planning a military coup, the premier to be shot on the podium during the Independence Day march-past. At this, Zogu summoned loyal battalions (with plenty of Mati clansmen) to put a cordon around his residence. When 28 November passed without incident, the tension did not relax. Armed factions patrolled the capital, spoiling for a fight. The mutineers gained access to an army storeroom and doled out ammunition by the haversack.

This was the gravest crisis since March 1922, and Zogu again turned to the British Legation. Eyres was away, but the chargé Robert Parr heard him outline his three options: either resign and surrender, or play for time, or strike hard at once, crush the rebels, and hang the ring-leaders. This last response might entail 'semi-dictatorship'.[3] Urging restraint, Parr informally called together the senior diplomatic corps (envoys of Britain, Yugoslavia, Italy, and the USA) and let it be known that these four nations would refuse to recognise a Government which came to power unconstitutionally. The mood on the streets eased at this, but the gangs did not disperse. It took more ingenious diplomatic mediation to broker a compromise. As nobody in the cabinet could be trusted to administer public order impartially during the election, they would take turns as Interior Minister on a weekly rotation. In seven days, each incumbent could reverse appointments made by his predecessor and install his own cronies, but no faction would be in control long enough to put much pressure on the voters. In effect, central government was paralysed, and local gendarmerie officers and prefects received *carte blanche* to practise all sorts of electoral fraud on their own initiative.

The second and final round of voting took place on 27 December 1923. The outcome was indecisive.

Zogu felt dismayed yet not despairing. By his reckoning, the Zogists had won 50 seats out of 102, sweeping Durrës, Dibra, and Elbasan. The Opposition was fragmented, and he hoped to win over deputies from Berat, a prefecture dominated by the Vrioni family. He postponed the meeting of Parliament and opened private talks, which proved long and tiresome, as Sami Vrioni initially aspired to the premiership himself. Meanwhile, there was nothing to ease the protracted atmosphere of menace. Entire units of the armed forces continued to repudiate the Prime Minister.

It was not until 23 February 1924 that deputies gathered to elect a new Government. Zogu had succeeded in striking a deal and anticipated a majority of twenty or so. Shortly after half-past-two, he left his office on the ground floor to go up to the parliamentary chamber for the start of proceedings. He was just on the turn of the stairs, when a young man appeared at the top and shot him. After two or three rounds, the pistol jammed and the assassin turned and ran.

Though wounded, Zogu simply drew his revolver and carried on. The deputies, who had instantly fallen silent, turned to see the double-doors of the chamber thrown open as the Prime Minister staggered in. 'He looked deathly pale,' related Ekrem Vlora, 'but he held himself straight, pulled himself together, smiled even, went confidently to the Government bench, and sat down in one of the armchairs set aside for the secretaries.'[4] The stillness was unnerving. A hundred men hovered on the brink of a shoot-out.

Then fresh rounds sounded in the lobby. Some deputies dived beneath their desks while others started pushing and shouting and waving their guns. The assassin had in fact locked himself in the lavatory, where he was singing patriotic songs and firing through the door. Ringed by supporters, Zogu summoned up strength to call out, 'Gentlemen, this is not the first time in the world that such a thing has happened in a parliament. I ask my friends to leave it alone and deal with it afterwards.' His appeal for calm was remarkably effective, even though, as he later admitted, 'it was not so easy to stay calm myself'.[5] Contrary to Zogist legend, he did not then make the longest and most brilliant speech of his career, but he did remain in his place for 15 minutes with every appearance of composure. The bullets had injured his left wrist, thigh, and lower abdomen. 'It hurt like the devil,' he remembered, 'but I knew that I must not show my pain.'[6] After first refusing to let anyone touch him, he finally allowed a doctor who had been in the public gallery to apply temporary dressings. When his own physician arrived, Zogu asked that the assembly carry on quietly and left with obvious difficulty.

No Government was elected that day. Wild accusations and counter-accusations flew across the chamber until business had to be suspended. Zogists warned of an imminent *coup d'état*. The Opposition posited a private feud, but news that the telegraph line to Mati had been cut indicated a conspiracy. Astonished at his survival, some adversaries alleged that he must have staged the incident himself for some Machiavellian purpose.

In fact, though his life was not in danger, Zogu had been badly hurt. Rest was essential on medical grounds, and that may not have been the only factor. By the laws of the blood feud, the victim of an attack should not leave his house until avenged. Of course, Zogu the social reformer professed to be above the Law of Lek. Some later accounts of his remarks in the chamber even include, 'The culprit must be entrusted to the

Justice of the State.'[7] But Zogu the chieftain needed to retain the respect of his clansmen. Next morning, he resigned as Prime Minister.

After a few days, a predominantly Zogist ministry was formed by Shevqet Bey Vërlaci, a landowner said to be the richest in the country. A political opponent till 1922, Zogu had managed to gain his support (and that of some other reactionary beys) by pledging to marry his daughter Behije. This was no love-match – the couple scarcely knew each other – but a traditional arrangement between a prominent bey and a rising politician. The Opposition depicted Vërlaci as keeping the seat warm for his future son-in-law.

In or out of office, Zogu remained the focal point. Hundreds of well-wishers visited his home, where he lay on a couch, tended by his mother. By custom, a wounded man was obliged to receive his friends, no matter how ill he felt, and to try and keep up a polite conversation. Zogu did so brilliantly, despite a fever. Not an angry word passed his lips; he seemed totally unconcerned (which, to guests attuned to the psychology of feuding, conveyed his certainty of vengeance). His assailant, Beqir Walter, was brought before him. Zogu knew this eighteen-year-old from Mati and judged him incapable of having acted alone. In return for a lenient three-year gaol sentence, Walter pointed the finger at a group called *Bashkimi*, the Union of Young Albanians, who aspired to emulate the Young Turks or the Bolsheviks.

Eight weeks later, the leader of Bashkimi was gunned down in the street. It was Avni Rustemi, the celebrated assassin of Essad Pasha Toptani. A morose little man, he had long expected the Toptani clan to exact retribution, and his killer leased a mill on one of their estates, but many people suspected a red herring. It suited Zogists who paid lip-service to the justice of the state to talk up the Toptani link in order to exculpate their hero. Everyone else, given the Law of Lek, assumed that Zogu had Rustemi killed in revenge for the attack on himself.

In cases like this, he scorned denial. Clear evidence of his direct involvement in murder was never to be had, but, while dual standards operated in Albania, he likely judged that, on balance, his standing was enhanced if people believed him responsible. At the cost of upsetting a liberal minority, he won the respect and fear of the rest. If he expected to derive any advantage in this particular instance, however, Zogu was making a serious mistake.

The backlash began with an open letter from 'the patriotic youth' of Vlora, warning that Avni Rustemi's assassination 'had driven the people to the extremity of despair, since it is felt to be a death blow to the idealistic conception of the State'.[8] The anti-Zogists had found their *cause célèbre*. Even those who had had no time for Rustemi when alive, eulogised him in death as 'the national hero-martyr' – the foe of despotism who first saved

Albania from Essad Pasha and then sacrificed his life in the effort to save it from Ahmed Zogu. For what was the latter if not a replica of Essad? Both aspired to autocracy. Both had sold out to the Serbs. If Zogu resumed his public career, what chance would there be for anyone else?

The funeral of Avni Rustemi turned into an Opposition rally. Inflammatory speeches over the coffin called for Zogu to stand trial for murder and denounced the Vërlaci Government for shielding him. Afterwards, twenty-two members of the Opposition declared that they would boycott the tainted Tirana Parliament until the malefactor had been driven into exile. They invited honourable deputies to join an alternative assembly at Vlora.

One of the first to respond was the Finance Minister, Luigj Gurakuqi, a pioneer of Albanian education, who came from Shkodra, where the Zogists had been trounced in the general election. This town, a former Ottoman provincial centre, had resented the choice of Tirana as the national seat of government. When led to believe that a new regime would move the capital, Shkodra followed Vlora in rejecting central authority. In the north, clan discontent was sharpened by sheer desperation in 1924, as three years of drought culminated in failure of the maize crop. Reduced to eating grass, the Mirdites were ripe for revolt, and Kosovar guerrillas led the way. When Bajram Curri attacked the village of Kruma, diplomats feared the start of civil war. Conspiracy theories arising from the apparently motiveless murder of two American tourists added to the sense of alarm.

Zogu remained convalescent in Tirana. Friends and enemies alike anticipated some dramatic riposte on his part, yet weeks went by without a sign. Though his health was improving, and he even grew uncharacteristically plump, his spirits were slower to revive. Always susceptible to the occasional bout of pessimism, this time he was downright depressed. An Englishman seeing him in early June found him 'a picture of indecision . . . by no means impressive'.[9] Though kept informed of the spread of the revolt, he appeared obsessed by the fact that he held no place in the Government, yet, by now, the Government scarcely signified.

Pathetic vacillation had been the hallmark of the Vërlaci ministry. It was too reliant on Zogu to expel him and seemingly incapable of acting without him. The rebels, some five thousand, were scattered and without a single leader. Sooner than take the field, however, the Government argued over tactics and observed the daily defection of gendarmerie and army units hitherto loyal. By the end of May, both major garrisons at Përmeti and Shkodra were taking their orders from Vlora (where forty deputies had assembled), and mutiny acquired the momentum of revolution. Vërlaci resigned and fled to Italy. His successor, Ilias Vrioni, managed to negotiate a one-day ceasefire but hardly knew what to do with it. First, he invited Zogu to take command of the northern district. Then he forbade him to leave Tirana, for fear that the town itself would rebel. On 7 June, Vrioni implored the British Legation to intervene. Eyres refused.

Two days afterwards, Zogu made his long-awaited appearance on the streets of the capital to appeal for support against the advancing insurgents. He still had some six hundred clansmen and gendarmes behind him, but the majority of the inhabitants turned their backs on a losing cause. When he asked a public meeting to choose between resistance and surrender, the verdict was almost unanimously for the latter. Everyone of importance had already left town. As the white flags went up, Zogu and his dwindling band did the same.

In extremity, his power of decision returned. He first went east to Elbasan, skirmishing *en route*, and then headed north to Homesh in Dibra. There Elez Jusufi, the local chief, was still bound by the besa that they had sworn in March 1922. As long as he stayed in Dibra, Zogu would be safe. Curri's guerrillas, who had been in pursuit, found their way blocked at the edge of the region. Thus Jusufi fulfilled his obligation, but, in respect of the rebellion, he declared neutrality. For ten days, Zogu strove to persuade him that Dibra should ally with Mati in the cause of Gheg solidarity. The old man would not be moved. On 22 June, Zogu paid off his clansmen and slipped across the border into Yugoslavia with 170 gendarmes.

Eyres was sorry yet unsurprised: 'He placed far too much faith in his own capacity for intrigue' and had disgusted even the 'well-meaning deputies by his inveterate habit of promising everything to everybody'.[10] In summer 1924, Balkan commentators penned the political obituary of Ahmed Zogu, aged twenty-eight, 'a young man with a quiet, diffident manner, full of physical courage, but lacking in moral grit. His faults were his inability to judge men and to keep his word, and a lack of decision in critical moments. He had in him, however, the seeds of patriotism and some real administrative ability.'[11]

CHAPTER TWELVE

Fan Noli

The new regime in Tirana was a motley coalition of liberals, Kosovars, opposition beys, and mutineers, united by antipathy to Zogu. They had at their head, however, an extraordinary polymath: His Grace Fan S. Noli, Bishop of Durrës, leader of the Democratic Party, League of Nations delegate, Bachelor of Arts, biographer of Skanderbeg, translator of Stendhal, Maupassant, and Molière, liturgist, composer, and orator.

A stocky Tosk with a big beard jutting above his clerical collar, Bishop Noli had been an actor in Athens, a schoolmaster in Egypt, a lumberman in Buffalo, a canning-factory worker in New York, a cinema organist in Boston, and a student at Harvard before settling in Albania in 1921 at the age of thirty-nine. He was Orthodox purely in the confessional sense, and even that was questionable. Ordained a deacon by the Russian Orthodox archbishop of New York in 1908, Noli founded an Albanian Orthodox Church in the USA with himself as its sole priest. Privately, meanwhile, he claimed to be a Nietzschean and, at various times, labelled Christianity a capitalist instrument of enslavement and stated that the whole truth was in Omar Khayyam. He admitted subordinating religion to politics in the best Albanian tradition. His church was intended to promote national consciousness among Christian Tosks hitherto attached to Greek Orthodoxy. He translated the liturgy and made himself a bishop by persuading an assembly of Albanian-Americans to acclaim him as such in 1919. Despite his pioneering work, it was only with reluctance that the new native Albanian Orthodox Church accepted him. Some fanciful critics even alleged that he wore an artificial beard in order to look more episcopal.

During fourteen years in the USA, Noli had won pre-eminence within the Albanian community there, which numbered over twenty thousand. He went to London in 1913 to lobby for independence and campaigned for international recognition after the World War. It delighted foreigners to engage in intellectual discourse with an Albanian bishop. He was a complex man whose style was often self-mocking. Sometimes he sounded sure of his messianic significance; moments later, his tone might be flippantly cynical.

Zogu and Noli were the two most famous Albanians of the inter-war period. The events of 1924 focused attention on their rivalry, and there was subsequently a tendency to present it as the defining issue of an entire era of Albanian history. Émigré writers portrayed a clear moral contest: Bishop Noli symbolised enlightenment, democracy, and progress, while King Zog connoted ignorance, autocracy, and reaction; and the worse man won. This overlooked the fact that it is generally easier for politicians to display idealism when out of office than when confronted by the harsh realities of power. Noli's reputation as a democrat, moreover, owes much to two extraneous factors. First, he spoke excellent English (along with myriad other languages): 'It was only natural for a Harvard graduate to introduce democracy into his native country.'[1] Then he became the unintended beneficiary of communist historiography. Marxist-Leninists talked up 'the Bourgeois Democratic Revolution of 1924', casting Noli in the role of a premature Kerensky. To some westerners, this was practically an encomium to the lost leader.

Whatever he may have claimed in retrospect, Noli came to power by unconstitutional means, established a mixed military-civilian cabinet without reference to Parliament, and seemed in no hurry to hold elections. England was the curse of Europe, he said, as free institutions copied from Westminster were nothing but 'a bloody farce'.[2] Perhaps Noli and Zogu had more in common than Albanian liberals care to admit. The tragedy was that they were incapable of working together. They had begun as allies of a kind. While Zogu fought to secure the Provisional Government at home in 1920, Noli worked to win it respect abroad. They had both belonged to the Popular Party, indeed, though the bases of their support were very different. Noli sat in Parliament as the representative of the diaspora. The Boston Albanians subsidised him and the thousands returning from America in the early 1920s were his natural followers, along with a small band of foreign-educated intellectuals who resented the dominance of chieftains and beys in national life.

Noli held the post of Foreign Minister in the Government formed after Zogu's coup in 1921, but he resigned three months later (during the Kosovar revolt) in protest at its 'reactionary' policies. He then formed his own Democratic Party and became the most eloquent critic of successive ministries. Noli demanded to know why more was not done to modernise Albania. Where were the new roads, the hospitals and schools? In September 1923, in the confidence debate, he delighted the Chamber with a tale of Till Eulenspiegel, the rascal of German folklore (whom he likened to the proverbial Turkish rogue Nastradin). Once upon a time, Till was paid by a baron to paint some murals. After squandering the money without lifting a brush, he summoned his patron to admire the non-existent paintings, explaining that bastards might not be able to see them. Everyone said the murals were superb till a serving girl cried, 'God have mercy on my poor mother!' This gave rise to a parody of a Zogist song:

> Long live Ahmed Zogu,
> The joker of progress!
> May he be remembered for ever
> As the grandson of Nastradin.[3]

Noli felt that the Prime Minister, if he had ever been genuinely progressive, had now sold out to beys resolved to block reform. Rather than trying to win him back, the Bishop turned to those who wanted him swept from the scene entirely. It is not hard to see why these two men resented each other. Noli was far better educated; Zogu came of a higher social class. One of the Bishop's supporters at this time later described the King as 'an ignorant mountaineer who has lost all the virtues of the primitive man and acquired all the defects and none of the qualities of civilisation'.[4] Was there an element of Tosk versus Gheg here? Ghegs tended to distrust Tosks, whom they regarded as less purely Albanian than themselves; Tosks scorned the backwardness of the Ghegs. Some even detected a divergence of political mentality: the Gheg clansman was self-reliant and heedful of traditional authority; the Tosk peasant was more inclined to collective action and hated his Turkified bey.

When Avni Rustemi was shot in 1924, Noli did not hesitate to channel popular outrage into revolutionary activity, arguing afterwards that his 'spiritual fathers' – Napoleon, Skanderbeg, and Jesus – would undoubtedly have done the same.[5] He instigated the breakaway Vlora Assembly, and the varied insurgents rallied around him. Absence abroad had made him something of an outsider, able to stand above clan jealousies. His manifesto of June 1924 promised 'to suppress the medieval privileges which impoverish the Albanian people' by delivering roads, bridges, health-care, education, prosperity, and, far more contentiously, 'economic emancipation of the peasants'.[6]

The first act of the rebels on taking Tirana was to release the assassin Walter. Noli then set up a political court which in due course sentenced Zogu to death *in absentia*. Lesser opponents were force-fed cod liver oil until they soiled their trousers (a technique copied from Fascist Italy). Such proceedings made a bad impression abroad, and Greece was the only country to recognise the new regime. Here the influence of Harry Eyres played a part in holding Italy, Yugoslavia, and the USA to their pledge (made during the election campaign seven months earlier) to withhold recognition from any cabinet formed unconstitutionally. Britain was seen to be backing Zogu on account of the oil concession.

Foreign hostility dismayed Noli, who aimed to finance his reforms by means of that elusive cure-all: a League of Nations loan. He daringly absented himself for seven weeks to attend the League Assembly in Geneva, where he took to the podium on 10 September:

But do tell me, Mr Secretary-General, why you refuse to give Albania a loan to enable her to get on her feet? We need only 300,000,000 gold francs. Too much, you say? Well, I am going to climb down elegantly to the modest sum of 200,000,000 gold francs. You are shaking your head. Well, I am willing to negotiate for a smaller sum, say 100,000,000 gold francs. I beg your pardon? Do you mean to say that you have never met me in your life, and that you would not lend me a penny? . . . Perhaps the Secretary-General meant to say that he is unwilling to negotiate a loan with a revolutionary Government without a Parliament like that presided over by my reverend humility. But do you know what a Parliament is? . . . A Parliament is a hall where heartless politicians meet to vivisect their own race, a hall full of poison gas, of asphyxiating gas, of tear-producing gas, of laughter-producing gas, of tango-producing gas, and of all the other gases with which the last war was fought to end all wars . . . But since you insist, we are willing to have new elections, and to convoke that pest, that calamity, that abominable superstition, the Parliament after, say, two, or rather three, years of paternal government. Will you then Mr Secretary-General, after three years, give me the loan of 400,000,000 gold francs which we agreed upon a few minutes ago? You say 'No' again? I knew it.[7]

It was a remarkable performance and he came away empty-handed.

Recent events had made the Great Powers more certain than ever that Albania was unfit to handle a loan. News of shootings, famine, and revolt revived the old anti-Albanian line:

The Albanians are barbarians who have not evolved beyond the tribal stage and who have consequently no conception of any higher unity; a race of men whose principal pursuits consist of fighting and raiding other people's lands and conducting blood feuds on certain punctilious lines . . . the League of Nations, while refusing to find a loan for a nation whose territorial and other stability can in no wise be guaranteed, should seek to entrust the destinies of its people to a more competent rule.[8]

This author, Dudley Heathcote, advised that, if anyone could keep Albania in order, it was the Serbs. Others were equally confident that it was the Italians. Their rivalry, more than anything else, preserved Albanian independence. While pledging non-intervention, Italy and Yugoslavia each contemplated sending troops to Albania lest the other do so first.

Noli returned in October to find his regime unravelling. The Kosovars were angry at lack of progress on frontier revision. The Clique was conspiring as usual. Curri and Gurakuqi rejected plans for a republic. Without a loan, Noli hardly knew what to do next. In retrospect, he rationalised his failure thus: 'By insisting on agrarian reforms, I aroused the wrath of the landed aristocracy; by failing to carry them out I lost the support of the peasant masses.' In fact, the peasants showed scant interest in his fate, as pessimism born of experience made them sceptical of change. More revealing is his second admission: 'My Government colleagues, and the majority of the army officers, were either hostile or at best indifferent to these reforms.'[9]

Enemies of the regime seized on another point. In seeking international aid, Noli had not neglected the Soviet Union, with which Albania had previously had no relations. This was bound to be controversial, since the Balkan monarchies were all vehemently anti-communist. King Alexander of Yugoslavia had spent ten years in St Petersburg, and Belgrade was a haven for Tsarist refugees. Ninčić, the Yugoslav Foreign Minister, explained: 'We were faced with the only situation in which it is possible to interfere to a certain extent in the internal affairs of another country, that is, when there is a menace of Bolshevism. Fan Noli was altogether in the hands of the Bolsheviks.'[10]

This was a gross exaggeration. When he realised his mistake, the Bishop backed away from diplomatic recognition, but a Soviet mission arrived in Tirana in December 1924 regardless, disguised as church choristers. Though Noli refused to see them, the damage was done. By the time the Russians left on 20 December, Zogu and his fighters were just 10 miles away, and the days remaining to the Noli Government could be counted on one hand.

CHAPTER THIRTEEN

'The Triumph of Legality'

The whereabouts of Zogu in the autumn of 1924 were a matter for speculation. It was variously put out that he was in Austria, Switzerland, or France. His desire for foreign study cloaked the embarrassment of exile, and, when he asked for a passport at the Albanian Legation in Belgrade, he had spoken of spending several months in Paris. In all probability, however, he went no further than Vienna to meet his mother and sisters (who had fled Albania via Italy). While Ninčić promised the Italians that the Albanian fugitive would be expelled as an undesirable, secret services of interested nations knew that he remained at the Hotel Bristol in Belgrade (there winning renown as 'a lion with the ladies'[1]).

Even before Noli's entanglement with the Reds, Zogu had plied the Yugoslav Government with arguments for intervention. The ambiguities of the Bishop's revolution were such that his own supporters among the intelligentsia were unclear whether it was the harbinger of communism or the counterpart of Mussolini's March on Rome. Initially, Zogu exploited the latter suggestion, telling Yugoslav officials that Noli received Italian money via the Vatican. If the Kosovo Committee endorsed the new regime, it had to be anti-Yugoslav. When Noli stopped in Rome on his way to Geneva, the implication was obvious. Indeed, with Great Britain and France against him, Noli did court Italian recognition.

From the start, Zogu gave the impression that he expected to be 'recalled' to Albania very soon. Marinković, the Foreign Minister when he arrived, recognised his counter-revolutionary potential, and it fell to Pašić and Ninčić to agree the detail. In practical terms, the Yugoslav contribution amounted to some two thousand men, two artillery batteries, thirty machine guns, and a large quantity of ammunition. As the *quid pro quo*, it is safe to assume that Zogu pledged antipathy to the Russians and Italians, acquiescence in the loss of Kosovo, and readiness to see the frontier finalised on Yugoslav terms. The Serbs wanted the southern shore of Lake Ochrid, because of the monastery of St Naum, but nothing was put in writing.

While Zogu negotiated in Belgrade, his secretary, Jak Koçi, acted on his behalf in Rome. For a donation of two million lire, Italy was offered an Albanian foreign policy that would guarantee it definite control of the Adriatic. The line taken here was the need for Italo-Albanian co-operation against the Slavs. Koçi told Mussolini that Zogu realised that

Italy alone could help develop his country. For Britain, it was 'the habit of centuries to take without giving and it is certainly not going to change out of sympathy for me'.[2] The *Duce*'s insistence on a formal contract prevented any deal. Italians could not forget that Zogu had played a leading part in driving them from Vlora in 1920.

The Anglo-Persian Oil Company may have been more trusting: it allegedly paid out 50 million dinars as an advance on oil revenues. The money was used to hire mercenaries from the White Russian army of General Wrangel. Zogu toured frontier districts by car to recruit ethnic Albanian volunteers. He paid three gold napoleons per month, offsetting his lack of popularity in Kosovo. Rich Albanian families were asked to make contributions and many feared to refuse, given that Zogu plainly enjoyed the support of the Yugoslav authorities. A key figure in all this was Ceno Bey Kryeziu, the husband of his sister Nafije. Recently Mayor of Djakovica, Kryeziu was a Yugoslav citizen and one of the principal Kosovars to co-operate with the Serbs.

It is sometimes assumed that Zogu chose to act in December in order to surprise his opponents. In fact, Albanians held that the bright and frosty days of midwinter were better for warfare than the wet seasons that preceded and followed them. He also had a political reason for not waiting till spring. In a last bid for international recognition, Fan Noli had on 13 November proposed elections for 20 December and 20 January (under the existing indirect voting system). Zogu judged that he had to strike first. The date was set for 17 December. The Zogists, all dressed as Albanian irregulars, divided into seven columns to invade from all sides at once, and the sound of firing across the mountain-tops would be the signal to advance. Small bands starting from Montenegro and Greece were essentially token efforts, intended to suggest that the movement had support throughout the nation. The columns led by Zogu from Macedonia and Kryeziu from Kosovo comprised the fighting forces.

The operation did not start as planned. Hearing gunfire from the north on the night of 13 December, Zogu guessed (correctly) that Kryeziu had become prematurely embroiled with Bajram Curri's kaçaks. He ordered his own column into Dibra at once, only to be driven back by Albanian frontier guards. The Yugoslavs came to his rescue with a brief bombardment and the invasion went ahead at the second attempt.

For months, Zogu had been making secret overtures to Elez Jusufi of Dibra, who disliked the Noli Government, seeing it as a Tosk regime. On the other hand, he could not stomach the idea of collaborating with the Serbs. When the time came, Dibra chose to resist. Battle was joined near Peshkopi, but when Jusufi fell mortally wounded, his clansmen wavered. At Homesh on 17 December, Dibra came to terms. Zogu had no wish to seem vengeful. He had already been ordering his men to fire over the heads of their opponents. By claiming British backing, moreover, he played down his links to Yugoslavia. After Mati naturally rose in his support, other Gheg fighters swelled the ranks. Just as importantly, news from Dibra demoralised Curri, who had beaten off Kryeziu's first attack. Now, however, he withdrew into the highlands.

Despite there being a minimal response to his mobilisation order, Noli placed his faith in the Albanian army led by Shevqet Korça. Its troops were concentrated in the mountains to the east of Tirana, where the Zogists would have to use passes so narrow that single file was necessary. Noli judged that a few machine-gunners on the summits could keep them entirely covered.

Zogu's column first encountered regulars at Guri i Bardhë on 19 December. After a token assault, the Zogists took to the mountains, their advance made easier by Korça's decision to pull back outlying units to reinforce his stronghold at the Shkallë Gorge. This was virtually impregnable, as the Zogists discovered on 21 December. They appeared to have been halted, but in fact they were just drawing fire, while small detachments crossed the lower slopes of Mount Dajti undetected to reach the far side of the Priska Pass. A few shrapnel bursts over the army command post on the night of 23 December proved decisive. Imagining himself surrounded by substantial forces, Korça fled, declaring that all was lost. Aghast, Noli wired to Geneva that Yugoslav irregulars were overrunning his country. He hoped that the League would sanction counter-intervention by Italy but he could not wait for a reply. With the contents of the Treasury in their bags, the Government left in two taxis and chartered a fishing boat to Brindisi. The counter-revolution was a fact.

There was no resistance when 150 Dibra tribesmen arrived in Tirana on the morning of 24 December, henceforth to be called 'Legality Day'. They had come via Kruja to fight for Ahmed Zogu but found themselves surplus to requirements. The man himself was delayed by the need to disarm the conscripts still at the Shkallë Gorge. He entered the capital the following afternoon at the head of eight thousand fighters, who whooped with excitement and fired into the air; some had never seen a town before.

While dignitaries queued to welcome him, Zogu dispatched a series of telegrams. One of the first conveyed his greetings to the Italian Minister at Durrës, while voicing regret 'that the Italian press should have given currency to tendentious reports that his forces had contained non-Albanian elements'.[3] (Several hundred White Russians were even then demanding payment outside the Yugoslav Legation in Tirana.) He claimed legitimacy as the last commander-in-chief appointed by a legal Government. True, he had left six months ago to avert civil war; now he had come back to restore the constitution.

Even more shameless was his circular to prefectures, which relayed the good wishes of Benito Mussolini for the independence and prosperity of Albania. That the Italians should be offering congratulations was incredible – and utterly untrue. The message was an isolated extract from an Italo-Yugoslav joint communiqué on non-intervention issued a few weeks earlier. By the time Rome had disavowed it, however, it had served its purpose, which was to give the impression that Zogu was not a Yugoslav client.

Finally, Albanian Legations abroad received notification of the flight of the 'Revolutionary Government'. They were asked to explain that Ahmed Zogu had assumed personal power with the title of Commandant-General because of 'an overwhelming and spontaneous popular movement within Albania'.[4] In truth, the most that could be said was that he encountered little popular opposition. Thanks to Yugoslav arms and money, he had a strong fighting force behind him. Furthermore, domestic politics had been polarised by events. All his main adversaries had aligned themselves with Noli in June 1924; now, at a stroke, they were scattered. A ban was placed on the Kosovo Committee, the Clique, and Bashkimi. That left only politicians ready to defer. It did not matter that many great beys continued to look down on Zogu. The threat of losing their lands under Noli's 'Bolshevist' reforms induced them to submit to the lesser evil. The wife of one Tosk magnate remarked, 'In my youth, when the Mati came to market in Tirana . . . the people closed their doors and windows. Today we have entrusted not just property and possessions but even our lives to these robbers!'[5]

In these circumstances, the Commandant-General had no need to share power with anyone outside his immediate entourage. All the same, he attended to constitutional niceties for the sake of foreign opinion. In Zogist history, his seizure of power became 'The Triumph of Legality', as its alleged objective was purely to restore the legal Government of Ilias Bey Vrioni, which had fleetingly held office before Noli's revolution. On reassuming the premiership, Vrioni understood that all he had to do was to resign. A half-forgotten Regent, unearthed to do the honours, then asked Zogu to form a ministry on 6 January 1925.

The new Prime Minister first published a justification of his action in putting an end to 'a very dangerous' situation:

> The revolutionists, supported by the regular army, took the power from the legal Government and set up one of their own, under the premiership of Mr Fan Noli and dismissed the members of the Constituent Assembly. Their regime, which lasted six months, was characterised by imprisonments, confiscations of property, and burning of houses. The programme, good or bad, which they had

promised the people, was never carried out. These abuses against your liberty were committed with the direct assistance of army officers in active service, whom you expected to see defending the State and the honour of the nation. A place where life, property, and, above all personal honour, are not respected, that place with communistic ideas, cannot possibly exist in the present century.[6]

He then announced his Cabinet, and a most perfunctory one it was: all the posts were held by Zogu and two Tosk lieutenants, Kostaq Kotta and Myfid Bey Libohova – and they were only there to show that it was not an exclusively Gheg regime.

The principal lieutenant was too busy elsewhere to join the Cabinet until April. Ceno Bey Kryeziu spent the intervening weeks stamping out the Kosovar guerrillas in close conjunction with the Yugoslav army. The end of the kaçaks might be dated to 29 March 1925, when, tracked down to a hideout in the Dragobi caves, Curri turned his gun on himself. An alternative story of how he fought till he dropped enhanced his status as an anti-Zogist martyr.

By the time the Special Tribunal for Political Offences had passed death sentences on the ousted leaders *in absentia*, several had already been killed. Exile was no guarantee of safety. Luigj Gurakuqi was gunned down in a café in Bari. Noli managed to reach Vienna, protected perhaps by his international fame. Zogu worried about the survival in Italy of Hassan Prishtina; for years, they were to plot against each other. With lesser enemies, though, he could be more lenient. The first amnesties dated from April 1925 and pardons were granted to all but the most recalcitrant émigrés over the next three years. A few even resumed their political careers – as obedient Zogists. Zogu was ruthless but not vindictive: he forgave men whom he ceased to fear. In early 1925, however, his aim was to intimidate.

Parliament met on 17 January. Two-thirds of the deputies dared to appear; there was virtually no opposition. Elected over a year ago as a Constituent Assembly, it now addressed its task under Zogu's direction. Unity was the watchword, 'because we are at war, not with an opposing party, but with Bolshevism'.[7] One deputy later wrily recalled how 'hitherto very questionable and dubious friends of Zogu suddenly revealed themselves to be his most passionate partisans'.[8] Four days in, they abolished the phantom monarchy. Then, on 31 January 1925, President Ahmed Zogu was voted a seven-year term. Only the third Muslim to be president of anywhere, he was not yet thirty.

The new constitution bore a superficial resemblance to the American model, but its effect was to emasculate the Chamber of Deputies and empower the President, who could veto legislation without appeal. 'The real purpose of the move', remarked Harry Eyres, 'is of course, to legalise Ahmed's position as virtual dictator of the country, and this is thoroughly understood.'[9] The civil service was packed with Zogists, and the army reduced to 1,200. Zogu explained 'that the keystone of the arch of his building was reorganisation of the gendarmerie'.[10] He rewarded the chieftains who assisted his coup with gendarmerie commands: Muharrem Bajraktari in the north-east, Fiqri Bey Dine in the north-west, Prenk Previsi in central Albania, and Xhemal Herri in Tirana. These four were certainly worth propitiating, yet the President needed to stop the security forces furthering any political interests but his own. How could this be achieved? He sent Colonel Stirling, one of two remaining foreign advisers, to London to recruit half a dozen gendarmerie inspectors. In the sphere of public order, declared Zogu, 'Englishmen alone had the requisite racial characteristics':[11] they should be immune from Albanian conspiracies and answerable only to him.

In April and May, the Albanian people supposedly gave its verdict in a general election. 'I assure you that there will be no push and pull on the part of the Government,' Zogu had sworn. 'The elections are free and must be free . . . everybody should understand and feel the sovereign power of the people, for which I have the greatest respect.'[12] In fact, no one critical stood, the outcome was entirely predictable, and the turnout failed to reach 20 per cent. More important was the ceremonial gathering of 540 Gheg chieftains and elders in a field outside Tirana on 25 June to swear their besa to the President. He told them to keep away from foreign intrigues, to entrust the enforcement of law to the state, and to treat their people as a father treats his children. They promised to set aside old enmities and go forward 'Shoulder to shoulder and hand in hand'.[13]

The mere proclamation of a republic ended an era in foreign reporting about Albania. Imaginative speculation about candidates for the throne, starting in 1912, had revived in the early 1920s. Would Prince Jerome Bonaparte become Prince of Albania? Or Prince Ferdinand of Orléans, Duc de Montpensier? A Romanian named Prince Albert Ghika had been using the title for years. In America, oil millionaire Harry Sinclair and tin-plate tycoon William B. Leeds featured in reports. The prime British contender had been Aubrey Herbert, the pro-Albanian MP who died in 1923, but Lord Lonsdale, the sporting earl, and Lord Inchcape, the shipping magnate, also merited a mention, along with cricketer C.B. Fry.

Albanian diplomats said that these stories were invented by hostile agents to make their country appear ridiculous, yet many actually had some basis in unofficial initiatives by enterprising emigrants. Even in Tirana, royal speculation was a divertisement on days when there was no other news. A few republicans (such as Noli) could be found, but most politicians supported a monarchy. At this point, the consensus collapsed, as each faction wanted to place its own candidate on the throne in order to reap the expected rewards. Debate became hypothetical to the point of fantasy, as schemers bandied names without even bothering to learn much about them. Zogu played these games with the rest, telling Parr of the British Legation that 'many difficulties might have been avoided if an English prince could have assumed the throne'.[14] He acquiesced in an approach to the 8th Duke of Atholl, whose private army of Highlanders made him attractive, but the Foreign Office warned off the would-be 'King John'.

The story completed its transformation from coffee-house gossip to international joke in August 1923 when the *Evening News* carried the front-page headline: 'Wanted, a King: English country gentleman preferred – Apply to the Government of Albania'.[15] The European press took it up so eagerly that even Noli at the League of Nations cast an eye over C.B. Fry, a substitute delegate for India, so as to have his own nominal candidate to hand. (Fry described Noli as 'the nearest replica of W.G. Grace I have ever seen'.[16]) In Tirana, the Prime Minister was abashed to receive over seventy applications, most from suburban London. A ballet-teacher wrote that her ability to soar in the air like a bird fitted her to be Queen of the Sons of the Eagle, and an offer from a dentist prompted Zogu to quip that the man 'doubtless considered himself a specialist in gold crowns'.[17]

Now that sort of nonsense was over, though some exiles were loath to admit it. From 1925, the face of His Excellency Ahmed Zogu appeared on postage stamps for all the world to see.

CHAPTER FOURTEEN

Lira Imperialism

The seizure of power had indeed been a triumph – maybe not of legality, but certainly for Zogu and his Yugoslav backers. In domestic terms, he had fixed the essentials of his dictatorship within six months. The international shock-waves, however, took three years to settle. In the meantime, the President observed, 'he was on a volcano, there was no knowing from day to day what trick either Italy or Yugoslavia might play on him'.[1] Nor, some would have added, what trick he might play on them.

His return caused consternation in Rome. The Italians had tentatively inclined to Noli, and it stung Mussolini to discover that Ninčić, a placid-looking law professor, had been more daring and duplicitous than himself. His first idea was to seek a League mandate to send in troops, but, when he summoned a council of ex-premiers and generals, it transpired that he was alone in judging military action worthwhile. The Duce habitually cited the Italian withdrawal from Albania in 1920 as one of the humiliations to be erased by Fascism: 'When I heard of the evacuation of Valona, I wept. And that is not just a rhetorical phrase.'[2]

In reality, Mussolini himself knew that Italy was not yet ready for war. But there were ways and means: 'The Fascist State is will to power and domination,' he wrote, and 'One can imagine an *Imperium*, that is, a nation that governs other nations, which does not require the conquest of a single square mile of land.'[3] Mussolini believed that the pre-condition for Italian expansion in north-east Africa and the Middle East was informal domination of the Balkans and the eastern Mediterranean (to balance French supremacy in the western Mediterranean). The first obstacle to this strategy was Yugoslavia, a bumptious new creation with the audacity to act like a regional power. The Duce decided to cut the Serbs down to size, and Albania could yet be the means to do it. No opportunity should henceforth be missed to bolster Italian influence in Tirana.

This response was not wholly unwelcome to Zogu. He needed to live down the accusation that he was simply a usurper imposed by Serbian bayonets, a traitor who had sold out the Kosovars in order to gain the presidency. The easiest way for him to shed the Serbophil label was to show partiality for Italy. Before he could proceed very far down this path, however, one item of outstanding business had to be settled. The contract with the Anglo-Persian Oil Company was 'of supreme importance to Albania', he said.[4]

This provoked a belligerent outburst from Mussolini, keener than ever that the prospecting rights should go to Italian firms. Albania would 'feel the force of Italian displeasure', he warned, if it ratified the Anglo-Persian deal.[5] Confrontation loomed for a day or two in February 1925, until direct Anglo-Italian talks resulted in 50,000 hectares being earmarked for a subsidiary of Italian State Railways. Happy with the compromise, Zogu thanked Britain for standing firm. What he really wanted, he told Eyres two days after ratification, was a British undertaking to protect his country from attack. The British Minister urged him to trust to the League of Nations. But what if the League were busy with more important places? This kind of exchange became a ritual of Anglo-Albanian relations.

After taking special powers to approve foreign concessions without reference to Parliament, Zogu renewed his invitation to international capitalists. The other oil companies bought small-scale prospecting rights to keep a foot in the door. Then, less predictably, there followed an orchestrated rush of offers from Italian firms to construct railways, docks, mines, and drainage schemes – and to set up a bank.

Albania needed a national bank, not only for investment but for easier trade. Its currency was purely notional: no specie had ever been minted, so gold napoleons, sovereigns, and dollars were mixed together and valued by weight, with change given in coinage of half a dozen countries. Most people resorted to barter. Zogu knew what he wanted: a modern money economy, but, beyond that, he was out of his depth. Where were the Albanians competent to advise on high finance? 'Believe me,' he assured Eyres, 'never will I fall into the arms of Italy.'[6] Yet he authorised the Italo-Albanian bank agreement of 1925.

The details were negotiated by the Libohova brothers. Myfid Bey Libohova, the Finance Minister, had assisted in the 'Triumph of Legality', but, prior to entering the Zogist camp in 1924, he had been seen as definitely pro-Italian. His courtly manner and ostentatious extravagance were hallmarks of the last generation of the Ottoman élite. Ekrem Bey Libohova, six years his junior, headed the Albanian Legation in Rome.

If only as a bargaining ploy, Zogu did invite rival offers, but the terms suggested by the Midland Bank sounded nowhere near so generous as those which the Italian Finance Ministry arranged. To launch the economic development of Albania, the Italians were willing to couple the creation of a national bank with a loan of 50 million gold francs to be paid over five years. This was the equivalent of £2 million at the time – a very significant sum for the Albanian Government, whose total annual revenue in the years 1926–30 ranged between 19 and 30 million gold francs. An advance of one million would be available at once. Zogu found the money irresistible. Though 7.5 per cent interest was not particularly favourable, the Italians seemed relaxed about repayment. In any case, he was gambling on the oil; Anglo-Persian began drilling near Fier in the summer.

Thus, in the course of 1926, the qindar, lek, and gold franc (or *franga ari*) at last became tangible, courtesy of the Bank of Credit and Issue: one hundred qindar to the lek, five leks to the Albanian gold franc. The design of the currency attracted adverse comment at once: the one franc note and two franc coin bore the Roman eagle and not the double-headed Albanian one. It was very apt symbolism. The Albanian national bank was actually an Italian bank operating overseas under Italian law, with its reserves held in Rome and its banknotes redeemable only in lire. This deprived Albania of control over its own currency, especially as the terms of the deal had been subverted. Fifty-one per cent of the capital of the bank was supposed to be subscribed by Albanians, but Myfid Libohova failed to publicise this information till the time limit for share applications had expired. For this service, and others, the Italians made him a secret gift of one million gold francs.

The scandal did not end there. The Libohova brothers agreed that the tempting loan advance would actually remain in Italy to pay for three purchases of very questionable value. Large amounts of ammunition for the Albanian army proved to be so old and damp as to be useless. Two second-hand patrol boats, renamed *Shqipnia* and *Skanderbeg*, became the entire Albanian navy. (After two years rusting off Durrës, they were sold for scrap.) The remainder went to buy a gorgeous uniform for the President: a white silk tunic with thick gold frogging, epaulettes, and a black-red-black sash, white breeches, a white fur hat with plume, a black cloak, and white patent leather boots with gold spurs. Zogu modelled it for a portrait in oils, but he apparently grew self-conscious when people remarked that no other president wore anything like it outside Latin America. The famous white uniform was seldom seen in later years.

The squandering of the first million was a small matter, however, compared with the political ramifications of the loan, which was secured on the Albanian customs and state monopolies. The funds were to be administered by the *Società per lo Sviluppo Economico dell'Albania*, purportedly an independent development company. In fact, the investment made no commercial sense and *SVEA* (as it was called) was subordinate to the Italian Finance Ministry, whose negotiators called the loan 'a mortgage on the whole Albanian economy, surpassing our most optimistic expectations'.[7] The money was to be spent on public works, and the national bank would award the contracts, giving preference to Italian firms. Maybe Zogu did not grasp the significance of the deal till he read independent analysis in the European press. Feigned naivety was one of his favourite ruses, admittedly, but he seemed shocked to find the experts instantly concluding that Albania was irretrievably bound in the coils of lira imperialism. Though all the Balkan nations owed large sums, Albania was unique in being effectively indebted to a single foreign government.

Zogu looked for a scapegoat. Not only was Myfid Bey Libohova dismissed, but a special inquiry scrutinised the negotiations for corruption. Cynics assumed that its real object was to find some grounds for unilaterally denouncing the deal. An Italo-Albanian row seemed imminent, but nothing happened. Parliament and press simply ceased to mention the subject. Mysterious silences were a feature of politics in the Zogist era, when explanation became a rare commodity. The bank agreement stood (while the Libohova brothers went to Italy for a while). Privately, Zogu commented that he would have to make the best of a bad bargain.

This left observers to speculate on his reasons for failing to see the matter through. Some suggested that diplomatic balance required that the Italians should keep the national bank, because the British took the lion's share of oil rights. Others correctly guessed that the President, just like the Libohovas, had accepted a 'tip' of a million gold francs from Rome. Throughout his career, Zogu appeared to think that refusing a bribe was like looking a gift-horse in the mouth. As the Yugoslavs were fast learning, he did not consider receipt to entail an obligation: 'It was easy to buy Zog, but he would not stay bought.'[8]

He had plenty of other grounds for favouring Italian loans. Albania, he believed, would never become economically developed without major foreign aid. The League of Nations was clearly not going to deliver this, and only Italy and Yugoslavia showed much interest. Neither relished Albanian independence, but one of them was rich and might be ready to pay to prevent strategic territory falling under the exclusive sway of the other. Moreover, Italians were better qualified than Serbs to be agents of westernisation. Mussolini meanwhile reckoned that he had turned a fiasco into a triumph. In December, Ahmed Zogu acquired power as a puppet of the Serbs. By June, Albania was destined to be 'an Italian province without a prefect'.[9]

An Italian gunboat anchored off Durrës half a dozen times during the summer of 1925. While it was there, a man was rowed ashore each night to spend a few hours at an isolated house by the beach. The visitor was Alessandro Lessona, a minor Fascist deputy, and his host was the Albanian President. Zogu told the Duce's special envoy precisely what he wished to hear: that he hugely admired Mussolini, that Fascism inspired his own effort to construct an authoritarian regime, that he desired Italian mastery of the Adriatic. The inexperienced Lessona rejoiced to discover that Zogu, far from being a creature of the Serbs, was in fact 'the winning card' for Italy.[10]

Then the Albanian asked for more money, and bargaining began in earnest. Mussolini wanted Albania to recognise the Declaration of Paris, the formula that stipulated that any intervention there by the League of Nations would be undertaken by the Italian army. It was tantamount to a protectorate, and Zogu refused to endorse it. No other independent nation had its relations with the League preordained in this way. He nevertheless expressed interest in an Italo-Albanian military agreement which would guarantee his country 'against all possible surprises'. Who better knew how easy it was for Yugoslavia to meddle in Albania?

The late-night talks became intricate and sometimes tense. At one point, Zogu demanded (and obtained) a loan of 6 million lire within three days to pay his armed forces. At another point, Lessona threatened to invade with his squad of blackshirts unless the President gave more ground. The negotiations culminated with a confidential exchange of letters between Zogu and Mussolini in late August 1925, which set out the terms of an alliance. Italy would guarantee Albania, and, if Italy were attacked by a Balkan state, Albania would declare war if requested. In the event of joint military action resulting in territorial changes, Italy undertook 'to obtain for Albania territory inhabited by people the majority of whom speak Albanian'.[11]

Lessona was proud of his work and expected it to lead to a formal treaty, but the Italian Foreign Ministry was aghast at the letters. Did Italy want to risk being dragged into a struggle for Kosovo? Could Zogu be trusted not to provoke such a war? The Duce had second thoughts and let the matter drop.

Zogu could congratulate himself. He had not obtained a solid guarantee against Yugoslavia (for the exchange of letters was not legally binding), but he had given nothing away. If Albania were ever menaced by the Serbs, moreover, he could publish Mussolini's letter and thus cause an international storm. In addition, he had pocketed at least 6 million lire. The informal military compact did oblige him to refrain from abolishing the army: Albania could not be Italy's secret ally if it had no regular forces. He agreed to employ three Italian military advisers too – the first of many – but he drew the line at Italian gendarmerie inspectors. He had originally intended to have Serbs, he lied, so the recruitment of British officers was in itself a conciliatory gesture.

By the end of 1925, the Italians were getting the measure of President Zogu. 'He is clever enough,' conceded Mussolini, 'but no hero, and he loves intrigue.'[12]

CHAPTER FIFTEEN

Avanti Italia!

During the winter of 1925–6, the diplomatic environment in Tirana and Durrës underwent a transformation, as two changes in personnel signified the end of one era and the beginning of the next. In December, Harry Eyres was finally pensioned off with a knighthood. He had become an institution, hailed by many locals (though not the friends of Noli) as a godfather of the Albanian nation. The new British Minister, Edmund O'Reilly, had formerly served in Bolivia and Guatemala. He soon confessed: 'I thought that South America had taught me something about monkey tricks, but it was an infant school to this job.'[1]

The other new arrival in March 1926 was Baron Pompeo Aloisi, who was later to become well-known as the mouthpiece of Fascist Italy at the League of Nations. An aristocrat, cultured, poised, and monocled, Aloisi was one of the few career diplomats ever to win favour with Mussolini. Perhaps this reflected his readiness suddenly to cast aside good manners and become overbearing; his colleagues in the diplomatic corps detested the way in which he propositioned their wives. Charles Hart, the American Minister, remarked: 'Baron Aloisi has been sent here to get the goods and is the kind of guy who'll get them soon enough.'[2]

Armed with the lever of the five-year loan, Mussolini aimed to control Albania in fact if not in name. This meant keeping out rival influences. He shrank from a straight alliance in deference to the views of his Foreign Ministry, but still he hankered after some sort of formal recognition of Italy's exclusive role in the country. Zogu, however, had no desire to tie himself to just one foreign partner. Grand strategy aside, he valued his freedom to touch anyone and everyone for funds.

For three months, Aloisi did not press the issue, but, once he fully appreciated the extent of his power, he could not resist exploiting it. Through *SVEA*, Italians controlled around one third of public expenditure. The Baron looked forward to an arrangement that 'would completely monopolize in Italy's favour the internal and foreign actions of Albania'.[3] This was what Mussolini wanted to hear. In June, he authorised fresh negotiations for an Italo-Albanian treaty. The opening bid was merely the promise to defend Albania under the terms of the Paris Declaration. Zogu responded by suggesting that he would need to discuss such a pact with the Duce in person – a typical stalling device.

Aloisi began to talk about possible delays in loan payments, but Zogu was unimpressed. For three weeks, he managed to fob off the Baron, while treating Edmund O'Reilly to his most winning ways. A new Anglo-Albanian commercial treaty was mooted and a trade pact actually signed with Yugoslavia on 22 June 1926.

The Italians struck back two days later. Exactly what passed in the presidential office will never be known, but Zogu hastened to give other legations his version of the interview. Aloisi, he alleged, had read out what he said was a telegram from Mussolini, demanding that the Albanian Government subscribe at once to the Declaration of Paris. In return, there would be arms and money in plenty. If Albania refused, however, Italy would instantly break off relations. Aloisi had then explained how his secret service could stage a fake incursion from Yugoslavia to justify invasion by Italian troops. For his part, the Italian Minister flatly denied that there had been any ultimatum. He had merely offered Zogu a treaty of friendship. When this was rejected, it so happened that he had to leave Durrës at once by warship for consultations in Rome.

O'Reilly of the British Legation knew whom he was inclined to believe: 'when he talked to me about the Italians, he seemed like a fascinated rabbit in front of a snake'.[4] Confronted with external crises, Zogu displayed a kind of pathetic stoicism that rarely failed in its appeal to British and American diplomats at a personal level. O'Reilly was especially susceptible. He wanted to continue 'the Eyres tradition' of moral support for Zogu, but, almost inevitably, he lacked the old man's attitude of indulgent cynicism. Eyres liked Zogu but took what he said with a pinch of salt. Keeping him straight was 'a rather forlorn task', he would probably end up 'murdered or something', and the best reason for backing him was the quality of the alternatives.[5]

O'Reilly seemed more disposed to rate the personable young President at face value: 'With the slenderest education, though with some great natural talents, he has to bear the whole burden of administration with no disinterested person whom he can trust, and without capable advice.' Now, proud but shaken, Zogu related how roughly Mussolini was bullying him: 'I am up against forty-three million people led by a madman.'[6] O'Reilly urged him to stand firm and telegraphed the Foreign Secretary in London.

Sir Austen Chamberlain, half-brother of Neville, had been in charge of British foreign policy for over eighteen months, but Albania had not often demanded his attention. For years, indeed, relations with Tirana had been effectively left to the man on the spot. Now Chamberlain, prompted to reassess the situation, took a detached view of Balkan affairs. These political storms in the Adriatic affected British interests in so far as they exacerbated hostility between Italy and France (as patron of Yugoslavia), for dissension among the Great Powers impeded European reconciliation and disarmament. Sir Austen judged that Mussolini had the makings of a responsible statesman. 'The more one knows the Italian Prime Minister, the more one loves him,' he wrote in 1925. 'I trust his word when given and I think we might easily go far before finding an Italian with whom it would be as easy for the British Government to work'.[7] It would be foolish to allow somewhere as insignificant as Albania to damage Anglo-Italian relations.

Tension over ratification of the oil concession in February 1925 had first alerted him to the possibility of unpleasantness. He had been sorry to hear that the British Minister in Durrës was seen as anti-Italian, and that his relationship with the Albanian leader was exceptionally close. Everything Chamberlain knew about President Zogu suggested untrustworthiness, and this latest Rome–Tirana incident looked very suspicious. Was it really coincidence that it broke just before HMS *Dauntless* paid a courtesy visit to Durrës? Zogu could have exaggerated or invented the ultimatum in order to provoke a breach with Italy. His motive? It would allow Albania to denounce the disastrous national bank agreement while hiding behind British protection. Chamberlain could not be sure. Questioned by the British Ambassador in Rome, Mussolini admitted that Aloisi might have exceeded instructions. On the other hand, the Italians reported that when their chargé asked Zogu why he was spreading alarmist rumours, the Albanian denied doing any such thing and insisted that O'Reilly must have misunderstood him. Under neutral British scrutiny, both sides were watering down their stories.

Thus the immediate deadlock resolved itself. HMS *Dauntless* made its prearranged visit. Italy did not break off relations. Zogu risked no further anti-Italian moves. Ten days after making his dramatic exit, Aloisi simply returned with a draft treaty of friendship containing no mention of the Paris Declaration. Zogu cannily proposed that Albania should sign identical friendship pacts with all its neighbours. The Baron disparaged 'an accord devoid of any political content whatever' and ended the talks.[8]

In thwarting Aloisi, Zogu had won a Pyrrhic victory. The lasting significance of the episode was Chamberlain's resolution that Britain must never get entangled in Italo-Albanian squabbles again. On 29 July, he told the Italian Ambassador that he would recall O'Reilly from his post. 'His Majesty's Government have themselves no special interests in Albania', he explained, 'and have no desire to obstruct legitimate Italian expansion in that country.'[9] The new British envoy, William Seeds, was instructed not to question Italian activities. 'It is impossible to state in advance the exact point where Italian aspirations in Albania may cease to be "legitimate"', conceded Chamberlain, who added:

It is Ahmed Bey's constant endeavour to obtain the support of His Majesty's Government against Italy, and he would appear to have been unscrupulous in his use of the British Minister's name when he desired an excuse for refusing an Italian demand. . . . I must impress upon you the need for the greatest circumspection especially in regard to any advances or suggestions made to you by Ahmed Bey.[10]

Chamberlain had decided that stability in the Adriatic was best served by treating Albania as an Italian sphere of influence. In return, Mussolini swore to respect its independence, presumably in the way that Britain respected the independence of Egypt.

Zogu understood the implication when officially informed of O'Reilly's recall on 23 August. (He had in fact received the news from an exultant Aloisi several days earlier). He sat quite silent for a moment and then said, 'The Italians do not leave me in peace either day or night.'[11] Deprived of moral support from London, he feared that he might have to resign. Hyperbole aside, he spoke truly enough when he added that Italy would exploit the situation to the full. Summer 1926 was a turning point. Looking back in later years, Zog observed with understatement, 'It is a pity that Great Britain was disinterested in us, leaving us to Rome, Belgrade, and Athens.'[12]

On 10 September, Baron Aloisi once more raised the issue of an Italo-Albanian treaty. Zogu was now reduced to his crudest bargaining techniques. Italy promised him money if he signed a treaty. How much? Starting with a demand for 5 million lire, he would raise the figure when the Italians tried to strengthen the wording of the draft. The talks dragged on for three months. Gatherings of anti-Zogist exiles at Bari and Brindisi increased the pressure, as did the state of the Albanian Treasury: public sector pay was once more months in arrears. Zogu tried telling Anglo-Persian Oil that it had 'a moral obligation' to lend him half a million pounds. Piqued at rejection, he retorted that money 'would be obtained without difficulty elsewhere'.[13]

By 10 November, Zogu had yielded to Aloisi on most of the substantive points. Though he held out against acknowledging the 1921 declaration, he was ready to seal a 'Pact of Friendship and Security'. As usual in dealings with Zogu, however, a last-minute hitch occurred: he worried that Parliament might refuse to ratify the treaty. How could this reluctance be overcome? An extra 5 million lire might do it. Aloisi would have to ask the Duce.

On 20 November, news came from Shkodra that the northern highlands were in full-scale revolt. The Roman Catholic tribes of Shala, Shoshi, and Dukagjini descended on the town and shot the local gendarmes. Their leader, a priest named Dom Loro Caka, voiced the usual grievances: the men of Tirana were worse than the Turks, and Shkodra should be the capital (if not of Albania itself, then of an autonomous Roman Catholic province). It was far the gravest challenge to Zogu since his return, and he had to move swiftly to contain it. Ten thousand men spent ten days defeating and dispersing the rebels; the violence did not end there. Though Zogu said that he wanted to 'spare the misguided mountaineers so far as possible', he also argued that 'Balkan races respected forcible rather than conciliatory methods'.[14]

More will have to be said of the domestic consequences of the 1926 revolt. For the moment, it need only be noticed how it played into Italian hands. It may be the case that the Italian secret service engineered the uprising in order to step up the pressure on Zogu. The involvement of Roman Catholic priests was superficially suggestive. The Belgrade press pointed the finger at Hassan Bey Prishtina and his 'Independent Political Group of Albanian Refugees' at Zara. On the other hand, several observers – not all of them Italian – suspected participation by Yugoslav agents aimed at preventing an Italo-Albanian pact by scaring or ousting Zogu. The question of foreign responsibility has never been resolved, and, in a sense, it was academic. Zogu assumed that Italy and Yugoslavia were both conspiring against him, independently, and Albanian rebels would seek weapons and gold from every source. Never mind who was backing them, they simply had to be crushed, and for this he needed money to pay his fighters and keep the chieftains in line. Aloisi handed over the first 200,000 gold francs on 22 November, and the Pact of Tirana was signed five days later:

> *Art.1.* Italy and Albania recognise that any disturbance threatening the political, legal and territorial status quo of Albania is contrary to their common political interests.

> *Art.2.* In order to safeguard the above-mentioned interests the High Contracting Parties undertake to afford each other mutual support and cordial co-operation; they also undertake not to conclude with other Powers any political or military agreements prejudicial to the interests of the other Party as defined in this agreement.[15]

Italy had bought a pretext for interfering in Albanian affairs, and Zogu had sold the right of Albania to an independent foreign policy for the next five years. Of course, he did not admit as much. 'I have concluded the Pact,' he said obscurely, 'because I was convinced that it is and will be a guarantee for peace in the Balkans, and that it will have historical consequences.'[16] Bribes secured prompt ratification, and propaganda evoked the partnership between Skanderbeg and the Venetian Republic.

Unveiling the pact to the British Minister, Zogu lamented that no one in his Foreign Ministry was competent to judge what it denoted in international law:

> for his own person and interests he cared little: he bore on his body seven wounds already incurred in his country's cause and he confidently expected that number to be doubled before he was finally done with. He pleaded for Albania; even in her name he did not ask for financial or military assistance: he only begged from Great Britain sympathy, advice and guidance.[17]

William Seeds did his duty and turned a deaf ear. The meaning of the pact was indeed unclear. What precisely was 'the political, legal and territorial status quo' which Italy promised to safeguard? Zogu's domestic position would be stronger if he could hint that any revolt against him would bring down the Italian army on Albania. On the other hand, Italy itself might foment rebellion as a pretext for invasion.

Coming on top of the bank deal, the Pact of Tirana implied that Albania was a virtual Italian protectorate. If other nations treated it as an annexe of Italy, that was effectively what it had become. Zogu wasted his breath when he assured the Yugoslav Minister that he intended to sign a similar treaty with his country. Italy would never allow it. Knowing this, Bogoljub Jevtić cut him short and denounced the Pact of Tirana as an unfriendly act. This was the cue for a war scare.

1. H.M. King Zog I of the Albanians in his study in Tirana. On the wall hangs a portrait of his mother Sadije. (Associated Press)

2. *Ahmed Zogolli, the future King Zog, when a schoolboy. (C. Dako,* Zogu the First, *Tirana 1937)*

3. *Xhemal Pasha Zogolli, his father, hereditary governor of Mati. (Z. Xoxe,* 10 vjet mbretni, *Tirana 1938)*

4. *The ruins of Castle Burgajet, ancestral home of the Zogolli family.*

5. *A shepherd tending his flock in the upper Mati Valley, a few miles south of Burgajet.*

6. *Prince Wilhelm of Wied, sovereign of Albania in 1914. He held the throne for a mere six months.*

7. *Essad Pasha Toptani, who strove relentlessly between 1912 and 1920 to make himself ruler of Albania (or part of it).*

8. *The young officer: Ahmed Bey Zogolli in Austrian uniform c. 1917. (C. Dako,* Zogu the First, *Tirana 1937)*

9. *The young politician: Zogolli on his return to office in 1921. (*Shqipnia më 1927, *Tirana 1927)*

10. Four rivals of Ahmed Zogu: Hassan Bey Prishtina, leader of the Kosovars, shot dead in Salonika in 1933. (Shqipnia më 1927, Tirana 1927)

11. Bajram Curri, celebrated guerrilla commander, shot dead near Tropoja in 1925. (S. Haxhija, Flamurtari i Kosovës Isa Buletini, Munich 1967)

12. Fan Noli, revolutionary bishop, exiled from December 1924. (A. Logoreci, The Albanians, London 1977)

13. Shevqet Bey Vërlaci, a prospective father-in-law, who took offence. (Albania, Rome 1939)

14. The ruler: President Ahmed Zogu in his famous white uniform, c. 1926, with aides-de-camp Zef Sereqi (left) and Llesh Topallaj (right). Topallaj was killed in the Vienna assassination attempt of 1931. (Marubi)

15. Some of the ruled: a typical family in northern Albania between the wars. (D.R. Oakley-Hill, An Englishman in Albania, *Centre for Albanian Studies 2002)*

16. *A stalwart British aide: Major-General Sir Jocelyn Percy, Inspector-General of the Royal Albanian Gendarmerie 1926–38.*

17. *A formidable adversary: Baron Pompeo Aloisi, Italian Minister in Albania 1926–27, foreign policy adviser to Mussolini 1932–36. (The Illustrated London News Picture Library)*

18. *Locals supposedly 'celebrating' the signature of the Pact of Tirana, whereby Italy secured a virtual protectorate over Albania in November 1926.*

19. Old and new in central Tirana: the eighteenth-century Mosque of Ethem Bey was joined in 1932 by the prefecture building, designed by Florestano di Fausto and opened by Princess Maxhide.

20. Italian civil engineers faced great challenges in Albania: part of the new road from Kruja to Burreli in Mati.

21. A Zogist postcard from 1928 (printed in Italy) shows the two approved faces of Albanian monarchy: the medieval hero Gjergi Kastrioti Skanderbeg and his self-styled successor after 460 years.

22. *Albania becomes a kingdom: 1 September 1928, as covered in the* Illustrated London News. *Note that the family group is incorrectly captioned: Zog was still a bachelor, and the photograph actually shows his mother Sadije, seated, with (left to right) his nephew Salih, sister Maxhide, half-sister-in-law Ruhije, half-brother Xhelal, sister Myzejen and nephew Hysein. Foreign journalists frequently guessed what they did not know about the Albanian royal family. (The* Illustrated London News Picture Library*)*

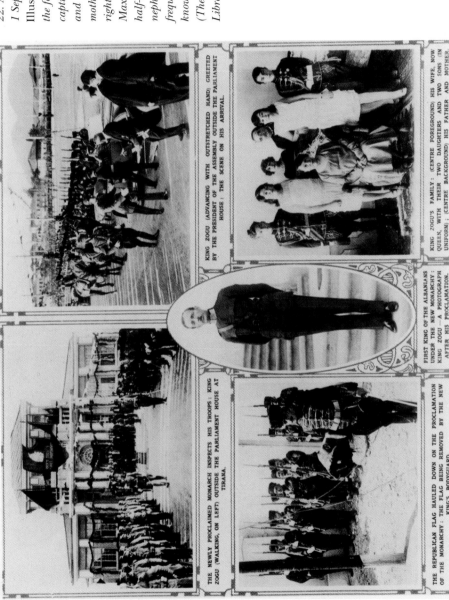

KING ZOGU (ADVANCING WITH OUTSTRETCHED HAND) GREETED BY THE PRESIDENT OF THE ASSEMBLY OUTSIDE THE PARLIAMENT HOUSE: THE SCENE ON HIS ARRIVAL.

KING ZOGU'S FAMILY: (CENTRE FOREGROUND) HIS WIFE, NOW QUEEN, WITH THEIR TWO DAUGHTERS AND TWO SONS (IN UNIFORM); (CENTRE BACKGROUND) HIS FATHER AND MOTHER.

FIRST KING OF THE ALBANIANS UNDER THE NEW MONARCHY: KING ZOGU — A PHOTOGRAPH AFTER HIS PROCLAMATION.

THE NEWLY PROCLAIMED MONARCH INSPECTS HIS TROOPS: KING ZOGU (WALKING, ON LEFT) OUTSIDE THE PARLIAMENT HOUSE AT TIRANA.

THE REPUBLICAN FLAG HAULED DOWN ON THE PROCLAMATION OF THE MONARCHY: THE FLAG BEING REMOVED BY THE NEW KING'S BODYGUARD.

23. *A newly royal family. The King in 1928 with five of his sisters, a nephew, and a niece: (left to right) Myzejen, Senije, widowed Nafije with son Tati, Zog, Maxhide, Ruhije and Teri. (Popperfoto)*

24. *The Palace in Tirana, Zog's principal home from March 1928 to April 1939. This picture, taken in 1938, shows recent improvements: the avenue of trees, dormer-windows and the huge wooden extension that housed the ballroom. (Associated Press)*

25. *King Zog presides at a military parade in Tirana to celebrate his birthday, flanked by successive Prime Ministers Kostaq Kotta (left) and Pandeli Evangjeli (right), with bearded Leon Ghilardi. (Hulton Archive)*

26. *His women-folk look on: (left to right) Nafije, the Queen Mother, Senije, Myzejen, Ruhije, and Maxhide.*

27. With Albanian–Italian relations in crisis in 1933–34, it was time to appear especially patriotic: (left to right) Senije, Ruhije, Hysein, Nafije, Sadije, Zog, Myzejen, Maxhide, Tati, Teri and Danush in national costume. Zog may be forgiven for looking self-conscious: the kilt was not traditionally worn in his native region of Mati. (Popperfoto)

28. An aerial view of south-east Tirana in the 1930s. The royal compound can be seen beyond the Mosque of Suleiman Pasha (with minaret).

29. *The Summer Palace at Durrës, completed in 1932. Note the statue of Skanderbeg above the entrance. Though it was Zog's grandest residence, he spent only a few days there each year. (Associated Press)*

30. *The royal family posing in summer uniform at Durrës c. 1937: (left to right) Ruhije, Senije, Tati, Zog, Myzejen and Maxhide. (Hulton Archive)*

31. Count Galeazzo Ciano, the Italian Foreign Minister, inspects the guard of honour at Tirana airport at the start of his official visit to Albania in April 1938. Escorting him are General Xhemal Aranitasi (left) and Zef Sereqi (right). (Hulton Archive)

32. The royal wedding of 27 April 1938: Queen Geraldine signs the marriage register, watched by Prince Abid (in white tie). Behind her stand Count Ciano and Zog, between whom can be seen Musa Juka, the feared Interior Minister, and Colonel Hysein Selmani, Commander of the Royal Guard. (The Illustrated London News Picture Library)

33. *The height of Albanian royal splendour: Zog and Geraldine entering the ballroom of the Summer Palace during celebrations to mark the tenth anniversary of the monarchy in September 1938. (The Illustrated London News Picture Library)*

34. *Francesco Jacomoni, Italian Minister in Albania 1936–39, Italian Viceroy of Albania 1939–43. (Albania, Rome 1939)*

35. *Abas Kupi, leader of Legaliteti, the Zogist guerrilla movement during World War II.*

36. The exiled Zogists' greatest public relations assets: Queen Geraldine and Crown Prince Leka in London in December 1940. (The Illustrated London News Picture Library)

37. Facing a bleak future: King Zog at Parmoor House in December 1945, shortly after Britain and the USA recognised the communist regime in Albania. (Hulton Archive)

38. *A sick man: Zog, followed by his wife and son, boards the liner taking them from Egypt to his final place of exile in France. The date was 1 August 1955; he was not yet sixty. (Associated Press)*

CHAPTER SIXTEEN

The Breach with Belgrade

'Goodbye, friend of today, enemy of tomorrow.'[1] Legend has it that these were the words uttered by Nikola Pašić, the Prime Minister of Yugoslavia, as he watched Zogu leave Belgrade on his way back to Albania in 1924, but even the worldly-wise Serb could not have expected him to switch to Italian patronage so entirely within two years. Most Yugoslavs were downright furious. Ninčić, the Foreign Minister, had to resign when the Pact of Tirana was published. King Alexander, a Spartan military man, seemed braced for early war with Italy. Mussolini was cultivating Hungary and Bulgaria and encouraging Croatian and Macedonian separatism, so, strategically, it was disastrous that Albania should be turning into an Italian bridge-head in the Balkans.

Where had Yugoslavia gone wrong? The first signs of trouble between Zogu and Belgrade had emerged soon after the 'Triumph of Legality', when he offered to drop Albania's claim to the region around the monastery of St Naum – but only on condition that the Serbs make concessions elsewhere. The President did not want St Naum to look like payment for services rendered. Ninčić, however, viewed this horse-trading as a breach of faith. Though Yugoslavia won practically all it sought when the Conference of Ambassadors finalised Albania's frontier in July 1926, ill-feeling persisted.

In truth, the Yugoslav Government was divided from the start over how to handle its Albanian protégé. Ninčić and his diplomats wanted Albania to be an independent buffer state that did not try to recover Kosovo: inevitably, President Zogu would manoeuvre to balance Yugoslav influence with Italian – so long as the outcome *was* a balance, that was acceptable. As Italian involvement grew, however, hardliners in the Yugoslav army demanded that Albanian policy be brought into line with that of Belgrade: if Zogu did not do as he was told, he should simply be replaced by someone who would. The basic ambivalence of the Yugoslav Legation grew manifest. Successive ministers, Lazarević and Jevtić, sounded sympathetic enough, yet the military attachés were intriguing constantly with disaffected chieftains.

In retrospect, the contest between Italy and Yugoslavia for supremacy in Albania appears very one-sided, for it boiled down to money: there were more lire to be extracted out of Rome than dinars out of Belgrade. Though at first Zogu was as importunate with the Yugoslavs as with the

Italians, he found it a waste of effort. One peasant state could not afford to bankroll another. The Yugoslav Government had imagined that the British would help keep the Italians in check. When this illusion was stripped away, the fundamental imbalance became clear: Italy managed Zogu with the stick and the carrot; Yugoslavia could only use the stick – and that proved counter-productive.

The spring and summer of 1927 saw a rare influx of foreign reporters to Tirana, waiting to become war correspondents. Italy issued a formal diplomatic protest in March about Yugoslav plans to overthrow the Albanian Government by armed intervention. Zogu sent troops to Shkodra, with several Italian instructors in tow, and began requisitioning horses. It troubled him to observe how generously the Yugoslav Government treated anti-Zogist refugees: pensions and sinecures sustained Rexhep Shala, Interior Minister under Noli, and Lazar Gurakuqi, brother of the murdered Finance Minister, as coffee-house conspirators in Kosovo. The Yugoslavs denied everything and accused Italy of engineering the scare as a pretext for occupying Albania themselves.

No invasion or revolt came to pass, but, in June, Belgrade broke off diplomatic relations after the Albanians arrested one Vuk Djurasković in Durrës on espionage charges. Djurasković was an Albanian citizen employed as an interpreter at the Yugoslav Legation, and the ensuing dispute about the scope of diplomatic immunity turned into a tense 'affair of honour', which it took weeks of outside mediation to resolve.

In these crises, Zogu was a nominal protagonist only. Seeds rightly concluded that the Djurasković Affair showed the Albanian Foreign Ministry to be 'to all intents and purposes a mere branch of the Italian Legation'.[2] The brusque Aloisi had left Albania in February 1927 – mission accomplished – but his successor, if less intimidating face-to-face, was every bit as ambitious. Ugo Sola, young and round-faced, spoke so openly of his influence over the Government that Baron de Vaux of the French Legation wryly asked if Signor Sola were perhaps the new Prime Minister. The Italians rated the Djurasković Affair a triumph: it was stage-managed by them to alienate Zogu from his former patrons and make Albania more reliant on Italian protection.

While Sola loudly seconded 'Albanian' complaints about spies and diplomatic insults, the President himself took refuge in arch simplicity to claim that:

he could not understand the lack of tact and *savoir-faire* which the Yugoslavs had displayed ever since the Treaty of Tirana. Surely it ought to be in their interest to come up smiling, make the best of things, and instead of sulking try to prove to the Albanians that they were even more friendly to this country than were the Italians.[3]

Thus the supposed strong man of Albania disclosed 'his natural political timidity'.[4] Perhaps he simply realised his impotence. He was not one of those pro-Italian Albanians who swallowed the line that Yugoslavia would break up under military pressure and let Kosovo fall into their laps. On the contrary, his continued readiness to compromise with Belgrade exasperated Ugo Sola, who reported to Rome that it was 'no easy task to make someone born a sheep assume the posture of a lion'.[5] If Zogu joined in stoking up Albano-Yugoslav tension at times, it was because he needed to deflect domestic critics, who would be more likely to tolerate Italian interference if they believed that Yugoslavia posed an even greater menace. All the same, he thought that any Adriatic war was bound to turn out badly for the weakest nation involved: 'there was complete incompatibility of temper between Italy and Yugoslavia and . . . Albania was the predestined victim'.[6]

He also suspected that he himself could be a 'predestined victim' – of an assassin in Italian or Yugoslav pay. Mussolini might want to replace him with one of his more reliable clients of long-standing, such as Prishtina or Vërlaci, while the Serbs had obvious reasons for wishing him dead. Zogu probably felt in more danger in 1927 than any time before. Autocratic though his regime might be, he had been unable to switch from Yugoslav to Italian patronage without friction among his followers.

Ceno Bey Kryeziu always advised against collaboration with Italy. Aside from his status as brother-in-law, Kryeziu owed his influence with Zogu to his effectiveness as an intermediary with Belgrade. If Albano-Yugoslav relations lost their importance, so might he. As a conciliatory Kosovar, he wanted co-operation with the Serbs to reduce barriers to cross-border travel. The Kryeziu were a powerful clan; Ceno was quick, confident, and similar to Zogu in age and looks. Cronies proclaimed him the only possible successor to the President. This was careless talk.

Rumours of a rift between the two men began in July 1925, when Kryeziu left the Interior Ministry after only four months with no reason given. An extended trip to France then prompted talk of banishment. Pundits could only attribute his return in 1926 to Sadije's soft spot for her son-in-law. He did not stay long in Tirana, as Zogu appointed him to the Albanian Legation in Belgrade. There Kryeziu helped mollify the Yugoslav Government for a while, until the Serbs realised that his stubbornly anti-Italian views were hardly an accurate representation of official Albanian policy. Ceno Bey yet had his uses for them. From spring 1927, he was in receipt of financial support from the Yugoslav Interior Ministry: he had been 'turned' and barely concealed it. During the war-scare in March, Kryeziu gave newspaper interviews dismissing any Yugoslav threat as fantastic and voicing mistrust of Italy. Then he refused to leave when Zogu recalled him during the Djuraskovié Affair.

Insubordination did not incur dismissal. Instead, Zogu named him as Albanian Minister to Czechoslovakia in addition to his present post.

Events now took a dramatic turn. Kryeziu had just arrived in Prague to present his credentials when he was shot dead in a café on 14 October 1927. His assassin, Alqiviadh Bebi, was an Albanian student who argued that Ceno Bey deserved to be killed 'because he wanted to sell his fatherland to Yugoslavia'.[7] Six weeks later, Bebi was himself shot dead in the dock of a Prague courtroom on the first day of his trial. The killer this time was Zia Vuçiterni, a servant of Kryeziu's brother Gani, so it appeared to be a feud. The Czechs sent Vuçiterni to gaol but freed him after fourteen months on account of psychological problems. He went to Belgrade where he too was shot dead.

Three rounds of murder confounded all attempts to elucidate the original crime. The killing of Kryeziu is the most debated assassination of the Zogist era. At the time, attention focused on links with Noli's National Revolutionary Committee in Vienna. The Bishop, however, condemned the crime. Graver suspicion must attach to the Italian secret service: Ceno was the only leading Zogist still opposed to Italy's special role in Albania.

The third suspect is Zogu himself. He knew that Kryeziu was ambitious for power and willing to work with the Serbs to secure it. On this theory, the assassination was intended to eliminate a leadership rival. The Kryeziu family drew their own conclusion and left for Yugoslavia, where the brothers, Gani, Hassan, and Said, became zealous anti-Zogists. Chalk up another blood feud. On the other hand, it is hard to see why Zogu would have chosen to have Ceno Bey murdered in Prague. The European press classed Albania with Bulgaria as a den of assassins. Zogu had liked his brother-in-law and seemed sincerely distressed, but that could point either way. Ceno received a grand burial in the historic Suleiman Pasha mausoleum.

Few people set eyes on the President during October and November 1927. There was speculation about threats to his life, a mysterious illness, and secret disputes with Italy. Diplomats who did obtain an interview found him thoroughly out of sorts; a 'depressed invalid' indeed.[8] In most ways, Zogu was a master of self-concealment, perfectly controlling his words, voice, and expression, but he could not prevent anxiety revealing itself in physical symptoms. Slender at the best of times, at the worst he grew haggard, and self-assured utterances did not ring true when his face looked drawn and old. Even if he failed to hide his worry, however, he usually disguised its cause. The truth might become discernible later, when his return to fitness coincided with some particular political development.

This time the connection was obvious. Zogu was back on form by 22 November when he received the heads of foreign legations in his office to reveal that a new Treaty of Tirana had just been signed. It was a straightforward military alliance between Italy and Albania to safeguard each other against attack from without. This was the kind of commitment that Zogu had sought in 1925–6. Mussolini had declined to trust him then, but by now the Italians had isolated Albania and deprived it of an independent foreign policy. An alliance thus became almost free of risk for Italy – and largely redundant for Albania. Negotiations had started immediately after the Djurasković Affair, with Zogu dawdling and demanding money in his usual way. In September, he temporarily broke off the talks when he discovered (or was allowed to learn) that Italy was still funding Hassan Prishtina and his group at Zara. Sola deftly explained that the subsidies prevented anti-Zogist emigrés becoming dangerous pawns of Yugoslavia. The ending of payments to Prishtina constituted another bargaining chip, and the talks made faster progress after the death of Ceno Bey.

To the Yugoslav Minister, Zogu hinted that Italy had forced him into the alliance against his will. He also played games with the British Minister. After explaining that Albania was 'a weak and tiny country which could not exist without the protection of a stronger Power', he swore that he would tear up the treaty if Britain disapproved: 'British advice is law to me.'[9] Despite his determination not to intervene, Chamberlain was in fact slightly perturbed. Eleven days earlier, a Franco-Yugoslav Treaty had been signed in Paris that promised joint consideration of threats to external security. Great Power rivalry in the Balkans echoed the years before 1914, yet Mussolini protested that Italian policy was in no way sinister. Sola had based the wording of the Treaty of Tirana on the Anglo-Portuguese alliance of 1810. Italy viewed Albania 'as her little sister to be protected and cherished'.[10]

The twenty-year alliance set the seal on the international position of Albania. Although it was presented to the locals as extra protection against Slav expansionism, Europe viewed it as confirmation that here was an Italian client state, ready to be used as a military base. Guardhouses, patrols, and checkpoints multiplied on the Albano-Yugoslav border until travellers said that it seemed more like half a dozen frontiers. Forests were cut back to facilitate surveillance, and white wooden crosses marked where people had been killed while crossing illegally. In Tirana, Jevtić, the Yugoslav Minister, shut himself away in his Legation, and anyone who had contact with him attracted police attention. Relations with Yugoslavia were frozen in sullen hostility.

The Italian Legation meanwhile grew large and intrusive, its head known locally as 'Sign Please'. And President Zogu did sign. The following year witnessed a series of inter-linked deals, some public and some not, wherein he exchanged favours with Mussolini. Most welcome was a moratorium on loan repayments: Albanians would have nothing to pay till 1930. Zogu accepted an Italian military mission, under General Pariani, which would act as an alternative general staff. He promised to expand the army and engage military advisers from nowhere else. Italians in Albania would be subject to Italian law, not Albanian. Finally, Italian State Railways, holders of the oil concession, channelled a gift of ten million lire to the President. He required this money for a specific purpose, as one crucial component of all these deals was not written down and had yet to transpire.

CHAPTER SEVENTEEN

On the Steps of the Throne

Compared with what had gone before, the three-and-a-half years of the Albanian Republic might almost be rated a time of domestic tranquillity. Zogist propaganda, as usual, went so far as to compel disbelief:

> The unemployment problem was solved: everybody had a job and money was no longer scarce. . . . The people were too happy and content to have time to think of fighting for politics' sake and then, the entire population of the country was favourable to the President.[1]

This writer could only attribute the very substantial northern revolt of November 1926 to the jealous machinations of Balkan neighbours who 'realized that Albania would progress too fast with Zogu at the reins'.

Surviving a serious armed challenge certainly enhanced his prestige. The Zogist regime relied on violence. Too many of its opponents were murdered – and too many police enquiries allowed to lapse – to leave any real doubt about it. In managing beys and chiefs, Zogu preferred persuasion, bribery, and intimidation, yet their effectiveness could only be increased by the tacit threat of assassination. Men who opposed him understood the risk. Most would have been equally ready to kill him if ever they had the chance. In politics, the time-honoured blood feud merged into modern gangsterism.

The violence unleashed in Dukagjini in the winter of 1926 was of a different kind, being 'pacification' on the old Ottoman model. The rebel Roman Catholic clans of Dukagjini, Shala, and Shoshi were punished by the warriors of Dibra and Mati plus the gendarmerie led by Muharrem Bajraktari under the supervision of Interior Minister Musa Juka: all of them Muslims. The Government forces burnt villages and pigs, and flogged men of fighting age more or less at random. The total death toll ran into hundreds. Suspects were crammed so tightly into Shkodra gaol that some of them suffocated. Zogu denied excessive severity, and foreigners shrank from overt criticism, as they feared that civil disorder in Albania could easily end in war between Italy and Yugoslavia. After this brutal episode, ordinary Albanians might think twice about insurgency. November 1926 was indeed the last significant clan uprising until the Second World War. Opening Parliament on 15 September 1927, Zogu commented:

The past year saw a movement in the brave Dukagjini mountains but the rapid disappearance of this movement proved that the State organisation is capable at no matter what moment of maintaining the Statute and laws of the Republic. This movement against the State is now forgotten: if it is ever remembered it is remembered only as a lesson.[2]

By then, he had even paid an official visit to Shkodra. The Cabinet and most of the deputies were obliged to accompany him, in sweltering August heat, as he intended to show the northerners 'that Albania was not governed purely by himself, and to convince them that his Government was a reality'.[3] Citizens marked out a big 'AZ' on the side of Mount Tarabosh and prudently cheered as the President passed beneath decorative arches in his armoured car. Since the revolt, a compulsory 'benefice' had built him a holiday home at Shiroka on Lake Shkodra, but this example of central European spa rococo was discovered not to be ready. Luckily, the Grand Hotel off Shkodra square was the best in the country (which implied a comparative absence of bugs).

His Excellency did not set foot outside for a week. All the chieftains had to come to him to be conciliated with pleasantries and gifts and to swear their loyalty in return. For light relief, he chatted about roads to two British tourists (who described him as 'a figure who might have stepped out of a London band box'[4]). On his eighth morning in Shkodra, ringed by crimson-clad guards, Zogu finally emerged to review a parade of 'militia': clansmen from Mirdita and Dukagjini, as well as Mati and Dibra. Then he summoned the diplomatic corps at one day's notice to the first ever Albanian state banquet. In the modest garden of the Grand, guests dined in full uniform with orders. One of them observed that the President 'was obviously somewhat embarrassed' by the novelty of the occasion, though he bore himself with his usual natural dignity.[5] Zogu did not choose to repeat the experience for almost a decade.

It shocked locals to see women at the banquet, but they danced in the street when the President pardoned seventy-four rebels and reduced the sentences of the other four hundred-odd. His triumphal fortnight in the north, coming after the events of the winter, was the kind of performance of which a sultan would have been proud. Before he left, the town council begged him to accept the title 'Prince of Shkodra'. He declined because of his republican oath, but the burghers were not alone in thinking that this might not apply much longer.

Some simple Albanians already believed that they were ruled by a prince or king. Exile groups repeatedly warned that he would declare himself ruler for life. Robert Parr remarked in 1926 that Zogu used to argue that internal jealousies made a native dynasty wholly impracticable,

'But the President has a childish tendency towards the grandiose and he may well be contemplating action.'[6] At the Italian Legation, they knew this for a fact at least from the summer of 1927. Zogu discussed the matter with Sola, for it would cost money to elect a monarchist constituent assembly. He accepted the Treaty of Tirana on the basis that funds would be forthcoming for this purpose in due course, although it would hardly do to make the connection too obvious.

These efforts at discretion did not prevent rumours of an announcement in the run-up to every national holiday. 'Legality Day' (24 December) was widely tipped, but Zogu held back, and Parliament merely voted him the title of 'Saviour of the Nation'. Next came a change of premises in March 1928. The President had hitherto rented two adjoining houses, living in one and using the larger as offices. Now he moved into a substantial villa on the southern side of the town centre which had formerly served as the Foreign Ministry. Built in Italianate style with Turkish touches and a roof of simple red tiles, it was not highly distinguished, but a double staircase, balustrades by the steps, and mouldings above the windows proclaimed it the residence of a wealthy man. The interior began to suggest a little palace when fitted with French and Italian furniture.

Articles began to appear in the press proposing that, after three whole years, it was time to review the constitution and see where it might be improved. No sooner proposed than adopted: the elections to the Constituent Assembly would be held on 16 July and 16 August. Now the monarchist campaign started in earnest. Telegrams flooded in from all corners of the country calling for a kingdom. Doubtful newspapers mysteriously ceased publication. Zogu made a few day trips to show himself to the people, though death threats put him off visiting Korça and Gjirokastra. The latest 5 million lire payment from Italian State Railways helped in many ways. The Roman Catholic chieftains had to be detained for days at Shkodra (and generously compensated for the inconvenience) before they would put their thumbprints to a petition.

Zogu said that he could understand why Albanians wanted a king: 'We are a primitive and backward people, accustomed to the hereditary principle and unable to appreciate the meaning of a republic.'[7] The clan system was deeply engrained, yet there was no reflection of it in the current constitution. 'Something more in harmony with national ideas was needed.' In mid-August, he explained his predicament to the Heads of Legations:

He was being impelled by an ever-increasing volume of opinion in the direction of a change in the character of the régime. . . . The people felt the need of a permanent authority which would rise superior to the conflicts of personal interests and political groups. The Crown would be such an authority; it would inspire confidence and serve as a pledge that justice was to be had. Also, it would give the idea of continuity. What Albania chiefly needed and had been lacking in the past was a stable Government which would encourage the people to set to work and build up the State on a firm foundation. . . . He had resisted the impulsion so far for various reasons – recognition by foreign Powers might be withheld for a long period and a disastrous interregnum might ensue; he felt, too, the natural repugnance to putting himself forward in a way that must inevitably be ascribed to him for ambition, though, in fact, he was actuated by no such motive. . . .[8]

He pretended not to know whether he should yield to the pressure or withstand it.

Monarchy had one basic attraction for the ruler of Albania: a king would not need to stand for re-election. The calculation was not quite as crude as this might suggest, though, as Albania was already a dictatorship. By the 1925 constitution, the chamber of deputies elected the President, so the dictator would continue to require the return of a puppet Parliament. Here money was the crucial determinant. When Zogu sought re-election in 1932, there was likely to be a hostile chamber only if Italy had switched its funding to somebody else. Seeing that Zogu had first seized power as the protégé of Yugoslavia, Mussolini might want to install an Albanian of his own choosing. The foundation of a monarchy would make this much more difficult. Therefore the deal in 1927–8 was not so much collusion against Albanian 'democracy' as a straight *quid pro quo*. When the Italians agreed to the idea of a kingdom, they voluntarily gave up their prime opportunity for replacing Zogu by pseudo-constitutional means. He reciprocated by letting them strengthen their military presence in his country.

The Constituent Assembly opened in Tirana on 25 August. Zogu made a fleeting appearance, in full uniform, to hand in a type-written message expressing his desire to give the country modern organisation, maintain good relations with neighbouring states, and foster industrial and agricultural production. A few days later, unsigned proclamations ordered people to throng the streets, waving flags and singing the national anthem. 'The whole population of the capital, without any exception of class or calling, must take part,' said the posters. 'No Albanian man or woman shall sit during the demonstrations in a coffee-house, shop, restaurant, or street; all must accompany the population in their manifestations.'[9]

At a quarter past nine on the morning of 1 September, the two-hundred-strong Assembly unanimously passed a brief resolution offering the 'illustrious crown of the historic Albanian throne' to the Saviour of the Nation. A delegation in white tie and tails at once conveyed the invitation to the palace. Tirana newspapers reported cheering crowds, pealing bells, and brilliant sunshine: 'The day had come, the day so long waited for; the throne of Skanderbeg was no longer empty.'[10]

CHAPTER EIGHTEEN

His Majesty

The ceremony of acceptance was scheduled for five o'clock, but by half past four the white-washed chamber of the Parliament House was already crowded. From its high windows, sunlight shone down on deputies, civil servants, and mountain chieftains, tailcoats and white wool fezzes. The heads of foreign missions were also present, though trying to look inconspicuous. The occasion raised difficult questions of protocol, so, pending the verdicts of their Governments, the diplomats had opted for morning dress with no decorations. To show that their attendance was informal, they squeezed onto the floor of the modest hall, leaving the box reserved for them to the Associated Press correspondent.

Knowing looks consequently greeted the arrival of eight carloads of Italian dignitaries in full-dress uniforms of purple and gold. The verdict of their Government was never in any doubt. The Yugoslav Minister, Dr Mikhajlović, was meanwhile nowhere to be seen – still on summer leave apparently – so there was not much doubt about the attitude of his Government either.

Less than half-a-mile away, a trumpet fanfare sounded, and an open car with a cavalry escort began to make its way through the narrow streets beneath a series of triumphal arches topped with the monogram 'AZ'. On one side of it rode Xhemal Aranitasi, Commander-in-Chief of the Army, and on the other, Leon Ghilardi, Inspector-General of the Army. Hundreds of cheap flags had been imported from Italy, so every household could afford to display the black eagle rampant on a blood-red ground: the standard of Skanderbeg. Leafy green boughs, brought down from the mountains and already beginning to fade, decked the doors and windows of all the old mud-brick cottages. Multi-coloured Turkish carpets hung from the balconies of more prosperous villas. Hand-painted banners stretched across the street proclaimed (with slightly varied spelling) *Asambleja Konstituante* and *Monarkija*.

The trappings of a conventional procession were in place, but, to those unused to the ways of the 'Saviour of the Nation', the scene presented a curious spectacle, since, apart from lines of soldiers, the streets were entirely empty. It was awkward that a man ostensibly elevated to the throne by the will of the people should not have been able to enter into closer contact with them, but Zogu had to be mindful of security. He made a point of arriving either early or late for public engagements.

The short parade entered Skanderbeg Square and halted on its southern side. It was now twenty minutes to five. A slender man in an olive-green uniform stepped from the car, shook hands with the President of the Constituent Assembly, and walked briskly up the steps, under the stone lintel inscribed *Parlamenti*, into the chamber, and down the central aisle. Looking pale and nervous, he mounted the dais and falteringly raised his right hand to support the constitution. The room rang with cheers, which he acknowledged with grave bows to right and left. Then, while the saluting of guns outside made a deafening noise, he swore an oath on the Koran and the Bible:

I, Zog the First, King of the Albanians, on the occasion of ascending the throne of the Kingdom of Albania and taking into my hands royal power, swear before Almighty God to maintain the national unity, independence, and territorial integrity. I will faithfully adhere to the Constitution and act in conformity with its provisions and the laws in force, keeping always before my eyes the will of the people. May God help me.[1]

At that moment on Saturday, 1 September 1928, President Ahmed Zogu became His Majesty King Zog I, and Europe gained its latest kingdom and its only Muslim king. He had thought seriously about calling himself Skanderbeg III, but direct descendants in Italy claimed sole right to the name. King Ahmed sounded far too exclusively Islamic, so he chose to adopt his own surname (which in Albanian means 'bird'). Inevitably, *Zog I Mbret i Shqiptarvet* was sometimes translated as 'Bird the First, King of the Sons of the Eagle'. By the rules of Albanian grammar, when the noun Zogu is either preceded by a title or followed by an ordinal number, it assumes the indefinite form and loses the final letter: hence the monosyllable by which he was henceforth known abroad.

The new monarch signed his oath and made a short speech in deeply earnest tones. He looked upon it as a point of honour to serve Albania to the best of his ability, and, if necessary, to give his life for it. 'The world has understood that if the Sons of the Eagle are left in peace they can build a state.' His peroration was brief but effective: 'Gentlemen, may we come forth with honour in the eyes of history!'[2] It was still not yet five o'clock, when, to cries of '*Rroft Mbreti*! Long live the King!', he hurried from the hall, with his aides bumping into each other in their effort to keep up. At what was now the Royal Palace, half a dozen new Princesses and a Queen Mother awaited him.

Six days of public holiday followed. Troops were reviewed and bonfires lit. Rocket after rocket went up to the glory of Zog I. Sheep were slaughtered in front of the palace. Italian planes dropped streamers and confetti. Six colonels were promoted to the rank of general. Two thousand prisoners were pardoned, and state employees received bonuses equal to one month's salary. The main towns vied to present the monarch with handsome properties, lest they appear disloyal. Every shop and café prominently displayed his picture, as failure to do so incurred a fine of 50 francs. Even devout Muslims had to overcome their objection to human images and buy the crudely coloured standard portrait. Any genuine enthusiasm for the monarchy was obscured by heavy-handed efforts to force the note of public approval.

Some predictable criticism was voiced abroad. From Munich, Wilhelm of Wied protested that he was still Prince of Albania. From Vienna, Bishop Fan Noli denounced 'an odious crime against the Albanian people'. The Zogist monarchy was 'a farce prepared at Rome and played at Tirana'.[3] Noli, who had lately translated *Macbeth* and *Julius Caesar*, spoke for KONARE, the émigré group dedicated to freeing Albania from imperialism, feudalism, and Ahmed Zogu. Exiled beys in the rival *Bashkimi Kombëtar* were equally indignant.

More significant was the reaction of Yugoslavia. For a few weeks, the Yugoslav Minister in Tirana remained unavailable for comment, and the Yugoslav Foreign Minister declared himself too busy to meet the Albanian envoy in Belgrade. They took exception to the fact that Zog had chosen the title 'King of the Albanians' as opposed to 'King of Albania', which was widely interpreted as a declaration of authority over ethnic Albanians in Kosovo. This objection had been foreseen, and French diplomats especially had lobbied for the uncontroversial formula. Zogu had equivocated and explained his powerlessness as 'a mere thing in the hands' of the Constituent Assembly.[4] Two friends of Italy, Vërlaci and Alizoti, were credited with swaying his judgement. Nationalists, said Zog, had spread expectations which he could scarcely disappoint. 'The throne was offered me by the Albanians so that I cannot be called other than King of the Albanians', he argued, and he did have a debating point in his favour.[5] Was not the monarch of Yugoslavia officially 'King of the Serbs, Croats, and Slovenes'? There was also the Tsar of the Bulgarians and the King of the Hellenes – both titles chosen with frontier revision in mind.

Belgrade recognised the kingdom on 18 September. Another breach in Yugoslav-Albanian relations would only have played into the hands of Mussolini. Italian recognition had been so swift as to underline their sponsorship of the regime. The first official visitor to the Royal Palace was Ugo Sola, delivering an effusive message which barely cloaked the link with the Treaty of Tirana:

My Government saw with great satisfaction that change of status of Albania which brought Your Majesty to the throne which the faithful ally of Italy, George Kastrioti Skanderbeg, left vacant for five centuries. I am sure that Your Majesty will be inspired by the traditions of this great predecessor, in upholding and strengthening more and more an alliance whose value, force, and duration are made close by historic traditions and geographic considerations.[6]

Zog answered that the alliance would 'long outlast its term; in fact it will last forever'. To the Duce, he offered immutable friendship and gratitude.

It annoyed the King of the Albanians that Britain and France waited three weeks before acknowledging his elevation (to save Yugoslavia from appearing isolated). Sir Robert Hodgson, the new British Minister, reported that poverty-stricken people would find things no easier because their dictator had succumbed to the whim of calling himself *Mbret* (derived from the Latin *Imperator*), though 'Certainly, the Albanian understands a King better than he understands a President'.[7]

In formal terms, Zog had placed himself above the chieftains and beys and enhanced his status abroad. His vernacular title was actually the same as that used by Prince Wilhelm in 1914, but the new *Mbret* stipulated its translation as 'King', not unreasonably, given that the only sovereign princes in Europe reigned in Monaco and Liechtenstein. The King of Albania assumed first place in the *Almanach de Gotha* (thanks to alphabetical order by country). His use of the numeral, Zog I, accorded with continental practice, though it struck English-speakers as premature and pompous.

Most Heads of State reacted to the creation of the kingdom with a modicum of politeness. Not so Mustapha Kemal, President of Turkey, who thumped the table on hearing the news:

> What! Accept that? No, no! I will not recognise him! Perhaps I will be alone in the world. That doesn't matter. I swear to you, I give you my word that I will not recognise him. It is necessary to set an example! A man elected by the people should not betray his oath. Never, never![8]

The future Atatürk, who may not have been entirely sober, ordered that his words be published verbatim. Later he hailed an Albanian diplomat with the query, 'Asaf Bey, I see a lot of funny pictures in the newspapers. What's going on in Albania? Are you performing an operetta?'[9]

Kemal had much in common with Zog. Of partially Albanian descent, he was educated in Monastir and Istanbul. His hero was Napoleon. He visited Vienna in 1917. He led resistance to the partition of his homeland and established himself as a dictator committed to modernisation. Yet the

Turk was contemptuous of the Albanian's lesser achievement and especially of his reliance on Italy. A desire to quash stories that he would make himself King of Turkey may also explain his vehemence. 'Zog goes backwards,' he exclaimed. 'Why should he in this day and age become King?'[10] Diplomatic relations between Tirana and Ankara lapsed for over three years. King Zog affected indifference: after centuries of Ottoman domination, Albania had reason to distance itself from Turkey. In truth, he felt deeply offended.

The operetta gibe was endlessly repeated. Journalists wrote that Zog instructed his sisters not to be photographed too often in Albanian costume lest foreigners be reminded of Act II of *The Merry Widow*. The image of Franz Lehár's 'Pontevedro', he thought, had contributed to the downfall of independent Montenegro. Maybe he should have gone further and stopped the youngest princesses appearing in the military uniforms of white poplin which equally suggested the travestie chorus from *The Desert Song*. The outside world had never taken Albania very seriously, but King Zog would have been the last person to realise that the sudden elevation of a spivvy-looking man with a bizarre name had not helped.*

The ruler of Albania wanted to be the equal of his Balkan neighbours. Yugoslavia, Romania, and Bulgaria all had kings (and Greece was only briefly a republic), but the new royal faced the same sort of derision as the new rich. It was said, for instance, that Ettore Bugatti refused to sell Zog a *Royale* limousine for fear of devaluing the brand. The Romanian, Bulgarian, and Greek dynasties belonged to the cosmopolitan cousinhood of European royalty. Hohenzollern-Sigmaringen, Saxe-Coburg-Gotha, and Schleswig-Holstein-Sonderburg-Glücksburg looked askance at Zogu-Mati. There was a closer parallel with the Karadjordjević kings of Yugoslavia. The original 'Black George' became leader of the Serbs by his own violent efforts in the early nineteenth century, and his grandson had regained the throne after the murder of his rival in 1903. Since the War, however, Alexander I of Yugoslavia had sealed his respectability with a dynastic marriage. Politics aside, the Karadjordjević family would still not have been eager to associate with their replacements as the black sheep of European royalty.

Though sensitive to even the most trivial snubs, King Zog could console himself with the reflection that these were simply the penalties of exceptional success. So what if the inheritors of thrones regarded him as an outlandish upstart? It stood to reason that every royal dynasty had to begin with somebody.

---

* In Britain, *Zog* was the brand name of a well-known cleaning product, a powder applied with a damp cloth to sinks, linoleum, etc.

CHAPTER NINETEEN

King and Capital

It was the wont of journalists outside Albania to depict King Zog as a capricious voluptuary. Their editors looked for something colourful from the Balkans, a requirement easily met with the familiar story of how the resources of a poor little nation were squandered on women, wine, and song. This was the classic Ruritanian recipe with a pinch of democratic censure. Ivor Novello put it on stage in *Glamorous Night*.

What newsmen could not learn about the King, they very often guessed, for how many readers of the popular press could possibly know any different? Zog was labelled 'the last ruler of romance', the supreme overlord of a wild and rugged land whose life brimmed over with danger and adventure.[1] Many of the fantasies were quite harmless, even flattering, yet there were generally no Albanian spokesmen to complain when inaccuracy verged upon absurdity and libel. Even in Rome, London, Paris, and Washington, where Zog maintained legations, protests could simply be ignored. What did it matter if Albania took offence?

One caricature emphasised the Muslim background: Zog the decadent oriental despot, taking on where Sultan Abdul Hamid II had supposedly left off. He spent his days lounging on cushions while dancing-girls diverted him with a thousand-and-one tales. Photographic evidence of silk tie and pinstripes undermined this travesty while giving rise to another. Here he was a millionaire playboy, addicted to champagne, fast cars, roulette, and a harem of Hollywood starlets. Up-to-date ideas of royal debauchery owed a good deal to the King of Romania, but, while Carol II retained foreign friends and diplomatic influence, Zog I had neither. The socialites of St Tropez and Capri did not defend the Albanian, because they knew nothing about him.

That King Zog should so rapidly have had the character of a frivolous cosmopolitan projected upon him says much about the stereotype of Balkan royalty. The illusion was sustained by the curious frequency of press reports about his travel intentions, though he never had the chance to make or receive a State visit, and basic obstacles stood in the way of his going abroad even in a private capacity. In theory, Albania was a sovereign state; in practice, it was subordinate to Italy, which had no intention of letting Zog onto the international stage as an independent actor. Foreign governments therefore left well alone. There was no point in exchanging platitudes with a docile Italian puppet – and Zog in any other guise would be a mischief-maker, clouding relations with Rome.

In any case, the King did not feel secure enough to venture outside his kingdom, as the chances of usurpation, insurrection, civil war, or invasion raised doubts about the likelihood of his ever returning. While leaders of more reliable nations undertook actual foreign visits, Zog could only supplement his diplomacy with orchestrated speculation about possible ones. In 1934, for instance, when relations with Italy grew especially bad, it was reported that he was going to Turkey to meet Kemal. Then Italo-Albanian tensions eased, and no more was heard of the Turkish trip. King Zog really went abroad only once during his entire reign: reluctantly, to Vienna for medical checks. The haunt of this Balkan king was his home city.

Tirana in the 1920s was in a class of its own among European capitals, and not just because of its largely Muslim population. Covered in slimy mud in winter and ghostly dust clouds in summer, it was variously likened by western visitors to a gold-rush town, a recent target of shellfire, and an abandoned building site. These excessively unflattering descriptions reflect the fact that Tirana satisfied neither those who expected a conventional modern metropolis nor those in search of the exotic east. The Albanian 'city' was Zog's creation in many respects. He had favoured it as provisional capital in 1920 and confirmed its status in 1925, although it had not been an obvious choice.

Tirana was then a small provincial town which had grown up undramatically over fourteen centuries. The Emperor Justinian had sited a modest fortress there in 520, but the settlement did not amount to much until Suleiman Pasha Mulleti, a local feudal lord, added a mosque and some Turkish baths eleven hundred years later. The eastern quarter of the townlet was named after him. Recently, a few beys had built retirement villas in Tirana. Its situation, about 200 metres above sea level, between Mount Dajti and a low chain of hills, made it a mild and sheltered spot. One drawback was a poor water supply. The River Llana was little more than a stream – in summer a succession of stagnant pools. Behind high mud walls in quiet streets, red-tiled bungalows of uncertain age multiplied slowly over decades in their surprisingly lush little gardens. In its own ramshackle and lethargic way, old Tirana had a certain charm. In 1916, the Austrians reckoned the number of residents at around twelve thousand.

The attraction of the place to Zog derived from its central location, which meant that it was better insulated from hostile foreign influences than any of the alternatives. Shkodra, though mainly Muslim itself, was ringed by Roman Catholic districts and dangerously near Yugoslavia. Durrës and Vlora stood on the coast and therefore too close to Italy. Greece claimed Gjirokastra and Korça. Tirana was safe from border raids, yet overseas visitors would not have to journey far inland. Zog may have valued one other factor: the town lay within striking distance of Mati.

Zog engaged a team of Italian architects after 1925, headed by Armando Brasini, a celebrated urban planner. They promised to transform the place, but the project was forever hampered by lack of funds and poor workmanship. Hard toil on a construction site was beneath the dignity of many Albanians: a proud man fought and farmed for himself, he did not drudge for others. Gypsy labourers needed constant supervision. Despite these problems, by the mid-1930s an Italian town of concrete and stucco had been patchily imposed on the mud-brick village. Tirana now sprawled a couple of miles, though the country was never more than ten minutes' walk away. The population had doubled to the delight of local landlords. Rents were astronomic.

The city had electric lighting after 1927 – a row of trees with fairy lights was at first a popular novelty – but there was no piped water or sewerage for almost another decade. (Drinking water for the palace came by lorry twice a day from a spring some 15 miles away.) Most residents threw refuse into the street to rot, the stench not wholly masked by wood-smoke and the pervasive smell of mutton fat used for cooking. The other distinctive odours of Tirana were coffee grounds and mud.

Cypress trees and minarets retained their charm, and the eighteenth-century Mosque of Ethem Bey, brightly frescoed with fruit and flowers, survived the demolitions to give a touch of architectural distinction to the dusty expanse of Skanderbeg Square. For six days in the week, this much enlarged marketplace was a gaping hole in the heart of the city. It came to life only on Thursdays when buffalo wagons, pack trains, and women brought firewood and produce down from the hills. Not only did the women carry huge bundles on their backs, they also worked handheld spinning wheels as they walked. Their male protector was now more likely to bear a stick than a gun when in town. He did the buying and entertained onlookers with the ritual of ferocious barter. The variety of traditional dress to be seen on a market day was astonishing, as every valley boasted its own distinctive mode of trousers, jacket, and sash. The fez vied with the skull cap, the colour of either being black, white, or red, according to faith and locality.

On one side of the square, the medieval bazaar preserved its picturesque decrepitude of old while gaining an added measure of animation. The rough cobbled alleys, narrow and crowded, wound between ancient open-fronted shops, darkened by broad eaves. Here silversmiths worked on filigree rings and long cigarette-holders tipped with amber. Rams bleated and stamped in butcher's shops. Illiterates waited on the public letter-writer. Dancing dervishes pierced their cheeks with skewers. Hard-faced peasants discussed the respective merits of wooden ploughs. Bits of old motor-tyre and string were sold as shoes. A mountain clansman with a rifle in one hand and an umbrella in the other chatted with epauletted officers. Half-naked beggars wailed for alms. Timid Muslim women drew black robes across their faces, and water carriers with ponies and old petrol tins did brisk trade all year round.

Officious policemen directed foreigners away from the old town to go and admire the jerry-built structures and semi-western manners of new Tirana. Among the most striking innovations were Boulevard Zog (billed as 'the broadest boulevard in the Balkans') and Boulevard Mussolini. These 40 metre-wide roads, asphalted and lined with trees, stretched north and west from Skanderbeg Square to nowhere of importance. Eminent persons were intended to build their houses along them, but the economic slump after 1929 left most of the plots half-finished or empty. The ravine at the end of Boulevard Zog served as an unofficial tip.

Traffic in Tirana was minimal. There were no buses or trams, and the battered Model-T Fords which passed for luxury hire-cars did not begin to proliferate until the mid-1930s. The rich still travelled in four-wheeled carriages which had known better days in Vienna or Budapest before the World War. People walked in the middle of the street except when soldiers with bayonets forced them to use the pavements. The boulevards were an outstanding example of the misapplication of Italian aid.

More justifiable was the complex of government ministries completed by the Italians in 1931. The eight three-storey blocks of white stone and redbrick dwarfed the little parliament on the edge of the square. Decorated with mustard-coloured facings and a Skanderbeg helmet above each entrance, they were a remarkable improvement on scattered ex-Turkish offices with smashed windows, broken locks, and infamous latrines. In the 'Albanian Whitehall', self-important officials delighted in telephones and typewriters which made them feel at the forefront of westernisation.

Most educated young men faced three career options: emigration, teaching, or the civil service. Emigration became difficult after the USA introduced quotas. Teaching meant living in some remote village on basic pay. The civil service offered prestige, perks, and plentiful opportunities for extra income. Dark-suited bureaucrats were the new men of Zog's Albania. Not everyone was favourably impressed. 'They made me think of Al Capone's bodyguard,' remarked one reporter of the American-speaking staff of the official publicity bureau.[2]

It was the new men's wives who sustained Rruga Mbretnore or Royal Street: two blocks of single-storey concrete shops selling imported goods at high prices to raise money for a second floor. These few bareheaded women in flesh-coloured stockings, patrons of 'The Drapery, Progress', were the beacon of Albanian social reform. 'The enlightenment and uplift of the women of Albania is an absolute necessity', proclaimed the King,[3] but attitudes were deeply entrenched. Even at royal functions, the sexes gravitated to opposite sides of the room. Westernised women found themselves practically unemployable. There were no businesses wanting secretaries, no big stores requiring assistants, and a waitress in a restaurant would never have got round the tables. Men openly propositioned unaccompanied women – all the more after abolition of the veil. The lives of peasant women meanwhile changed not at all. Zog's eventual answer in 1937 was to have his unmarried sisters tour the nation in tight skirts. 'We believe in being modern girls', they said. 'Although our country is semi-Oriental, we have no shyness in introducing such innovations as going to the cinema regularly, wearing abbreviated bathing costumes and beach pyjamas, making up, and doing without the veil.'[4]

In Tirana, ideas for fashion *alla Franka* did indeed come direct from Hollywood on Saturday nights. Drama was almost non-existent (despite the foundation of amateur societies at royal command), so the National Theatre filled its programme with films. Most were silent, and a man at the side of the screen called out the subtitles in translation. Local tastes in cinema could be surprising. Westerns, war films, and gangster stories – in other words, pictures involving gunfights – were scorned as pitifully unrealistic. *Felix the Cat* enjoyed a ready following, but Tirana liked best of all to see 'high life': dinner jackets, ballroom dancing, and glamorous women in nightclubs. The dressy young ladies of Rruga Mbretnore wanted looks like Greta Garbo or Marlene Dietrich and homes like Manhattan apartments. They did their best with shoddy Italian clothes and cosmetics and Czech glassware and pottery.

Even the stock of the bookshops came from abroad. Cheap editions of world classics, the thrillers of Edgar Wallace, and gruesome Italian penny-dreadfuls were the standard fare. With an extremely small literary heritage and under a hundred thousand readers, Albania did not print many vernacular publications, so education beyond elementary level inevitably entailed learning a foreign language. This troubled Zog, who appreciated that the Albanian tongue was fundamental to the sense of nationhood. 'It is our duty, therefore, to love it with all our heart; to guard it as the most precious jewel against any danger, to study it carefully,' he decreed, 'for a national language is always wiser than the wisest of those who speak it.'[5] His efforts to foster Albanian literature centred on the Grand National Poet, Father Gjergj Fishta, a Franciscan friar who produced quantities of patriotic verse, most notably *The Lute of the Mountains*, a thirty-canto epic about fighting the Montenegrins. Although their relations were sometimes strained when the writer dabbled in politics, Zog handled Fishta carefully, and royal patronage had its value. Ambitious young men in public service were eager to be seen at 'The Bookshop, Beauty' buying the subsidised magazine in which his work appeared. An Englishman found that 'everyone automatically cries "our greatest poet!" if you so much as utter "fish"'.[6]

Tirana's tiny class of intellectuals took more interest in Joyce, Gide, and Gorky. Graduates of foreign universities, some of whom seemed like foreigners in their own country, they were nevertheless an important part of a definite cultural revival. Educated young men received new ideas with genuine excitement – and so many ideas came fresh to Albania in the 1920s and 1930s. Predictably, the intellectuals could rarely find work consistent with their expectations. Some swallowed their pride and accepted posts in high schools or government offices; others dabbled in journalism. Few had any liking for a regime which promoted illiterate chiefs. But political discussion could be dangerous. It was safer to talk about surrealism or psychoanalysis.

The King may later have regretted introducing a small number of scholarships for higher education abroad. One beneficiary was Enver Hoxha, the future communist dictator, who first picked up Marxism at Montpellier University. Others came back from Rome or Milan with a comparable enthusiasm for Fascism. Such people had to be watched. They were the seeds of a new kind of underground opposition, but as yet there were not very many of them.

Albania's disaffected intelligentsia skulked in sawdust-strewn cafés where loudspeakers blared out Broadway hits from a few years back. Establishment types preferred the *Kursaal*, the smartest coffee-house in Tirana. At little tables in its shady willow-fringed garden, politicians, beys, and diplomats sat for hours with tiny cups of Turkish coffee and mulled over the news of the day. The city was invariably rife with rumour, much of it trivial and repetitive, and some of it utter nonsense. Political gossip thrived, because the state-controlled press was dull and circumlocutory. Personal gossip thrived in *alla Franka* circles, because everyone knew everyone else.

At six o'clock, the cafés closed and patrons of the Kursaal divided. Pro-Italians normally went to the bar of the new Hotel Continental to carry on their intrigues. Its Italian management confidently advertised the best accommodation in Albania. Less pro-Italians (anti-Italians even, though it was hardly prudent to say so) preferred the Hotel International or 'Internasional' according to its sign. This was an older Albanian establishment which still rented out beds in rooms as distinct from bedrooms. The International had enjoyed its moment of glory in the early 1920s when it installed the first water closet in the country. Cheering crowds escorted the pan through the streets, but its full potential could not be realised without piped water.

While the hotel bars were good enough for most of the native élite, a very select few might yet win admission to the sanctuary of the *corps diplomatique*: the pavilion of the tennis club at the rear of the French Legation. There cocktails and bridge were on offer to those who satisfied the dress code. The expatriates in Tirana, who numbered a hundred or so, kept up a strenuous social calendar. The central figure, as in so much else, was the head of the Italian Legation. Though Sola, a widower, had not been much of a party-giver, the Marchese Antonio Lupi di Soragna changed all that after 1930. It henceforth required an extensive wardrobe and an excellent cook to compete with the Italians.

If the weather were fine, the ordinary people came out of their homes for the *xhiro*: the customary stroll in the evening. The boulevards were at their busiest then, though the strollers were quiet and the pace relaxed. Men walked arm-in-arm under the bitter-orange trees, greeting acquaintances with wishes of long life and puffing out clouds of smoke. Albanian cigarettes were cheap, but expensive matches (a state monopoly) meant frequent requests for a light. Friends squatted at the roadside to gamble at cards, dice, the toss of a coin, or anything else that could give rise to a wager. The crowds dispersed around eight o'clock, and respectable folk did not go out after dark.

For a little while longer, plaintive music drifted across from the Gypsy quarter on the south side of the Llana. That was where the belly-dancers were, along with hereditary prostitutes who strutted the streets in billowing harem trousers. Zog banned such entertainers from the city-centre coffee houses. When flutes and tambourines fell silent, there was only the croaking of bull frogs and the crowing of Albanian cocks – fowl notorious for anticipating the dawn with cries of prodigious duration.

Such was daily life in Tirana under the monarchy. King Zog saw extremely little of it, and it saw even less of him. This was not because he was away. He just very seldom went out.

CHAPTER TWENTY

Inside the Compound

The royal compound in Tirana consisted of the Royal Palace and half-a-dozen smaller buildings within several hundred yards of perimeter railings and balustrades, ornamented here and there with Lalique glass lamps. In fact, the Royal Palace was the same villa that had been selected for President Zogu in 1928 and there was nothing inherently regal about it. There were plans to build a brand new residence, fit for a king, a couple of miles to the south of the city. In the meantime, Zog stayed put. Nowhere else would have been so convenient for the Royal Guard: five-hundred infantry and thirty cavalry who wore distinctive carmine facings on their functional grey-green uniforms. The most regularly paid regiment in the army, the Guards were recruited exclusively from the Zogolli branch of the Mati. They stood on sentry duty at the palace gates, beside the doors, and under the windows, usually in pairs with fixed bayonets.

Here in the compound, the King passed his days. He did not mind admitting why he submitted to voluntary incarceration. 'I've nothing against dying in battle,' he said. 'But I don't intend to be shot in the street like a dog.'[1] He claimed that he owed it to Albania to take sensible precautions, as he wanted to do as much as he could for his country before he was killed, as he frankly expected to be. His struggles with rival beys, Kosovars, Noli-supporting radicals, and Dukagjini rebels left him at blood with dozens of families. Those with a grievance sometimes sent him a bullet in an envelope with the promise of the next one in the neck. A British visitor once ventured to suggest that the Head of State should be exempt from feuds. His guide replied, 'Our King, Excellency, is one of us – not like your King!'[2]

It thus became second nature to King Zog to stand away from windows, scan the rooftops of surrounding buildings, and reach for his gun at the first sign of trouble. Even inside the palace, he had to be alert. A parliamentary deputy was shot dead in the adjutant's room in 1932 (by a fellow Mirdite in a seventy-year-old feud). That said, the traditional laws banned killing in the home. When foes met as guest and host, etiquette demanded every courtesy. The King could thus come face to face even with bitter enemies. During especially awkward interviews, he allegedly kept a loaded revolver hidden under a handkerchief on the desk by his right hand, just in case his hospitality should be abused.

Official engagements beyond the compound routinely entailed clearing the streets and searching or evacuating the houses which overlooked the route. The people of Tirana were able to see their King taking the salute at military parades on national holidays: a uniformed speck on the far side of Skanderbeg Square surrounded by Royal Guards. While it was true that the masses in many other countries came no closer to royalty, this remoteness seemed more pointed in a quiet little town than in a modern metropolis. When Zog attended a reception at the new premises of the United States Legation in 1930, diplomats watched bemused as he leapt from his car, dashed into the building, listened to the speeches, and dashed back out again. The opening of Parliament was equally hasty on those rare occasions when he delivered the King's Speech in person. 'Foreigners here enjoy a lot of cheap sneers at him,' lamented Rose Wilder Lane, the American writer who lived in Tirana and became his friend and admirer.[3]

There were impromptu royal appearances, now and then, when Zog would take a short walk arm in arm with his mother across the triangular public garden between their residences. This miniature park was a municipal showpiece, with rose borders and bandstand, where *alla Franka* society came on Sunday afternoons. With Sadije at his side, he was safe from assassins who respected the Canon. For more vigorous exercise, the King might assemble his cavalry escort and go for a ride: either a few circuits of the nearby parade-ground or a gallop past the olive groves beyond the city limits. Day-trips by car were an infrequent treat, usually an outing to Mati with his sisters, taking lunch at his chalet at Qafë e Shtamës. Excursions involved alternative routes, false information, bomb checks, and last-minute itinerary changes.

Many Albanians tacitly assumed that the King would sooner or later go the way of Essad Pasha and Ceno Bey Kryeziu, so they did not find his circumspection remarkable: 'A man with an enemy is like a hare sitting on its form, he must watch all the time.' Powerful people had always lived behind high walls with plenty of body-guards, and self-imprisonment was often the only defence for a man at blood. Everyday experience informed the adage: 'A rifle doesn't care for bravery, a rifle kills.' It was foreign critics who accused King Zog of cowardice and paranoia. William Seeds felt a need to dispute the common view:

> he is not the pallid tyrant trembling in his palace that some would have him to be; he has in his favour youth, good looks, physical strength and a most courteous and amiable manner; while the fact that he has so borne himself in war as to command the respect of his wild tribesmen outweighs, in one's personal relations with him, the vacillations and lack of principle which mark his inexperienced attempts to deal with high politics.[4]

If Zog had the idea that hundreds of people wanted to kill him, he could not be called deluded. Rose Wilder Lane protested, 'if he walked down the street he would live about ten minutes, and when he's gone, Albania's gone'.[5] Nonetheless exiled opponents could chorus: here is a ruler so hated by his subjects that he dare not show his face.

The King's fear for his life may yet have been exaggerated. Other more secure national leaders could entrust their safety to the police; Zog found it necessary to oversee his own protection in detail. It would not be surprising if the danger preyed on his mind sometimes. Some in his immediate entourage subtly fuelled his fears, since the greater his isolation, the greater his reliance on themselves. The diplomatic envoys of Italy and Yugoslavia also tried to frighten him by passing on secret service reports about conspiracies among Albanian émigrés. A warning was often a threat in disguise. The revolutionary committees at Zara, Belgrade, and Vienna, regularly incited his murder. They would have become far more dangerous had foreign backers provided enough gold for them to buy a traitor within the royal compound. Zog knew that he was surrounded by Italian spies who would be able to supply crucial intelligence to Hassan Bey Prishtina if ever Mussolini sought a change of leadership in Tirana.

At times of international tension, as during 1926–7, fear of assassination at the behest of Italy or Yugoslavia heightened his anxiety, so, when foreign relations went badly, his instinct was to strike at domestic enemies. Summer 1928 had been an uneasy season: the last chance for rivals to stop him becoming king. In July, three men (two of them Bulgarian) received death sentences for plotting to plant bombs beneath a road along which he was to travel. In such cases, the gallows would be raised in Skanderbeg Square on market day to guarantee an audience. The crowd surged forward at the end to get slices of rope as good-luck charms.

Zog never complained about the threats. 'Such incidents are part of my job,' he would state. 'They are risks that every head of State must take.'[6] When going out was such an ordeal, however, it was much easier to stay at home. The palace complex contained a tennis court and gymnasium, although the King did not use them often. Old-fashioned Albanians could not conceive why westerners took violent exercise without compulsion. Sport was a feature of modern European society and a means to physical fitness, however, so Zog occasionally wielded his racquet. Those who extravagantly praised his game knew no standard for comparison. Another sport, fencing, played a larger part in his memories of Vienna than in his current regimen.

The routine of this prodigious chain-smoker was anything but healthy. 'He was a human chimney,' recalled one reporter: 'I have never seen a man smoke so rapidly and continuously.'[7] According to this source, Zog claimed that in the 1920s he was in the habit of smoking 250 cigarettes a day. This works out at about 15 per hour, stopping only for sleep. Perhaps other inveterate smokers can best judge whether consumption of tobacco at this rate is physically possible, but everyone agreed that he smoked long and hard even by Albanian standards. Journalists with an eye for picturesque detail sometimes detected a preference for exotically scented Turkish brands, but others say that he was not very fussy so long as he obtained his nicotine. His smoking must have related to nervous tension. He suffered from a hacking cough.

Zog professed to rise at six and retire at midnight. He was normally at work in his plain overheated study by eight o'clock, and timetables pinned up prominently in the aide-de-camp's office showed appointments spread over a fourteen-hour day. (As a Zogist poet phrased it: 'The rivers do not sleep, the seas do not sleep; Neither sleeps the King.'[8]) He did in fact observe the customary siesta, and, when possible, spent the next hour with his family. The Princesses lived a stone's throw away in a street named Rruga Carnarvon.

His meals came from the Queen Mother's palace in a sealed box, as he trusted only Sadije herself to cook them. Hence they were normal Albanian fare (resembling Greek and Turkish cuisine): lamb and rice, peppers, courgettes, and vegetable compotes, along with such local staples as whey, white cheese, heavy brown bread, and *byrek* (a kind of layered pastry with cheese or nuts). One of his favourite dishes was stuffed aubergines.

The King seldom catered for guests in any substantial way at the palace. A silver-plated dinner service had been purchased for official dinners, but, for most of the reign, these were held in the town hall or a hired room at the Tirana Club. The Albanian palace servants appeared idle and over-familiar to Europeans: an English butler engaged to train them took to drink and had to be sent home. Such a cloistered existence provided little scope for protocol. The royal lunch was latterly borne across the road by a waiter in dinner-jacket and gloves, flanked by soldiers.

When Zog wanted a break from work, he played with his pets, a Scottish terrier and a Hungarian sheepdog, and walked around his garden, which was partly sunken so he could not be seen from outside. The gravel paths and borders were unremarkable, but the tall cypress trees cast a pleasant shade, making the garden seem an island of calm, where the pigeons cooing on the roof sounded louder than the asses braying in Skanderbeg Square and muezzins calling the faithful. Next to the garden was a modest zoo, with wolves and bears, open to the public twice a week. The wild cat answered to the name of Mussolini, according to a photographer from the *Daily Sketch*, but the King favoured the birds of prey. 'Like eagles the world over,' he would say, 'the Albanian eagle is proud, defiant, courageous, and independent. Therefore we made it the symbol of our national liberty.' He added with a smile: 'My people bring them to me in such numbers as gifts that I now have enough to export some to America.'[9]

King Zog read a good deal, and here there was no clear line between work and leisure, as he could enjoy following the twists and turns of international relations for their own sake. Parcels of books and periodicals came regularly from Vienna. He retained his interest in military history, especially the Napoleonic era, and a small bust of Bonaparte adorned his desk beside a ceramic plaque of Skanderbeg. Often, after finishing work, he would play cards for money with a few of his adjutants and ministers. These men-only parties were an occasion for informal politicking. Zog learnt the latest gossip from his guests and started rumours on his own account. The Albanian court was devoid of courtiers of a purely social kind. It is easy to see why the King liked foreign visitors, especially if they were women.

Zog usually left the capital only once a year. In the height of summer, Tirana seemed peculiarly subject to thunder, so people of means preferred to escape its oppressive atmosphere and swarms of flies. The royal household journeyed in convoy to Durrës each June to spend three or four months near the sea. The Decauville railway, built beside the road by the Austrians during the war, had long since fallen into disrepair, but the 25-mile trip only took an hour-and-a-quarter by car.

Durrës had been the capital in the days of Prince Wilhelm and Essad Pasha, though there was not much to show for it except the burnt-out shell of the former palace and a small memorial to Colonel Thomson, a Dutch gendarmerie officer killed by rebels in 1914. The town looked a rough work-a-day place, at least to eyes untrained to recognise the vestiges of past glories. It was said to have changed hands thirty times since the year 1000. The port of Dyrrachium had once been a centre of Roman commerce; business had slumped in the later Ottoman centuries and never recovered. Sea-breezes stirred eddies of dust in the deserted streets while the afternoon sun gleamed on a couple of silvered oil containers. Most people nowadays wore shoddy western clothes, and earthquake damage from 1926 supplemented war damage from 1916. Old cottages (and sections of the Venetian city walls) had more recently been demolished to make way for one macadamed road, inevitably called Boulevard Zog. On bad days, the sirocco whipped up sand to scour the peeling façades of the mock-Venetian houses.

Zog hoped to develop Durrës as 'The Gateway to Albania'. It was one of the best anchorages in the Adriatic, according to the Albanian Government. Visiting seafarers were not so sure: 'There were no buoys to show us where to go, but the wrecks and masts of sunken ships told us where not to go.'[10] The Italians built a breakwater in 1927 and added facilities for the Bari ferry. With regular dredging, the harbour would have been admirable; without it, passengers had to come ashore by barge in rough weather. The population stuck at around nine thousand, and health was a worry till the malarial lagoon was reclaimed by planting pine trees.

It was here in Durrës, in anticipation of a more affluent future, that King Zog chose to erect his Summer Palace. Several eager-to-please municipalities had presented him with a house or land at the time of the proclamation of the monarchy. He usually placed these properties in the care of a government ministry to be used as barracks or a hospital. His holiday villa at Shiroka, for example, became a school for officers (and cynics said that this particular patriotic gesture was prompted by its dangerous proximity to the Yugoslav frontier). When a public subscription in Durrës raised funds for a royal mansion, however, he wheedled a further donation out of Mussolini and proceeded to build (with Italian contractors) a residence rather grander than his present home in Tirana. The aim was probably to tempt foreign statesmen to cross the Adriatic – eight hours by sea, thirty-five minutes by air – and spend a few days on the eastern shore.

Nobody disputed the scenic merits of the location. The palace was erected on a promontory hill above the port with an outstanding view over the town to the broad sandy beaches which stretched several miles to the south. Its architecture was more controversial: a flat-roofed multi-level structure, with a four-storey central tower and port-hole windows, painted terracotta pink. Isabel Anderson, shown over the palace while it was still under construction in 1929, learnt from her official guide that its multiple stairways had been devised so that Zog could find exercise without going out.

It was characteristic of the King to favour an international style, but one traveller in search of the real Albania complained that the first building he saw was 'like the casino in one of the minor Belgian sea-coast resorts'.[11] No one approaching Durrës by boat could possibly miss the palace. Its only Albanian features were kitchens separate from the main building and an equestrian statue of Skanderbeg above the entrance. The interior featured a Louis Quatorze reception room, an Empire dining room, and a Marie-Thérèse bedroom. The entrance hall was all black marble, polished like a mirror. The music-room ceiling was coffered in gold with the double-headed eagle motif, and, most famously of all, the bathroom boasted every modern convenience, set around a huge 'white marble bath, constructed on Roman lines (without exaggeration almost the size of a small room), with the water flowing from the parted lips of a bronze nereid'.[12]

The project was a failure in one sense only. As the steward on the Bari-Durrës ferry would explain, 'He built this palace for distinguished guests. But he never seems to have any.'[13] Foreign dignitaries stayed away, so it was shockingly under-used. On his annual arrival from Tirana, the King would spend a couple of days there, receiving local officials and beys. Then he usually became tired of dwelling in marble halls and left for his favourite home a few miles south of the town. 'Palaces do not appeal to me', Zog would say, when he welcomed foreign journalists to the double row of pastel-painted wooden bungalows built right on the beach, with the brilliant blue Adriatic before them and the scrubby mountains behind.[14] His own pink and green residence stood on stakes over the waterline, so sitting on the verandah was like being on the deck of a ship.

Here daily life was even quieter than in the capital. While sentries stood for hours in the sun, courtiers languished indoors under the blistering red tin roofs. The bolder of them might swim out to a raft moored a little way offshore. Albanians appreciated that beach holidays were modern and western but they were usually too self-conscious to sunbathe. Zog ventured into the water most days, however, followed by guards in a rowing boat. Troops camped amid the sand-dunes, and a getaway vessel remained on standby.

At the seaside, the King swapped his customary grey suit for white flannel trousers and a blue blazer with brass buttons. ('He looked like those Englishmen one sees on a summer's afternoon poling their punts at Henley.'[15]) Most of the time, he stayed in his study, a tidy office impersonally furnished with a couple of easy chairs, a coffee table, and desk. Views by local artists of mountains and peasants decorated walls tapestried in pale pink, grey, and white. Damp was a problem in the chalet on the shore, so lady visitors were asked not to wear heels that might pierce the floorboards. As fewer people came to see him away from the capital, Zog made regular use of his telephone. Albania was not linked to the international network, but lines between palaces, ministries, prefectures, and gendarmerie posts were reasonably reliable, as they used copper wire. (Three hundred-odd private subscribers had to make do with zinc and bad distortion).

In the late afternoon, when the air grew cooler, there was sometimes music from the Royal Band, or the King might bring out his gramophone with discs of light classics and dance band hits. Filmshows often followed in the cinema bungalow. His sisters and their children liked to watch Charlie Chaplin and Shirley Temple. Everyone went to bed early.

Contrary to common belief, lavish balls and banquets were not a conspicuous feature of the Zogist monarchy for the greater part of its existence, but there are other forms of extravagance besides merry-making and high-living – and luxury, like poverty, is relative. The 1928 constitution set the King's civil list at 500,000 gold francs per year (around £20,000), plus allowances for staff, clerical, and even travel expenses. The Queen Mother and Princesses received 120,000 in addition. Compare the budget of the foreign ministry for 1929–30 at 892,160 francs. Though far less than the sums paid to the Kings of Yugoslavia and Romania, the Albanian civil list seemed tremendous in a land where annual revenue barely exceeded £1 million and the treasury always ran a deficit. In the barren highlands, whole communities subsisted on maize bread and salt. GNP per capita was about £12.

Towards the top of the social scale, gradations in standards of living were skewed by the fact that an *alla Franka* lifestyle was absurdly expensive. As civil servants in Tirana knew all too well, there were hardly any home-produced substitutes for western manufactures imported at puffed-up prices. This did not deter the royal family from having nothing but the best. When Zog made any purchases himself, it was by overseas mail order. He was generous to a fault to his relations, and along with books and cigarettes, he liked to buy clothes of the finest quality.

As diplomats appreciated, his ostentatious expenditure was, at least in part, a conscious attempt to outstrip the wealthiest beys. He endeavoured to embarrass them with his munificence when it came to an exchange of gifts. Prestige was also one motive for his acquiring half-a-dozen limousines (mostly Mercedes-Benz). He did not drive himself, but mountain roads warranted big engines. To impress more traditional chieftains, the King displayed his collections of exquisite oriental rugs and antique weaponry, in whose design and history he took some interest.

On top of all this expense, it appears that King Zog paid two or three times the market value for almost everything which the royal household bought locally as a matter of routine. Each official expected to take his cut and reach mutually beneficial arrangements with his cronies in the retail trade. Conceivably, the King did not realise that his grocery bills were inflated; more likely, he knew perfectly well: the goodwill of Tirana's merchants was worth a premium.

CHAPTER TWENTY-ONE

Zog and the Zogists

The hardest working king in inter-war Europe may well have been the occupant of its least splendid throne. Though his title changed in 1928, the duties of the Albanian Head of State stayed nearly the same, without much resemblance to those of ceremonial monarchs in better established kingdoms. How often does it make sense to compare Zog to Wilhelmina of the Netherlands or Haakon of Norway? His name is as likely to be found near the bottom of a list that begins with Hitler and Stalin, and carries on via Mussolini and Franco, down to Horthy, Salazar and Metaxas.

Monarch or dictator? In south-east Europe, the distinction was somewhat blurred. Yugoslavian, Bulgarian, and Romanian kings all resorted to choosing ministers without regard to parliament. But Zog took that much for granted. 'Ahmed Zogu is a ruler whose initials are symbolical of his permeation of the affairs of his country,' remarked Sir Harry Luke, the Governor of Malta. 'It is literally the case that everything in Albania from A to Z comes under his notice and is vitalized by his energy'[1] (so the King could congratulate himself on that audience). His subjects also said that not a gendarme could be appointed nor a schoolteacher dismissed without His Majesty's knowledge – and it was almost true. Such direct personal rule smacked less of European kings or European dictators than of Middle Eastern rulers. King Zog disliked the comparison, but many foreigners who did business with him discerned beneath the 'western' exterior a basically 'oriental' mind. 'Ahmed Bey moves by devious ways,' advised a British diplomat; 'the straight line as a means of reaching an objective is unknown to him.'[2]

The King sat at his desk practically all day every day, yet he wrote as little as possible. This was a golden rule, which he urged his retinue also to follow. The transmutable subtleties of thought were of more use to him than the crude permanence of the written word. His work consisted of talking, usually one to one, to an endless queue of envoys and subordinates.

Zog had an excellent memory. It behoved his underlings to defer to it, regardless of their own recollections. In this way, doubts about the outcome of previous meetings were dispelled and disputes over the details of verbal agreements swiftly resolved. Anyone not immediately convinced of the King's version of events soon found himself abashed by a string of precise circumstantial details. His blue eyes radiated honesty. The senior staff of the Italian Legation judged Zog a brilliant liar, and, on this point, their Yugoslav counterparts agreed. Radoje Janković claimed to have calculated a dishonesty rate of 53 per cent.

Working for the King was never easy. His favourite weapon was uncertainty. Officials desired to say the right thing, but what *was* the right thing? Zog rarely voiced clear opinions and never cared to explain his reasons for a decision. In meetings, his demeanour was passive. He sought advice without giving any real indication as to whether he agreed with it. Concluding an interview with warm words and smiles, he might do entirely the opposite of what had been proposed.

Once he had made up his mind, he would explain the problem to the relevant minister and ask him to suggest various courses of action. Everything would meet with a critical response, while Zog steered imperceptibly towards his chosen option. Eventually, when his own ideas were put to him, he would reluctantly resign himself to the scheme – 'because I see you wish it'.[3] His skill consisted in the cleverness with which, instead of appearing as the instigator of a policy, he gave an impression of falling in with the desires of others.

Unable to rely on a loyal state apparatus – bureaucracy, army, or police – Zog could not afford to put his authority to the test by barking out commands. None but the clansmen of Mati were sure to obey him. Since they only came into their own in a crisis, so, in a sense, did he. In a few hectic days, he could divide his opponents by intimidation and appeasement until the immediate danger melted away. Everyone recognised his skill at drawing disgruntled chiefs back from the brink of rebellion at the eleventh hour. This was fundamental to the survival of his regime, but routine administration demanded more than a talent for manipulating Gheg elders.

The tiresome psychological games played out in his office were designed to secure flexibility and safeguard his prestige. If a decision turned out to be a good one, Zog took the credit. If not, a minister would be blamed for talking him into it. In difficult cases, it might be worth his while to allow a second minister to extract approval for an alternative policy. Nobody dared accuse him of inconsistency – and secrecy came easily to the King, who had a liking for mystification. It amused him to supply different people with different versions of innocuous events for no apparent reason.

What sort of men were willing to serve such an exasperating master? Avaricious ones, mostly. A foreign sympathiser explained:

> His followers are *not* 'deserting him in droves'. He has no followers worth mentioning. Those who might be called his followers are figureheads who do what they are told and get what they can in graft.

He has consistently tried to get followers, helpers among the best men in Albania, but they have all been Fan Noli's in one way or another.[4]

Zogist administration was once summed up as '*corruptio ad absurdum*'.[5] Though it can hardly have been more corrupt than the Ottoman bureaucracy in which most of its officials had commenced their careers, even the Turks accused Albanians of having a great love of money. Salaries were not as generous as they sounded, for *alla Franka* living was dear and job security poor. Peculation had become the established norm at every level. Anyone wishing to see a prefect, magistrate, or minister, had to slip some coins to his clerk, or the official would never be free. Bureaucrats purloined a percentage of all cash that passed through their hands. Friends and families expected favours. A coffee house quip of the 1930s: 'True, there are no brigands in Albania; all of them have gone to Tirana, where they rob with authority from behind desks.'[6]

The King pretended to demand higher standards; in reality, he concentrated on dividing the spoils. It is no exaggeration to say that Zog created and sustained the Albanian state by bribing local leaders to submit. He went on imbursing them for 'military reserves' and awarded scholarships to their sons, who would then be taken into government employ:

> First you make the fullest enquiries about a man's abilities and loyalty. You have him spied upon, to see that he is not too friendly with, let us say, the Yugoslav or the Italian Legation. Then you give him a good job and treat him with apparent confidence. After a bit you sack him, to ensure that he shall realise his complete dependence on the throne. Presently, you relent and put him back in office, always, however, making sure that you know what he is doing, and that some rival of his shall have every opportunity of catching him out if he leaves the beaten track.[7]

Loyalty (so-called) counted for more than competence. Even the cabinet was run on the same basis. Ministries came and went with some frequency – the longest lasted only two years and ten months – but a change of Government was really little more than a reshuffle, designed to intensify the contest for royal favour and shift around patterns of patronage. While every ministerial career had its ups and downs, the same old names reappeared as if in rotation. Cabinet-making was mainly a matter of balancing sectional interests: Gheg and Tosk, landowner and merchant, Christian and Muslim. Zog promoted a disproportionate number of Christians to compensate for the fact that he was a Muslim.

The political opinions of a minister rarely signified much; the cabinet made few collective decisions and sometimes did not meet for months. Nevertheless, the office of Prime Minister (or President of the Council) was revived under the monarchy. The principal incumbents were Pandeli Evangjeli and Kostaq Kotta.

Evangjeli was an Orthodox Christian from Korça who had been a wine merchant in Bucharest before the Balkan Wars. Although his spell as premier in 1921 had ended in humiliation, the very fact that he was not a powerful figure qualified him for a post under Zog. There had always to be a place for a middle-class Tosk, and Evangjeli was a polite old gentleman. Neither as President of the Parliament nor as Prime Minister for five years from 1930 did he need to show initiative. Tact was his strong suit, combined with sufficient vagueness to leave no doubt that power lay elsewhere. By 1935, his admitted age had been seventy-three for some years.

Evangjeli alternated with Kostaq Kotta, another Orthodox townsman from Korça, who was Prime Minister 1928–30 and 1936–9. A token Tosk in the 'Triumph of Legality', previously employed in the Education Ministry, he did as he was bidden 'without too searching an enquiry into methods or objects',[8] while his own handling of everyday matters won him a reputation for nepotism and vindictiveness. Kotta struck people as a small man on the make: small, that is, in the social sense. His plump face and solid build suggested good living.

Both Evangjeli and Kotta were superficially presentable. The Zogist politician who really caught the imagination of foreigners was Ilias Bey Vrioni, the stout former premier with a toothbrush moustache who posed as a *boulevardier*. Garrulous even when sober, Vrioni was in the habit of emitting a bizarre laugh at unsuitable moments. When drunk, he raved and fired bullets in the air. Well-intentioned he might have been, but who could have taken him seriously as Foreign Minister between 1927 and 1929? Though ministers tried to be formal to the point of stuffiness in public – with top-hat, frock coat, and a gendarme following fifteen paces behind – several of them only attracted notice on account of their weakness for alcohol, gambling, or loose women, while more temperate ones were often obscure bureaucrats. To idealists, the personnel of the regime constituted an affront to national pride.

King Zog summed up his ministers thus: 'If intelligent and energetic, they are rogues; if honest, they are incompetent or idle.' He chose subordinates too elderly, inept, or unpopular to rival their master. How often did he have to spell it out to foreigners? 'Don't bother to talk to my ministers . . . If you want anything, come and see me.' They only ceased to be nonentities when he needed to refuse a request. Then he would insist on his own willingness to accede and regret the obstinacy of a cabinet united in opposition. 'What can I do? They are all the same!'[9]

Ordinary Albanians were also often heard to express dismay that their King was so 'unlucky' in his appointments.

Sheer jealousy motivated his perverse choice, according to Faik Bey Konitza, Albanian Minister to the United States:

> Having watched him since he was eighteen, I never caught him telling a truth. He has never kept his pledged word. . . . He is greedy, selfish, callous, and dishonest. He hates all those who have something – be it culture, birth, wealth, a capacity in any field, or simply a rugged and honest patriotism.[10]

The diplomat detected elements of Zog in Shakespeare's King John and Dogberry and Marlowe's Young Mortimer and the Jew of Malta.

Konitza was himself an example of Zogist man-management. A graduate of Dijon and Harvard universities, who spent most of his life abroad, he was the most cultivated Albanian of his day. That he had not entirely abandoned the habits of a bey was yet evident from his attitudes to money and politics. Konitza aligned himself with Essad before the World War and Noli after it. He befriended Zogolli in Vienna, only to become one of his sharpest critics in the early 1920s as editor of the Albanian-American paper *Dielli*. Then he dropped Noli after 1924 and accepted the Washington job, without bothering to conceal his contempt for the monarchy. The King did not dismiss Konitza, however; it seemed wiser to carry on paying him to stay 5,000 miles away.

Zog had no real friends as distinct from henchmen. Indeed, Ekrem Vlora submitted, 'With his character, a genuine friendship was scarcely possible.'[11] His closer associates, habitués of the compound, were generally dubbed 'the Old Gang', the qualification for membership being an unbroken record of Zogism dating back to 1924. Veterans of 'The Triumph of Legality' wore the Order of My Friends; rumour had it that they could get away with anything.

There was usually some overlap between the Old Gang and the cabinet – Kotta for example – but it was inclusion in the former group which conferred the greater influence. Access to the King being everything, many a minister counted less than an aide-de-camp. The senior adjutant was Colonel Zef Sereqi, notable for his caddish good looks. A product of the Shkodra Jesuit school, Sereqi owed his eminence to the fact that there were very few Roman Catholics in the inner circle, yet the King needed links to this confessional group. After service in the Austrian army, in the early 1920s Sereqi distinguished himself fighting the Serbs as a lieutenant of Bajram Curri. It is unclear what made him switch to Zogu. Nor is it obvious why the King trusted him with so many confidential missions, apart from his fluency in languages (German, Italian, and

Serbo-Croat). His ingratiating style did not suit every taste. No more popular was Ekrem Bey Libohova, the richest Tosk landowner in the Old Gang. Once an officer in the Sultan's palace guard, then equerry to Prince Wilhelm, he now served as an officious Minister of the Court.

The notorious members of the cabal, though, were two less ceremonious personages: Musa Juka and Krosi.

Musa Juka was probably the most feared man in the country. People preferred not to mention him by name: he was just 'MJ' or 'the man from Shkodra'. His crushing of the Dukagjini revolt had made him a national figure, and he sealed his evil reputation by running the regime's largest network of informers as Minister of the Interior from 1930 to 1939 with an interval of only thirteen months: a record incumbency. A big slow-moving middle-aged man, with bushy eyebrows, thick moustache, and a saturnine expression, Juka was unusual among the Zogist élite in observing the outward forms of his Muslim faith with solemnity. The best that could be said of him was this: where MJ took charge, things got done. His earlier career as mayor of Shkodra had ended with locals burning his house down and driving him into exile in 1924. By aiding the 'Triumph of Legality', he earned promotion to prefect and went on to demonstrate his usefulness. MJ made a fortune from blackmail.

If anyone was more hated, it can only have been Abdurrahman Mati, usually known as 'Krosi' (meaning bald or scabby head). He stood closer to Zog than anyone else, often literally, and his presence at court was as conspicuous as his formal function was obscure. He spoke only Albanian and interpreters gave up on his homespun parables and long-winded anecdotes. All the same, few diplomats could ever forget the sight of him dancing attendance on the King at levées: 'A prehistoric monster whose age cannot be estimated.'[12] Krosi had a white moustache, thick lips, and a lantern jaw. 'His morning coat was well cut but it fitted badly, and the line of its swallow-tail was spoilt by at least two ill-concealed bulky pistols in the back pockets.'[13] Nothing was too bad to be believed of this podgy old illiterate, whose name was a byword for fraud and favouritism: he forced butchers to buy anthrax-infested sheep, he sold bad fish, he had his commercial competitors thrown into prison. Few businessmen in Tirana could make much money and keep it without paying him a commission.

His only official role was as parliamentary deputy for Mati, the King's native valley, whose inhabitants grew rich on pensions and sinecures – and none richer than Krosi himself. His value lay in his ability to parley with the clan elders of Mati, Kruja, and Dibra. For centuries, his ancestors had been bailiffs at Burgajet and attendants to the chief, so it is hardly surprising that Zog should have chosen him to carry messages and taste his food. More remarkable is the way in which Krosi became the hub of the court camarilla. If deputies did not know how the King desired them to vote, they took their lead from Krosi. The man somehow retained royal favour, even while his abuses were bringing the monarchy into disrepute. Zog allegedly described him as 'a first-class robber, but lacking the courage to be a murderer'.[14]

Some Albanians proffered the explanation that Abdurrahman was the King's natural father, but there is no reason to believe them, least of all physical resemblance. If Zog kept Krosi at his right hand, it was probably because he had always been there, he had definite uses, and his loyalty was such that even the Italian secret service had despaired of him. Although diplomats sometimes referred to him as 'the Albanian Rasputin', Krosi was not really the power behind the throne. Being 'a tiresome old ruffian with an insatiable appetite for land and money',[15] his main interests were patronage and contracts. Petitioners queued at his door to obtain little slips of paper bearing his mark: 'Do as so-and-so tells you. He is my friend.'[16] Krosi did not decide policy.

The same holds true of the Old Gang as a whole. They could make or break a career, a business, or even a life – Krosi and MJ oversaw the murderous side of the dictatorship – but coffee-house whispers that the King was their puppet were essentially ill-founded. Krosi, Kotta, MJ, and the rest had irrevocably linked their fates to his, and the loathing in which they were widely held was a kind of guarantee. How long could any one of them expect to stay alive if ever he lost royal protection?

Thus Zog maintained a formal pyramid of placemen to give an impression of modern administration, while the Old Gang did the dirty work of authoritarian rule. Neither group undermined Joseph Roucek's judgement: 'Albania was a one-man country – and Zog was the man.'[17]

CHAPTER TWENTY-TWO

The Inspectors-General

Even a ruler as diligent as King Zog in a country as small as Albania could never have supervised every government activity in person, and obviously not without leaving the royal compound. Yet it was part of his pose to appear prodigiously well-informed on everything from the availability of schoolbooks in Shkodra to the fish-stocks of Lake Ochrid. To some extent, his omniscience could be bluff, but he clearly needed agents to act as his eyes and ears. He also found it convenient to assign urgent errands straight to individuals. The Old Gang fulfilled many functions; a visit from Sereqi or Juka was quite enough to put the fear of Zog into the staff of an out-of-the-way sub-prefecture. Special sensitivity nevertheless attached to dealings with the security forces, and here the King employed more definitely disinterested intermediaries. Among the regular attenders in his smoke-filled room were four foreign military men, two originally from Austria–Hungary and two from Britain: Myrdacz, Ghilardi, Stirling, and Percy. They were the Inspectors-General (except Myrdacz who was Chief of Staff). Taking instructions directly from Zog and answerable only to him, they effectively wielded the power of viceroys when they had his full support. But neither they nor anyone else could be sure that this would be so on any given occasion. A confusing system of dual control was the (doubtless intended) result.

Myrdacz and Stirling were survivors from the batch of seven foreign advisers recruited in 1923. They seemed to offer the attractive combination of administrative competence and political impotence. This was too straightforward to last. As soon as Italy secured its virtual protectorate, the Inspectors-General acquired a symbolic significance out of all proportion to their actual influence, for the Italian Legation disliked the continued presence of outsiders near the heart of the regime. Why, asked Sola, did Albania need them now that Italy supplied advisers? The honest answer could never be given: Italian experts were more or less spies who would sooner obey Mussolini than Zog. From having been dispensable, the Inspectors-General became entrenched, since, if ever one left, it would be hard to avoid replacing him with an Italian. The King therefore kept them on – partly because he valued their advice, partly because he could use the issue of their dismissal as an extra bargaining chip in negotiations with Italy.

Thus the Italian military mission which arrived in 1928 did not officially supplant the existing army staff. General Alberto Pariani was called the Head of His Majesty's Military Household, while General von Myrdacz remained Chief of Staff. The functions of the Military Household duplicated those of the General Staff. The one was dominated by Italians, the other was not. Since the Italians held the purse-strings, however, the King preferred to let Pariani prevail when serious differences arose. Myrdacz was reduced to a cipher after the Treaty of Tirana: 'when we were taken without being beaten', as he himself put it.[1]

A military engineer by training, Gustav von Myrdacz had held the rank of brigadier-general in the Austro-Hungarian army at the end of the World War. Having briefly served in Albania, he struck up a friendship with Colonel Zogolli in Vienna, his native city, and this led to the offer of employment five years later. He was a quiet bespectacled man, who resembled more an academic than a soldier. From the first, he recommended that Albania needed only a very small standing army, but, once Zogu became entangled with Italy, this policy had to change. Myrdacz was intelligent enough to understand perfectly how he came to lose such influence as he ever possessed. As his savings would not go far in Austria, he stayed on the army payroll, while devoting much of his time to music and gardening. The efforts of General Pariani to convert the Albanian army into a modern fighting force evoked his wry amusement. Chief among his own problems was an acerbic wife, unhappy at the prospect of living out her days in Tirana.

The Inspector-General of the Army seemed the antithesis of the Chief of Staff. Leon Ghilardi was a big black-bearded Croat, by turns taciturn and voluble, whose conceited manner suggested to many an operatic *buffo*. Others, more taken with his physical strength, compared him to a circus performer. This was the same Ghilardi who had rivalled Zogolli for command of the guerrillas recruited by Austria–Hungary in 1916. He had once been a hussar in the Austro-Hungarian regular army, before an affair with the wife of a brother-officer compelled him to depart in haste. He had surfaced in Albania in 1913 and become the first foreigner to take its citizenship, finding work as a mercenary.

Ghilardi was with Zogolli when he raised the flag at Durrës in February 1916. This alerted the Austrian military authorities, who used threats of a court-martial to persuade him to sever his latest attachment to the Bulgarians and instead recruit Albanians to fight for the Habsburg Empire. Despite their jealousies at the time, King Zog evidently bore no lasting grudge against Ghilardi, whom General von Trollmann had rated by far the abler of the two. In 1918, rather than join the White Russians, the Croat opted to become a captain in the new Albanian army. Though Zogu found him useful in the defence of Shkodra, his zeal for fighting the Serbs caused another estrangement for a couple of years.

Ghilardi dramatically returned to favour in the autumn of 1924 when he swam the River Drin to join the Zogist forces on the far side of the frontier. His part in the invasion earned him Old Gang status and rapid promotion: major and aide-de-camp in 1925, colonel and inspector-general in 1926, general in 1928. He lived in the royal compound. The advent of the Italians did not affect Ghilardi so much as Myrdacz, for the Croat was more of a general factotum. Despite Italian ancestry – his full name was Ghilardi della Ghianda – he was used by the King as a personal envoy.

Ghilardi, Myrdacz, and Pariani were all nominal advisers of the native army commander, Xhemal Aranitasi, an archetypal Zogist placeman, whose utter inconsequence made him a fixture from 1925. His prime qualification was lack of ambition, though Zog enjoyed the dunder-headed rudeness with which he riled the Italians.

Having opened up his army to Italian instructors, Zog strove to exclude them from the gendarmerie by retaining his little team of British officers at all costs. The gendarmerie, as an internal security force, always meant far more to him than the army. After 1926, moreover, it came to symbolise national independence as the most important institution in which Italians played no part. The British Government repeatedly denied any connection with British nationals in Albanian service, but it could not prevent the King making sly insinuations to the contrary. To sustain the illusion that Britain cared about his country and would oppose an Italian takeover, he wanted people to surmise that his British staff were agents of imperialism, like British personnel in Egypt or Iraq.

It was easy to arouse this suspicion. The first Inspector-General of the Gendarmerie came with exactly the right pedigree. Lieutenant-Colonel Walter Francis Stirling – Frank to some, but Michael to his intimates – had fought with T.E. Lawrence in the Arab Revolt, advised Emir Feisal, and governed Sinai and Jaffa before taking a position in Tirana. His motto was 'Safety Last'.

He was certainly intrepid and energetic, but his stock had fallen low with Zog by the time of the monarchy. For one thing, Stirling had failed to foster any closer links with the British Government. Even before summer 1926, his personal relations with the British Legation had gone from poor to downright poisonous.* He quarrelled with the gendarmerie instructors too, whom he had recruited in haste and then found incompetent. Worse: he seemed to get on excellently with Baron Aloisi.

---

* Stirling told influential friends in London that Eyres displayed the mentality of a Turk and that Parr drank to excess. Eyres countered that Stirling had entirely gone to seed, worn out by the demands of his young wife.

The thought occurred to President Zogu that Stirling might even be an Italian spy. He need not have worried. When Stirling tried to be civil, he only made the Italian secret service more suspicious. His tolerance of Aloisi and Sola probably reflected his basically imperialist outlook. If Britain sadly declined to take Albania in hand, he saw no objection in principle to Italy having a go. In 1926, Zogu removed Stirling from the gendarmerie by ostensibly promoting him to the new post of Inspector-General of Civil Administration. Possibly he was too much of a political intriguer on his own account to be the perfect aide. He gave out that he was the King's supreme adviser and said that Zog should be more autocratic.

The Stirlings were prominent figures in Tirana. Frank was smart with grizzled hair and he wore his Hashemite decoration at court. Marygold, his wife, was younger and uncommonly tall. The King encouraged her to accompany her husband to remote regions, so that the highlanders might see an emancipated woman. It was her daring as an equestrienne which usually impressed them.

Officially-speaking, it was never quite clear what Colonel Stirling was supposed to be looking for when he inspected civil administration. Investigation was primarily a threat to be held over civil servants whose loyalty was questionable. The colonel overstepped the mark therefore in 1929 when he amassed evidence to show that Musa Juka had been siphoning large sums out of the Ministry of Agriculture. The King was always interested to hear about corruption, but he preferred to hold the information back for purposes of political blackmail rather than proceed with a prosecution. This was especially the case with MJ, who knew too much to be touched unless he committed crimes far more serious than the misappropriation of public funds. Zog called a halt to the investigation and issued a statement saying that an enquiry had found his conduct to be irreproachable.

Stirling now had the Old Gang gunning for him as well as the Italian Legation. In 1930, a parliamentary vote halved his salary without warning. The King simulated regret. Next, Stirling learnt that the Inspectorate-General of Civil Administration was due for abolition. After a painful altercation, Zog found him a year-long sinecure in the Ministry of the Interior, after which he returned to London and became an assistant porter at Marks & Spencer. When Stirling wrote his memoirs twenty years later, however – with his self-esteem restored by intelligence work in the Second World War – he recalled his departure from Tirana as voluntary and did not stint his praise: 'Of all the statesmen of the Middle East – and I have met most of them – I consider Zog to be by far the most brilliant, the most cultured, and the most far-seeing.'[2]

Having felt obliged to throw one British adviser overboard, the King clung more tenaciously to the other. Major-General Sir Jocelyn Percy, the last Inspector-General, played an active part in sustaining the regime until its final year. He was, said Zog, 'a far better man than Colonel Stirling'.[3]

The King had Sir Harry Eyres to thank for finding this much-decorated soldier and persuading him to take over responsibility for the Royal Albanian Gendarmerie. Aged fifty-five on accepting his appointment, Percy had a commanding presence: stern-visaged, straight-backed, over six feet tall, with a sober grey moustache and an unflappable temperament. A veteran of the Hindu Kush, the Boer War, and the Somme, he had served as Chief of Staff of the Fifth Army in 1917–18 and headed a military mission to Southern Russia. His civilian careers – as an apple-farmer in Canada and a central heating salesman – had not prospered, however, which explained his arrival in Tirana.

Stirling had not progressed far in the Sisyphean task of instilling discipline into a force of heavily-armed policemen so seldom paid that many of them lived by crime. Relays of British instructors came out, found conditions unbearable, and went home out of pocket. Percy was very nearly one of them. The King only just talked him out of resigning after six months. Theirs was a relationship based on mutual respect, but it called for maximum forbearance on the General's part. Year after year, Zog eagerly endorsed reform of the gendarmerie, and then obstructed it at every turn, or so it seemed. Their weekly meetings became a ritual of protest and mollification.

In the late 1920s, Zog diverted funds from the gendarmerie to the army as a gesture of appeasement whenever he annoyed the Italians. Even more damagingly, he kept promoting and dismissing officers without any regard to merit. General Percy discovered in 1928 that four regional gendarmerie commanders (appointed for political services in 1924–5) were routinely corrupt. Those in charge of frontier posts were smuggling. Others quartered their men in remote villages to quell imaginary unrest, ordered them to live off the land, and pocketed the field allowances. When confronted, Fiqri Dine and Hysni Dema insisted that they acted with the full knowledge of the King and paid him 75 per cent of all monies thus obtained. Zog refused to dismiss the four young men but sent them to Italy for training. Less than a year later, one of the four, Muharrem Bajraktari, returned as Commandant-General of the entire force.

Percy's resignation threats became a devalued commodity, as he failed to overturn this appointment until 1931, when the King selected Bajraktari (now chieftain of Luma, a strategic frontier district) to be his aide-de-camp. The essential problem remained. King Zog employed a British Inspector-General to extend the rule of law and an Albanian Commandant-General to carry out nefarious political acts. The gendarmerie improved by the slow progress of two steps forward, one step back.

Thanks to Sir Jocelyn Percy, wrote Seeds, British prestige in the highlands stood at 'a truly Kiplingesque height'.[4] He did keep in touch with the two or three British diplomats in Albania and sometimes told them of his conversations with the King. This did not worry Zog: Albania needed British spies to offset dozens, if not hundreds, of Italian ones. The number of British officers serving under Percy never exceeded a dozen, of whom only two, Edmund de Renzy Martin and Dayrell Oakley-Hill, stayed very long. The latter found time to help run the Society for the Protection of Animals and the football league. Other British residents were the writer Joseph Swire (until expelled for reporting corruption), the philologist Stuart Mann, the anthropologist Margaret Hasluck, and the nurse Ruth Pennington (of Lady Carnarvon's relief fund). Contrary to some press stories, Zog did not keep a Cockney minder called 'Battler Smith'. Expatriates from France, Germany, and the United States (except Albanian-Americans) were even fewer. Italians numbered over two thousand.

The King liked his Inspectors-General. Myrdacz and Ghilardi were probably the nearest he had to friends, and, with Stirling and Percy too, he could drop his façade of infallibility. All the same, nobody presumed too far. Zog always kept his distance from subordinates in order to play one against another: Ghilardi against Myrdacz, Myrdacz against Pariani, Pariani against Percy, Percy against Stirling, Stirling against Juka, Juka against Krosi.

He tried to offset groups and interests in just the same fashion: Old Gang against cabinet, prefects against chieftains, Ghegs against Tosks, landowners against tradesmen, army against gendarmerie, Muslims against Christians, Roman Catholics against Orthodox, and clan against clan. Excepting the Mati, no class or sector of Albanian society ever gave the King its whole-hearted backing. Communist historians argued that the monarchy relied on rich reactionary beys. That was a plausible half-truth. To stay in power, Zog relied on the beys to tolerate his rule so long as he did not attack their economic privileges. But he could never rely on their active support. Many of them hated him. Unable and frankly unwilling to have much faith in any group of his people, Zog strove to keep all classes in unstable equilibrium. Through hours of hideously convoluted talk, he obsessively manipulated his assorted underlings (nearly all older than himself) in an effort to exercise personal control from seclusion.

One summer evening, Pietro Quaroni, First Secretary of the Italian Legation, sat down to take a cup of tea with the King on the verandah of his bungalow at Durrës. Zog, who seemed unusually relaxed, was lamenting that he never had enough time for reading and study. Quaroni plucked up the courage to ask what many other people had naively wondered: 'Your Majesty, what is the point of being a king? You work like a convict from dawn till dusk, you never take a day off. Why don't you select a President of the Council to deal with day-to-day administrative affairs? A young man like you must surely want a little pleasure out of life?'

Zog looked thoughtfully into the distance. After a moment, he answered slowly, 'Yes, perhaps you're right. But you don't know what it is to have power. To command men.'[5]

CHAPTER TWENTY-THREE

Royal Family

King Zog had a saying: 'Family harmony is one of the most important things in human life.'[1] Politically, he may well have been the loneliest ruler in Europe, but he never lacked devoted companions: his mother and sisters. To sit with an indulgent expression amid the small-talk of half a dozen doting women was his favourite relaxation.

Nobody meant more to Zog than the Queen Mother. He trusted her completely, desired her approval, and respected her judgement. They met every morning at breakfast time to discuss the business of the day. Sadije alone could – and did – address Zog candidly and critically on any topic. She was vivacious, intelligent, and instinctively authoritarian. If ever he really annoyed her, she would refuse to speak to him until he apologised. Here then, if anywhere, was a power behind the throne, but it was impossible for outsiders to deduce her opinions. Imbued with traditional moral values, this blunt-featured cigar-smoking Muslim matriarch guarded her privacy. Zogist hagiography presented the Queen Mother as 'the apotheosis of the historical-heroic woman',[2] yet the people of Tirana saw only a dumpy, unapproachable figure in a heavy fur coat, with a dour expression and greying hair tied in a tight bun. The warmth of her personality and sharpness of her wits showed themselves exclusively at home.

An audience with the Queen Mother was a privilege reserved for very honoured guests. Thus even the Italians did not form a proper estimate of her before their Foreign Minister Dino Grandi paid a three-day visit in April 1929. When she made a speech of welcome, they initially assumed that she had learnt it by heart; Grandi talked to her and discovered her political nous. It came as a surprise. At parties, Sadije effaced herself so thoroughly that most observers agreed with Edward Hadwen, a British Vice-Consul, who described her as 'a simple old country body, wrapt up in her son and his welfare, who seems oddly out of place in her present surroundings in Tirana. Her daughters do her less credit than her son', he continued, 'for it is difficult to imagine a more uninteresting posy of young ladies.'[3]

Again, he was not the only one to think so, yet, in justice to King Zog's six sisters, it should be noted that the people who disparaged the Princesses did not really know them. Nor did anyone else, except their family and servants. It would be hard to think of adult royal personages in twentieth-century Europe who, without being invalids, lived less in the public eye. The norms of Albanian society saw to that: no respectable man would speak of his womenfolk to strangers. Women were not even mentioned by name; they were so-and-so's mother, wife, or daughter.

Even though Zog repeatedly expressed himself in favour of 'cultural freedom for women and their equality before the law', he was not ready to outrage public decency.[4] More importantly, the women of his own household felt the force of conventional inhibition within themselves. The six Princesses – Adile, Nafije, Senije, Myzejen, Ruhije, and Maxhide – accepted that they should be known to the world as King Zog's sisters. Those who met them seldom elicited anything beyond the most predictable small talk. Newspapermen could not tell them apart. In public perception, the half-dozen royal highnesses comprised a single entity.

According to Antoinette de Szinyei-Merse, a latterday lady-in-waiting, the Princesses were 'gracious and amiable ladies of such simplicity and modesty as can rarely be found among western women'; their life-style was almost puritanical.[5] Nevertheless, the portrayal which has gained wider recognition is exemplified by the post-war poet, Dritëro Agolli:

> In their palace Zogu's sisters, in company with
> young dandies,
> Sweeten'd and soothed their mugs, with Parisian
> creams and candies.
> Princess Senije wandered abroad, as well as
> Princess Myzejen,
> They felt homesick for Paris, for Wall Street
> and for Wien . . .[6]

In a series of memorable photographs, they appear as vampish brunettes sheathed in satin or lamé and decked with diamonds, their faces heavily made-up and their bobbed hair crimped and lacquered. Even before 1928, they were said to be 'living like princesses' in Vienna, with Zog indulging their every whim.[7] He did allot them official duties. 'I am in charge of leading the modern artistic movement in Albania', said Ruhije; 'Myzejen is the pioneer of women's sports, and Maxhide is in charge of tourism'.[8] The work was purely nominal. Though Senije might head the Association of Albanian Women, an emancipation movement, it looked as if their interest in the modern western woman stopped short at her dresses and jewellery. Apart from very occasional appearances at parades, they passed their time smoking, drinking black coffee, flicking through imported fashion magazines, and watching three films a day in their private cinema. They went abroad for a few months each year on extravagant holidays.

This picture is a caricature, based on elements of truth. Some of the Princesses were indeed regular visitors to Nice and Monte Carlo, where they succumbed to the lure of the casino. The smart set nicknamed them 'the Zoglets'; their popularity was not great. The Princesses once found themselves in a hotel lift with young Otto von Habsburg. The exiled heir to the Austro-Hungarian thrones wished them good morning, and they cut him. 'Why didn't you accept the Archduke's greeting?' asked their attendant. 'He has fallen,' they replied.[9] The tale is probably apocryphal, but it gives some idea of the impression they made on outsiders who failed to realise that their apparent hauteur was very largely shyness. 'Once they were barefooted girls, busy in their snow-topped mountains making goats' cheese,' explained an American journalist with poetic licence. 'Now alas they are princesses, and weird and wonderful is their idea of how princesses in the Great World dress and comport themselves.'[10]

In the 1920s, the status and prospects of the six women had been radically transformed, although not all were affected to the same degree. The Princesses were distinct individuals; even their physical similarity was not really so pronounced. Some had sharp profiles inherited from their father. Others, notably Maxhide, shared the rounder face of Sadije. Ruhije had protruding teeth. Myzejen looked fragile and oriental. Senije most resembled Zog, albeit with fuller cheeks. Above all, the two elder Princesses need to be distinguished from the four younger ones. This was because Adile and Nafije married before their brother became leader of the nation.

Princess Adile did not fit the caricature at all. Seen from a distance, the unglamorous lady in the plain hat and coat looked a generation older than the others. Her one experiment with make-up was a family joke: she had put lipstick on her eyebrows. This Princess was more often to be seen baking and bottling fruit than lounging on a chaise-longue. Since her sisters knew nothing about domestic duties, Adile oversaw the management of their household. Her other concern was her children: three sons and two daughters. Albanians called them princes and princesses out of courtesy. All went abroad for education, yet, given a fifteen-year gap between eldest and youngest, they were never all away at once. Salih and Hysein attended the French military academy of St Cyr. Politics dictated that Sherafedin (known as Dine) completed his schooling in Italy. Teri and Danush, who were younger than their brothers, went to a boarding school in England in 1934. Before that, they lived with their mother, grandmother, and aunts.

What about their father? The question was often asked. Adile had been given in marriage to Emin Agolli Doshishti of Dibra back in 1909. The Doshishti were a leading family which owned sizeable properties near

Lake Ochrid. The couple must have stayed together until 1925, but they had separated before the proclamation of the monarchy. The reasons for this are unclear (divorce being a taboo subject for Albanians), but politics may have been a contributory factor. The marriage had started as a strategic alliance between influential families. Once it ceased to be advantageous in this respect, there was less incentive for the couple to put up with each other. Emin Bey 'lived alone, and did not appear in public, being somewhat inclined to alcohol'.[11] His children long thought that he died in 1938. After the fall of communism, it transpired that Doshishti had lived on in Dibra until 1988.

Princess Adile herself was rarely around in the early days of the monarchy. She and Danush developed tuberculosis and spent several years at a sanatorium in Switzerland, during which time Sadije brought up Teri. All the children loved their grandmother and uncle, who effectively took the place of their father. As an endearment, Zog sometimes called them his sons and daughters. He never ceased to feel responsible for them. Adile recovered and lived with her brother or children for the rest of her life.

The fate of Princess Nafije was far more tragic. She was the widow of Ceno Bey Kryeziu, the pro-Yugoslav politician shot dead in Prague in 1927. That marital alliance, celebrated in 1922 but arranged well in advance, had certainly paid political dividends in its time, when Zogu needed contacts in Belgrade. Then it came to be viewed as an obstacle to close relations with Italy. Then Kryeziu was assassinated. Nafije never got over the trauma. The fact that she returned to Tirana and took up residence with her mother and sisters in close proximity to her brother is seen by some as proof that she did not suspect him of complicity in the killing. How could she possibly have faced him day after day for the next twenty-seven years if she entertained any doubts as to his innocence? Against this, however, must be set the severity of her psychological reaction to the crime. It is sadly all too easy to identify Nafije in the few photographs of the Princesses in which she features: she is the one with the down-turned mouth and the hunted look. The rarity of her public appearances, along with her demeanour when she did appear, gave rise to speculation that she was mentally disturbed. She was manifestly chronically depressed: idle, uncommunicative, and incapable of taking much interest in anything. Although her sisters tried to engage her in family life, she never really escaped her private misery.

The upbringing of her son fell to Sadije in the first place. Tati (sometimes called Essad) was three years old when his father died. Reared in the bosom of the Zogu family, surrounded by aunts and cousins, the fair-haired little boy attracted greater public interest than the Doshishti children. For a start, it seemed that King Zog was grooming him as a successor. The two posed together in uniform for official photographs. Tati was a general from the age of four and he bore the popular (if provocative) title Prince of Kosovo, which many took to be the equivalent of Crown Prince. Newspapers described Tati as a guiding star for Albanian youth.

More interesting to the gossips, however, was the fact that Tati was a Kryeziu. He had no contact whatever with his father's family, for obvious reasons. The Kryeziu clan remained convinced that Zog had arranged the murder of Ceno Bey, whose brothers were living in Yugoslavia and plotting retribution. They would try and reach the Prince when he grew up to tell him of his duty to kill the King. This sensational prospect excited much discussion – in private in lowered voices. According to hearsay, Zog took special care that Tati never had access to firearms while inundating the boy with expensive gifts. From the age of ten, he was driving a little red sportscar up and down Boulevard Zog.

In truth, Tati adored his uncle Zog and knew nothing at all about the murder allegations. The King no doubt hoped to preserve his ignorance, but the motorcar held no particular significance: Teri received one around the same time. Sadije apparently thought that youngsters should learn to drive at the same age as earlier generations had learnt to ride.

The four younger sisters of the King also took up motoring. An Italian farmer named Liberti made money by leaving his tractor on a sharp bend on the Tirana–Durrës road and accepting a reward each time he hauled their car out of the neighbouring ditch. This was almost as close as the Princesses ever came to people outside the royal circle in Albania. Senije, Ruhije, Myzejen, and Maxhide led a very sheltered existence. They were grown-up women who had never left home.

The Queen Mother and the Princesses dwelt in interconnected palaces opposite the royal compound and next to the old Ministry of the Interior. The palaces, which were pre-existing villas with vaguely Turkish or Moorish facades, looked out upon the municipal rose garden. Adile, Nafije, and Senije each had a self-contained flatlet, but all seven royal ladies lived together in practice, along with the younger children not at school. No one questioned the right of Sadije to rule the roost. As visitors were few, the family preferred to gather in the ordinary sitting-room upstairs rather than use the grand drawing-room and dining-room, where the children sometimes went during siesta hour to play amid the silk draperies and porcelain cabinets. There were plenty of servants but no courtiers: a pair of ladies-in-waiting materialised only when the Princesses went to public events. The sentries outside alone distinguished the palaces from a grandiose family home.

The Princesses did not make or receive social calls. Tirana society, which revolved around the diplomatic corps, knew better than to invite them to picnics or evening parties, for they were certain to refuse. The King did his utmost to insulate them from politics. Their untaxing days slipped by in a quiet, even rhythm, punctuated by meals, dancing lessons (Albanian and western), and horse-riding with Captain Fraghi, an Italian cavalryman. 'It was a stirring sight to watch them all out together,' recalled Pietro Quaroni of the Italian Legation. 'Fraghi would ride in front, at a respectable distance from the sisters, who followed in Indian file, dressed alike in green – dark green leather boots, somewhat lighter green breeches, light green blouses, and colonial topees with veils, in the best nineteenth-century manner.'[12]

In the summer, they decamped with their brother to Durrës, where the younger Princesses added sunbathing to their routine. When President, Zogu had arranged for his four unmarried sisters to attend finishing schools in France and Switzerland. The piano lessons had not made a lasting impression, but they continued to learn French and a little English for their annual trips abroad, shepherded by Albanian Legation staff and a trusty from the Old Gang. That is when they acquired their sybaritic image. Senije, Ruhije, Myzejen, and Maxhide did love shopping in the Faubourg Saint-Honoré. Travel also supplied them with things to say at court receptions.

It would be hard to argue that the King's younger sisters led full and rewarding lives. They did not undertake the usual royal duties of visiting schools, hospitals, and barracks till the late 1930s, and these do not seem to have been very joyful occasions to judge by the photographs. Most of them show three nervous-looking women in chic little hats and suits surrounded by unsmiling clansmen with the menacing figure of Musa Juka in the background. Usually, the Princesses whiled away their time in seclusion, as the daughters of beys and chieftains normally did – until they married. There was the nub of the issue. The Albanian woman was a wife and mother. Years went by, and the Princesses remained single.

Most, perhaps all, of them had once been engaged, back in their days at Burgajet. Just as Sadije found Doshishti for Adile and Kryeziu for Nafije, she had taken the trouble to arrange good matches for her younger daughters. The contracts were sealed, but the rise of Zogu destroyed the matrimonial calculus on which they were based. How could the first family favour three or four clans without incurring the jealousy of others? Postponements sufficed for a time. Then, between 1925 and 1928, President Zogu undertook the painstaking and delicate task of extricating his sisters from their engagements. This had to be by mutual consent, if possible, since failure to deliver a promised bride automatically triggered a blood feud (unless she pledged herself to lifelong virginity). The redundant prospective brothers-in-law extracted compensation in terms of professional advancement and help in arranging good alternative marriages. Xhemil Bey Dino, once engaged to Myzejen, became Albanian Minister to the League of Nations.

The Princesses expected their brother and guardian to make new marriage contracts compatible with their rank. No Albanians were eligible. The House of Zogu-Mati needed to rise above beys and chieftains. But where were princes at once pro-Muslim, pro-western, and willing to marry into a parvenu dynasty? All four younger sisters were dark and slender with tiny size-three feet. Their glamorous studio portraits, however, probably harmed their chances by raising false expectations. 'No one would have claimed they were beautiful', wrote Quaroni.[13] Even if they had been, the fate of Kryeziu would still have deterred potential suitors.

It was not until January 1936 that Zog had the satisfaction of marrying off Senije to Prince Abid, the bespectacled youngest son of the late Sultan Abdul Hamid II. The engagement, announced just four days before the wedding, caused more of a stir than he anticipated. An Ottoman prince, albeit deposed, had considerable prestige in the Muslim world, but, to the other Balkan countries, Abid was the offspring of a hated despot. Atatürk, moreover, took it into his head that the match was part of an Italian conspiracy to undermine the Turkish republic by reviving Ottoman monarchism. In consequence, some half-a-dozen nations boycotted the ceremony. Personal insults of this kind brought out the proud chieftain in King Zog, who had the Turkish, Yugoslav, and Romanian Ministers replaced over the next six months. This contretemps was welcomed in Italy, where the royal couple spent their honeymoon. A large dowry may have played some part in inducing Prince Abid, a law student, to wed a woman several years his senior. The King made him Albanian Minister in Paris.*

Undaunted, Zog tried next to secure Prince Mohammed Abdel Moneim, only son of Khedive Abbas II Hilmi of Egypt. He had been heir apparent until the deposition of his father in 1914 and he was still heir to $50 million. No diplomatic obstacles presented themselves: the world knew Prince Moneim primarily as an expert on tropical fish. In 1938, he seemed willing, but the old Khedive objected to his marrying beneath himself, so Myzejen had to carry on waiting, along with Ruhije and Maxhide.

These three became very coy about their age – and about the date of their father's death. In the first years of the monarchy, Xhemal Pasha Zogolli was reckoned to have died in 1908. Myzejen was said to have been

---

* Zog also found a sinecure for Abid's nephew and bosom friend, Prince Mehmet Orhan. Previously an aerobatic performer in Latin America, he became personal pilot to His Majesty (who had no aeroplane).

born in 1905, Ruhije in 1906, and Maxhide in 1907. By 1933, the official year of Xhemal's death had been advanced to 1911, and his daughters' dates of birth were 1909, 1910, and 1911. The process did not stop there. To prevent the emergence of a suspicious gap, the ages of the elder Princesses were also brought forward: Adile was born between 1891 and 1894, Nafije between 1893 and 1900, and Senije between 1897 and 1908. In each case, the supposition must be that the earliest date is the true one. It is nowadays thought that Xhemal may have died as early as 1904 or 1905, with Myzejen born in 1900, Ruhije in 1902 and Maxhide in 1904.

The marital prospects of the Princesses Zogu were virtually destroyed by their questionable royal rank. It might even be said to have blighted their lives – at least by the standards of their own society – but they would never have admitted it. Spinsterhood did not worry them. The man who mattered was the King. 'Father, brother, husband, head of the family and of the clan, national hero, such are the multiple functions which Zog without doubt fulfilled in the subconscious of the Princesses to the point where their individual existence held little significance in their eyes compared to their communal life.'[14]

The highlight of each day came immediately after the siesta, when the family gathered in the drawing room of the King's palace for coffee and conversation. Zog individually greeted his mother, his sisters, and his nephews and nieces, and each person embraced every other on arrival and departure. If ever he merely shook the hand of one of his more remote relations, this was understood to be a mark of disapproval. His sisters and the children invariably received a hug. Then he took his place on the sofa in the middle of the room, with Tati, Teri, and Danush beside him.

Zog himself was not much given to chit-chat, but he knew how to put the right question to set others talking. Then he sat back and listened, intervening now and then to move things forward or inject some gentle humour. He liked to hear about the little ups and downs of his sisters' lives: their lessons, their purchases, their horse-rides, their magazines. Everyone desired to please him, and even the youngsters found it easy to join in. 'He was not only very calm and kind. He made everyone feel they were something special,' recalled Teri. 'Each one of us expected that, if anything went wrong with us, he should know and he ought to put it right.'[15]

While extremely solicitous in attending to the concerns of his family, Zog usually appeared positively serene about his own affairs, which is just a way of saying that politics were taboo. If ever he did discuss them with his sisters, it could only have been in private with Senije. In a family not immune from sibling jealousy, her claim to the rank of favourite sister nevertheless went unchallenged. Zog and Senije had been especially close from earliest childhood, as only a few years separated them, and they still teased each other. She sometimes spoke for all the sisters and acted as an intermediary between them and the King. Personal problems which might cause dissension within the family were not to be raised during the coffee hour but referred to Senije. 'You must tell *me* if something isn't right,' she would say.[16] Zog did not contradict or reprimand any member of his family in front of the others if he could possibly avoid it. No unkind words passed his lips. His voice was never raised in anger. If somebody upset him, and a single glance failed to put her right, she would hear of his displeasure from Senije the following day.

When Zog relaxed with his sisters, perfect harmony reigned. Often he played them a few operatic arias or a symphonic movement from his record collection. His own love of classical music dated from his years in Vienna, and the Royal Band played a significant part in bringing western music, popular and classical, to a land where it had previously been almost unknown. The Princesses, not really appreciating the more demanding composers, found diversion in backgammon. Sometimes Zog played too, but he generally looked on, giving advice and betting a lek or two on the outcome. After about an hour, he would rise, initiate a final round of embraces, and bid everyone farewell till they met again the next afternoon. Only the most urgent crises disrupted this pattern.

One further member of the royal family neither appeared at public events nor took part in these cosy palace gatherings. This was Xhelal Zogu, the King's half-brother, who was not only still alive but even flourishing in his way. Albanians considered sons of the same father to be brothers without distinction. When his sisters became Princesses, Zog made Xhelal a Prince. He lived in a handsome white villa at Burreli, the small town now growing up around the gendarmerie post in Mati, and he seldom came to Tirana or Durrës. Coincidentally, it was at Burreli that Zog imprisoned his most dangerous enemies, not that their wretched conditions in any way resembled those enjoyed by the Prince. Every material comfort was his, on the understanding that he kept well clear of politics. This suited Xhelal. A loafer, corpulent and scruffy, he had none of Zog's ambition and few of his social graces.

Prince Xhelal might have been forgotten entirely but for the persistent rumour that the details of his personal life would not bear inspection. Some people satirically suggested that he might be reviving the Muslim practice of polygamy. It had never been common for Albanians to have more than one wife at a time, and it became illegal in 1929. Then wits gibed that the Prince was making full use of the new divorce laws. The embarrassment had begun in 1912, when Xhelal parted from his first wife. She was Ruhije Doshishti, a sister of Adile's husband. Sadije took the side of the deserted wife and invited her to live with her in-laws, which she did for the rest of her life (so there were two Ruhije Zogus in the household). Xhelal achieved notoriety as a Bluebeard after his elevation to royalty. In 1931, he married Ikbal, who died after bearing him a daughter in May 1932. Then he wed Faika, who had a son in June 1933. That same year, he married Hirijet, who gave him four children.

Scandalized by these goings on, Sadije refused to recognise any of these very young women as her daughters-in-law and decided that Xhelal was unfit to rear his own offspring. The babies came to Tirana, where nannies helped bring them up with their cousins. Zog again played the father-figure, as nobody respected 'Uncle Lal', who displayed scant interest in his children.

Thus the Albanian royal family comprised Princesses without husbands and a Prince with too many wives. The crucial difference was that the King was responsible for the women in his household. Anybody whom one of his sisters married would be regarded as his choice. Xhelal headed a separate household, and his selection of brides was his own affair. His belated fecundity did prompt some comment, for by 1938 he had three little sons: Skender, Mirgin, and Genc. If anybody mentioned the succession, however, Xhelal insisted that Zog would soon marry and have a boy of his own.

The family life of King Zog struck foreigners as strange. It did not seem 'normal' that a wealthy middle-aged man should choose to live with his mother, his sisters, and nearly a dozen children not his own; and that this domestic arrangement should continue (as it did) even after his eventual marriage. True, the King did not actually sleep under the same roof at this time, but he was always next door or just across the road. In later years, they would all lodge together.

Albanians saw nothing unusual about this. It was thoroughly conventional. Zog carried out his duties as head of the family in an exemplary fashion. He revered his mother, cherished his sisters, and treated their children as his own. By custom, they had a right to share his home, yet they never needed to assert it. Everything was taken for granted, and Zog would not have had it otherwise. All the family depended on him and deferred to him. The sole peculiarity was his failure to marry off his sisters, and Albanians understood this. The traditional subordination of women likely arose from fears about conflicts of loyalty: would a wife side with her husband or her brother?

The close relationship between King Zog and the Princesses was not altogether exceptional. If they clung to him, it appears that he wanted them to cling. He took pleasure in pleasing them, and, in their eyes, he could practically do no wrong. Consider the following from anthropologist Berit Backer:

> Sibling links are emotionally loaded in Albanian society, and that goes
> not only for brothers but for sisters as well, and for a sister and a

brother. The closest male to a woman, with whom she openly recognises emotional involvement, is the brother, as the husband is not necessarily to her liking, being chosen by the family. Much of a woman's love may be invested in her favourite brother, whom she will continue to see and who will care for her children in return. In correspondence, the maternal uncle, the *daja*, is the figure seen as a male mother, being generous and indulgent with his sister's children.[17]

Sadije Zogu held to the established conception of Albanian family life and imprinted this so firmly on the minds of all her children that their later 'westernism' never effaced it. In this regard (as in others), King Zog, for all his rhetoric, could not and would not westernise himself. What interwar travel writers found picturesquely 'ethnic' in High Albania, however, did look more curious when the patriarch wore Savile Row suits and his womenfolk were dressed by Worth.

CHAPTER TWENTY-FOUR

The Public Face of the Regime

The 1928 constitution declared: 'Albania is a democratic, parliamentary, hereditary monarchy.'[1] Nothing in this definition was true beyond disputing – not even the noun, for the mystique of an historic throne defied easy replication. A coronation amid the dramatic ruins of Skanderbeg's citadel at Kruja, planned for 28 November 1928, never came to pass. The Austrians refused to hand over the helmet and sword which the King claimed as regalia from the museum in Vienna. Zog chose not to buy a new crown and sceptre. Muslims had no tradition of crowning in any case.

Young royal houses elsewhere in the Balkans purported to revive the glories of ancient civilisations or medieval kings. Ferdinand of Bulgaria and Marie of Romania revelled in pseudo-Byzantine lore. Albania had more trouble finding a monarchical past to reinvent. A cult of the Pelasgians and assertions that ancient Macedonia, Epirus, and Illyria were all Albanian states enabled nationalistic historians to provide Zog with a list of precursors that included Achilles, Alexander the Great, Pyrrhus of Epirus, Queen Teuta of Illyria, Diocletian, Constantine the Great, and Justinian. However, not even claims that Alexander came from Mati could disguise the fact that none of them had actually thought himself Albanian.

More recent local potentates presented problems. Ali Pasha Tepelena, the 'Lion of Janina', was famed for defying the Turks in the early nineteenth century, but he had ruled what was now northern Greece as well as Gjirokastra and Vlora. Moreover, he carried too much odium as a torturer and pederast to embellish Zogist history. A Gheg counterpart, Kara Mahmoud Bushati, who governed Shkodra, had likewise come to a violent end.

The royal heritage of Albania was therefore narrowly defined as Gjergj Kastrioti Skanderbeg, a hero to both Gheg and Tosk, who already monopolised nationalist literature. By positing some kind of continuity or equivalence between the events of 1444 and 1928, the regime strove to inculcate the notion that Zog and Skanderbeg were the twin faces of legitimate Albanian kingship. Did not some old papal documents refer to the Lord of Kruja as *Rex Albaniae?* It was rather as if the historical basis of the British monarchy had been exclusively Henry V. Few opportunities were missed to point similarities between King Zog and the Herculean demigod in the horned helmet. Propagandists claimed that they both had a special birthmark denoting greatness, and Sadije was supposed to have dreamt the same dream as Vojsava Kastrioti before giving birth. 'After Alexander the Great, Pyrrhus, and Skanderbeg, history had reached a new high point'. Zog was God's gift to his people, the 'Executor of the Divine Will', 'the most intelligent man in the country', and 'the brightest star that ever rose upon the Pelasgian horizon'. This genius 'accomplished in politics what Michelangelo had achieved in sculpture'.[2]

> The noble set of his head on his broad shoulders is proof against any weakness. The high and slightly broad forehead defies the clouds of anxiety to settle for long. But it is his eyes that draw and reveal the innate greatness of the man become ruler. They are clear, grey-blue, shining eyes of the Seer, who ever keeps his goal in sight and marches steadfastly onward.[3]

This description was actually intended for an American audience. Admiring foreigners sometimes called him *Pater patriae*, but, in a land where fathers really were respected, people did not rush to acknowledge Zog as such. Although he made out that the Ghegs revered him as supreme chief of the united clans, many saw him as a successor to the sultan.

Officials stencilled 'Long live the King' on the walls of prefectures, barracks, and schools, and checked that cafés still displayed his picture. The major efforts at monarchist publicity were parades in Tirana and regional centres on national holidays. The proximity of Monarchy Day (1 September), the King's Birthday (8 October), and Independence Day (28 November) annually placed a strain on state finances, and hiring Fox Movietone News to film the 1929 festivities cost a fortune. In private, King Zog was capable of charm approaching charisma. In front of a crowd, it was a different story: 'He had nothing of the art of cultivating personal popularity on a wide scale.'[4]

At these outward displays of loyalty, participants marched in regimented groups suggestive of unity and progress. First came the Royal Band, followed by the frock-coated festival commission. Behind them trooped the *alla Franka* ladies of the Association of Albanian Women, schoolchildren in red and black uniforms, the cycling club, the mounted Royal Guard, the *Enti Kombëtar* youth group, scholarship students, priests and hodjas, civil servants, judges, journalists, writers, athletes, artists, the chamber of commerce, and provincial delegates in local costume. All joined in singing the Hymn of Zog, which ascribed to him over numerous verses the most admirable characteristics of the lion, the fox, the elephant, and other animals. In front of the podium, right forearms swung stiffly across chests to make the Zogist salute (flat hand over heart, with palm facing downwards). The stage management owed a lot to fascist models, yet this gesture – a Roman salute gone wrong – neatly symbolised relations between Zog's Albania and Mussolini's Italy.

Inevitably, the reputation of the King has been tarred with the brush of fascism – chiefly by people who use the term merely as a synonym for dictatorship. Albania differed so fundamentally from Italy and Germany that fascism – on any precise ideological or sociological definition – was scarcely applicable. Mussolini exported his creed across the Adriatic only in superficial form, and usually for ulterior motives. The National Organisation for Albanian Youth, the *Enti Kombëtar* did resemble the *Ballila* in Italy: youngsters in red shirts marched, sang, and played sport. Italian advisers set it up in 1929 to undermine the efforts of certain British gendarmerie instructors to promote scouting.

The regime increasingly indulged in sloganising, yet Zog's 'Discipline, Sacrifice, Progress' had neither the menace nor the ring of Mussolini's 'Believe, Obey, Fight'. Albania lacked a state ideology beyond the commitment to national unity and westernisation. King Zog used violence but he did not glorify it. Among authoritarian states in eastern Europe, his kingdom stood out as one where the military did *not* play a major political role, if only because it was no more cohesive than any other organ of government.

Anti-semitism was not an issue, since only Vlora had a tiny Jewish community, and, if Zog himself had any ethnic or religious prejudices, he never advertised them.* Maybe the single advantage of the 1913 borders was the fact that a small Albania meant high levels of ethnic homogeneity: 92 per cent. The most substantial minority were the Greeks in the south (4.7 per cent). The issue of Graecophone schools generated ill-feeling, yet the consensus of international opinion was that Albania treated its Greeks no worse than Greece treated Albanians. Minorities complained more of neglect than of persecution.

While Mussolini boasted of trampling on the putrid corpse of liberty, Zog kept up the pretence that Albania enjoyed free institutions, though even he sounded unsure whether the country had actually arrived at democracy or was still only on the path to it. Of course, the 234-article constitution was pretty much a sham. The King exercised complete executive, legislative, and judicial powers; the one domestic constraint on

---

* Albania was notably liberal in granting visas to Jewish refugees from Nazi Germany.

him was fear of rebellion. The illiterate populace accepted bey governance and only bothered to vote in elections when gendarmes rounded them up and escorted them to the poll. Official turnout figures of 90 per cent contrast with independent estimates of 10 per cent. In the second round, an oligarchy of electors picked deputies from an approved list, after 'unqualified' and 'undesirable' candidates had been excluded. Parties did not exist.

A parliamentary deputy was merely 'a big man to whom the King granted a large salary, and who in turn granted small salaries to smaller men for keeping the peace'.[5] Though Zog did not demand total unanimity in the chamber, deputies who wanted to keep their privileges would try to vote in accordance with royal desires. Sometimes he perplexed them by giving mixed signals. Now and again, he even let the Government go down to defeat. It did not necessarily mean anything, as Zog explained to Sir Robert Hodgson after one such instance in January 1930:

> Ministers were prone to adopt a hectoring and discourteous attitude in their relations with members of the Chamber, and their arrogance had made them personally unpopular. That was all. As Albania needed above everything internal tranquillity, he had patched up the quarrel. . . . The Cabinet was independent in its outlook. This being the primary virtue he demanded of it, the Cabinet would remain in power.[6]

Thus he reminded the ministers that he could have them ousted by the deputies whenever he wished, and reminded the deputies that they could not oust the ministers except when he wished.

Perhaps the best known parliamentarian was Hiqmet Delvina, a Tosk bey with a row of gold teeth, who made amends for opposing Zogu in 1924 by offering him prolix eulogies. The papers reported him in full and ignored any speakers who hinted at censure. Until 1933, the constitution stipulated that censorship could not be imposed except in an emergency. In reality, it operated all the time. A leader had to guard his honour. To be criticised in public was an insult, and to tolerate it shameful. Few Albanians could have respected a king too weak to silence his enemies.

Beyond this, censorship seemed capricious. Unfavourable comment on Italy was generally prohibited, yet Zog occasionally found it convenient when bargaining with Rome. Similarly, adverse press reaction to particular policies or ministers could suit his purpose, but every editor was likely to upset the authorities at some stage. After the State Press Bureau came into being, this could mean losing a 5,000 gold franc deposit or even gaol. More normally, official harassment forced a temporary closure. For a land with few readers, Albania spawned a surprising number of periodicals, with such titles as *Rebirth, New World,* and *Albanian Effort.* The Interior Ministry, in the name of culture, paid subsidies which became the levers of control.

Naturally, King Zog banned political groups which advocated revolution. 'Albania needed a couple of centuries of capitalism', he once observed, 'before there was any use of even considering the undoubted merits of communism.'[7] The number of communists in Albania was minuscule. Ali Kelmendi founded the first secret cell in Korça in 1929, but he spent most of the next decade in prison or in Moscow. This did not prevent Musa Juka applying the label indiscriminately to disaffected young men whose politics were not obviously tribal. His 'Red Scare' rhetoric later allowed the real Albanian communists to claim more credit for anti-Zogist protests than ever they deserved. The 'demonstration for bread' broken up in Korça on 21 February 1936 was a case in point.

The authorities cracked down hard on strikes, regarding them as incipient revolts, and the use of informers helped keep unrest to a minimum. Civil liberties meant little. The opening of mail was common knowledge, and foreigners often complained of their hotel rooms being searched. A shocked American reported:

> Practically every third man in the country was a paid spy. Italy, of course, had her complete espionage system; so also did the jittery king; the police had their own close-meshed spy network; every member of the Cabinet had his own separate espionage service. It was fantastic.[8]

Yet Zogist repression, although sometimes harsh, was anything but thorough, and the example of Enver Hoxha belies communist claims to the contrary. The dictator-to-be lost his scholarship to study abroad, either for neglecting his course or for contributing some anti-Zogist reports to *L'Humanité* in Paris. Hoxha actually joined the Communist Party there in 1935. Then he returned home and took a job at Korça *lycée,* probably the most prestigious school in the land. This despite Circular No. 666 of the Ministry of Education:

> The teacher must not concern himself with propaganda of principles differing from those instituted by the State, neither should he tolerate such by the student. It is his duty to seek to fire the students with feelings of love towards the organizations of the State, towards His Royal Highness the King, towards the flag, the nation and the fatherland. Those who do not carry out these duties should not stand in the ranks of those responsible for the education of our youth.[9]

It was in the classroom that echoes of totalitarianism were most clearly heard. Children sat under red and black patriotic banners and chanted poems about Skanderbeg and Zog. The King explained:

> You must understand that the average Albanian knows nothing about nationality. He has always looked up to the head of his tribe, or his Bey, as the supreme authority. He has got to be taught gradually to transfer this local allegiance, admirable in itself, to the central government. He must learn in fact that while remaining the member of a tribe, he is also a citizen of the State.[10]

In setting out to raise national consciousness, Zog followed the lead of writers whose doctrine of unity through education, known as *neoshqiptarizma* (or New Albanianism), dated from the struggle against the Turks and derived its distinctive zeal from a desire to efface religious cleavages. In the words of the poet Pashko Vasa: 'Let not mosques and churches keep you apart. The true religion of the Albanian is Albanianism!'[11]

Differences of faith did underscore social and regional divisions, despite the lack of fanaticism. Muslims referred to pig-eating infidels; 'All Muslims stink,' swore Roman Catholic clansmen. Asked about exaggerated fears of communism, the King answered that 'he had three religions to cope with, as it was: he could not afford a fourth'.[12] The way in which he coped was by making Albanian Islam, Orthodoxy, and Roman Catholicism more 'national' and by showing them equal respect. Albanians enjoyed twenty-one public holidays per year (a European record) to mark the festivals of all three faiths. Sunday was the weekly rest day from 1929, but Muslims could still take time off on Friday.

Zog remained a nominal Muslim all his life. 'We must pray and have faith in God,' he would say in perilous times, though diplomats judged him a secular man, who, if 'not actively anti-religious, is at all events without sympathy for religion in any form'.[13] He and his sisters celebrated Ramadan and Bajram by exchanging lots of presents, just as they celebrated Christmas and Easter; only the Queen Mother could be called devout. This syncretic approach found most favour with the Bektashis: Muslims who drank alcohol and ate pork. Islamic traditionalists feared westernisation, and Catholics caused political problems disproportionate to their numbers. To improve relations with the Vatican, Zog opened talks on a Concordat; they soon broke down, as the Church opposed his introduction of divorce in 1928. This exasperated him. Did the Pope not understand the alternative?

> There is a case here in Tirana just now. The wife of a Roman Catholic left him and spent a week with another man: the priest

rescued her and induced the reluctant husband to take her back. She has now run off again, with the priest in pursuit, but if the worthy man brings her back a second time the husband will certainly shoot her. And then I shall have to tell my gendarmes, judges, and executioners to get to work. Now, divorce would stop all that.[14]

The new marriage laws went ahead in the face of condemnation from the pulpit. Open protest on this scale was a rarity. Zog reminded the Archbishop of Shkodra that 'any priest whose enthusiasm ran away with him beyond proper bounds would soon be provided with a tree with adequate strength to support his weight'.[15]

The Roman Catholic Church worried Zog because of its Italian connections, especially after the rapprochement between Mussolini and the Vatican. Italy did indeed subsidise Albanian Catholicism, and Aloisi inspired a move to bring the Albanian Orthodox Church into communion with Rome: a Uniate Church opened at Elbasan on 21 September 1929. The same day, the King proclaimed a law on religious communities giving him control over appointments and finances. Priests accused him of anti-clericalism.

These controversies did not usually touch the man in the street, whose right to religious freedom was respected (though proselytising was discouraged). Zog had no desire to eliminate religion. While Catholicism was associated with Italy, however, and Orthodoxy with Greece, he could not ignore church politics. Nor did he see any objection to school-children reciting the 'New Albanian' catechism:

Q: But man himself, what does he love in life?
A: He loves his country.
Q: Where does he live with hope? Where does he want to die?
A: In his country.
Q: Where may he be happy and live with honour?
A: In Albania.
Q: Where does the mud seem sweeter than honey?
A: In Albania.[16]

CHAPTER TWENTY-FIVE

A Fragile Stability

Zog's top priority was to 'establish exemplary order and discipline throughout the country'.[1] A network of four hundred gendarmerie posts extended state power to places which had never before experienced it. Admittedly, a gendarmerie post might be nothing more than a tumbledown shack with a tattered portrait of the King on the wall. Policing in remote areas still depended on co-operation from the local chief, moreover: powerful men often went unpunished. Order was not the same as law, and gendarmerie methods were rough and ready. When Stirling put a price on the head of three bandits, he did not anticipate that one of them would deliver the others' severed heads in a bag, but it soon became standard practice to send one brigand band to wipe out another and thus win a pardon. The gendarmerie impressed the British Minister as the one Albanian institution that worked with a semblance of efficiency.

Zog's drive to disarm the civilian population continued in an intermittent and selective fashion. Only about 180,000 rifles were ever confiscated, but the mere fact that weapons now had to be kept hidden was itself a tremendous social change. Previously, an Albanian would as soon appear in public without his gun as an Englishman would without his trousers.

Of 1,832 murders officially recorded between 1930 and 1938, blood feuds accounted for 756 – and this was probably an under-estimate. It was difficult to convince Albanians (including the policemen) that it was necessarily wrong to kill, steal, and lie in the interests of the clan. The Canon of Lek defied repeal. Not just a code of laws, it had moulded Albanian morality. Vengeance was traditionally a matter for boasting: a murderer sent word to his victim's family to fetch the body. The authorities could say what they liked: if the rules of feuding sanctioned the killing, witnesses would not testify. It was not only traditionalists who criticised attempts to prosecute in such cases, as driving honourable killers from their homes boosted the number of bandits. Judges used their discretion. A man who killed his adulterous wife and her lover, displaying their bodies as the Canon required, might go to prison for two or three weeks.

The British gendarmerie officers sometimes tried to resolve long-standing feuds. The normal procedure was to investigate the original cause, tally the killings on each side, value each life lost in terms of cattle, strike the balance, and finally arrange the transfer of an appropriate number of cows. When the parties to the feud were men of high status, the King himself often had to adjudicate at a face-to-face meeting in his office.

It was only in towns that the Law of Lek gave way to the Law of Zog. 'Albanian justice registers unforgettable days of glory,' claimed the King. He instructed teams of lawyers to draw up a new civil code (1929) and criminal code (1930) to replace Ottoman law with judicial procedures based on the French model. 'With its new laws, Albania enters the European family,' he said.[2] In practice, there remained far to go. Prisoners in leg-irons were herded into barnlike gaols, after trials that ranged between the perfunctory and the chaotic, often with blatant political interference. Zog 'administered justice less with regard for the law than with an understanding of when harshness or mercy would most impress the public mind'.[3] Hence draconian sentences and early pardons.

By 1937 the murder rate had fallen below twenty per month, and travellers judged Albania no more dangerous than other Near Eastern countries. The decline of outlawry brought relative calm to ravaged frontier districts, which came as a relief to Balkan departments in Europe's foreign ministries. There had initially been international apprehension at the speed and completeness with which Zog had succumbed to the Italians, but, by 1930, it was clear that alliance with a Great Power had not turned his head. He assured the British that he had long ago 'made up his mind to regard Kosovo as lost to Albania'.[4] Though Yugoslavia still complained of terrorists operating out of Dibra, border raiding on a large scale was a thing of the past.

King Zog had achieved some kind of stability in Albania. To most outsiders, that was all that mattered. His dictatorship had its failings, they acknowledged, but, in their domestic politics, all the Balkan states were somewhere between Tsarist Russia and Latin America. Powerless peasants submitted to misgovernment by a king-dictator who left them alone in their private lives. 'In Albania the process of state building and nation making confronts difficulties not encountered elsewhere to the same extent,' wrote one political scientist.[5] The weakness of the rule of law could partly be blamed on the recency of Ottoman misgovernment. The Kingdom of Albania stood comparison with Greece in the 1830s, Romania in the 1860s, or Bulgaria in the 1880s. Britain and France were simply pleased that Zog and Mussolini had taken Albania off the list of immediate crises. Or so they thought.

In December 1930, reports came from Tirana that the King might be gravely, even terminally, ill. Ever since 1925, there had been bouts of speculation about his health, notwithstanding his youth, and the predictions were always dire. Tuberculosis, syphilis, cancer, angina, liver disease, malaria, gallstones – all had been credited with bringing Zog to death's door. Poison also loomed large in the popular imagination. The fact that he was not seen in public for weeks at a time allowed these tales to gain a hearing, but his repeated survival had been turning them into a joke. Cynics said that he invented the rumours himself to dissuade assassins from taking the trouble.

This time, however, those with access to the palace did know that something was wrong with him. Acute abdominal pains were the main symptom. Ulcers seem a likely explanation, but, whether from ignorance or by intent, Zog kept everyone guessing. He was said – almost everything about this is hearsay – to be a trying patient: terrified of surgery, suspicious of drugs, and loath to exercise. After the King cancelled all meetings and retired to his bungalow in Durrës, diplomats heard that he had suffered twenty-four hours of agony and lost six kilograms in days. Austrian doctors brought huge cases of X-ray equipment, but it could not be used. In mid-January, word came that he was well on the way to recovery. Just days later, however, on 25 January 1931, an official bulletin stated that he would be leaving tomorrow for Vienna for medical tests. The Italian cruiser *Quarto* took him as far as Venice, to avoid his having to travel through Yugoslavia.

This news caused a sensation. Everyone who knew the King supposed that he would not have risked absenting himself from Albania unless his life was really in danger. This assumption had two effects. First, every political faction began secretly preparing to battle for the succession. Second, however, the very gravity of his illness made would-be revolutionaries hold back. A *coup d'état* was more likely to succeed, especially in securing foreign recognition, once the King was dead. Serious plotters determined to wait and see. There were whispers of a republican conspiracy in the south, a Mirdite uprising in the north, and an invasion led by Gani Bey Kryeziu from Kosovo.

The Italians were meanwhile fuming. Zog had refused to tell them what was wrong, refused to let Italian doctors examine him, refused to name an heir, and refused to go to Rome for treatment. Now Soragna had to scout around for possible substitutes in the event of his death. It was not easy: Zog had ensured that no one possessed enough prestige to step into his shoes. The old Italian standby, Hassan Prishtina, would be a red rag to the Yugoslavs; and how could the Italian Legation plausibly promote yet another Albanian commoner to royalty? Soragna considered Prince Michael or Prince Paul of Montenegro, nephews of the Queen of Italy. He overlooked the younger members of the Zogu dynasty.

Albanian politics were suspended in limbo. Everyone waited for news from Vienna, some hoping for the death of the King and some for his recovery. And Zog himself? Although thin and tired, he was up and about, evidently not in much pain. With a suite of twelve (including Krosi), he took a floor of the Hotel Imperial and consulted a succession of eminent doctors in a surprisingly leisurely fashion. Whatever they told him, he kept to himself. At night, he went to the theatre, often with two unknown young ladies. This created the impression that his visit was turning into a holiday, and the Austrian authorities took a dim view. Given the presence of various anti-Zogist émigrés, they felt obliged to provide round-the-clock protection.

On 20 February, King Zog attended the double-bill of *I Pagliacci* and *Josephs-Legende* (a ballet by Richard Strauss) at the Opera House, a few hundred yards from his hotel. His usual caution had not deserted him entirely: he left by a side door shortly before the curtain at half past ten, having ordered two limousines to be waiting in the queue of taxis in the Operngasse. The seven Albanians were just getting in when the first shots rang out. Çatin Saraçi, consul in Vienna, explained:

> I saw the two assassins approaching from the colonnades of the Opera. I recognised them instantly as two disaffected Albanian nationalist ex-officers, one of whom was at one time in relation with the Communists. I instantly drew my revolver and fired at them. At the same time they opened fire on His Majesty.[6]

The detective in the front of the first car leapt out, and Zog, who was already in the back, made a move to do the same. Major Topallaj, an aide-de-camp standing on the running-board, lurched forward and fell on top of the King, however, pinning him to the back seat while shielding him from bullets. Zog drew a gun from inside his tail-coat and returned fire, as did Libohova, Sereqi, and the chauffeur. Krosi and Bashko, the court doctor, crouched in the second car, while a gun-battle ensued in the lamplit side-street. Bystanders threw themselves down in the dirty snow and panic spread to the crowd emerging from the auditorium.

Over twenty shots were fired in all. Libohova suffered a wound to his leg. Zog emptied the five chambers of his revolver and then asked Topallaj to hand him his pistol, unaware that the Major was already dead. Fearing attack from the other side of the car, he squeezed past the body and ran back into the Opera House, shouting in German, as the police appeared and seized everybody involved. The assassins, both in evening dress, cried that King Zog was a traitor ruining their country. They were identified as Aziz Çami and Ndoc Gjeloshi, formerly of the gendarmerie.

The King had escaped without a scratch, despite four bullet-holes in the bodywork of the car where his head and chest would have been and another three bullets in Major Topallaj. Possibly Zog owed his life to the fact that his adjutant was of the same height and build: the initial shot had hit the wrong man.

The news was announced in Parliament in Tirana the next day to dramatic effect. Everyone in public life had felt the tension of the preceding month. Now uncertainty vanished. Providence had spared His Majesty, so who would dare appear less than ecstatic? The deputies marched to Rruga Carnarvon to congratulate the Queen Mother – a pilgrimage to 'her who bore the Christ of Albania' in the words of Hiqmet Delvina.[7] Prefects inundated Musa Juka with pleas that 20 February be declared a public holiday, services of thanksgiving packed mosques and churches, and to the rhapsody repertoire was added *The Ballad of Llesh Topallaj*:

> Only look after my wife and children:
> Majors are as common as the sands of the sea,
> But such another King you will never find.[8]

The political background to the assassination attempt seemed every bit as murky as such things usually are. Çami and Gjeloshi, between them, had connections with virtually every Albanian exile group in existence. Amid all the conjectures, one portentous fact stood out. Both men had entered Austria on Yugoslavian diplomatic passports. The Belgrade Government at once denied complicity, but unconfirmed reports that hundreds of armed Albanian émigrés had massed on the Kosovo border on the night of the attack impressed international opinion. 'The organisation of bands on our frontier disturbs order and weakens our finances,' Zog told an Austrian newspaper, 'thereby hindering the consolidation of Albania and endangering peace. Such activities obviously make empty words of the finest assurances.'[9]

It is hard to credit that the leaders of Yugoslavia wanted to destabilise Albania and risk war with Italy in February 1931, when Croat separatism was causing them so many internal problems. Since the events at Sarajevo in 1914, however, it had been well-known that Serbian military men, even high-ranking ones, dabbled in secret operations of which their masters were unaware. To Zog, this seemed a likely explanation and he did not press the point. The new Yugoslav Minister in Tirana, however, managed to strain relations even further by alleging that the King had shot Major Topallaj himself by mistake. Evidence presented at the trial of Çami and Gjeloshi seven months later disproved this suggestion but otherwise shed little light on the affair. They were given sentences of seven and three years after their lawyer presented extracts from the writings of Faik Konitza to show that Zog was a murderous despot. In the meantime, the journalists of Tirana and Belgrade resumed their usual exchange of insults.

In the excitement, the reason for Zog's visit to Vienna had been half-forgotten. It does appear that his abdominal pains went away of their own accord. Sooner than suffer exploratory surgery, the King accepted a diagnosis of nicotine poisoning, so he said, with fresh air and exercise the only prescription. He cut back his smoking to a hundred cigarettes per day. Zog left Vienna on 11 March, spent a week in Venice to appease the Italians, and received a tumultuous welcome at Durrës. After embracing Sadije, he made straight for his car and Tirana. The trip to Vienna had cost 300,000 gold francs; he ruled that the Treasury could not afford an additional public holiday each February.

So passed the curious 'crisis' of 1931. Nobody believed in nicotine poisoning as an explanation. Both the Yugoslavs and the Italians continued to suspect that Zog had some obscure malignant disorder. In April, he assured Hodgson that his actual infirmity had been 'a dropped intestine', which a series of injections put right.[10] The physicians may have told him this, but science has since dismissed the whole notion of displaced organs. There was no end of speculation, but diplomats did not take it seriously, and simple people contented themselves with tales of 'the Evil Eye'. By the autumn, Zog looked very robust as he joked about needing 'all his clothes let out in order to accommodate his recovered girth'.[11]

One more mystery made no difference to a state addicted to secrets. Paramount was the fact that King Zog had survived absence, illness, and assassination. He could report that 'exemplary peace has continued to reign throughout the kingdom'.[12] The gunfight in the Operngasse confirmed his reputation abroad as a dashing royal gangster. Foreign observers inclined to indulgence: alone of all Albanian leaders since independence, this upstart king displayed the combination of skill and luck required to keep a troublesome little land in order and thus contribute to peace in the Balkans. The relief felt in the British Foreign Office, however, provoked a counterblast from Sir Robert Hodgson:

What seems more likely than that Zog should come to an untimely end is that he will deteriorate and become a small-size, indolent oriental potentate. . . . He has already lost much of the power of decision which characterised him a few years ago, and he seems to be gradually losing his hold on the threads of government.[13]

Slow Progress

King Zog told Parliament in 1928:

> We are decided, with your collaboration, to begin a new period of wide reforms in our social life. The customs imposed by the various occupations of past times, which are unsuitable to the character and interest of our nation, shall be made to yield place to the customs of civilised peoples. We will not permit the desired reforms to be pushed to excess in respect of things which are not harmful to the Albanian race; on the other hand, We will not permit the continuance of those retrograde customs that damage the State morally and materially. We must understand that the geographical position of our State forces Albania as soon as possible to enter the ranks of civilised States.[1]

His internal policy, he informed reporters, was 'to try and leap over a few centuries when all was decay, and bring Albania into line with modern ideas and modern needs'.[2]

While blaming the Ottomans for the state of his realm, Zog indisputably derived part of his notion of modernisation from the Young Turk ideology which he had espoused in his youth. He could also draw (unacknowledged) inspiration from the contemporaneous efforts of Kemal Atatürk to modernise Turkey itself. Legislation ended polygamy in Albania, abolished the veil, banned unseemly combinations of western and traditional clothing, established secular law, and introduced regular surnames. Endeavours were made to standardise the language on the basis of the Elbasan dialect.

The problem with these reforms was enforcement. Outside the towns, Albanians continued to view the state with suspicion. What was the chieftain of Mati to them? To counter this predisposition to anarchy, Zog needed to show that national government conferred benefits. The premium could be education, health care, transport, electrification, anything that clearly improved living standards. Unfortunately, however, the government could still not afford to do much, as there was no serious effort at fiscal reform. Income tax remained a farce, and plans to replace the tithe with a land tax never materialised, as Zog still shrank from confronting the rich. In the short term, he had the Italian *SVEA* loan to bridge the gap between revenue and expenditure. For the long term, he looked to royalties from oil concessions.

The fierce competition for prospecting rights in 1923–5 had given rise to great expectations. Strikes were made. The oil was there. Why did the bonanza not occur? It transpired that Albanian oil was saturated with bitumen, which made it so thick and heavy that it could not easily be pumped unless refined or heated, and declining bitumen prices led all the firms to suspend operations in 1930. Anglo-Persian Oil retained the Patos field on a 'stand-still' rent for a few years till financial desperation drove Zog to demand that the company either work the concession or abandon it. To his dismay, Anglo-Persian took the second option and left Albania in 1934; superior oil could be had much more cheaply in the Middle East. The minor oil firms also quit, leaving *Azienda Italiana Petroli Albania* a monopoly. Lacking alternative energy sources, Italians sank enough wells to be taking 175,000 tons a year by 1939. This brought £40,000 into the Albanian exchequer, but it was not the outcome which Zog had desired.

Nor could other mineral reserves deliver instant prosperity to Albania. 'Her rocks are a geologist's delight, for numberless specimens exist, but a prospector's despair, for the quantities are almost always too small to be worth working.'[3] In time, the prospectors in fact discovered significant amounts of coal, iron, and chrome, but large-scale mining hardly began before the Second World War. Though get-rich-quick fantasies lingered in the minds of reformers, modernisation would have to be financed by more piecemeal economic growth – from a very low base.

According to official statistics, the number of 'industrial concerns' rose from 127 in 1928 (employing 2,000 workers) to 244 (with 7,435 workers) in 1938. Nearly all of them processed agricultural products: cheese, olive-oil, flour, cigarettes, and tomato purée. They generated no more than 5 per cent of national income. When people called Korça 'the Manchester of Albania', the sobriquet was entirely relative. Only eight towns had over 5,000 inhabitants.

The King continued to appeal to foreign capitalists, but genuine commercial investment by companies unconnected to the Italian Government was minimal. The flotation of the Albanian National Brewery Company in London in 1929 turned into a well-publicised fiasco, after the prospectus added a nought to the annual beer consumption figure. Equally embarrassing was the visit in 1930 of an American millionaire, who negotiated for public works contracts and offered $22 million for a tobacco monopoly. The King invested him with the Order of Skanderbeg. Then the millionaire left, his cheques all bounced, and Zog learnt that he had hosted John Dekay, a notorious criminal.

Domestic capital for industrialisation could only come from an agricultural surplus which did not yet exist. Peasants engaged in subsistence farming, because market towns were so distant and communications so slow that produce would have rotted in transit. Lack of access also prevented exploitation of the forests which covered a third of the country. The Ministry of Agriculture promoted stock-breeding and tobacco-growing, but Albanian cigarettes were unfit for export. Plans to revive the highland economy with silkworms and vines came to nothing. Even where market-based farming was viable, entrepreneurial spirit was scarce. A clansman prided himself on being a good fighter rather than a good farmer. Tosk peasants were too poor to build up businesses, while their beys were too rich to bother. Sixty per cent of arable land belonged to 150 individuals. Enterprising people emigrated.

Intellectually, the King understood the need to give farmers the means and motive to grow more. Politically, he hesitated, for fear of upsetting forty-odd great landowning families, with names like Vërlaci, Vrioni, Libohova, and Vlora. They had supported him at the end of 1924 precisely because his return lifted the threat of land confiscation posed by Noli. Agrarian reform had then been synonymous with Bolshevism in Albanian politics – until 1929 when the press suddenly extolled its merits. The new cabinet employed an Italian economist to draw up a scheme, and the King went into print in its support:

> It is clear to us that the results, which our reforms in this area will produce, must be good, even when many people today still view what we are about to do with less than friendly glances. Those who do not want to understand the current situation will have to learn that national interests take priority over all others.[4]

By Zogist standards, this qualified as straight talking.

Under the Agrarian Reform Bill, each landlord would enjoy inalienable possession of up to forty hectares of land, plus an extra five hectares for his wife and each child. Of land held in excess of this limit, one-third would be expropriated at twenty gold francs per hectare and resold to the peasants on easy terms over ten years. The landlord could retain the other two-thirds provided that he worked the land to its capacity. This was the most radical piece of legislation ever presented to the Chamber of Deputies, which suddenly came to life, as the magnates hotly protested, led by Shevqet Vërlaci. The King's usual techniques of parliamentary management had little effect, for what bribes could induce rich men to surrender their property? Compensation would not even be in cash but in shares in an agricultural bank. How far might the beys go in their opposition? The King worried about the attitude of the Italian

Legation. Instead of praising the reform, Sola was going out of his way to show favour to the very beys who obstructed it.

After months of delay, Zog used loyal Gheg votes to get a version of the Bill onto the statute book, but this was merely a matter of saving face. Land registration proceeded at a pace so sluggish that beys had plenty of time to subdivide estates among their relatives; only a few thousand hectares changed hands under a reform programme practically aborted. Albanian farming remained primitive. Peasants did well to make one gold franc per day. When harvests were bad, they went hungry. 'Better a dog in America than a man in Albania,' said poor Tosks.

With neither minerals nor agriculture yielding substantial profits, the only significant investor in Albania was the *SVEA* development company, disbursing the 50 million gold francs borrowed from Italy. Half the money went on building hundreds of miles of roads and over a thousand bridges to link the towns of the western lowlands. The Italian engineers also struggled to improve some mountain roads, all of which made a considerable impact. In 1923, there had been only three cars in the entire country. By 1938, there were about two thousand. When the first bicycle reached Mati in 1936, women screamed and men asked where the bullet came out. By then, many mountaineers were already used to seeing the 'silver birds' of *Ala Littoria* overhead. Zogu originally granted the air monopoly to Adria-Aero-Lloyd, but this small private company was bought up by the Italian Government. Tirana airport offered flights to Shkodra, Vlora, Korça, Salonika, and Brindisi. They operated at a loss, courtesy of the Italian taxpayer. Nationalists boasted that Albania progressed straight to the aeroplane from the mule, which was one way of saying that it was the only European nation – besides Andorra – without railways.

The new roads made the kingdom easier to govern. Whether they made economic sense was questionable. Few Albanians wanted to travel from one end of the country to the other. Small local projects to link fertile valleys to towns might have stimulated growth by allowing specialised farming. Instead, Albania had national trade routes and virtually nothing to trade. What commercial need was satisfied by spending 8 million francs on Durrës harbour? The nation exported olives, cheese, tobacco, and hides in very small quantities. In 1933, imports were worth 15.9 million and exports 5.7 million gold francs.

The combination of regular ferry links, better roads, and a desire for foreign currency encouraged Zog to found the *Klubi Turistik Automobilistik Mbretnor* to provide tourist information:

This thriving country, seen from the air, seems to glitter and shimmer under a bright sun amid the encircling majestic heights of the mountains, leaving the observer a well-stored memory of the

ageless mystery of the country, the charming graciousness of the
people, and scenery never to be forgotten. . . . The Albanians are by
far the most hospitable people in South Eastern Europe. Their doors
are never closed and a friend can never ask too much. They are
charmingly naive in their manners and delightfully quaint in their
customs. There is nothing of the hurried, hysterical existence in
Albania; the natives are leisurely and get the full benefit out of their
sunny, mellow days. . . . The price one pays a day in the average
European capital would serve for three or four luxurious days in
Albania. . . . The vacationer lives as only he has dreamed possible. . . .
There are countless large and small restaurants throughout the
country – spotlessly clean – serving the most delicious tasty food –
European, American, or Oriental. . . . The old saying of 'being killed
with kindness' is literally true in this unique kingdom.[5]

Despite much more in similar vein on the historic mosques and
monasteries, excellent hunting, and curative waters of Shpat –
'considered usurpers of Carlsbad' – foreigners failed to come. The only
real step in the direction of mass tourism was the building of a hotel on
the beach at Durrës in 1938.

With the economy stagnant in early 1930s, little could be expended on
social welfare. The Italian loan paid for a couple of showpiece hospitals,
and the Rockefeller Foundation drained some malarial swamps. It was a
modest start to tackling daunting health challenges: tuberculosis in the
mountains, malaria on the plains, syphilis and malnutrition everywhere.
Life expectancy was thirty-eight years in 1938, when there were a
hundred doctors (one to every ten thousand people). The majority had
to rely on traditional medicine. A cure for typhus was sugar and frog guts,
placed warm on the sufferer's head. In some villages, if someone had
fever, everyone stopped work and fasted to avoid upsetting the stomach
of the sick person.

'The country's crying need is education,' said the King, whose words
adorned many a classroom wall: 'The people who have the best schools in
the world will be the leaders of the world: if not today then tomorrow.'[6]
In the decade to 1937, the number of elementary schools rose by 14 per
cent. The number of pupils nearly doubled in that time, according to
ministry figures, for attendance was compulsory where possible from
1934. That still meant that under 40 per cent of the relevant age-group
went to school. Eighteen secondary schools had 4,627 pupils, and 428
Albanians were at university abroad. Four out of five Albanians still could
not read, but it has to be remembered that serious efforts to combat mass
illiteracy had only begun in 1920. Time was needed for there to be
enough literate people capable of teaching the rest.

In fact, all the reforms required time – and an evolution in popular attitudes which could only come from the passing of several generations. Young apostles of westernisation expected the overnight transformation of Albania and blamed Zog when it did not occur. He complained that the idealists underestimated the difficulty of remoulding their compatriots after a thousand years of misdevelopment. 'We must make long and rapid strides towards the culture of western civilization,' he reiterated in 1937, though public lectures on sanitation and weaving looked more like small steps.[7] There was yet substance to the boast of greater change in a decade than in the previous four centuries. An American, taken to the right places in Tirana, Durrës, and Korça, could summarise King Zog's Albania as, 'New schools, new hospitals, new barracks, new government buildings, new business blocks, new factories, new harbour facilities, new highways, new homes, new bridges, new pavements, new foreign legations, new residential sub-divisions, new everything.'[8]

At the same time, the majority of Albanians carried on as before, scraping a living from the soil, conducting themselves according to the Law of Lek, and knowing no way of life except their own. Outsiders were not meant to see this, and old hands at Near Eastern travel gave offence when they said that Albania seemed more Turkish than Turkey did by the 1930s, what with fezzes and veils, and calls from the minaret in Arabic. Zog tried to turn the comparison with Atatürk to advantage:

> He was convinced that the Turks of today were largely influenced by Bolshevik methods. They were . . . creating a gulf between the past and the present which was not a good thing. To his mind, conservatism in itself was not a bad thing. He hoped to use it as the base upon which to build up the future and to modify it according to the practical needs of the country.[9]

No doubt many Albanians resented being told how to behave by foreign-educated youngsters. Secular society distressed devout Muslims. Clansmen wanted children to tend goats rather than go to school. To critics, however, Zog's failure to impose reforms with more rigour revealed not sensitivity but indolence, or at least a wish to let sleeping dogs lie.

Above all, his refusal to grapple with tax reform and his climbdown over land reform damned him in the eyes of intelligent observers. Nobody expected the King to engineer an economic boom during a world slump, but he might have laid the foundations of market agriculture and state solvency. The evil consequences of turning a blind eye to these fundamental problems were political as well as financial. Contrary to his pledge, Zog had manifestly failed to teach the beys that 'national interests take priority over all others'. Daring in the pursuit of power, he appeared to be losing his nerve in the exercise of it. Procrastination characterised the whole regime; the time-lag between the conception of a project and its adoption preceded a still greater delay before its execution. Often the money ran out, but even cheap reforms seemed to be repeated several times over, since the preliminaries dragged on for years. The ban on women wearing veils, finally enacted in 1937, is a prime example.

Surveying development in the mid-1930s, Ronald Matthews made three points. King Zog needed to spend more on the peasantry and less on boulevards and bureaux, to tax people with wealth instead of those without, and to stop devoting half the entire budget to the armed forces. Matthews described Albanian progressives as 'a group of people, sometimes corrupt, more often well-intentioned, perpetually talking and almost always inefficient, setting about the building of a nation on the principles of *The Cherry Orchard*'. When asked about finance, they often answered, 'Oh, we can get money from Italy.'[10]

Since material advance depended on public investment, and the state budget depended on Italian subsidies, the progress of Albania was crucially bound up with Italian foreign policy and international relations in the Mediterranean. This explained a lot about the priorities of *SVEA*, at least to opponents of the so-called experiment in international collaboration. The Bari–Durrës ferry was an Italian troop-ship thinly disguised, Tirana aerodrome resembled an Italian airforce base, and the new roads led to the frontier. No wonder Italy did not press the King to persist with land reform. Albania was to be developed, not as a viable nation, but as a dependency.

'It is not a country. It is not even a possibility,' said Mussolini. 'We are pouring money into Albania and we shall have to go on doing so, or Zog will tumble back into the arms of Yugoslavia. He thinks he has the best of us because that choice is always open to him, but some day we'll have a return for our money and our work. You know that anything that gets done over there is done by *us*.'[11]

CHAPTER TWENTY-SEVEN

Debtor and Creditor

Italian dominance in Albania was never a secret. Nobody in authority would publicly acknowledge it, but the truth was plain to see. An opulent new Italian Legation opened right next to the palace in Tirana in 1928. Cars on Boulevard Mussolini were nearly all Fiats, carrying the Italian officers, engineers, agronomists, surveyors, and doctors who came to spend the *SVEA* loan. By 1930, 245 Italians 'assisted' the Albanian Government: in addition to 100 army officers, there were 47 in the Ministry of Public Works, 29 in the Finance Ministry, and 39 at Education. Italians ran the airports and harbours. Italian concessionaires extracted raw materials. Italian farmers leased land near strategic sites. Italy broadcast an Albanian radio service from Bari. In cafés, alongside the picture of the King now hung a second portrait: 'Benito Mussolini, Duce of Fascism, loyal friend of Albania.'[1]

In interviews, Zog felt the need to make a point and labour it:

We have no intention of surrendering our independence to any other nation. I can only point to history. Albania is the only country in the Balkans which has always maintained her independence in spite of many invasions. The character of the Albanian race is based on a love of freedom under their own chiefs. We will never allow ourselves to be ruled by Italy. The people will never submit to Italian domination. . . . We are still a nation, and our own masters, and we will never allow ourselves to be dictated to or exploited in the interests of another.[2]

At the same time, he would catalogue the material benefits which the Italian connection brought to Albania. The associated perils did not require any elaboration. 'A friend's embrace,' Zog told General Percy, 'when the friend becomes over-intimate, is prone to become a hug, and a hug may mean broken bones.' He had 'no thought of getting Albania's ribs broken for her'.[3]

The Duce assured the King that he could reckon on Italian friendship as 'perfectly loyal, deeply sincere and scrupulously careful not to commit any action or utter any word that could be interpreted as an intervention in the internal affairs of the Albanian state'.[4] Just as predictably, he remarked in private: 'Zog knew he would have to be a puppet.'[5] Pulling the strings in Tirana was the Italian Minister. Ugo Sola relied on invincible patience and untiring repetition. He did not expect honesty or consistency from Zog. Conversation between equals in Albania, he recognised, was a decorous ritual of compliment and confirmation. Offensive truths were always to be avoided; oblique approaches were best. When instructed to promote the independence of the Albanian Orthodox Church from the Greek Patriarchate, Sola instead plied the King with arguments for the ecclesiastical status quo. His perplexed interpreter challenged him afterwards. 'Ah, you don't know Zog,' was the reply.[6] A few months later, the Church took its next step towards autocephalous status. Perhaps Sola was familiar with the Albanian proverb: 'Do not ask your friend for advice; ask your enemy and then do the opposite.'

Diplomatic interviews put the King on the defensive. 'He is naturally shy,' Robert Parr noted, 'and his consciousness of the limits of his education and of his knowledge of the world greatly increases his reserve.'[7] Unless sure of his ground, Zog preferred to smile, listen, and refer to his problems by veiled allusions. Only the Italians managed to provoke him to visible anger:

> Occasionally, very rarely, he would utter a 'No' which had the force and immediacy of a rifle-shot. Then the man would become transformed; blood would drain from his face, his features became drawn, his lips a thin line, into his eyes would come a fixed, gloomy, almost malicious look. He suddenly seemed twenty years older. He would twist his moustache nervously with his left hand, while pressing the sides of his chair with his arms.[8]

Usually, however, he was so suspicious that he was at great pains to hide his suspicion. He adopted 'a dry, ironical-humorous way of talking', which allowed his infrequent forays into frankness to be made with a jesting tone.[9] 'When I agree, you still won't be content,' he told Sola at the end of a meeting. 'You'll only be wanting something else. So why the hurry?'[10]

It is noticeable that foreigners usually credited Zog with 'a humorous outlook on life', while Albanians reported quite the reverse.[11] There are two explanations for this. The King thought it necessary to seem dignified before his subjects, who were not especially known for jocularity. The intelligentsia however saw a sense of the absurd as a mark of sophistication: they remarked on Zog's lack of it in order to put him down. With his sisters, he actually enjoyed occasional banter and even gave a parrot to Senije which shrieked, 'Horrid woman! You liar!'[12]

Despite his comparative informality with foreign envoys, he did expect to be flattered, and no compliment was too extravagant for him.

Albania's problems were at an end, said Sola, now it was ruled by 'one of the ablest men in Europe'.[13] His vanity was seen as another feature of the oriental psychology, like his aversions to haste and straight answers. Quaroni wrote that Zog 'was an odd mixture of positive and negative' qualities: 'Complex, tortuous, diffident, he had a fundamental decency and honesty.'[14]

Sola himself might not have agreed. Even his patience had been exhausted by the time he left in 1930, 'disgusted with the Albanian and all his works'. He felt satisfied, however, that he had finished building Italy's special position: it only remained for his successor 'to give his creation a coat of paint'.[15] This was overly sanguine. The Marchese di Soragna never acquired so deft a technique of handling Zog, and he inherited from Sola an incipient problem in the shape of their compatriot, General Pariani, Head of His Majesty's Military Household.

Alberto Pariani is mainly remembered as the Chief of the Italian Army Staff from 1936 whose wildly optimistic assessment of Italian might egged Mussolini on to ever greater bellicosity. He has since been described as 'a cold-blooded maniac . . . totally divorced from reality'.[16] In Tirana, 1928–33, the rigidity of his mind was already growing apparent. Pariani believed that an Italo-Yugoslav war was 'not only inevitable but necessary'.[17] To guarantee control of the Adriatic, Italy would need its ally to hold back the Yugoslavs in the opening days while it ferried troops across to Durrës and Vlora. For this, the General judged, Albania would require a standing army of ten thousand men, with three hundred Italian officers, plenty of modern weaponry, and a network of fortifications.

Thus it came about that Albania around 1930 was devoting a higher proportion of public spending to the military than almost any other nation in Europe. Quantities of matériel were imported from Italy, and the *SVEA* loan paid for ugly army camps near most of the larger towns, where the bugle became a common sound. With a world disarmament conference in the offing, Zog lamely pointed to educational benefits as justification: Albanian barracks were 'schools of patriotism and of discipline'.[18]

The Italians were delighted that the King seemed so ready to take Pariani's advice. 'The army is now thoroughly efficient,' Luigi Villari could report after two years. 'Military service is popular, and the Italian officers have succeeded in gaining the confidence and affection of the men.'[19] Such lies told the Duce what he wanted to hear. Insubordination was endemic, ammunition vanished onto the black market, and conscripts were crippled by foot ailments, having never worn boots before. With uniforms in rags after six months, youths spent a year-and-a-half loafing about on dismal parade grounds.

King Zog took a realistic view of the military value of his army. With the Italians, however, he encouraged the delusion that its transformation into an efficient fighting machine only needed a little more time and a little more money, and Pariani doggedly pursued his goal. New barracks and forts were excellent news for provision merchants (and brothel-keepers). The General, with his ever open purse, became the best liked Italian in the land.

Official speeches and press editorials constantly testified to the warmth of Italo-Albanian friendship. Otherwise there were few signs of it. In Tirana, Italians kept to their own hotels and cafés, saying that Albanian ones grossly overcharged them. Sullen hostility and derision were the commonest local attitudes to rich *makaronis*, many of whom came to regard the Albanians as shiftless rogues: too proud to work, not too proud to scrounge. Each group seemed to think the other stupid, and Albanians felt no gratitude for new roads, schools, and hospitals. Why should they? Italy had made them borrow the money to pay for them, often at an inflated price, since the tendering process was rigged.

Therefore King Zog had constantly to reckon with underlying opposition to his pro-Italian stance; and, naturally, young men in suits, the prime beneficiaries of Italian-funded westernisation, objected more than most to arrogant Italian colonialism. Foreign observers feared that Zog, unable to free himself from the coils of Italy, was preparing instead to pander to the nationalists by challenging Yugoslavia over Kosovo. What else could explain his apparent enthusiasm for Pariani's militarism?

The answer began to emerge in 1930. That was the year when Albania received the last instalment of the *SVEA* loan, and had supposedly to start repayment. Everyone knew that default, more loans, rescheduling, cancellation, or foreclosure were the only possibilities. But first came a war of nerves. To show willing, the Albanian Treasury scraped together 900,000 gold francs for *SVEA*. Then Zog admitted that he could see no way of paying the full instalment without huge defence cuts. He might even have to phase out the army entirely. It saddened him to think that Pariani's excellent work would all go to waste, but alas!

Back in 1928, the appointment of an Italian general to King Zog's military household had been seen as a cunning move on the part of Mussolini: while Sola cajoled, Pariani could bully. In practice, however, Zog had turned the situation to his advantage. Faced with two Italian representatives with different priorities, he ingratiated himself with the military mission and exploited the divergence. Whenever Soragna piled on the pressure, Zog could squeeze the army, and Pariani squealed. That left the Italians to argue among themselves, and there was every chance that the Duce would support the sabre-rattling General.

This mechanism worked like a charm in 1931. Soragna went on saying until April that fresh loans were out of the question. In June, the Italian Government agreed to lend Albania enough money each year to bridge the gap between revenue and expenditure, up to a maximum of ten million gold francs (roughly the cost of the Albanian army). Zog, who negotiated the deal himself, thanked his 'Dear and great Friend' in Rome for this 'magnificent gesture'.[20] The loan programme, intended to last ten years, would be subject to annual renewal, conditional on the 'continuation of full and sincere technical and political collaboration'.

On the face of it, this gave the Italians great leverage, but Zog felt so confident in 1931 that he began to push his luck almost at once. The Pact of Tirana, whereby Italy had proclaimed its sphere of influence in 1926, was due to expire in November. Mussolini had proposed renewing it during the loan discussions, but Zog had persuaded him to wait for the sake of appearances, lest anyone say that Rome was buying its special relationship with Tirana. When Soragna next raised the issue, however, he coolly replied that Albania no longer wanted Italy to underwrite its political status quo: 'If after the Pact of Tirana has been in operation for five years, the regime it was intended to buttress still stood in need of support, that regime must surely be a poor thing, doing little credit either to the King himself or to the Italian effort to help him.'[21]

Soragna retorted that the current calmness of the kingdom was actually a direct consequence of the Pact of Tirana, so its lapse might well give the cue to rebels and bandits. The threat was not very subtle. Nor were the delays that suddenly affected subsidy payments. It was the old loan agreement, however, which allowed Italy to exert most pressure. Mussolini had 'persuaded' *SVEA* to grant Albania a moratorium on its debt in 1931. Zog now heard that this would not be extended. Unless eight million gold francs were repaid by 15 January 1932, Italy could invoke its right to take over Albanian customs and state monopolies.

The King did not panic. For one thing, so many countries were defaulting on debt in the early 1930s that foreclosure would have caused an international outcry. For another, he could repeat his proven tactic: Albania would cut its army to nothing in order to pay *SVEA*. It was obvious but it worked: Italy advanced 500,000 francs within a week; *SVEA* agreed a fresh moratorium in March.

Thus King Zog had freed his country from the most flagrant legal infraction of its sovereignty, the Pact of Tirana, without incurring any financial penalty. Surely this should convince the restive young nationalists that their King was not a mere puppet? The Italian Legation consoled itself with the reflection that the end of the Pact made no practical difference to its preponderant position. But how much was that position really worth? Italy had now spent around a billion lire on its ally since 1926, without reaping any significant reward. One embarrassed Italian diplomat protested, 'You wouldn't believe how much poetry there is in the attitude of Mussolini towards Albania.'[22]

In July 1932, the Duce resumed direct control of the Italian Foreign Ministry. This in itself did not signal any change in the patron–client relationship, since he had insisted on supervising policy towards 'the young allied nation' even when Grandi was the Foreign Minister. However, his choice of chief of cabinet should have struck Zog as ominous: it was Baron Aloisi, the man who had defeated him in the diplomatic stand-off of 1926. Six years on, Aloisi surveyed Albanian affairs with a sharp eye – and he did not much like what he saw.

CHAPTER TWENTY-EIGHT

Hard Times

Italo-Albanian wrangling over debt was becoming an annual fixture. In January 1933, Zog once more informed the Italians – for small nations 'cannot afford to be anything but frank' – that he would not be able to find eight million francs for *SVEA* in the coming year without decimating the army.[1] Albania was already 23 million in arrears, but no one seriously expected anything else. What angered the Italians was rather the Albanian attitude: Zog imperfectly recognised their right to call the tune.

The first sign that he was not going to have so easy a ride this year was a secret proposal (direct from Aloisi) for customs union between Italy and Albania. The King promptly leaked it to Reuters, and this had the desired effect. When Yugoslavia, Great Britain, and France voiced concern, the Italian Foreign Ministry first denied all and then claimed that it was Zog who had raised the idea and Mussolini who rejected it. The Albanian saw no need to put the record straight but pressed on with his own agenda.

Was it not time to face the fact that rapid economic growth was impossible in a poor little country in the depths of a world depression? What Albania needed, he argued, was not another one-year moratorium but thorough revision of the *SVEA* contract. When this was refused, he waxed indignant:

He himself, it was true, had placed Albania in her present predicament, for it was he who had shackled her with the *SVEA* loan. He had done so trusting to the fair words of his creditors, who had assured him time and time again . . . that the signature to the contract was a formality, that he could with complete tranquillity accept the obligations to which he was putting his name inasmuch as he would never be pressed to meet them. . . . Yet now when the burden has become intolerable, he finds no disposition on the part of his creditors to alleviate Albania's lot.[2]

He talked about taking his case to the League of Nations. What was *SVEA* anyway? 'Nothing more than a screen which the Italian Government has set up to suit its own convenience.'[3]

The new Italian Minister in Tirana was having none of this. Armando Koch, a small, jerky young man, full of garrulous self-confidence, owed his promotion to Aloisi and shared his resolve to take Zog down a peg. It came to the usual point: without an agreement on rescheduling debt by 31 March, the King warned, he would have to reduce the army to 2,000 men. 'A very good thing to do,' replied Koch '– it is all you can afford.'[4]

The King had heard that sort of talk before. But what would General Pariani say? The dogmatic soldier was as anxious as ever to preserve his departmental budget. Yet Zog underestimated Koch. This Italian Minister admitted quite openly what his predecessor merely hinted: that Pariani's military build-up in Albania since 1928 had been 'a complete fiasco'.[5] He did so in the knowledge that Baron Aloisi was working to convince Mussolini that Italian strategic interests would be adequately met by a naval base (at Durrës), an airbase (at Tirana), and thirty military advisers.

The 31 March passed without any deal. The King went on threatening massive defence cuts, unaware of how pointless this tactic had become. Enlightenment began to dawn on him when Italy recalled all its officers from His Majesty's Military Household. General Pariani, an Italian ally in more ways than one, left on 30 April. Incensed, Zog at once packed the Military Household with Albanian placemen, but this intended snub entirely missed its mark. Mussolini now appreciated how dual representation in Tirana had misfired. Henceforth the residue of Italian soldiers, more or less genuine instructors, would answer to the Legation.

This was a serious blow to Zog, who lost his favourite device for evading Italian financial pressure. What would the Italians now want in return for a moratorium? Sooner than wait to find out, he had seized the initiative even before Pariani departed. His choice of battleground may seem odd: failing defence, education. In April 1933, Albania suddenly banned private schools.

This had been desired for some time by nationalistic 'New Albanians', who objected to independent schools, because many were religious foundations subsidised from abroad. The previous autumn had seen some steps towards reorganising education; now the whole system was nationalised at a stroke and plunged into confusion. Nearly sixty private schools, including the leading secondary schools, closed within weeks, even in places lacking any alternative state provision. Where state schools existed, they could not cope with the extra pupils.

Why should this matter to Italy? The closure of seventeen Roman Catholic schools would mark the end of an historic conduit of influence to northern Albania: virtually all the teachers had been Italian-born or Italian-educated. Italians had helped found Albanian secondary schooling, in order that theirs would become the second language. Nationalisation was a rejection of Italian culture. Mussolini had lately denounced restrictions on Italian language-teaching in Malta. To be insulted by the British Empire was bad enough, but by Albania? The closure of private schools, fumed Koch, 'was an act of crass and reasoned spitefulness'.[6]

Zog's response was downright flippant: 'it was his custom, whenever he had taken a decision, to put it into effect without delay – more especially if it was a wrong one'.[7] The reform, he argued, advanced his policy of minimising religious differences, yet it is hard to resist the conclusion that he expected Italy to buy a compromise: Roman Catholic and Italophone education in return for a generous debt settlement.

Mussolini refused to oblige. The 1931 Italo-Albanian loan presupposed 'cordial collaboration'. Koch told the King that, unless this base insult to Italy were withdrawn, Albania could expect no more financial assistance. The axe fell on 18 May: contractors departed on the Bari ferry, leaving roads, bridges, and schools unfinished.* Most Italian advisers in government service followed, as the subsidy had paid their salaries.

By June, the deadlock was complete. Koch would not discuss money until Albania reversed the school closures, and Zog would not discuss schools until Italy continued the 10 million annual loan. The King told Percy (not for the first time) that Albania was finished with Italy. Mussolini was equally adamant that Zog should 'go to Canossa' (a reference to Henry IV's submission to the Pope in 1077).[8] The Italian Legation, Koch observed with menace, had worked hard in the past to prevent unrest among the Roman Catholic clans. Zog ordered 260 more gendarmes to Shkodra and retired to his beach-bungalow complaining of stomach pains. Economies took the simplest form: state employees went unpaid.

With government and diplomacy at a standstill, the dramatic news of the summer was the assassination of Hassan Bey Prishtina, Zog's old Italophil rival, at a café in Salonika on 14 August. The timing seemed more than a coincidence. Condemned *in absentia* in 1928, Prishtina had since been flitting between Rome, Vienna, Budapest, Sofia, and Istanbul, pursued by Zogist agents. People speculated that the King had him murdered to thwart the Italian secret service and cow other anti-Zogist émigrés.

After this act of defiance came an effort at appeasement. A royal decree on 29 August made Italian a compulsory subject in secondary schools and required that 80 per cent of scholarship students attend Italian universities. Not enough, said Koch, who held out for the reopening of all confessional schools. He even confronted the King with an exercise book covered in corrections to show that the Italian lessons given by Albanian teachers were awful. By now, Zog was trapped by his own propaganda. To whip up public support, he had presented the state

---

* They also left 160,000 francs worth of dressed stone beside the castle mound at Burgajet. Zog had been planning to rebuild his ancestral home. The stone was destined never to be used.

monopoly of education as an issue of profound importance, making it hard for himself to offer any further compromise.

When Parliament met in October, its task was to sanction spending cuts of 20–30 per cent across the board (including the civil list). 'We express our very great satisfaction at the lofty virtues of the Albanian people,' said His Majesty, which, 'now in the period of grievous crisis, is showing the greatest self-sacrifice'.[9] One of the ironies of the situation was that the armed services still swallowed half the budget, as, when it came to it, he shrank from dismissing many of his eight hundred army and gendarmerie officers for fear of their turning against him. Only the navy swiftly contracted to ten men. Civil servants took a 22 per cent cut in salaries already six months in arrears. Many *alla Franka* shops soon closed for lack of trade.

Zog returned to Tirana on Independence Day to silence fresh stories that he was dying. Against expectation, the celebrations were especially lavish this year. It was the twenty-first anniversary of 1912, and he had to try and hide his financial weakness from the clans. Torrential storms washed out the parades, but the evening saw half a dozen public dinners and a grand ball at the Foreign Ministry. The Albanians' hospitableness embarrassed the British Minister, but 'To them there is nothing incongruous in regaling guests with Mumm Cordon Rouge while they themselves are on the border of starvation'.[10]

National pride was meant to sustain the Albanians. Rumour had it that the quarrel really concerned a plan to colonise the coastal plain with Italian immigrants. Intellectuals once again took up the cry of 'The Balkans for the Balkan people', and the press carried favourable references to Yugoslavia for the first time since 1926. Zog had the audacity to ask King Alexander as early as June 1933 for a loan of 2.5 million gold francs.

The Yugoslavs viewed the rift between Tirana and Rome with satisfaction but did not rush to exploit it. Their expansionist ambitions had faded away in the face of internal troubles. King Alexander now insisted, 'I would not take Albania as a gift.'[11] The chief Yugoslav interest was simply that the Italo-Albanian estrangement should continue. This meant providing a modicum of succour to Zog (to prevent him despairing and giving in to Mussolini) while refraining from bold anti-Italian intervention (which might impel Mussolini to submit to Zog). There would be no dinars for the bankrupt Albanians but plenty of kind words.

The main plank of Yugoslav foreign policy at this time was the creation of the Balkan Pact, signed in Athens on 9 February 1934. Yugoslavia, Greece, Romania, and Turkey mutually guaranteed the security of all their Balkan frontiers. The signatory nations had such diverse objectives that the Pact was bound to be a shaky alliance, yet Zog desperately desired an invitation to take part, if only to show the Italians that Albania had other friends. The Yugoslavs were actually willing to consider Albanian involvement, but the Greeks vetoed it. Nevertheless, Zog could anticipate that the Balkan Pact – intended by Yugoslavia to promote unity against Italian expansion – would work to his advantage. If Mussolini had four Balkan countries ganged up against him, would he not indulge his little Balkan ally? Again, the Greek Foreign Minister dashed Zog's hopes. So emphatically did Demetrios Maximos proclaim that Greece had no intention of being dragged into any war against a Great Power that the Pact lost its anti-Italian thrust.

The Greek Government was generally in no mood to help him. Nationalisation of Albanian education had destroyed schools for Greek-speakers in the south. Athens accused Tirana of violating minority rights and appealed to the League of Nations. Zog made concessions in 1934 but failed to halt the bitter war of words. At one point, he threatened to dismiss every Greek-Albanian in public service, and there was also talk of swamping the Greek minority district with refugees from Kosovo.

When, eventually, the Permanent Court of International Justice gave its advisory opinion in favour of Greece, Albania complied in full and Greek private schools reopened. 'A death blow' to national unity, grumbled Zog, if only for the sake of form.[12] However well it had played with Albanian nationalists, the dispute with Greece had proved a debilitating distraction from his real problems: an empty treasury, a deflated economy, growing urban poverty, and no sign of a resumption of Italian aid. He hit upon the formula that Italo-Albanian relations had now touched bottom and would soon improve again, but he found himself repeating this month after month. How could it be that the central mechanism of his foreign policy had jammed? Playing Italy off against Yugoslavia did not seem to work any more.

CHAPTER TWENTY-NINE

Ill Winds

Nineteen thirty-three is a year remembered for one fact above all other: Adolf Hitler became Chancellor of Germany in January and set about the construction of the Third Reich. The domestic triumph of extreme German nationalism gave a jolt to statesmen in many European capitals. But in Tirana? The German consulate-general nominally became a legation and a huge swastika went up outside. Otherwise, nothing changed in German-Albanian relations. Weimar Germany and Nazi Germany alike showed minimal interest in the country (which Zog deemed a matter for regret). Indirectly, though, the rise of Hitler rapidly had an effect on international politics in the Adriatic Sea, where, on the face of it, little had altered since the Italo-Albanian and Franco-Yugoslav alliances of 1927.

Italo-Yugoslav relations remained bad – satisfactorily so, from the Albanian perspective. Mussolini funded Croat terrorism, and King Alexander had resorted to dictatorial powers to try and ward off disintegration. He complained that the Italian military presence in Albania was 'like an arrow in our body', and refused to consider any entente with Rome which did not restore Albanian neutrality.[1] Yugoslavia instinctively clung to its alliance with France, but it was here that the shock-waves from Berlin quickly made themselves felt. Faced with a German leader openly resolved to smash the Treaty of Versailles, the French hastened to revise their foreign policy priorities. Never mind the fifteen years of Mediterranean rivalry with Italy; now they wanted to reconstruct a Franco-Italian front against Germany. Ideally, this would not require the sacrifice of a Balkan ally, yet France would not be standing squarely behind Yugoslavia in future Adriatic troubles. French diplomacy aimed at Italo-Yugoslav *détente* in 1933–5, so it discouraged the Yugoslavs from taking advantage of the rift between Zog and Mussolini.

The attitude of Fascist Italy to Nazi Germany was decidedly ambivalent. 'The victory of Hitler is also our victory,' declared Mussolini in January 1933, but once he recognised that his status as Europe's great dictator was being usurped, jealousy increased his receptiveness to the argument that a resurgent Germany would threaten Italian interests.[2] Could Italy really tolerate Greater Germany on its northern border? Strategists advised Mussolini to co-operate with France in order to resist the union (*Anschluss*) of Germany and Austria. To win better relations with France, it would be necessary to go easier on Yugoslavia. The Duce himself was reluctant to modify his Balkan ambitions, but Aloisi warned him that, if Italy squeezed Yugoslavia any more, King Alexander might retaliate with a German-Yugoslav alliance. Preventing the German absorption of Austria must come first. Therefore most of the policy-makers in Rome rather welcomed the cooling of Italo-Albanian 'friendship,' on the grounds that it should calm the Yugoslavs and thereby assist a Franco-Italian *rapprochement*.

Thus one of the many repercussions of the advent of Hitler was the diplomatic isolation of Albania. King Zog was finding it unprecedentedly difficult to attract Italian attention, let alone Italian money. Hitherto Albania had been pursued and harassed by two determined suitors. Now Italy had turned its back, and, when Albania flirted with Yugoslavia, the response was too tepid to inspire jealousy. If Zog appealed to the Italian Legation for help, Koch simply told him to rescind the nationalisation of schools. Barring a humiliating climbdown, the King could only wait on international developments, in the hope of something occurring to restore his leverage.

In the meantime, the situation was bleak. For 1934–5, the Albanian budget shrank to 18 million gold francs: a drop of 40 per cent in two years. It was now that Zog issued his ill-fated ultimatum to Anglo-Persian Oil to work its concession or leave. Efforts to borrow abroad met with total failure. By driving out Italian teachers in an excess of chauvinism, surely Albania had cut off its nose to spite its face?

State employees, their wages unpaid, struggled to feed and clothe their families. The commercial boom in late 1920s Tirana had turned to bust, and discreet yet strenuous efforts were made to ensure that the odium attached to the Italian Legation rather than to the Palace. Signor Koch, the most hated man in the city, tried to regain favour by opening a soup kitchen. It attracted 1,600 people a day, till the police broke up the queues and transported the indigent back to their native villages.

With the stalemate in its second year, the sheer passivity of the Italian Government disconcerted Zog, yet nerves were also fraying at the Italian Legation, which had never expected him to hold out for so long. Koch had misjudged his antagonist: the one thing which an Albanian chief did not concede was an open gesture of submission. Even in 1934, Italians could not remain entirely indifferent to Zog's talk of adhering to the Balkan Pact, still less to rumours (false but probably officially inspired) of a secret military treaty between Albania and Yugoslavia.

At half past four in the afternoon of 23 June, nineteen Italian warships dropped anchor off Durrës. No notice had been given of their arrival. When the local prefect enquired whether this constituted a military demonstration, the first Italian officer ashore replied that, on the contrary, here was a goodwill visit by the Adriatic fleet. The Albanians nevertheless began digging trenches. More ships arrived the next day, and fear of invasion swept the nation. King Zog, however, displayed commendable calm. He refused to receive Koch and let it be known that there could be no discussion of Italo-Albanian problems until an atmosphere of serenity had been restored. The Italian Minister could only suggest that the request for Albanian permission for the naval visit must somehow have gone astray. The French Legation urged politeness on both sides.

After two days, most of the Italian squadron slipped away, and all the ships were gone within a week. The main consequence of this half-hearted essay in gunboat diplomacy was a rare (and short-lived) outpouring of domestic support for the King. Even Gjon Marka Gjoni, the senior Roman Catholic chieftain (and son of the late synonymous rebel), telegraphed to Zog that he could count on Mirdita's loyalty to the last drop of blood. This was reassuring, since relations with Italy reverted to stagnation – until stirred by extraneous events.

Engelbert Dollfuss, the Chancellor of Austria, was murdered on 25 July 1934 during an abortive Nazi coup. Mussolini rushed troops to the northern border and promised to defend Austria from German invasion. At once, the Yugoslav army also took up advance positions – to attack Italy. Yugoslavia saw Italian intervention in Austria as encirclement. There ensued three weeks of tension in the Adriatic, during which an Italian insurance-broker named Rocco called at the royal beach colony in Durrës. He was really a secret emissary from Aloisi, who wanted to talk to Zog about resuming subsidies in return for various concessions: Italian leases on naval and air bases, merging of the gendarmerie and army, Italian lessons in schools, and much else.

The old game had reopened, and the King looked forward to quibbling, stalling, cadging, and bluffing till the demands were whittled down to something acceptable. The sudden departure from Tirana of Armando Koch (blustering about 'family reasons') spoke of a fresh start, but only briefly. After a few weeks of secret discussions, Aloisi lost interest in Albania again, leaving King Zog more or less where he started. (France had been so impressed by Mussolini's anti-German stance over Austria that it increased its efforts to broker an Italo-Yugoslav entente in the autumn.) Six months after the arrival of a new Italian Minister, Zog was complaining that he had still not had any serious conversation with Baron Mario Indelli, an aloof and gloomy personage well-suited to executing a policy of masterly inactivity.

On 9 October 1934 – a vintage year for political murder – an assassin despatched King Alexander of Yugoslavia at the start of a state visit to France. The French Foreign Minister, Barthou, also died. Their killer was a Bulgarian hired by Croats. Italian complicity has never been proven, but the suspicion lingers that it may have been a last effort by Mussolini to trigger the break-up of Yugoslavia (against Foreign Ministry advice). As such, the assassination failed in its effect, and the Yugoslavs were ready to turn their fury on Italy, but French diplomats went to great lengths to restrain them, as the new Foreign Minister of France, Laval, was even keener to appease Mussolini.

Thus the Marseilles outrage created no diplomatic openings for Zog. It probably weakened his position, for, notwithstanding the war-scares, it had suited him to have a hard man in Belgrade to balance the hard man in Rome. The new Yugoslav monarch, Peter II, was eleven years old, and, under the regency of Prince Paul, the country would follow an increasingly passive policy.

The breakthrough in Italo-Albanian relations, if such it can be called, ultimately came about as a result of events more distant still. In December 1934, an Ethiopian border commission clashed with Italian-led tribesmen at Walwal on the frontier of Italian Somaliland. Within the month, Mussolini had determined on a war of conquest in Africa sometime in 1935. Great Britain and France were so preoccupied with Hitler, he reckoned, that Italy need wait no longer for its empire. Rather to the relief of his Foreign Ministry, Ethiopia replaced the Balkans as his *idée fixe*, and all that he immediately desired in the Adriatic was an end to uncertainty.

In February 1935, Italy 'had the goodness' to give Albania 'spontaneously and as a token of the sincere friendship existing between the two States a sum of three million gold francs'.[3] So much for making Zog go to Canossa. The money enabled him to pay his armed forces up to the previous November. He was so grateful that he promptly asked 'Albania's natural protector' for a loan of 15 million.[4] Financial negotiations resumed, unhurriedly but with purpose. While the League debated the Walwal incident and thousands of Italian soldiers headed for East Africa, King Zog could once more cheerfully bemoan his country's fate in terms reminiscent of the old days:

> Somehow or other, he declared, Albania would contrive to deal with her difficulties, even with the miserable revenue she manages to collect nowadays, if only people would leave her alone. They won't! The Italians are continually badgering her for her collaboration and the more they protest the purity of their intentions the less he believes in it.[5]

The Italo-Ethiopian War broke out on 3 October 1935. The League of Nations condemned Italian aggression by 50 votes to 1. Albania abstained. 'Our relations with our ally Italy, based on the Treaty of

Alliance, are very friendly,' affirmed Zog on 15 October.[6] When the League imposed sanctions, Albania refused to operate them, officially because of the likely damage to its own economy. The King did appear slightly uneasy when confronted by British diplomats. Albanian oil might at last make some money, he laughed, before changing the subject.

There was some apparent danger in early 1936 of the war in Ethiopia producing an Anglo-Italian confrontation at sea, if the British tried to enforce an oil embargo or close the Suez Canal. Eager for mastery of the Adriatic, the Italians saw their way to dropping some of the demands which Zog found objectionable (such as a forty-year lease of Durrës harbour and Italian gendarmerie inspectors) and prepared to dig deeper into their pockets. The spectacle of one weak country doing its best to profit from the demise of another was to become common enough over the next few years, but it fell to King Zog to set the precedent. After the fall of Addis Ababa, he congratulated Mussolini on a conclusive victory 'covered with imperishable glory by magnificent actions which appealed to the admiration of the whole world'.[7] Albania was the second country (after Germany) to recognise King Victor Emmanuel as Emperor of Ethiopia, just as it was the third to hail General Franco as ruler of Spain.

The new Italo-Albanian relationship rested on a package of thirteen agreements made public on 19 March 1936. For a start, the 1931 loan deal was annulled. Italy wrote off 18 million gold francs lent in its first eighteen months. Then came all the fresh credits: 9 million to cover the intervening deficits, 10 million for agricultural development, 3 million to form a state tobacco monopoly, 4 million to enlarge Durrës harbour yet further, and various lesser handouts. Albania stood to receive something in the region of 40 million gold francs between 1936 and 1940. In addition, the Italian Government 'persuaded' *SVEA* to waive all payments due to it for the next five years. Italian ministerial advisers would return, but not so many as before, and – heaven forbid that anyone should posit a link – two months later, a royal decree permitted Roman Catholic schools to reopen.

The three-year struggle between Albania and Italy came to a close. Who had won? Among international commentators, instant reaction damned the Albanians. Greek writer Doros Alastos: 'The Treaty represents nothing less than the complete capitulation of Albania to Italian Fascism.'[8] The historian Arnold Toynbee: 'an ignominious surrender which left Italy in full possession of her base of operations in the Balkans'.[9] George Slocombe: 'Albania has become an Italian colony, like Eritrea. And its chief port, Durazzo, threatens to become another Massawa, the jumping off place for the next Italian imperial adventure.'[10]

These assessments, made in the shadow of the Ethiopian War, say more about the transformation in attitudes to Mussolini than they do about the relationship between Tirana and Rome. To those who assumed that Zog's objective had been to sever his links with Italy and join the Balkan Pact, no doubt the 1936 settlement did look like total defeat. On the other hand, the King can scarcely be accused of failing to accomplish what, in all probability, he never set out to attain. Diplomats who knew the Albanian leader gave more credence to Sir Robert Hodgson's verdict: 'King Zog's obstructiveness has had its reward for he has at last succeeded in extracting money from Italy without putting his hand to a document committing him to engagements encroaching on Albania's sovereignty.'[11] That said, it had taken three years of economic paralysis, and success depended on factors beyond his control.

The budget went back up to 21 million in 1936–7 and to 26 million the following year. As the last vestiges of idealism in international relations disappeared in the late 1930s, so there emerged a grudging respect for the way in which Zog manipulated Mussolini. 'Albania has had something for nothing,' deduced one expert. Forty million francs seemed a steep price for supplying a bit of threadbare diplomatic window-dressing to the Axis. 'The Albanian does not take kindly to foreigners,' wrote Sir Charles Petrie, 'but he realizes that he cannot get on without them, so he gives the Italians as much trouble as he can, and screws the maximum out of them.'[12] It might, however, have been better for Zog had such tributes not appeared in print.

When Count Ciano, the new Italian Foreign Minister, paid a visit to Albania in April 1937, the King did his best to fete him with dinners, fireworks, flags, and the Grand Cordon of the Order of the Besa. It nevertheless seemed fitting that the top Italian at the twenty-fifth anniversary celebration of Albanian independence was Count Thaon de Reval, the Minister of Finance (bringing with him an extra two million for road improvements and an orphanage). As King Zog remarked: 'There is nothing in the world more natural than the friendship between our two peoples.'[13]

CHAPTER THIRTY

Young Men and Old Men

For Zog, the acid test of success or failure was whether or not he remained in power. His own ambition and the interests of his country seemed to him inextricable, so the mere fact that he had kept his throne between 1933 and 1935, without foreign funding, registered as a triumph. Albania had shown a degree of internal tranquillity which few would have predicted. This was a tribute to the King's ability to divide and rule the chiefs. Such money as could be scraped together had gone to the right people; that is, it had been used to appease the men who could most easily have raised forces capable of overthrowing him.

There was a perpetual and not unreasonable grievance in southern Albania that the Zogist regime heavily taxed the hard-working Tosks in order to buy off the gun-toting Ghegs. Leading southerners had recently been cowed, however, by the suppression in 1932 of the 'Secret Organisation of Vlora'. This assorted band of Tosks had met the previous year to swear on the butts of their guns to seize power in the event of King Zog's death. Since then, they had done little or nothing, but the Special Tribunal saw fit to pass seven death sentences and send thirty-odd men to prison, twelve of them for 101 years. 'Nothing in the evidence justified anything more serious than a discharge with a caution,' reported Hodgson.[1] In response to appeals for clemency, Zog commuted the death sentences. What others saw as an overreaction, he judged a timely measure to prevent any revival of the Clique. (By 1936, only five conspirators remained in gaol after numerous pardons.)

With Musa Juka and his agents working at full stretch, the worst months of Italo-Albanian estrangement passed with nothing more dramatic than the flight of Muharrem Bajraktari to disturb the peace. This chieftain and royal aide-de-camp, whose staring eyes led some to question his mental stability, withdrew to his native district in September 1934, amid rumours that he planned a revolt. When Zog at length sent soldiers after him, he joined the anti-Zogist exiles in Yugoslavia.

More significant was the gendarmerie mutiny at Fier eight months later. Local reservists gathered in the market place on 14 August 1935 on the orders of Captain Kranja, who introduced a man purporting to represent a new revolutionary government in the capital. He was actually a maverick journalist called Kosta Çekrezi, who had spent three years in prison as a Vlora plotter. While he addressed the gendarmes and oil-workers, a car pulled into the square. Out stepped General Ghilardi, who happened to be passing through Fier. Shots were fired, Ghilardi fell dead, and the fictitious revolt became a reality. Çekrezi and Kranja led 130 men to take Lushnja. When the gendarmerie there fought them, however, they retreated, and, by the time troops arrived the next morning, the rebellion was practically over.

'Such occurrences must be expected in a country like this,' King Zog told General Percy, with a simulacrum of unconcern which did not extend to his actions.[2] Eleven gendarmes were immediately shot. Then 1,000 local people were arrested, 539 tried, 160 convicted, and 42 sentenced to death. Despite signs that the Fier revolt was part of a wider conspiracy, its pathetic failure made this response appear excessive; the British Minister wrote of 'a reign of terror'.[3] Inevitably, there was suspicion that Italian agents had staged the abortive revolt in order to frighten Zog back into the fold. Anti-Zogists meanwhile tried to portray it as a nationalist uprising designed to prevent a reconciliation with Italy. Albanian revolutionaries never hurried to disclose their exact objectives. Çekrezi, a Harvard law graduate, tried in exile to win French or British funding for an anti-Italian rebellion in Albania during the Ethiopian War.

The King commuted 41 of the 42 capital sentences passed at Fier to 101 years, as the 'unanimity and rapidity with which the people prepared to take action against the enemies of the State' proved that 'the Albanian nation has developed a mature national conscience'.[4] On Independence Day, the majority of the convicts were pardoned – clemency which seemed to confirm their probable innocence.

By then, the Zogist regime had apparently embarked on a new chapter in its development. To general surprise, on 22 October 1935 the King appointed an entirely fresh cabinet unlike any of its predecessors. Of the seven ministers, six were younger than forty, only two had held office before, and not one belonged to the Old Gang. These were the 'Young Men': members of the first generation to reach maturity in independent Albania, who had grown up with nationalism and received some western education. After a twenty-year time-lag, Albanian politics appeared to be transcending the decadent ethos of the late Ottoman Empire. Interestingly, such was the precocity of Zog, that nobody remarked that this generation was actually his own.

Although, at sixty, the new Prime Minister, Mehdi Frashëri, could not himself be called a young man (except in relation to his predecessor Evangjeli), he was widely respected as a bey of exceptional honesty and consciously liberal principles. 'He is by nature a theorist and something of a dreamer,' reported the British Minister, 'but he is also an enthusiast

. . . a chief who will assuredly do his utmost to raise the moral standard – at present deplorably low – of the Administration.'[5]

This really was a change of Government rather than a reshuffle, but the King offered no explanation beyond his desire 'to give some of the younger men a chance'.[6] Was it a reaction to the Fier revolt? The Frashëri Ministry suggested an attempt by Zog to make scapegoats of the old Government and reduce his unpopularity. By 1935, the café wits were jesting that, while totalitarianism advanced elsewhere in Europe, Albania retained its two-party system: 'Ahmed Zogu on one side and the Albanian people on the other.'[7] His intention may have been to broaden his narrow base of support by promoting ministers who appealed to the urban middle-class. At the start of the Ethiopian War, furthermore, it made sense to draw young nationalists into responsibility for Albania's return to Italian tutelage.

Mehdi Bey Frashëri promised to end internment without trial and payment of informers, to replace patronage with promotion by merit, and to reform the tax system. Albania should develop into a stable constitutional kingdom, 'And one of these days soon you will see the King walking through the streets of Tirana with me on his arm. And neither of us will carry any weapon more deadly than a walking-stick.'[8]

The political departure of 1935 has come to be known as the 'liberal experiment'. The adjective fits Frashëri, and it may be justified in a comparative sense, yet liberalism (as understood by English-speakers) was not the most obvious characteristic of the emerging generation. The Young Men stood for 'New Albanian' nationalism, efficient administration, and rapid modernisation. Few of them imagined that greater democracy could advance these aims in the near future. Why trust ignorant clansmen and peasants? Young Men willing to serve King Zog envisaged an 'enlightened dictatorship' on the model of Atatürk or even Hitler.

While national unity rhetoric was very much in vogue, the impact of the new cabinet on the Chamber of Deputies was far from unifying. When Frashëri talked about the need for liberal reform, Fejzi Bey Alizoti pointedly asked: 'Which Governments in Albania have been despotic then?' Hiqmet Delvina insisted that the Old Men deserved thanks from the Young Men, and, when one youngster dubbed him 'a lick-spittle', the sitting adjourned amid uproar.[9] An angry debate over whether to end the immunity of ex-ministers accused of corruption made two things clear. First, Zog was not 'managing' the Chamber very closely any more; but, second, if left altogether to themselves, most of the deputies would have opposed the new ministry outright.

The resumption of Italian loans in 1936 allowed Frashëri to announce that Albania 'was about to enter on a new and brilliant future'.[10] The

Government committed itself to raising the school-leaving age to fifteen and introduced the first Albanian Factory Act to limit the working hours of women and children. Idealists, however, felt disappointed at the slowness of economic recovery. Urban unemployment remained high, and the 'liberals' did not hesitate to use the gendarmerie to break up a strike by oil-workers and disperse demonstrations. Even so, it was not mass disenchantment that posed the main threat to the Government.

Everyone knew that the Chamber of Deputies was coming to the end of its four-year term in the autumn of 1936. If the Young Men had the chance to 'make the elections', many of the Old Men stood to lose their seats, their salaries, and their immunity. At this prospect, the beys became markedly restive. In September, the Old Gang newspaper *Besa* published a leaked circular from the Interior Minister, Ethem Toto, to prefects, asking them to submit profiles of likely candidates. With utter hypocrisy, the Old Men professed shock at interference in the electoral process. Toto investigated the leak (with revolver in hand) and learnt to his consternation that the source was Krosi, the King's so-called foster-father.

On 6 November, the Chamber was asked to approve a decree making all adult men liable to work on roadbuilding for 16 days per year. After a perfunctory half-hour debate, it rejected the proposal by 36 votes to 3. Frashëri promptly resigned. Four days later – and just one day before the dissolution of Parliament – Kotta was endorsed by 43 votes to 1 as head of a Cabinet full of familiar Old Gang faces. Thus the 'liberal experiment' ended.

Zog was as delphic about the departure of the Young Men as he had been about their arrival. According to him, it signified no policy change whatsoever, although:

> he really preferred, he said, the late ministry, composed as it had been of young and progressive men. There were, however, certain features of the internal situation which made it advisable to employ more experienced Ministers. He knew that the change was not altogether popular. He referred in particular to the appointment of Musa Juka to the Ministry of the Interior but said that he had given him most stringent directions as to what should be avoided and had told him that, if they were not observed, he would be finished for good.[11]

People could only speculate as to the real reasons for the turnabout. Was MJ blackmailing the King? Had the Frashëri Government actually been intended as a short-term manoeuvre? Maybe Zog had designed 'the liberal experiment' to make the Old Men less complacent and the Young Men more realistic. Or did it go much deeper than that?

Foreign apologists for the regime had hailed the appointment of the Young Men in 1935 as proof that Zog was really on the side of the angels. From their perspective, the Kotta ministry of 1936 looked like a serious relapse, and this led some people to wonder if the King was beginning to outlive his usefulness. Zog owed his success hitherto, they argued, to his being a Janus-faced figure, a compound of the Young and Old elements in Albanian culture, and therefore well-suited to the task of leading his country through the transition from Ottoman province to European nation. He knew the ways of beys and chieftains well enough to keep them in line, yet he also had sufficient cognizance of western civilisation to give Albania a strong shove in the direction of modern statehood. As Interior Minister in 1920, with his progressive face forward, he had been the first of the Young Men to gain power. Was he now, turning his reactionary face, destined as King to be the last of the Old Men to cling on to it? Perhaps, having brought his land so far towards modernity, he was incapable of taking it further and preferred to revert to old habits. It is true that even in the late 1930s, a retired diplomat could report that talking to Zog reminded him 'forcibly of interviews about 40 years ago with Turkish *valis*'.[12] But too much can easily be made of the events of 1936. While the Frashëri Cabinet better resembled a proper Government than its precursors, it no more ruled Albania in reality than did the Evangjeli or Kotta Cabinets.

This fact should be borne in mind when evaluating one other explanation for the return of the Old Men: namely, the wishes of the Italian Legation, which doubtless preferred to have Ekrem Bey Libohova as Foreign Minister rather than Fuad Asllani. The Young Men were too nationalistic and too pro-German. Half the outgoing Cabinet had been educated in Austria, and Mussolini did not want Nazi influence in his costly satellite state. In many countries, of course, the sacrifice of a Cabinet to outside pressure would be sensational. Zog may have judged it a cheap concession.

The Old Men could relax: Juka managed the general election in December and January so that all approved candidates won (and only eleven others stood). None of the fifty-eight deputies was a newcomer to Parliament. They might be reactionaries, wrote the new British Minister, Sir Andrew Ryan, but they were also wholly subservient. The King would go ahead just the same with reform of local government, training of nurses, marsh-drainage, and model farms. 'The sad thing,' added Ryan, 'is that he himself should cling to old-world methods even when he is disposed to embrace new principles. He is like a small Abdul Hamid groping with his cronies in a new world.'[13]

Opening Parliament on 10 February 1937, Zog added to his prepared text 'a blunt overture to the effect that there were not and would not be any parties in Albania and that all the elements in the State, Throne, Parliament, Executive, press, youth of both sexes, peasants and townspeople must co-operate in giving effect to the promised reforms'.[14] It sounded as if the recent outburst of antagonism between Young Men and Old had alarmed him, and he would not have been the first dictator to permit a measure of free debate and then recoil from the divisions which it exposed. State repression now increased or became more overt. The Law on Offences against the Social and Economic Order made it a crime to be a communist, and a year in prison awaited anyone found in possession of printed matter 'considered to offend the morals, good customs, or state regime of Albania'.[15]

Whitsun 1937 saw another forlorn little rebellion. A few gendarmes seized the sub-prefecture at Delvina, threw open the ancient prison in Gjirokastra, and marched on Tepelena. Within forty-eight hours, they were all rounded up. The only excitement arose from the identity of their leader: Major Ethem Toto, lately Interior Minister. He himself was reportedly shot while resisting arrest, four men went before a firing squad, and eighty were sent to gaol. Juka said Toto was 'a tool of the Comintern', but no one else seemed at all sure what it had been about.[16] Muslims against the ban on the veil? Nationalists against the Italian oil firm? Pundits wove theories about Italian spies, Greek irredentists, British gendarmerie instructors, the French Popular Front, and – of course – the King himself.

Who cared? Outside the phalanx of politicians, prefects, and officers – pretty much a closed shop by now – the twists and turns of Albanian politics seemed ever more inconsequential. The regime owed its durability, not to popular support, nor even to popular fear, but chiefly to popular apathy and fatalism. The few, who expected something from politics, desired it mainly for themselves, and found collaborating with Zog more lucrative than opposing him. The many, who expected nothing, endured this King because any other would have been as bad.

Foreign observers concluded that, if King Zog had hoped to strengthen the foundations of his regime, he had comprehensively failed. The best he could manage in 1937 was yet more parades and a ubiquitous new motto, *Atdheu mbi te gjitha*, 'Fatherland above all'.[17] Yet privately he was making progress on one other project which promised to help invest his rule with an air of monarchical permanence: his marriage.

CHAPTER THIRTY-ONE

Seeking a Queen

One of the legends of Zog runs as follows: The King of the Albanians was driving through Budapest when a lovely young woman caught his eye. 'Stop the carriage,' he cried.[1] He spoke to the girl, they fell in love instantly, and he took her to Tirana as his Queen. The reality was nothing like as simple.

For a long time, indeed, one of the remarkable things about Zog was the fact that he remained a bachelor. Even his mother was worried. Nobody doubted his ability to attract the opposite sex; he charmed lady visitors – from Rose Wilder Lane to Bapsy Pavry, a Parsee from Bombay – and seemed aware of the susceptibility of some western women to a semi-oriental despot with feline manners. Foreign writers served him well in this regard:

> The youngest ruler in Europe and the only unmarried one, he is one of the most picturesque and romantic figures of our time. Slender, handsome, a stranger to fear, retiring in manner but utterly ruthless when occasion demands, Zog might have stepped straight from the pages of a story-book or from the motion picture screen.[2]

His looks were compared to those of the Hollywood dandy Adolphe Menjou, whose films included *The Ace of Cads* and *A Gentleman of Paris*. 'He was a man who could throw a spell on any woman from the very first moment,' enthused Antoinette de Szinyei-Merse,[3] while René Vanlande mused on the soulful official portrait:

> King Ahmed Zogu is scarcely thirty-nine years old. But his life has been very full. His past is rather heavy . . . Hence no doubt the melancholic and disillusioned weariness which imbues his delicate, almost pretty face. The very elongated eyes have vivacity yet seem to doze under blinking eyelids. Two touches of black moustache, trimmed in the German style, leave uncovered a lip at once precious and morose. A romantic disenchantment can be read in his expression and his attitude. And this King of the Mountains makes one think of Gérard de Nerval's *Desdichado* – of that prince of Aquitaine of the shattered tower who 'bears the black sun of Melancholy'.[4]

Zog was habitually flirtatious (and probably sometimes more than flirtatious) with the foreign women he met. Maybe this owed something to traditional Albanian preconceptions about unescorted females, although he also took a quite untraditional delight in feminine conversation. Few opportunities could ever arise for him to relate to Albanian women (except family members) in a society where there was little middle-ground between the jealous chastity enjoined by the Law of Lek and the brothels in the Gypsy quarter. Handsome or ugly, gallant or misogynistic, an Albanian man was expected to marry.

The King naturally disdained speculation. His subjects heard that he was following the custom of a man not taking a wife until all his sisters had husbands. Skanderbeg had only married at the age of forty-six. Like him, Zog was too busy saving the nation: 'What have I to offer a wife living as I do?'[5]

A different explanation circulated in the highlands. When Ahmed Zogolli was young, he fell in love with Miriana Zougdidi. She returned his love, but her rich father considered Zogolli a poor prospect, even when he said that he would prove his worth by becoming King if need be. When the desperate youth tried to elope with Miriana, her father stabbed her sooner than let her go. Left with her lifeless body in his arms, Ahmed made three vows: to become King of Albania, to exterminate the Zougdidis, and to stay a bachelor all his days. This fantasy showed him in a better light than another tale, which asserted that he had a wife in Mati whom he deserted on moving to Tirana. She went to the palace with her father to confront him: 'Nobody has ever seen either of them again!'[6]

For political motives, Zogu had in fact become engaged in 1922 to Behije Vërlaci, daughter of the bey of Elbasan. Shevqet Vërlaci delivered him a measure of Tosk support and lent money to the Zogist campaign in the 1923 election. The alliance went awry when Noli forced them into exile. Zogu wanted to borrow a further 100,000 francs to help fund his invasion, but Vërlaci refused and failed to take part in the 'Triumph of Legality'. Thereafter, with the throne in view, Zogu had no intention of marrying any Albanian; domestic political jealousies precluded it. But actually breaking off the engagement was quite another matter. If a fiancée were rejected without justification (the only certain one being loss of virginity), her father had the right (if not the duty) to exact retribution. Although modern marriage laws had formally superseded the Law of Lek, neither Zogu nor Vërlaci could afford to lose face.

'Kill a man but do not insult him,' advises an Albanian proverb. The bullets flew when Shevqet Bey stepped from his car in central Tirana one night in December 1927. Leaping back into the vehicle, he drove off at top speed with holes in his clothes but no injuries. News of his survival allegedly caused panic in the presidential compound. The police made no arrests and Vërlaci made no accusations, but he put himself under the special protection of the Italian Legation. With an annual income of 240,000 gold francs from his Shkumbi valley estates, he could afford a flat in Rome and a troop of bodyguards. The Italians saw Vërlaci as their man in Albania, a possible substitute leader, so Zog did not dare to cross him again. The courtesy which they showed each other in public even led the British Legation to disbelieve the talk of a feud: this middle-aged man with a neat grey moustache was surely 'the most peaceable person in the Kingdom'.[7] Locals judged otherwise, though Vërlaci can hardly have been involved in half the treacherous intrigues ascribed to him. One thing was clear, however: the Zogu–Vërlaci engagement was off. Behije wed Xhemil Bey Dino, ex-fiancé of Myzejen Zogu, in 1934.

Zog was therefore an unattached bachelor when the monarchy came into being. Who was the heir presumptive? The constitution stated that, if the King had neither son nor grandson living, he could select a successor from among his relatives, provided that Parliament approved. He did not hurry to make a choice. At first, the favourite was Salih, his eldest nephew, born in 1910, whose zeal for military service made him rise at three in the morning to go to barracks. So said his admirers, among them a clique of army officers. This may have given his uncle pause for thought. The alternative was Tati, whom the King brought up like a son. Given his youth, his nomination would carry little weight, but Zog may have found it reassuring that no one could run the boy as a credible rival to him for many years yet. Salih's father, Doshishti, hailed from Dibra, a comparatively loyal district. Tati's paternal kin lived in Kosovo and were openly disloyal. Every spring brought rumours that Gani Bey Kryeziu was massing his followers on the frontier. Would naming Ceno Bey's son as heir appease the vengeful Kryeziu brothers or spur them on?

While hinting at Tati, Zog kept the succession open. There were even reports about the throne reverting to Wilhelm of Wied. Uncertainty would only end when the King fathered a son. He was now free to take a wife, but where would he find one? His Queen could not come from Albania. Nor could she come from one of the three nations interested in Albania without offending the other two. Zog assured Percy in 1928 that he had no plans to marry 'Miss Italy, Miss Yugoslavia, or Miss Greece'.[8] Already, however, he felt unable to refuse the services of Mussolini as matchmaker.

The idea of his marrying an Italian princess first arose in 1926, when Baron Aloisi was tempting President Zogu to accede to a formal protectorate. It then became a recurrent issue in Italo-Albanian relations. The offer at face value appeared flattering in the extreme. The House of Savoy was the oldest reigning family in Europe, and King Victor Emmanuel had two unmarried daughters, Giovanna (born 1907) and Maria (born 1914). But nothing could be taken at face value. The matrimonial question became a tortuous diplomatic ritual. Despite years of intermittent discussion, Zog never established whether Mussolini was serious about supplying a princess. Equally, the Italians never found out if Zog really wanted one. It was Zogist prevarication at its worst (or best).

The Albanian would usually begin by dismissing the proposal as laughable: 'I am not educated enough for an Italian princess. Look at my house! The way we live! How could an Italian princess adapt herself to this life?'9 He would harp on about his lack of eligibility until politeness compelled the Italian envoy to argue. Then Zog would concede, very hesitantly, that Maria or Giovanna might conceivably tolerate Tirana. It was now the turn of the Italian to equivocate, as the Duce was offering what was not his to give. Although compliant enough in politics, Victor Emmanuel was a stickler for dynastic rights and genealogy. His own dear wife came from Montenegro, yet this only made him more conscious of how native Balkan royalty was scorned. In his eyes, Zog looked little better than a bandit. Therefore, whenever the Albanian grew too keen on an Italian royal bride, the diplomats had to distract him with women from various noble families. He feigned an interest, but, of course, nobody now fitted the bill as well as a Savoy princess.

Only once did Sola think that he had the solution. The Marchese D'Auletta was a Neapolitan nobleman directly descended from Skanderbeg. How about one of his daughters? King Zog could make much of her Albanian ancestry. Mussolini vetoed the scheme. Believing her own propaganda, he said, such a queen would cease to be a proper Italian: the Queen of Albania must identify with Italy in order to ensure an Italian regency when the King died.

Zog probably realised that an Italian wife could take years off his life. A flat refusal would give offence, however, and for a real princess, he might take the risk. Giovanna wed King Boris of Bulgaria in 1930; Maria remained notionally available.

Zog stood no chance of winning a princess from any other reigning dynasty in western Europe. Balkan royalty came next in status. He ruled out Yugoslavia at once. Quite apart from the political obstacles, the Karadjordjević family had no females of suitable age. The Greek monarchy was exiled from 1924 to 1935, so that left Romania and Bulgaria. Albanians had nothing against Romanians – neither people were Slavs – and the Romanian Queen Mother, Marie, was already 'the Mother-in-law of the Balkans', having married her eldest daughter to George II of Greece and her second to Alexander of Yugoslavia. Her third, Ileana (born 1909), looked promising. Such a match would annoy the Italians, however, as Romania was allied to Yugoslavia. A Bulgarian bride might be better. Unhappy with the Balkan status quo, Bulgarians were not averse to Italian efforts to overturn it, and King Boris had an unmarried sister. Eudoxia was neither very young nor beautiful, but politics might prevail.

Gossips scouted these possibilities around 1930, but they had little material to work on. The King had no social contact with foreign royalty. He could not easily travel abroad and he preferred to avoid correspondence. This meant that courtship had to proceed through intermediaries, who operated in secret, lest the Italians learn of his plans. Royal parents, receiving verbal offers from mysterious Albanian agents, often suspected a hoax. In 1931, Princess Ileana of Romania married Archduke Anton von Habsburg-Lothringen. Princess Eudoxia remained a spinster.

Zog grew used to rebuffs. The fracas at the Vienna Opera House reinforced doubts about his reputation, and difficulties were increased by his refusal to consider Turkish, Egyptian, or Arab princesses: 'If I want to Europeanise my country, I do not need an Oriental, but a Christian.'[10] Mixed marriages, he said, were of patriotic value in a nation divided by religion.

Attention turned to non-reigning royal families. King Zog had yet to learn the extent to which deposed royalty stood on its dignity. He hoped some ex-King would welcome the chance to place his daughter on a throne that was actual if modest. He therefore went straight to the top and Archduchess Adelhaid Maria, daughter of the late Emperor Karl of Austria–Hungary, whom Colonel Zogolli had met in 1917. Over-zealous Zogists had latterly talked up his Viennese connections to the point of claiming that he had served as aide-de-camp to Franz Josef. Reportedly approached in 1933, however, Empress Zita was unco-operative. Zog went on thumbing through his *Almanach de Gotha*, while the Italians cheerfully anticipated that he would ultimately accept any contessa they deigned to suggest. Foreign magazines declared that he would marry anyone whose dowry exceeded $5 million. There were even allegations that he possessed a harem of wives already.

On a purely personal level, it is indeed probable that Zog felt no pressing need for a wife. A man with six devoted sisters never went short of feminine company. Moreover, it was known in Tirana that he kept a discreet mistress or two. Diplomats told jokes about a mysterious 'Madame Pompadourette', who reputedly passed her days hidden away in a plush little villa inside the royal compound. She eluded even the Italian Minister, although her existence was confirmed by an Italian doctor called in to examine her. Other people related how they had glimpsed after dark a tall woman in western dress who covered her face when caught in their car headlights in the vicinity of the palace.

This level of secrecy was preserved until Zog's visit to Vienna in 1931. During the opera interval, on the night of the shooting, he was seen talking to two ladies from an adjoining box. The anti-Italian newspaper

Stunde traced them to the Hotel Regina and published a piece which identified the 'Baronesses' Franciska and Maria de Janko as daughters of a gardener from the Ottakring suburb of Vienna. Franzi Janko, possessor of 'a pair of twinkling legs, a slim body, a snap of light chestnut-coloured hair, and a pair of brown mischievous eyes', had met Ahmed Zogu in 1924 while a cabaret dancer in Belgrade.[11] On his return to power, he invited her to live in Tirana at his expense with her sister for company. For most of the year, they stayed indoors, but, when the royal family went to Durrës each summer, they were smuggled out of the compound to take a holiday abroad. Franzi expected costly presents as compensation for enforced seclusion, and it amused her to address the King as '*Du Gebirgstrottel*' ('You mountain-idiot').[12] Zog declared that she brought him luck. Even the Queen Mother was supposed to be unaware that her son kept two women in a house across the road. If she did not have to set eyes on them, presumably, she need not take offence – a very Albanian arrangement.

The King was outraged when news of his mistress followed news of the assassination attempt around the world. No mention of Franzi Janko appeared in print in Albania, however, and Zog swore his entourage to silence. Thus the 'secret' was preserved, though hardly anybody remained in ignorance – not even clansmen in remotest Mirdita, who deplored his wasting money on a woman.

The clandestine company of the Janko sisters for eight months in the year failed to save Zog from further embarrassment in May 1934, when the dead body of 'Baroness' Dorothea de Ropp was found on a beach near Athens. Apparently a suicide, this lady, a German born in Lithuania, had lived in Tirana for three years from 1930. According to the Greek press, she had affairs with both the King and his Master of Ceremonies, Kemal Messare, now the Albanian Minister in Greece. It transpired, moreover, that Frau Ropp had been a double-agent working for Italy and Yugoslavia. Papers left in her room formed the basis of these reports. Naturally, the Albanian press completely overlooked the Ropp Affair, but it prodded the King into sorting out his private life. When Franzi left Tirana in June, she and her sister did not come back. A house in Vienna was his parting gift.

There was an additional reason why Zog sensed the lack of a wife more acutely after 1934. On 25 November, his mother died suddenly of a heart attack at her seashore bungalow. Her age was fifty-eight; she had been suffering from diabetes. Zog showed no emotion at the funeral, yet a few years later he confessed: 'In the difficult and in the beautiful moments of my life alike I think of my mother. Her memory gives me strength and multiplies my joy!'[13] A marble mausoleum, domed like an observatory, was built south of Tirana, and official delegations in future laid wreaths on the grave of *Nana e Kombit*, 'The Mother of the Nation'.

No wife could replace the Queen Mother as an adviser, but Zog took to heart her wish that he should marry. He lowered his sights from royalty to nobility and sent his sisters to scour the ballrooms of central Europe. Two retired Hungarian generals, Gyzy and Konkoly-Tege, acted on his behalf – with much circumspection, since ladies in whom they showed too obvious an interest risked being compromised by fervid Italian admirers.

Meanwhile, endeavours began in earnest to invest the court of King Zog with the panoply of majesty. The first formal royal banquet took place in January 1936 (to celebrate the wedding of Princess Senije). When the lire began to flow again later in the year, work resumed on the new royal palace, and the existing one was refurbished. Brocaded sofas and marble-topped tables adorned reception rooms decorated with draperies and gilt. A wooden pavilion, big enough for dances, went up on the site of the tennis court. The King engaged domestic staff from Austria and Hungary (along with an African pageboy) and commissioned a protocol of etiquette based on imperial Viennese practice.

In December 1936, there appeared to be a breakthrough when 25-year-old Countess Hanna Mikes and her father attended the New Year's Eve party at the palace (another court innovation, made daring by a ruling that ladies should wear *décolletée*). The Mikes were Magyar nobles from Transylvania. Hanna's uncle, Count István Bethlen, had been Prime Minister of Hungary. Zog found the Countess attractive, but her Calvinist faith raised the sensitive issue of religious education for any children. When Count Armond Mikes lost patience with Zog's vacillations and demanded that he propose by 15 January, the King let Hanna go home.

This gave the Italians another chance but they could offer no one more prestigious than a daughter of the Mayneri, Durini, or Cenci-Bolgnetti families. As a final bid, Mussolini persuaded Ferdinando Castriota Scanderbeg to take his sister to Tirana for the 1937 Independence Day ball, but even the famous name did not appeal to the King any more.

The restoration of the Greek monarchy had revived his hopes of securing a royal princess: namely Alexandra, posthumous child of Alexander of Greece, the king who famously died from a monkey-bite. Brought up by her mother, apart from the rest of the Greek royal family, sixteen-year-old Alexandra lived in Venice, where an Albanian envoy appeared to say that King Zog had never fallen in love until he set eyes on her photograph. Would she come and meet him in Durrës? He knew that the Princess had a passion for oranges: crates of the finest were waiting. In fact, Alexandra loathed oranges. King George II advised Zog that his niece was too young. (She wed King Peter of Yugoslavia in 1944.)

With Greece out of the running, central Europe returned to the fore, in time for the next New Year's Eve party. Just before midnight, it fell to

Princess Senije to introduce a new 'friend' to her brother. It was another Hungarian countess. Her Christian name was Geraldine. The King showed his shy young visitor to the buffet before leading her into a side-room to talk. He told her how much he liked Vienna, recalled his time there during the war, and spoke in general terms about his life and his hopes for his kingdom. At four o'clock the following afternoon, Geraldine was summoned to his study. Zog kissed her hand, offered her a seat, and asked her to marry him. She said she would, but he gave her ten days to make sure.

CHAPTER THIRTY-TWO

Geraldine

Countess Geraldine Apponyi de Nagy-Appony was a 22-year-old blue-eyed blonde with a broad smile and a charming look of innocence. Her photograph had appealed to the King, as did her family tree. The paternal side led to the old aristocracy of the Habsburg Empire. The Apponyis had been great landowners in Upper Hungary since the thirteenth century. On the maternal side were the monied families of the New World, specifically Maryland and North Carolina. Genealogists later traced this line back to an English colonist whose other descendants included Brigham Young and Richard Nixon.

The more immediate background of the Countess sheds some light on how it came to pass that she consented to marry a very foreign monarch within 18 hours of setting eyes on him. Not yet four years out of school, Geraldine had few experiences in common with her future husband, except for having been orphaned at a similar age. Her short life, despite material privileges, had not been especially easy.

Count Gyula Apponyi, first lieutenant of Hussar Regiment No. 13 (Reserve), had met Gladys Stewart-Strale while visiting Paris in the summer of 1914. Twenty-three-year-old Miss Stewart-Strale was the only child of the late John Stewart, sometime US consul at Antwerp, and the stepdaughter of Major Gustav Strale d'Ekna of the Swedish Legation. Four weeks later, the pair were engaged, but their plans were immediately thrown into confusion by the European crisis. At forty-one, Count Apponyi was too old to be called up in the initial mobilisation, but he was anxious to avoid internment in France. Therefore Gladys became one of the very first war brides – in Geneva on 29 July 1914. In Budapest thirty-six hours later, the new Countess met her in-laws.

The Apponyis were Magyar grandees of the first rank. Count Lajos Apponyi, the father of Count Gyula, had served Franz Josef as Grand Marshal of the Hungarian Court. His cousin, Count Albert Apponyi, was a noted nationalist politician. Gladys had lived in Paris from the age of eleven, but she was hardly prepared for the semi-feudal society of Nagy Appony. Count Gyula did not keep an establishment of his own, since his father had left him sizeable debts. His bride therefore had the choice of living in a country mansion as a kind of guest or sharing an apartment in Buda with her austere German mother-in-law. She was staying at the latter place when she gave birth to Geraldine on 6 August 1915. A second daughter, Virginia, followed sixteen months later.

With her husband absent on military service, Countess Gladys felt isolated and unhappy. By the time the United States declared war on Austria–Hungary in December 1917, she was staying with her mother and stepfather in Switzerland. Her husband and daughters also came to Montreux in September 1918, and it was from there that Count Apponyi observed the defeat of his country.

The sudden dissolution of the Habsburg Empire, accompanied by five months of Bolshevik revolution in Budapest in 1919, set the Magyar nobility reeling. Although he took his family back to Hungary in 1921, when Admiral Horthy had restored a semblance of the old regime, Count Gyula could not return to his estates. By the peace treaty of June 1920, Appony, renamed Oponice, formed part of Czechoslovakia, which denied him a visa. To make matters worse, his wife had lost her personal fortune (or he had lost it for her) by investing heavily in Hungarian war bonds, which were now practically worthless. With help from his mother, the Count could live in Budapest in reasonable comfort, but he brooded on his misfortunes. He died of lung disease in May 1924, not long after the birth of his only son.

Geraldine, now eight years old, was devastated. Her father had always seemed to her a kind and gentle man. After his death, Gladys Apponyi left Hungary and took the children to reside near her mother, Virginia Strale d'Ekna, on the French Riviera. Gerry and Ginny soon suffered another shock. 'My children, this is your father,' announced Gladys, introducing Colonel Gontran Girault in July 1926.[1] This secret remarriage struck Geraldine as an appalling betrayal, and several years of family discord ensued. The advent of a stepsister did not help. Nor did intervention by both grandmothers. Countess Margit Apponyi, a devout Roman Catholic, suspected Girault of anti-clericalism. She sent her nephew's wife, Muriel Seherr-Thoss (herself American-born), to negotiate the future of the Apponyi children, and by 1930 they were back in Hungary. Once drilled in German, the girls became boarders at a convent school in Pressbaum.

At eighteen, Geraldine was taken under the wing of her Aunt Fanny, Countess Laszlo Károlyi, an eccentric philanthropist famed for her ankle-length hair and her charitable village of Zebegeny, where aristocratic young ladies helped the war-wounded. Geraldine did secretarial duties and arranged entertainments. Her weekends were spent in Budapest society, for the Apponyi family organised her début. She won acclaim on account of her beauty – a magazine dubbed her 'The White Rose of Hungary' – but she did not gain a husband. Perhaps her manner was too ingenuous. Though outwardly glamorous, Geraldine never aimed at witty sophistication. There was also her unusual height (6 ft) and her known shortage of capital. The Czechoslovak authorities expropriated part of the Apponyi estate at a nominal compensation price.

In 1936, Geraldine accepted an invitation from her American grandmother to spend the summer at Nice. This did not please her aunts in Budapest. The marriage of her sister in January 1937 had the effect of isolating her further. Henceforth she had no fixed abode but constantly moved between friends and relations, dubbing herself 'the eternal guest' and 'the flying Dutchwoman'.[2] In her loneliness, Geraldine fell in love with a poor middle-class man, but he backed away from marrying a socialite, leaving her heartbroken. The Apponyis were not too sympathetic. They subsidised her lifestyle in order to help her make a good match, but her ideas on matrimony appeared to owe too much to the sentimental novels which were her favourite reading. To their knowledge, a millionaire had proposed to her at Monte Carlo.

In a bid for greater independence, Geraldine took a part-time job selling souvenirs at the Hungarian National Museum. Not long afterwards, Count Kari Apponyi, the head of the family, met an old acquaintance named Konkoly-Tege. The general said that he had taken the liberty of sending three photographs of Geraldine to the King of Albania. Would she like to visit Tirana with all expenses paid? Though taken aback, the Apponyis reminded their niece of what a Gypsy palmist had once foretold: 'Great luck, I see lovely lady. A crown I see in your hand. A golden crown.'[3] This story would later delight superstitious Albanians. Geraldine hesitated until it was settled that her friend, Katalen Teleki, could undertake a preliminary inspection of the Albanian court. Her visit coincided with celebrations to mark twenty-five years of independence, Zog spared no effort to please, and the report of Countess Teleki was extremely favourable.

Thus Geraldine arrived in Albania on the Bari-Durrës ferry on 31 December 1937, accompanied by General Gyzy and Baroness Rüling, her cousins' governess. 'A big swanky car' took them to 'a nice little villa' in Tirana. At eleven o'clock they went to the palace. In her nervousness, Geraldine let slip her champagne glass and it smashed to bits on the floor. 'Splinters bring luck,' said Zog. His quiet manner appealed to her, as they conversed in German, their common third language. 'It was so touching to see how our little friend was more and more attracted to the King's personality,' reported Baroness Rüling. 'I saw how he came to love more and more Geraldine's fairylike character; . . . two people had really found each other; two people whom God had created for one another; and I knew on that first evening that a love was born here which would last for ever.'[4]

This passage is perfectly representative of the way in which the royal engagement was presented to the world. The journalistic fantasy of

Albania as never-never land received its final fillip – and it was not *all* nonsense. The effusive accounts of 'a modern fairytale' mirrored the temperament of the bride-to-be, and her family and friends liked to emphasise the romantic note. Zog was now forty-two and looking old for his age; Geraldine, twenty years his junior, was a recognised beauty. Some harsh and derisive things were said in Budapest, and popular magazines always mentioned that she had been earning only a pound a week at the National Museum. The imputation was unfair. Though she may have been carried away by the adventure of marrying a king, Geraldine was never a gold-digger. As a museum porter declared, 'She was a nice sweet little countess.'[5]

All the same, the King overwhelmed her with his generosity. Each morning there was a bouquet on her breakfast tray, and each evening a present on her pillow. In addition to a 14-carat diamond engagement ring, he gave her crown jewels newly ordered from Vienna. The motif on the tiara was a representation of the Skanderbeg helmet. A French dressmaker came to Tirana expressly to measure Geraldine, so that two forms of her figure could be made in Paris for Chanel and Worth. With the aid of catalogues, Zog then selected her entire wardrobe, including lingerie, hats, handbags, and shoes, without once consulting her. Admiring his taste, Geraldine allowed this to continue. 'Though essentially a masculine man,' she later recalled, 'my husband was completely at ease in the world of women's fashion and always admired his sisters' lavish wardrobes.'[6]

Her relatives were suitably impressed when they came from Hungary for the engagement feast at the end of January. The King announced his intention of buying the expropriated Apponyi lands as a wedding present for his bride (and he duly secured three or four thousand acres of forestry and a hunting lodge in the Nitra Valley). Before the banquet, he declared:

> I should be very grateful if on this day of joy in my life, in this festival hour of my country, you would give a few moments of silent prayer to the memory of a woman who was dear and beloved to both myself and my people – more than anybody else. I know that the spirit of my mother is among us at this moment. Blessed be her memory.[7]

Next day, the Queen-elect scattered small coins and pieces of bread to the people of Tirana who gathered them as mementoes. Attention was drawn to various Apponyi ancestors who had fought the Turks, and the alliance between Skanderbeg and János Hunyadi was cited as a precedent for Albano-Hungarian co-operation. The wedding would take place on 27 April, the 487th anniversary of the marriage of Skanderbeg to Donika Araniti.

There was very little diplomatic reaction to the engagement. Count Albert Apponyi had been a conspicuous figure at the League of Nations in his later years, but no one could possibly regard it as a dynastic alliance. The political advantage of Geraldine was purely negative: she did not come from Italy.

Zog actually feared last-minute Italian sabotage. For this reason, he asked his fiancée to stay in Tirana until the wedding. In December, it had not occurred to her that she might be leaving Hungary for the last time. A friend of her family, Antoinette de Szinyei-Merse, 'Auntie Tony', agreed to be her companion. The King suggested that they move into the royal compound, as there happened to be a vacant villa which had been specially furnished some years ago for lady visitors. Its satin opulence and mirror-lined walls made Geraldine feel uncomfortable, alas, so Prince Salih placed his house at her disposal. The Hungarian ladies were closely guarded and instructed to see no one without permission. Reports that Zog would visit Budapest naturally came to nothing.

The King had three months in which to train Geraldine in 'the art of being a Queen'.[8] An intensive language course helped her add Albanian to her stock of Hungarian, English, German, and French, and all went well until the question of religion came to a head. Zog assured Geraldine that, although his family were Muslim, they welcomed the fact that she was Roman Catholic. This led the Apponyis to assume that he accepted the convention whereby the children of a mixed-faith marriage were raised in the mother's religion. In truth, his political sense still told him that an heir needed to be Muslim in a country three-quarters Islamic. Profiles of Geraldine in the local press did not mention her Catholicism. Zog persuaded her to agree to Islamic education for their children on the understanding that he would obtain a dispensation from the Pope. When the Vatican refused, he resolved to carry on regardless. Geraldine was deeply upset. Her Jesuit confessor told her that she would be no more than a concubine. Then he left for Rome – obviously a spy! Everything now became clear to Zog, but his theories of collusion between Italy and the Vatican failed to console his fiancée, who succumbed to a nervous disorder described as 'a possible aftermath of a brain fever she had suffered as a child'.[9]

Furious with the Pope, Zog ordered every Catholic Church in Albania to celebrate the royal wedding with a *Te Deum*. Geraldine meanwhile demonstrated her resilience. Her mother and grandmother arrived from the Riviera, and, after just a few weeks rest, she was herself again. 'I am looking forward to horse-back excursions in the Albanian Alps,' she told reporters on 25 April. 'It will be fun "roughing it" on long mountain expeditions.' How did she feel about marrying the King? 'I am so happy – it is all like a dream. My happiness is complete.'[10]

CHAPTER THIRTY-THREE

A National Event

The royal wedding was planned as the greatest celebration in Albanian history. Extended carousing had always been part of the traditional marriage, and beys and chieftains rivalled each other in the display of wealth. When Xhemal and Sadije married at Burgajet in 1891, the feasting lasted forty days. Recently, after the wedding of Gjon Marka Gjoni's son, relays of guests consumed 5,000 lbs of meat and 660 quarts of raki.

Despite the parades in Tirana, the House of Zogu-Mati had hitherto displayed little of the glamour associated with European royalty. Assassination fears had inhibited its inauguration, but, ten years on, the King felt able to put on a show for the outside world, whose sympathetic attention now seemed more desirable than ever. What was the foreign news? Hitler incorporated Austria into the Reich on 12 March. Axis-backed nationalist forces in Spain were dividing the republican area in two. In April, Nazis in Czechoslovakia demanded autonomy for the Sudetenland. The intensification of power politics threatened all small nations. Albania was used to living in peril, but Zog realised that any deterioration in its position could be fatal. He faced the future with his customary blend of objective pessimism and dogged hope. With Italian advisers back at his elbow, his room for manoeuvre was minimal. One thing he could yet do to keep Albania on the map was to make an exhibition of himself. Foreigners might care more about his nation's independence if reminded of its existence.

The wedding provided an excuse to flaunt the paraphernalia of an established monarchy in a belated effort to make Zog appear as regal as Carol, Boris, and George; yet western Europeans saw Balkan kings as theatrical. While earning more column inches in the international press than ever before, he was frequently cast in the role of comic relief. One cartoonist depicted Albania as a dancing girl in the midst of an anxious world. The accounts of royal gimcrackery in Ruritania brought smiles to some faces – and frowns to others. How could he afford gold-plated tableware and blooms from the Riviera? To those on the Left (and not only to them), the spectacle of luxury in a poverty-stricken land was almost obscene. Poor Albanians, however, likely took it for granted that a king would vaunt his affluence.

Albania had yet to develop an instinctive identification between crown and nation. The slogan embossed on commemorative stamps and medals struck a suitably didactic note: 'The Wedding of the King – A National Event'. For the village turned capital city, at any rate, it would mean a remarkably cosmopolitan week. Guests were coming from Italy and Hungary, along with the heads of all seventeen diplomatic missions (many of whom rarely left Rome or Athens). Even the Tirana soccer team prepared to play Bari.

To capitalise on the fact that Geraldine was half-American, the King had sent his three youngest sisters to the USA (escorted by Krosi). The Great Democracy did not feel any especial concern for the Land of the Eagles, but it proved all too easy to excite the American press. When the *Conte di Savoia* docked in New York on 28 February, the Princesses received the sort of reception more often accorded to film stars. Myzejen, Ruhije, and Maxhide were wholly bewildered. At an uproarious press conference, Faik Konitza interpreted as he saw fit. The youthful Princesses – aged twenty-nine, twenty-six, and twenty-four – had come to see how 'epic genius had turned a waste continent into a pageant of flourishing cities'.[1] The Girl Guides were their main concern, and no, they would not be visiting nightclubs.

Identically attired, the 'Zoglets' went to the headquarters of the Guides and a primary school before cancelling other public engagements and going into hiding. They were later spotted at the Empire State Building and the Rainbow Room nightclub. A high point of their tour was tea at the White House with President Roosevelt – the first time members of the House of Zogu had been officially received by a Head of State.

Equally symbolic was their trip to Boston, the centre of the Albanian-American community whose pre-eminent figure remained Fan Noli. 'The Fighting Bishop' had not prospered since his overthrow in 1924, despite the critical success of his literary work. After translating Shakespeare, he had tackled Ibsen and Cervantes. His annotated *Don Quixote* actually likened the Don to King Zog: both were perpetuating a 'feudal, medieval, backward situation', and, as for Sancho Panza, 'We grieve at the sight of the poor and ignorant peasant ready to die for his master, who fools and ruins him with empty promises and illusions'.[2] Given this rhetoric, it was not surprising that his émigré group in Vienna fell under the influence of the Comintern. In 1927, Noli attended a Congress of Friends of the Soviet Union, which earned him temporary detention at Ellis Island on his return to the USA. Illness then reduced him to poverty, until Zog decided on a show of magnanimity in 1934. In return for a pension, Noli had to provide a statement of respect for the King and to give up political activity. Now the Princesses sealed the public reconciliation with a visit to the Albanian Orthodox Church. When they invited him back to his country as a cultural luminary, Noli preferred instead to write a doctorate about Skanderbeg at Boston University. In this way, Zog's most eloquent critic was silenced. The three sisters left for Europe with trunks full of American clothes, and, if their tour had not exactly endeared Albanian royalty to the world, the steamer that conveyed them to Durrës on 22 April did also bring a fair number of special correspondents.

Banners, fairy lights, and arches mounted with the double-headed eagle decorated the streets of Tirana. Zog supervised the programme himself and, eager as he was to look European, he could not neglect the highland chieftains. On Sunday, 24 April, they came to the palace for a feast. The walls of the ballroom were hung with jewelled daggers, scimitars, and pearl-handled pistols. The King still had to condescend to old men in skullcaps and sashes who regarded themselves as his peers. Two from Dibra refused to appear until Zog interceded to arrange a besa, after which the all-male company danced to the bagpipes and squealing clarinet.

The Hungarians held a party at the Hotel International, 'which resembled a country inn of not quite first rank'.[3] The guest-list was an index of central European nobility: Apponyi, Berchtold, Esterházy, Festetics, Károlyi, Papendorff, Radziwill, Seherr-Thoss, Strachwitz, Thurn, Trautenberg, Urbán, Wenckheim, Wilczek, and several more. They drank the place dry, danced on the tables, and smashed their glasses against the wall (to the dismay of the landlord) till an equerry arrived with a message from the King, advising them to spare their strength for three days of official celebrations.

More annoying than the antics of Geraldine's relatives was the behaviour of the principal Italian guest. From the moment his plane touched down at Tirana (when chanting blackshirts swarmed onto the runway), Count Galeazzo Ciano seemed set on turning the event into a triumphal progress for himself. The King had asked him to be chief witness at the marriage to make up for the fact that the bride was not Italian. The irony of the choice emerged only later. Ostentatious and unprincipled, Ciano possessed zest and flamboyance liable to attract people who did not look too closely. His rise had been rapid. In 1930, aged twenty-seven, he had married Edda Mussolini (once tipped as a bride for Zog). Six years on, he was Foreign Minister. Ciano repaid his father-in-law with the sincerest form of flattery. He frowned and jutted his chin accordingly as he toured Tirana on 25 April 1938, giving the fascist salute at regular intervals. Unfortunately for Zog, the Foreign Minister was not a simple replica of the Duce, who played cat and mouse with Albania when he had nothing better to do. Ciano felt the need to prove his political virility. At the palace ball that evening, though, he intended to enjoy himself.

Designed to present a western image, the ball was the most ornate court function yet essayed. While the King and Geraldine stood on a dais draped in purple velvet, two hundred guests were to be introduced in order of precedence. Six couples in national dress would then lead the dancing with music alternating between the Albanian army band and a Gypsy orchestra from Budapest. All was ready at the appointed time except the guests of honour. The Italians turned up half-an-hour late. Perhaps this kind of petty rudeness was what Ciano meant when he spoke of imbuing diplomacy with *tona fascista*. Strictly speaking, the top Italian present was Adalberto, Duke of Bergamo, but it was Ciano who dominated the ballroom all night, flirting outrageously with Hungarian ladies. Zog looked on dourly. He seldom enjoyed formal parties, when his uninspired small talk could make people think him trivial. As for Geraldine, when the Gypsy violinist played *Red Roses for Easter*, she felt homesick and started to cry.

The highlight of Tuesday was a three-hour march past by the entire Albanian army: a monotonous stream of grey-green uniforms broken only by the crimson and black lancers of the Royal Guard and the novelty of three women's companies led by the Princesses. Earlier Zog and Geraldine had come to the gates of the palace to chat to fourteen couples who had just been married in Skanderbeg Square. Across the country, fifty peasant brides received a royal dowry consisting of a bed, blankets, and pillows. (Zog considered sleeping on the floor unhygienic and launched a public education programme on elementary bed-construction).

The King started his wedding day with a private visit to his mother's grave, while all mosques and churches gave thanksgiving. The marriage ceremony itself would be brief, for it could not be made religious without offending Muslim, Orthodox, or Catholic opinion, and traditional costume and folk music were unthinkable for a westerniser. Zog therefore declared simplicity the keynote, while ensuring that photographers would not be disappointed. The location, likened by the unkind to a film set, was the prefabricated ballroom adjoining the palace, now with a pillared balcony, green-draped walls, and a profusion of rugs to cover the floor. Rows of glaring naked electric lights dazzled the eye (and nearly set the place on fire). Costumes were varied, with the mix of long dresses and tailcoats supplemented by some extraordinary Magyar garb: hussars with vermilion cloaks, ladies in bodices and ruffles, and stout Uncle Anton Apponyi in doublet and hose. Imams and Orthodox bishops added touches of black. Two rows of soldiers formed an aisle down the middle of the hall.

At half past ten the assembly fell silent, as the royal couple entered arm in arm. Everyone thought that the bride looked radiant. Four young officers (including Prince Tati) carried the four-metre train of her wedding dress, and eight bridesmaids followed (four Albanian princesses and four Hungarian countesses). Geraldine was later at pains to point out that only her orange-blossom coronal made her seem taller than the King. He, in contrast, looked sombre and introspective. Nine stars on the left breast of his tunic proclaimed his status.* The pair came to a halt under the Queen Mother's portrait.

The Vice-President of the Parliament, Hiqmet Delvina, read from the civil code:

> The man and the wife accept reciprocal obligations to live together in loyalty and mutual assistance. The man is the head of the family; the wife follows the civil position of the man, taking his name, and is obliged to follow the head of the family wherever he sees fit to dwell. The man is obliged to protect his wife, to procure her a living according to his means. The wife is obliged to contribute to his nourishment if he is without means.[4]

Zog glanced at Geraldine with a smile as the last words were spoken. Each assented with a soft '*Po*'. Then the company shouted 'Bravo!' and applauded, as cameras clicked and a 101-gun salute punctuated the wail of the muezzin from the Mosque of Ethem Bey. Count Ciano, Prince Abid, Count Kari Apponyi, and the Hungarian Minister, Baron Frédéric Villani, signed the register as witnesses, dipping their pens in a silver inkstand inscribed, 'To Ahmed Zogu, President of the Albanian Republic'.

'The ceremony passed off with more dignity than one might have expected,' recorded Ciano in his diary. 'The King actually appeared moved.'[5] It had taken just six and a half minutes.

The reception was described as a small banquet (twenty-two different dishes) for honoured guests and families (150 people). The seating plan went by the board when a sudden downpour proved too much for the annexe roof. Everyone moved into the main body of the palace, where overcrowding amplified the gaiety. Old Gang politicians, bright young things from Budapest, cynical diplomats, and fascist functionaries ate French cuisine amid a babble of languages. Count Ciano felt that Zog's sisters were snubbing him ('the royal princesses are peasants'[6]). The Americans – Madame Girault, Mrs Strale d'Ekna, and Muriel Seherr-Thoss – showered congratulations on 'dear little Gerry'. The mother was cheekily quoted as saying, 'My daughter loves the man, not the King. He has given her six fur coats already.'[7]

Guests admired the 200 wedding presents. Admiral Horthy, the Regent of Hungary, sent a phaeton and pair of white horses. There was an equestrian statue from King Victor Emmanuel and, from Mussolini, four bronze vases that had once belonged to Napoleon. In addition, the

---

* Since 1925, Zog had received decorations from Yugoslavia, Italy, France, Romania, Hungary, Greece, Belgium, and Luxembourg.

Italian Government was promising King Zog a royal yacht. Hitler outshone them on the day, though, with a scarlet supercharged Mercedes convertible. King George VI sent only congratulations.

When the sun came out, a crowd surged around the compound and, to its own amazement, in through the gates. The King and Queen sat at the top of the steps to receive the homage of the people. Then they toured the streets in an open car while girls in white dresses strewed flowers before them. Soldiers lined the route, as always, but children stood in front and waved, while a biplane looped the loop overhead. Even conservative Muslim women perched on the roofs to watch. There were maybe 60,000 people in Tirana that day, joining in the revelry without overt signs of compulsion. Count Ciano alone reported that the populace 'remained indifferent and seemed, by contrast, more ragged than usual'.[8] Journalists with no strong motive to deceive recorded plenty of exuberance, although some may have erred in automatically assuming that Albanians loved 'The Big Bird' and his 'beautiful, smiling Queen'. Perhaps it was safer to infer only that Albanians enjoyed a party.

With Tirana still *en fête*, a long motorcade set off along the freshly repaired road to Durrës. Rumours of a honeymoon in Hungary were groundless. On reaching the palace, the newly-weds took coffee. Then Geraldine was shown into the gilded bedroom, where her husband joined her later: 'not as a King, but as a proud son of the Eagles'.[9] Next day, she discovered that her nightgown had vanished. Zog bashfully explained that proof of virginity was required by the President of the Parliament.

In at least one respect, their married life began as it was to continue: they were not alone together for long. Ciano arrived for lunch and stayed four hours. The King wanted him to intercede with the Vatican regarding Geraldine's marital status (later satisfactorily resolved). The union of Germany and Austria dominated discussion, however, since there were ramifications even for Albania. Greater Germany now bordered Yugoslavia. Zog suggested that Mussolini should avoid too closely tying himself to Hitler. Ciano replied that it was onerous having Germans as friends, but having them as enemies would be terrible. The outlook was uncertain, he agreed, but Albania could count on Italian friendship. He wished the couple a long and happy reign.

Fourteen years had passed since Zog pocketed his first three million lire. In official circles in Rome, it was observed with some frequency that there appeared to be a bottomless marsh on the far side of the Adriatic which swallowed up Italian gold. The lavish royal wedding made an impression on those who funded it. Count Ciano noted in his diary, 'I leave Albania more firmly convinced than ever of the need for a radical solution.'[10]

CHAPTER THIRTY-FOUR

Borrowed Time

King Zog and Queen Geraldine spent the greater part of 1938 at Durrës. When, at the end of June, the combination of heat and mosquitoes drove them from the Summer Palace, they moved down to their seaside camp, behind which the letters G.Z. had been etched on the mountainside several metres high. There the court resided till November, with Zog leaving his desk most days after only a few hours to swim, sunbathe, and learn to cycle with his bride. If life at the beach colony seemed unprecedentedly relaxed, this was thanks to an influx of young Hungarians. The Queen had her brother and sister to stay: fourteen year-old Gyula and 21-year-old Virginia (plus husband André de Baghy). She also found court appointments for a few impoverished friends, like Countess Rose Wenckheim, her private secretary.

Not everything changed. The six Princesses had joined the newly-weds two days into their honeymoon and stayed: a pointer to future tensions. Diplomats did wonder how a lady accustomed to Budapest and Vienna would adjust, but Villani, the Hungarian Minister, remarked that 'her previous existence had been in such straitened circumstances that the comfort and comparative luxury and security of her present life must seem like paradise'.[1]

Geraldine wrote to a friend, 'I am the happiest woman on earth!!!!!! It is lovely to be all the time, every moment with somebody you love and who loves you.'[2] The royal marriage was manifestly a relationship that worked on some level. The Queen liked to be liked, seemed eager to please, and tried always to look on the bright side. A husband resembling her father had been her explicit desire. The King had sought a loyal, attractive, and pliable wife. His face softened when he was with Geraldine, to whom he showed kindness, courtesy, and consideration (according to his lights). 'It was his gentleness that had a pull on me,' she later recalled.[3] His nature did not run to spontaneity. Keen admirer as she was, Madame de Szinyei-Merse yet identified grim reserve as the keynote of his personality, 'a more or less stable characteristic which he carried naturally, unostentatiously, like a well-cut fashionable suit. Often I thought that this very calm man did not know any emotions, any human affections at all.' He appeared to her to approach other people on the objective basis that to understand all is to forgive all. This impression is not dispelled by his recorded observation that, 'To govern well one has to know how to love people. Love and affection are the highest necessities of Society. Every State employee, the smallest and the greatest, must try to fulfil this necessity.'4

Zog had every reason to be pleased with his Queen. For one thing, she became pregnant within three months. For another, her natural informality promised to westernise the monarchy's image. At royal occasions, the King was belatedly learning how to smile and wave. His presence at the Durrës swimming races struck people as an encouraging departure – even if he did arrive late with an automatic pistol under his jacket. Still more boldly, he decided to visit southern Albania in mid-August. The Gheg King had never dared cross the River Shkumbi and put himself wholly in the hands of his Tosk subjects. He did not do exactly that now, but he borrowed a small Italian steamer, the *Cigno*, and took a four-day cruise of the dramatic southern coastline, where the Çika mountains drop sheer into the sea. At Saranda (renamed Zogaj in his honour), the royal pair went ashore at nightfall to attend an open-air feast. In the far south, people seemed happy to see them: support for the monarchy was a repudiation of Greek territorial claims. Next day, in enervating heat, Zog's party journeyed down the Straits of Corfu to inspect archaeological excavations at Butrint, where picturesque ruins stood beside a beautiful malarial lagoon. Then, steaming back to Durrës, they made unannounced calls at Himara and Vlora, where Zog gave a speech. For Geraldine, there was a moment of alarm – but only because enthusiastic citizens lifted her limousine onto their shoulders and carried it along the street.

A fortnight later came four days of festivities to mark the tenth anniversary of the monarchy, with, in addition to the usual parades, an official souvenir picture-book and a buffet reception for 300 guests at the Summer Palace, to which Albanians wore national costume, except for the King. This being the third Zogist carnival in a year, Faik Konitza complained that a nation once noted for tragic dignity was being lowered 'to the level of a cheap musical farce'.5 Everyone had to join in the songs:

> Zog the First with Albanian sword,
> A lightning-strike from the sky,
> Put to flight the treacherous horde,
> Like a lion that shines on high.
> Until the sun itself grow dim,
> Oh, may our land be ruled by him!6

It could all have been a fool's paradise – and for the young Hungarians it probably was. Optimistic schemes for social reform were the nearest Zog liked to get to politics when talking to his wife (who worried about the poverty of her subjects). He yet made a few unsettling remarks – 'I am giving you the jewels I can now, for tomorrow we may be without a penny' – and even a political innocent could see that his relations with the Italians were not such as might be expected between good friends. He had to start explaining, 'I distrust our ally more than our enemies.'[7]

Since the Italo-Albanian loan deal of 1936, the trading of material aid for political influence had continued week by week. Francesco Jacomoni, formerly deputy to Baron Aloisi, returned to Albania as Minister. Nobody questioned his diligence, even if his public demeanour – a mix of pomposity and false bonhomie – failed to diminish his inevitable unpopularity. Italy easily resumed its leading position. Import restrictions rigged the market in favour of Italian products. An Italian firm, *Pescalba*, monopolised local fisheries. Senator Prampolini came to supervise drainage schemes, Professor Montanelli revised the school curriculum, and Giovanni Giro set up leisure activities for workers. Zog viewed Giro with particular suspicion: an affectedly unconventional young man, he modelled himself on Lawrence of Arabia.

In March 1938, the Italian Government had duly 'brokered' a generous renegotiation of the *SVEA* debt. The interest burden was halved and 28 million francs of penal interest were written off. The deal did not come cheap: a few weeks earlier, King Zog had to give General Percy and his last three British gendarmerie inspectors their notice to quit. The perennial Italian efforts to oust them had redoubled after Britain denounced the invasion of Ethiopia in 1935. Previously, the British officers took some satisfaction in outwitting 'the wily Wops', but henceforth local Italian obstruction made their work almost impossible. Percy had wanted to leave in September 1936, but Zog begged him to remain Inspector-General 'for as long as he himself was alive and King of his country. "I may be a liar sometimes," said the King, "but I am not lying now."'[8] The last two years, however, had turned out to be humiliating. At his departure in September 1938, Percy blamed Zog for undermining his authority and giving him not one word of thanks. The British officers were nominally replaced by Albanians rather than Italians, but it made little difference. The last token non-Italian presence had gone.

International developments over the previous five years had fundamentally weakened the Albanian bargaining position *vis-à-vis* Italy by revealing just how empty was the threat of a return to Yugoslav patronage. Albania had been excluded from the Balkan Pact in 1934, and the Yugoslavs withdrew their lukewarm sympathy for its subsequent adhesion when they saw how Zog toadied to the Italians during the Ethiopian crisis. Since then, the Government in Belgrade had taken stock of the new European situation. Milan Stojadinović, Premier and Foreign

Minister from 1935, acquiesced in the waning of Franco-Yugoslav ties and aimed at appeasing the Axis in the name of neutrality. Yugoslavia disinterested itself from Albania in return for Mussolini curbing Croatian terrorism; a Treaty of Non-Aggression formalised the rapprochement in 1937. This was a grievous blow to King Zog, who had not been consulted by his Italian allies. Ciano lauded the realism of the Yugoslav leader: 'Stojadinović is a Fascist'.[9]

Elsewhere, Mussolini grew ever more bellicose, as British and French condemnation of the Ethiopian War led Italy to draw closer to Germany in the Rome–Berlin Axis. The price of German co-operation was acceptance of the *Anschluss*. Hitler reassured the Italians about the Alto Adige, but they still worried that Germany would inherit the traditional Austrian interest in the Balkans. Italian objections to Queen Geraldine related largely to her Viennese connections, which Nazis might somehow use to gain influence in Tirana. Despite such jealousies, Mussolini relished talk of a fascist Europe.

Italian and German forces were already fighting in Spain, where the outcome no longer seemed in serious doubt. The latest European crisis imperilled Czechoslovakia. In September, Hitler threatened to precipitate continental war unless the Sudetenland was ceded to the Reich. King Zog followed events as a spectator. He had no privileged knowledge of nations outside his own region, and his notions about the internal politics of democratic powers inclined to crudity. If anyone invited his opinion, he would say that he expected a peaceful resolution of the crisis, as certain powers were not yet prepared to fight a major war. Whether these unready powers were Germany and Italy, or Britain, France, and the Soviet Union depended on whom he was addressing. He told the British Minister that, even if there were a European war, it would be some time before it reached the Adriatic, because Italy was likely to wait and see which side would win before it became involved. In October, he congratulated Chamberlain and Hitler on the Munich Agreement. That said, Zog told Ryan that war had been postponed, not averted, as Germany would sooner or later take on the Soviet Union for control of the Ukraine. Earlier in the year he had argued that, if the British wanted to exert real leverage in eastern Europe, they should form a bloc on the southern flank by rallying the Balkan states – and be assured, 'If His Majesty's Government adopted the Balkan policy which he recommended, little Albania would be ready to do her little bit.'[10]

This was only one of his increasingly piteous attempts to interest somebody – anybody – other than Italians in his kingdom. The Japanese Minister to Albania heard about exciting commercial opportunities. The Anglo-Iranian Oil Company spent a year toying with the idea of a fresh concession after Zog approached them in 1937. Geologists advised that improved drilling techniques might now obtain better oil, but the Foreign Office would not hear of challenging Italy. Zog had been unwise enough to admit that his aim was to rid Albania of 'economic slavery'.[11] Simultaneously, he tried to talk the Germans into prospecting for Albanian oil. Why, he complained, did their great trade drive in the Balkans entirely ignore Albania? The answer, of course, was that any German interest in the place would infuriate Mussolini. Ciano advised the Nazi Foreign Minister, Ribbentrop, that Italy saw Albania as a 'family matter'. That, he noted, 'is the phrase they used for Austria and the Sudeten Germans. It means "Hands off".'[12]

The grouping of Albania with the Sudetenland was ominous. In fact, Zog's insouciance during the Munich crisis had been a sham, for he was shaken by reports that Mussolini would use it to distract from a strike in the Adriatic. Invasion scares were two a penny in the Europe of 1938–9, and the Yugoslav Legation may have been making mischief – its chief, Radoje Janković, was a leonine Serb nationalist of the old school – but Zog gave the rumours of attack enough credence to send Zef Sereqi to Rome with messages for Count Ciano. The first one in July attempted to divert him with a plan for a pro-Axis revolution in Turkey. It sounded a desperate ploy, though not so pathetic as Zog's appeal in October, summarised by its recipient thus: 'Albania is now in Italy's hands, for Italy controls every sector of the national activity. The King is devoted. The people are grateful. Why do you want anything more?'[13] On both occasions, the Italians inundated Sereqi with assurances of goodwill to take back to Tirana. They might be sincere or they might not, Zog explained to his wife: 'In any case I must pretend to believe them.'[14] He remained deeply disturbed – with reason.

Galeazzo Ciano had begun work on his memorandum advocating the annexation of Albania, 'the natural road to our expansion in the Balkans', while a wedding guest in Tirana in April 1938. With scant regard for accuracy, he set out every reason for an Italian takeover. The mineral wealth of Albania was tremendous, it would be a wonderful place for Italian colonisation, Albanians already loved Mussolini more than Zog, and educated youngsters longed to serve fascism. The Count knew how to appeal to his father-in-law:

Albania, which saw the destinies of the Roman Empire decided on the plain of Cruia (battle of Pharsalus, 48 BC) between Caesar and Pompey, reminds us that in recent times Italian troops withdrew hard-pressed by the ragged bands of tribesmen and that the retreat was so hasty as to resemble flight. In spite of all that has happened since, this picture has remained in the minds of too many Albanians, and it is a memory which tells against us still. The Duce will see to it that it is obliterated, just as he obliterated others of the same nature and of greater seriousness.[15]

This referred to the evacuation of Vlora in 1920, likening it to the Italian defeat by Ethiopians at Adowa in 1896. How could the great dictator fail to rise to such a challenge? On 19 May, he assured Ciano that he was 'ready to go into Albania, even at the cost of setting fire to the European powder barrel', but he had better seal the Italo-German alliance first.[16] The moment to act would be a year hence.

Ciano took Mussolini at his word and began preparing for an invasion in May 1939. Giro, the 'Strength through Joy' organiser, received orders to subvert important Albanians 'with expressions of mutual interest, with promises, and with corruption'.[17] Senator Prampolini, meanwhile, would drain the Durrës marshes to aid the military disembarkation. Ciano chivvied along Jacomoni and kept reminding the Duce of his next imperial coup.

Mussolini blew hot and cold, worrying about international reaction, but in the autumn he saw how Hitler managed to obtain the Sudetenland. The western democracies were feeble, and Ciano was right: he needed to show that the Rome–Berlin Axis did not exist solely for Germany's benefit. On 30 November, the Duce addressed his Grand Council: 'I announce to you the immediate goals of Fascist dynamism. As we have avenged Adowa, so we will avenge Valona. Albania will become Italian. I cannot yet – and I do not wish to – tell you how or when. But it will happen.'[18] Everyone present was sworn to silence, yet the gist of the speech reached Zog within a week. He hoped that his informant was lying and carried on showing a brave face, though the mask came close to slipping a few days later.

On 10 December, the King and Queen made their first (and last) voyage on the new royal yacht, *Illyria*, a sturdy vessel of the trawler type adapted by the Italians for cruising. As usual, complete secrecy surrounded their itinerary, but the presence of Foreign Minister Libohova (and the amount of luggage) suggested an Italian port of call. Leaving Durrës at sunset, the boat ran into choppy seas and Zog told the captain to turn back, because Geraldine felt unwell. She was in the fifth month of pregnancy. The sailors told him not to worry, so he had to insist. Though it was midnight when the *Illyria* reached shore, the royal pair refused to consider starting again next day and went to Tirana by hire car. Zog afterwards admitted that he had feared kidnap. There is no hard evidence, but, when Italy first agreed to pay for a royal yacht, Ciano had stipulated an Italian crew, so as to 'guarantee the impossibility of his escaping in any eventuality'.[19]

This mysterious episode was grist to the Tirana rumour-mill, but the King kept his own counsel, as always. The Italian menace, though widely sensed, could still not be acknowledged in cabinet even, and Parliament and press continued spouting the clichés of Adriatic amity. After all, the existing Italo-Albanian alliance was due to last until 1947.

In the royal compound, meanwhile, Geraldine and her ladies-in-waiting busied themselves with the innumerable little touches required to bring the Albanian court into line with conventional European standards. Never again would the soup tureen double as an ice-bucket, or embroidered placemats vanish from the dining room to decorate the walls of the garage. The new palace, under construction for almost a decade, on and off, would be finished soon. Big, white, and modern, it boasted panoramic bay windows and an internal glass wall-cum-aquarium.

Queen Geraldine brought the custom of the Christmas tree to Tirana and also the turkey dinner. Nevertheless, given religious differences, the chief palace function had to be at New Year. On 31 December 1938, the annexe once more served its purpose: down one wall a row of pot-bellied stoves, and down the other a buffet laden with delicacies, served on gold plate and Bohemian crystal. When the lights went dim at midnight, King Zog raised a glass of champagne and wished, 'Happy New Year to everyone in my home and everywhere.' The assemblage clapped as he kissed the Queen, resplendent in tiara and ermine. One bemused American recalled:

When the lights returned, people began to wave lottery tickets. . . . Somebody took my orange ticket and gave me a bundle. Inside I found a blue woollen muffler, brown socks, necktie and fancy handkerchief. Everybody got a present. Other men had shirts and ties done up in packages; bolts of material for suits; sweaters, suspenders. The women received fancy underwear, stuff for dresses, perfume, bunny rabbits containing pockets crammed with lingerie.[20]

Then the dancing started. Teri and Danush were popular. The King slipped out to tell a couple of foreign reporters about Albania's progress and his desire to see their countries. Hungarian ladies-in-waiting meanwhile tried to hide their disapproval of clansmen who ate with their fingers and stamped out cigarettes on Persian rugs. Once the guests had their fill of *foie gras* and ice-creams, they filed out into the quiet, damp night, past a line of yawning guardsmen and a couple of begging Gypsy children, to ramshackle droshkies waiting in the muddy street.

Tirana would not see another palace party, and some of the Italians present virtually knew it for a fact, as their impatient Foreign Minister had already recorded:

Our preparations in Albania are going ahead rapidly, so rapidly that we may have to advance our timetable, as the alarm may have reached the circles around the King. The operation is beginning to take shape clearly: assassination of the King (it seems that Koçi will undertake this for a reward of ten millions), riots in the streets, descent from the mountains of the bands we can trust . . . appeal to Italy to intervene politically and if necessary militarily, offer of the throne to the King Emperor, and a little later annexation. Jacomoni guarantees that all this can take place without trouble at a month's notice.[21]

CHAPTER THIRTY-FIVE

Into the Vortex

It was between 4 and 10 February 1939, most probably on Wednesday the 8th, that Zog heard the news that left him in no doubt that the Italian threat to his kingdom was specific and imminent. The Yugoslav envoy, Janković, his lips unsealed by a change of Government in Belgrade, confidentially divulged that Italy and Yugoslavia had been discussing a partition of Albania. Anti-Italian subterfuge could always be expected from this source, yet the admission of Yugoslav complicity and the strength of the supporting detail compelled belief.

Count Ciano had raised the issue during a six-day visit to Yugoslavia in mid-January. His personal relationship with Milan Stojadinović had flourished, and they were out shooting together when, with deliberate casualness, he started chatting about Zog. What an unreliable character! The portly Serb businessman agreed, adding that the answer would be to replace him or else partition the country in the cause of peace and stability in the Adriatic. To this, the Count replied that, if Italy were to occupy Albania, there could certainly be scope for frontier corrections, and the advantages for Yugoslavia might extend to Italian endorsement of its claims to 'Southern Macedonia' (northern Greece). Leaving the matter in the air, Ciano noted that the Yugoslav premier clearly had no insuperable objection to the end of independent Albania. He then sounded out the Regent. Prince Paul said, 'We have already so many Albanians inside our frontiers, and they give us so much trouble, that I have no wish to increase their number.'[1] Ciano understood this to mean that the Yugoslavs waived any claim to a share of the spoils, so he left Belgrade well pleased.

In fact, Stojadinović had not informed Paul of his outdoor conversation about partition. The Regent, a believer in Albanian independence, was furious when he learnt what his Prime Minister had proposed, and this compounded other grievances. Stojadinović seemed loath to address the Croat question, while his supporters had lately taken to wearing green shirts and hailing him as *Vodja* (leader). Prince Paul therefore engineered a cabinet crisis and replaced him with the less forceful Dragiša Cvetković in early February. Hence the revelation from Janković.

Zog was very agitated, in fear for his throne and his life. The spies whom he knew surrounded him assumed fresh significance. Everything had now to be interpreted in terms of an Italian plot. That very week in

Tirana, for example, seventy-three people from Shkodra (many of them secondary school pupils) went on trial for disseminating communist propaganda. Had the arrests been staged so Italy could intervene and 'save' Albania from Bolshevism? On Sunday 12 February, while walking in the gardens, Zog spotted the glint of sunlight on a gun barrel in an attic window. More than ever since 1928, he felt under siege.

Two days later, an improbable black comedy was played in the palace dining room. Unusually, the King and Queen had lunch alone with Jak Koçi, a shady Old Gang figure, who had served Zog on and off as private secretary ever since the World War. In more recent times, he had acted as one of his matrimonial agents, for, though physically unprepossessing, Koçi was well-mannered, quick-witted, and fluent in several languages. Today, however, he did not seem at ease. When dessert arrived, Geraldine and Koçi simultaneously each took a mouthful of apple strudel. She grimaced, and he spat his out. 'Try to be calm, Jak,' said Zog, seizing Koçi by the ear and pulling him to the door: 'You will never succeed in killing me. If necessary, it will be I who kills you!' He returned to the table a moment later, saying only, 'In two hours that one will no longer be on Albanian territory.'[2] Informed that Koçi was offering money to the kitchen staff to poison him, Zog had ordered his cook to fill the 'apple' strudel with cabbage. Koçi was indeed the assassin contracted by the Italians. 'Naturally, he is an old friend of the King's,' Count Ciano had written, 'but he feels he has been neglected by him.'[3] According to Geraldine, Koçi resented being refused permission to set up a counterfeiting operation in the palace cellars.

The King knew plenty of double agents. After lunch on 14 February, Murad Kaloshi, a chieftain from Dibra, came to the royal compound to confess that he had recently accepted a large sum in gold from Giovanni Giro, the fascist activist, as advance payment for civil disturbances. This was not an isolated case. Giro, whose audacity amounted to an insult, had bought a new house in Shkodra for Gjon Marka Gjoni. For months, maybe years, Zog had turned a blind eye, but now the reckoning changed: confronting Giro held fewer risks than allowing him to continue. While strenuously trying to avoid any hint of panic, the King told the cabinet of his concerns and spent the evening with his service chiefs: Aranitasi of the army, Shatku of the gendarmerie, and Colonel Hysein Selmani, commander of the Royal Guard. They agreed on a partial mobilisation, which meant calling out selected clans with minimal publicity.

Next day, King Zog summoned the Italian Minister and put to him the allegation that Ciano was contemplating the partition of Albania. Jacomoni naturally dismissed it as malicious Yugoslavian tittle-tattle, but the atmosphere remained glacial. Zog announced that Giro would be deported; a list of notable Albanians who had been accosted by him with subversive proposals, not omitting Jak Koçi, left the Italian abashed. The King ended with an assurance that the Italo-Albanian alliance would continue to be respected.

Italy did not protest at the expulsion of Giro, who left for Rome by air on 16 February, accompanied by Jacomoni (whose many trans-Adriatic flights during the winter of 1938–9 were put down to a need for medical treatment). Three days of acute trepidation ensued. While rumours of revolt and invasion swept across Albania like an epidemic to which only the press was immune, the King had extra bodyguards stationed around his office and 'spoke even less than his wont'.[4] Then the situation suddenly eased: just another scare, it appeared. The Italian Minister flew back with promises of friendship from the Duce; Zog affirmed his desire for cordial relations.

The Italians had been thrown off balance by these events in the first half of February 1939. It was not the quarrel with Zog that worried them so much as the change of ministry in Belgrade. Stojadinović they had known and liked, but, so far as they could tell, Cvetković was slightly more pro-Western while his Foreign Minister, Cincar-Marković, was more pro-German. Would they be as ready to accept the destruction of independent Albania? Mussolini and Ciano pondered two options: either they should try again to win Yugoslav collusion, or else they should seize Albania soon, before Belgrade could rally international opposition.

This uncertainty reactivated Mussolini's anxieties. Might a sudden Italian invasion of Albania precipitate the break-up of Yugoslavia? Of course, this had originally been a central aim of his Albanian policy, but changed circumstances made him fear the very outcome which he had once desired. Now Germany had absorbed Austria, the biggest beneficiary from the death of Yugoslavia would probably be Hitler, who might easily sponsor independent Croatia as a German satellite. Rather than chance 'the sight of a swastika in the Adriatic', Mussolini had finally come around to supporting Yugoslav unity.[5]

The logic of this argument pointed to leaving Albania alone, but the idea of a snap foreign policy 'triumph' greatly appealed to the Duce, and his Foreign Minister assiduously plied him with reasons for annexation. For Ciano, realising his brainchild had become an end in itself. After discussion, Mussolini reasserted that Italy would take Albania in any event, but he still judged it better to do so with Yugoslav connivance than without. On 6 February, he selected the first week of April for the invasion. Eight days later, he said it would have to wait upon victory in Spain and the signing of the Pact of Steel with Germany. In the meantime, the Belgrade Legation should sound out Cvetković and the Tirana Legation pacify Zog, while preserving the seditious contacts made by Giro. 'We must spread the most varied rumours,' Ciano added; 'like the octopus we must darken the waters.'[6]

In effect, Zog had been granted a respite. His task was to turn it into a reprieve. He was not sanguine about success, yet he clutched at the possibility that the Italians could be induced to stop short of actually killing or overthrowing him and instead satisfy themselves with employing these menaces to bully him into further concessions, as in 1926 and 1934. He badly needed to set up a bargaining process, be it about new gendarmerie inspectors, fascist party branches, experts in government ministries, Italian lessons in schools, or whatever. In the international climate of 1939, the longer Mussolini could be kept talking, the greater the chance of some crisis erupting elsewhere to distract him or place the Italo-Albanian relationship in a fresh context. Zog arguably owed his survival for the last five years to Ethiopia and Spain. Maybe Franco-Italian war over Tunisia would offer salvation to Albania. This failed to materialise, but Hitler soon gave the next terrific jolt to European politics.

The Führer did not consult the Duce before calling President Hácha of Czecho-Slovakia to Berlin on the night of 14 March and browbeating him until he agreed to a German protectorate on pain of invasion. Hitler made his entry into Prague within twenty-four hours, causing a sensation. In London, Neville Chamberlain faced the bankruptcy of his appeasement policy. In Rome, Mussolini felt indignation, wonder, jealousy, and downright fear of the growing power of his Nazi counterpart. For a few days, the Duce actually thought about backing out of the Pact of Steel and turning to Britain and France, assuming that the latter could be persuaded to buy Italian support with some concessions in North Africa.

Ciano encouraged this line of thinking while also arguing that the obvious answer in the short term was to pay Hitler back in his own coin by forcing a protectorate on Albania without any further delay. By demonstrating toughness and daring, Mussolini would restore his standing as an equal partner in the Axis and leave the Germans in no doubt that, whatever hegemony they might achieve in central Europe, the Balkans were earmarked for Italy. How Ciano imagined that he could simultaneously strike an expansionist blow in the Adriatic and improve relations with the democracies is a mystery. He depicted the Albanian riposte to Germany as quick, easy, and well-prepared.

After wavering, Mussolini concurred. The Germans had only just reached Prague, when the Italians determined to emulate them: King Zog would be told to request a protectorate or face invasion. That was how things stood on Wednesday evening, but, early on Thursday morning, the Duce commanded his son-in-law to postpone the ultimatum, since he had reverted to the idea that an Italian move on

Albania would simply provoke a German move on Croatia. It took Ciano another week to screw Mussolini's courage back up to the sticking-point. During this period, he crucially received the semi-inadvertent assistance of Ribbentrop, who, on realising how sore the Italians felt about Czecho-Slovakia, sent a letter to Ciano on 20 March. It said, among other things, that Hitler believed that in Mediterranean questions the policy of the Axis should be decided by Rome. He also denied any Nazi interest in Croat separatism.

On 21 March, Germany demanded of Poland the right to annex the Free City of Danzig. On 22 March, Lithuania ceded Memel to the Reich under duress. On 23 March, lest he be completely upstaged, Mussolini gave the go-ahead: 'Either Zog accepts the conditions which we lay before him, or we shall undertake the military seizure of the country.'[7] While Italian troops began concentrating in Apulia, Ciano settled precisely what those conditions should be.

The demands which Baron Carlo de Ferraris carried to Tirana in his briefcase on 25 March amounted to a compendium of Italo-Albanian unfinished business in the form of a draft pact: closer military alliance, right of intervention to restore public order, customs union, free use of ports and airfields, legations raised to embassies, reciprocal automatic citizenship rights, an Italian secretary-general in every ministry, plus a fascist organisation, an Italian chief of staff, and Italian gendarmerie instructors. Zog said that he would need to consult his ministers. Given the example of Czecho-Slovakia, he cannot have failed to appreciate the portent of this formidable list, but he elected to proceed on the basis that it was an exaggerated bargaining stance.

That same day – though whether earlier or later is unclear – the King received the British Minister and his friend Sir Thomas Hohler. Asked about the recent invasion scares, Zog admitted to some rather difficult negotiations but 'nothing to occasion any anxiety'. He murmured to Ryan in Turkish that 'he was willing to go a long way to meet the Italians', so far as was compatible with Albanian independence and integrity.[8] Hohler observed that, 'His whole attitude was of freedom from care, and anxiety only about his wife who was about to produce a baby.'[9]

As usual, Zog intended to deal with the Italians in person and in secret, and he felt that his façade of unconcern – vital to confidence in the regime – needed especially to be preserved in the presence of Geraldine and her family (who were arriving in Tirana for the confinement). Professor Weibel, her Viennese gynaecologist, had already warned that the birth could be slow and painful, since she had lost the water some months earlier. Rather than add to her worries, the King feigned the best of spirits and banned the household from mentioning the 'false' alarms in circulation. Ciano privately confessed:

There is above all a fact on which I am counting: the coming birth of Zog's child. Zog loves his wife and indeed his whole family very much. I believe that he will prefer to ensure a quiet future for his dear ones. And, frankly, I cannot imagine Geraldine running around fighting through the mountains of Mati or of Mirdita in her ninth month of pregnancy.[10]

King Zog sat alone for hours in his stuffy office, reading and rereading the draft pact, sucking in nicotine, and sipping his coffee, the silence broken only by rain driving against the windows. Meanwhile in Rome on Sunday 26 March, despite equally steady rain, Mussolini gave an oration to 200,000 people to mark twenty years of fascism. He dubbed perpetual peace a catastrophe and ended with the words, 'More guns, more ships, more aeroplanes at all costs and with every means, even if we must make a clean sweep of all we call a civilised life.'[11]

When Jacomoni came to the palace and pressed for an answer two days later, Zog tried his normal quibbling tactics, showing eagerness to accept the lesser demands and raising difficulties about the more significant ones. He was playing for time while scanning the political horizon: the Nazis had just accused the Poles of persecuting their German minority, and Cvetković had opened talks on Croatian autonomy. The Italian had to explain once more to him that Count Ciano's draft pact was a unified whole to be accepted or rejected as it stood. Zog voiced his sympathy for the scheme and regretted that his cabinet was so obstinate in objecting to some aspects of it. For forty-eight hours, the Italians went along with the fiction that the King needed to persuade Kotta, Libohova, and the rest. A concerted crescendo of rumour about imminent clan revolts increased the pressure – to no avail. On 31 March, Jacomoni had to fly to Rome to tell Ciano that, contrary to expectation, Zog was not willing to sign a treaty which formally and substantially violated the sovereignty of his kingdom. Zef Sereqi, appointed Albanian Minister to Italy that afternoon, came to the Palazzo Chigi to enlarge on what the King would and would not concede, but nobody paid much attention.

The time had come to prepare the ultimatum. Twenty thousand troops stood by at Bari and Brindisi (ostensibly reinforcements for the Dodecanese). Ciano had kept Mussolini up to the mark, and a warning from King Victor Emmanuel that it was senseless to risk war to 'grab four rocks' had merely provoked him into exclaiming, 'If Hitler had to deal with a nincompoop of a King he would never have been able to take Austria and Czechoslovakia.' Learning that Germans called him 'Gauleiter of Italy' behind his back stiffened his resolve, as did news of the fall of Madrid to Franco.[12]

Then another hitch occurred. General Alfredo Guzzoni, chosen to command the invasion force, judged its transport arrangements inadequate. The Italian army required an extra week to assemble more motorised detachments. This gave the Duce pause for thought, and his old fears returned, possibly heightened by news from London of Chamberlain's guarantee of Poland. If this led Hitler to slow down his drive for Danzig, would he then be taking more interest in Croatia? Mussolini instructed Ciano to reduce his list of demands to something which King Zog might be able to accept. The balance of advantage would not favour military action, he calculated, if Italy could obtain – instantly, by menace – a big enough boost to its special rights in Albania to impress world opinion when the new pact was unveiled at a grand ceremony in Tirana. Zog was given one more chance to 'co-operate'.

CHAPTER THIRTY-SIX

Holy Week

The limitations of the *Ala Littoria* schedule invested Italo-Albanian shuttle diplomacy with a certain piquancy. Jacomoni and Sereqi flew back to Tirana together on Sunday 2 April and, as the flight-path passed over Bari, they had a view of the warships and encampments of the invasion force. Arriving at dusk, Sereqi went to the palace to report to the King.

Public concern had been rising over the weekend, and a crowd of people, mainly young men, some with flaming torches, assembled at the railings of the royal compound to chant, 'Down with Italy! Long live the King!' (which latter cry was enough to convince the diplomatic corps that this gathering was not quite as spontaneous as a smaller one on Saturday). At length, the King and Queen came onto a balcony to wave. Someone shouted, 'Is it true that war has broken out?' Word had spread that Italian troops were going to land at Vlora that night. 'It is not true,' Zog answered. 'No war has broken out. I want peace! And you, too, want peace!'[1] This evoked a cheer, but he refused to say more and escorted Geraldine back indoors, lest she grow even more perturbed. Now very near her time and unable to walk down stairs, she wondered why foreign newspapers were not being delivered to her rooms. Musa Juka ordered the rally to disperse.

Around midnight, Kotta and Libohova arrived at the palace for a ministerial conference, having come straight from seeing Jacomoni at the Foreign Ministry. As usual, their task was not so much to give an opinion as to elicit that of the King. They remained in the royal study until four o'clock in the morning, by which time it had become apparent that Zog was not disposed to accept the modified Italian 'project' *in toto*, even though Ciano now made only four demands.

After a few hours' rest, the King went through the demands one by one with the Italian Minister. First, Italy sought the right to take control of Albanian ports, airfields, and roads in the event of national independence ever being endangered. This was the crucial issue: if granted the right, the Italians might well invent a bogus threat to justify their exercising it. Zog insisted that such an extension of the Italo-Albanian alliance would only be acceptable if the pact stipulated that no Italian troops could enter Albania except at his explicit request, for Albanians were alone competent to judge when their own freedom was in danger. The second demand, discussed a week before, was for an Italian secretary-general to be the top civil servant in each ministry. Zog queried its constitutional propriety and preferred to employ Italian staff on the present *ad hoc* basis. Third, Ciano requested full civil and political rights for Italian citizens in Albania. Civil rights he would concede, said Zog, but not political, as foreigners should not be allowed to stand for Parliament. The final demand presented no difficulty: the promotion of the Italian Legation to an embassy was a matter of protocol, designed to give the Italian envoy precedence.

The softening of the Italian terms had failed in its basic purpose: Zog did not jump at the deal. He rather felt encouraged to sustain the charade of free negotiation and voice 'confidence' about reaching an amicable agreement. In response, Jacomoni told him that the situation had become very serious, not least because intelligence had reached his Legation concerning secret plans for a rebellion later in the week. The King said only that Sereqi would return to Rome the next day to explain the Albanian position to Count Ciano.

After the meeting, Zog ordered Kotta to issue a statement asserting that Albania continued to enjoy the most friendly relations with Italy. Simultaneously, he told his generals to start mobilising reserves. The standing army and gendarmerie amounted to 14,000 men on paper, but maybe only a third of them were in barracks. Calling up regular reservists would bring the total to 30,000, and some spoke of raising 100,000 men, taking the clans into account. Statistics meant very little, however, since clan politics pervaded the entire armed forces, thanks to Zog's policy of incorporating chieftains into his regime by offering them commissions. The King had to spend hours on the telephone to individual officers, trying to coax them into action. He ceased to sleep with regularity and 'relaxed' only when he visited the Queen and pretended that nothing was wrong.

No formal state of emergency had been proclaimed, but the call to arms could not possibly be kept secret. Next morning, as if in reply, the Italian press accused the King of the Albanians of squandering millions of lire over the previous fourteen years. Thus fascist journalists commenced his hasty transformation from friend and ally to tyrannical wastrel. Tuesday 4 April was the first day when the existence of an Italo-Albanian issue received open acknowledgement. Italian external radio ran a short item:

> Following King Zog's explicit request, conversations are now going on for strengthening the defensive alliance between the two countries. The sympathy that Italy has for the Albanian people is known – it is a sympathy of which the Albanian people have had repeated proof. It is not the intention of the Italian Government to make attempts on the independence and integrity of Albania.[2]

Listeners who recollected the downfall of Ethiopia, Austria, and Czecho-Slovakia required no clearer notification of crisis.

In mid-afternoon, the King summoned the cabinet and senior parliamentary deputies to the palace. When the meeting broke up, former premier Mehdi Frashëri drove down Boulevard Mussolini to the Greek Legation where he relayed a verbal message from King Zog. Italy was making demands tantamount to a protectorate. If accepted, they 'would result in Albania becoming Italian from every point of view'. Zog would not surrender the independence of his kingdom and would resist invasion. He urgently appealed to the signatory states of the Balkan Pact (Greece, Yugoslavia, Turkey, and Romania) 'to make a collective statement with the view of stopping the contemplated Italian action'.[3] Frashëri then saw the French Minister before travelling down to the British Legation at Durrës.* Diplomats realised that Zog had kept silent until now for fear that disclosure would trigger attack.

Frashëri drove back to Tirana though rain and darkness to assure the King that his message had been delivered. The envoys would be consulting their home governments. After Munich and the demise of Czecho-Slovakia, Zog did not have much faith in Anglo-French intervention or Balkan solidarity, and in fact his appeal was even more futile than he knew, as the Italian secret service had taken preventive measures. Albania still had no international telephone connection. At the first sign of a surge in the number of long cipher messages, the Albanian telegraphic office started directing all cables via Rome. There 'technical problems' delayed transmission, ensuring that the reactions of foreign governments lagged behind events.

Late that evening, the Queen went into labour in the small whitewashed room especially prepared on the first floor of the palace. Four doctors, an Austrian midwife, her mother, her grandmother, and Princess Adile were all in attendance when, at half past three in the morning on 5 April, Albania acquired a Crown Prince. The big healthy baby was at once named Leka, the Albanian form of Alexander, and the Italians permitted this piece of news to reach the foreign press promptly. Popular papers relished the coincidence that Geraldine's sister, Virginia, had given birth to a daughter in Budapest at almost exactly the same time.

Geraldine had not been properly anaesthetised when Professor Weibel commenced the necessary small Caesarian. The doctors then over-compensated and put her out for six hours. It was therefore not until ten o'clock that family and friends were allowed in to see mother and son.

---

* Despite repeated requests from King Zog, the British had never moved their premises to Tirana.

To the sound of a 101-gun salute, Zog entered ceremoniously with a long polished rosewood box, which he placed on the bedside-table. From it he lifted a bronze pistol. He held the gun near the blue-eyed baby and gingerly placed its tiny hand on the carved ivory butt, saying in a loud voice, 'Be strong and courageous like your ancestors!'[4] Though slightly disconcerted by this Albanian tradition, the exhausted Queen rested happy in the belief that she had founded a dynasty.

Half an hour later, when the King returned to his study, he found Ekrem Libohova with a telegram from Ciano. With only trivial changes, the Italian Government presented the draft pact as an ultimatum to expire at noon the following day. The Italian Legation meanwhile instructed its nationals to assemble at ports and airports for evacuation, on the ground that their lives were in danger from armed bands (which were nowhere in evidence). The closure of the Hotel Continental, maybe more than anything else, convinced the Tirana élite that the danger was serious. They had lived through many an invasion scare, but never before had they lost their favourite bar. Nobody believed Libohova when he told journalists in late afternoon, 'There is no reason whatsoever to speak of a rupture in Italo-Albanian relations.'[5]

By then, Francesco Jacomoni had once more come and gone from the palace. After signing the book of congratulation on the birth of Prince Leka, he spent two hours with the King, who summarised their conversation thus: 'I refused to consider the demands which would result in a protectorate according to my view. The Italian Minister maintained that the demands would not constitute a protectorate.'[6] Jacomoni would not be drawn into bargaining.

Frustrated in his efforts to discover what was going on, the US Minister in Tirana, easygoing southerner Hugh Grant, sought out his countrywoman Muriel Seherr-Thoss (who had come to be with Geraldine) and asked her to get word to the King that the Foreign Ministry was preventing diplomatic access to him. The Turkish and French Ministers had had the same experience as himself, and they all suspected Libohova and Sereqi of working for Italy. Countess Muriel passed on the warning and returned with the reply that Zog 'knew very well that these men and many others were bribed'.[7] He probably also knew that the Italians decoded his ciphers, tapped his telephone, and opened Foreign Ministry correspondence.

Count Ciano therefore had no doubt as to the significance of his latest telegram from Ribbentrop, which stated, apropos of nothing, that Germany would welcome the strengthening of Italian influence. Italy had made a point of not consulting Germany about Albania, but, earlier in the day, the Albanian Minister in Berlin had gone to the Wilhelmstrasse and appealed for German diplomatic intervention to restrain Mussolini –

a sign of utter desperation, given that the Germans had rebuffed an earlier and less explicit approach from Zog with the assertion that Italy alone guaranteed the independence of Albania.

The Duce had recovered his nerve. 'He is calm, frightfully calm,' noted Ciano; 'he has decided to march, and he will march although all the world may be pitted against him.'[8] The fact of German knowledge probably fortified Mussolini more than apparent German approval, for how would it look to Hitler if he climbed down now? If the diplomacy of the Italo-Albanian crisis had a point of no return, this was it.

For King Zog, Wednesday 5 April had been an overwhelming day: he had become a father, received an ultimatum, realised that negotiation was futile, and played his last diplomatic card – the appeal to Berlin – without success. At nine o'clock, after a grim cabinet meeting, he went upstairs to see his wife. He admired the baby, gave her a string of pearls, and then explained, as gently as he could, that she and Leka must be ready to leave for Greece at very short notice. Geraldine was thunderstruck. Gladys Girault nearly fainted, and some Hungarian ladies-in-waiting wept as Mrs Strale d'Ekna tried to get them to pack. Professor Weibel advised Zog against moving the Queen until absolutely necessary. Despite the brevity of her actual labour, prolonged spasms of pain over the preceding week had left her too frail to stand.

Next day, the weather matched the mood in the towns of Albania. Though dry for the first time in a fortnight, it was unseasonably warm and close, and people waited for a storm which did not break. On the political front, the lack of official news did not prevent everyone sensing that matters had come to a head. Shops stayed closed and workplaces were deserted. Hundreds of young men milled about, looking angry and anxious, yet uncertain what to do. A report of three Italian warships off Durrës caused a flurry of excitement, but they were merely picking up the last Italian nationals.

Jacomoni called on the King in mid-morning and submitted the draft pact for signature. Even at the eleventh hour, with no hint of reprieve, Zog thought it worth trying to buy time, if only for his wife's sake. After reiterating his objections, he 'confessed' that some of his ministers were begging him to reconsider. He had therefore decided that Parliament should settle the matter during a special session. This ploy won him another six hours, but there was little or nothing to be done unless the Italians were willing to moderate their demands. They were not.

When the US Minister finally obtained his audience at noon, Zog glumly outlined the events of the week and held out no hope of averting invasion. Grant reported:

The King's general demeanour was calm but during the course of the conversation which lasted for nearly an hour he manifested strong emotion especially when he stated that Italian aggression would not be met in Albania as it was in Czechoslovakia. He said that he would not in any circumstances agree to sign away his country as the President of the Czechoslovak Republic has done. He referred with a touch of bitterness in his voice to the fact that the Italians launched their offensive at the very moment when the Queen was giving birth to a child. At this particular moment he gazed out of the window and I could see plainly tears welling up in his eyes. He controlled himself with difficulty at this moment. He gave the impression of a man who felt bitter disappointment and that he had been grossly betrayed.[9]

The King stated that military units had been 'placed in strategic sections'. Grant asked if any power had answered Albanian appeals for assistance. Only the Yugoslavs, said Zog, and they had simply told him not to worry. Cincar-Marković purported to believe that Italy was bluffing.

The most notable foreign reaction that afternoon came from London. Asked in Parliament if Britain had any interest in Albania, Chamberlain answered, 'No direct interest, but a general interest in the peace of the world'[10] – which Ciano thought very satisfactory. The British premier then left for a week's fishing in Scotland. This, after all, was the Thursday before Easter.

In Tirana, the young nationalists thronging the streets had gradually merged into one large crowd which surrounded the royal compound. 'Down with Italy! Down with Mussolini!' was the initial chant, which turned to 'Give us arms! We are being betrayed!' after Zog failed to appear. Across the rose gardens, Jacomoni and his remaining staff were barricading themselves inside their Legation and setting up concealed machine-guns for self-defence. After a couple of hours, the demonstrators moved on to Skanderbeg Square, where they were only silenced by the sight of fifty Italian war-planes flying high over the city. Radio Tirana, on air since November, broadcast a plea for calm from the King, which stated that 'he was still negotiating with Rome, but that Albania would resist in the event of attack'.[11]

The streets had cleared enough by six o'clock to allow the Italian Minister to drive unimpeded to the Foreign Ministry, as prearranged, to hear the decision of the deputies from Kotta and Libohova. They informed him that Parliament (doubtless taking its lead from the palace) had passed a resolution rejecting the draft pact and seeking more talks. The diplomat returned to his Legation without comment, and the cabinet ministers joined the King for what turned out to be an all-night vigil. The Albanian Legation in Paris issued a communiqué making plain that, since the Pact of Tirana lapsed in 1931, Italy could claim no legal right of intervention. Meanwhile, Zog sent a personal message to Mussolini, repeating the request for further negotiations and suggesting that his old friend General Pariani be sent to Tirana to conduct them. The reply was a telegram so double-edged as to offer no real hope. If Zog wished to negotiate, the Duce said, he should send a representative to see General Guzzoni after he landed in the morning. Guzzoni was leading the invasion force.

Into the small hours, Zog kept on telephoning prefectures and command posts. Sometimes the line went dead, and sometimes nobody answered. News arrived around three o'clock of an attack on Vlora. The report was in fact false, but shortly afterwards Sereqi cabled his resignation from Rome, which was the secret emergency signal. The King ordered the immediate evacuation of Geraldine, Leka, his sisters and nieces. From their boarded-up Legation, Italian diplomats heard the engine-noise as about a dozen limousines lined up outside the compound. Gladys Girault and her family had headed for Dubrovnik eighteen hours earlier. Mrs Strale d'Ekna, Madame de Szinyei Merse, and Professor Weibel remained with Geraldine and the baby, and one car was to collect her brother from the Korça *lycée*. Otherwise the drivers were told to avoid towns. To calm the Princesses, everyone spoke of coming back as soon as the danger was past.

It was almost four o'clock by the time the Queen was carried out on a mattress and wedged into a Chrysler from which the back seat had been removed. Zog leant inside to kiss her forehead and hand. 'Oh, God . . . it was so short,' he murmured, before watching the convoy disappear into the night and going back to his smoke-filled room.[12]

CHAPTER THIRTY-SEVEN

Good Friday

There is a story that when the first Italian officer stepped off the gangplank onto the breakwater at Durrës soon after five o'clock on the morning of Friday, 7 April, an Albanian official asked to see his passport. The soldier did not have one. 'We have come to occupy your country,' he explained.[1] A couple of hundred more soldiers were allowed to join him before the local gendarmes opened fire with two machine-guns. All the Italians left standing scrambled back on board their ship, and a short naval bombardment ensued. Then General Guzzoni ordered in 'whippet' tanks to secure the seafront. In under four hours, the Albanian resisters (300 men at most) had been forced inland. Disembarkation then proceeded unhindered.

The invaders faced even less opposition at Shëngjin, Vlora, and Saranda/Zogaj. Around eight o'clock, twenty-one bombers, in formations of three, swooped low over Tirana to scatter leaflets:

Albanians! Italian troops landing today in your country belong to a people who have been your friends throughout centuries and have often demonstrated this friendship with you. Do not oppose them with useless resistance. It will be wiped out. Do not listen to government or the men who have impoverished you and now would lead you to futile bloodshed. Soldiers of His Majesty the King-Emperor of Italy have come and will remain only for the time necessary to restore order, justice, and peace.[2]

Piloting one of the aeroplanes was Count Ciano, unwilling to miss the chance to witness 'his' invasion. He could report to the Duce that the sea was like a mirror and the road to Tirana wide open.

Even as the leaflets fluttered in the breeze, King Zog was at the radio microphone, appealing 'to France, Great Britain and the civilised world' and denying that Italian lives and property were in any danger.[3] He had left the royal compound at dawn, presumably for fear that it might be raided, and worked instead from the Prime Minister's residence and the Tirana home of Prince Xhelal. Since he travelled around the city in a car with closed curtains, and other functionaries did the same, a fair degree of secrecy was achieved, though every time he used the telephone, he probably gave away his whereabouts.

229

Choosing to take Mussolini at his word, on hearing that the fighting had died down at Durrës, Zog sent two emissaries to see Alfredo Guzzoni. The Italian military attaché, Colonel Gabrielli, escorted Rrok Geraj, the Minister for Economics, and Colonel Sami Koka, down to the coast. The proposal they brought from the King was this: if the troops and equipment which had already been put ashore were to be declared a gift from the King of Italy to the King of the Albanians, negotiations for a new pact could carry on as if nothing had happened. Guzzoni undertook to forward it to Rome, but he refused to discuss a ceasefire.

After waiting a couple of hours for an answer, which never arrived, Zog addressed the nation at two o'clock:

> Italy has made demands of Albania which would have deprived her of her independence. I and my Government will never accept such conditions aiming a blow at the freedom won by the blood of the people.
>
> In the face of aggression, I invite the whole Albanian people to unite today, in this moment of danger, to defend the safety of the country and its independence to the last drop of blood. I am convinced that the Albanian people, small in number but great in spirit and courage, will know how to give proof of those nationalist feelings which have inspired them and their ancestors.
>
> Sure that a nation united in this spirit will receive the Divine help, I appeal to every one of my people not to lose courage and the love for the Fatherland which, sooner or later, must assure to this land its natural rights. Long live Albania! Long live the Albanian people![4]

The message was repeated time after time (and relayed in French, German, and Italian), but not many of his subjects heard it: the number of radios in Albania was less than two thousand, and the Italians soon jammed the broadcast. Radio Bari meanwhile ran a speech by Marko Kodeli, prefect of Durrës, asking why years of Italian aid had failed to help ordinary Albanians. The answer, of course, was embezzlement by Zog and a 'court which can only recall the remote days of absolute kings and vampires battening on the unfortunate people'. Italy had finally cried 'Enough!'[5]

For several hours, the war of words was waged more actively than the war on the ground. According to Radio Tirana, the enemy had been thrice repulsed at Vlora and seven times at Durrës, and the morale of the Albanian forces was excellent. In reality, by far the greater part of the army, gendarmerie, and reserves had done nothing at all to resist the Italians. There were isolated acts of bravery by individuals, but no kind of co-ordinated defence materialised anywhere.

Why ever had the invaders not yet occupied Tirana then? That was just what Mussolini demanded to know. How long should it take to advance 25 miles against negligible opposition? Chaos reigned in the Italian expeditionary force. It appeared that raw conscripts had been arbitrarily assigned to specialist units, so there were wireless operators, lorry-drivers, and motor-cyclists who had never performed their tasks before. Vehicles broke down and blocked narrow roads. After the field command at Durrës lost radio contact with Italy and the three other columns, confusion grew till, in early afternoon, Guzzoni ordered all units to halt and report their positions. Filippo Anfuso, Ciano's assistant, wrote that 'if King Zog had possessed a competent fire brigade the Italian army must have been hurled back into the sea'.[6]

In Tirana, no one knew what was happening, beyond the fact that the Italians had stopped moving. Wondering if this indicated willingness to negotiate, Zog sent his envoys back to Durrës, but they probably did not get that far. The Durrës gendarmerie, which showed more spirit than the rest of the Albanian armed forces put together, had managed to destroy the bridge at Shijak. In one way or another, however, information reached the King by five o'clock that the invaders were simply pausing and would soon resume their offensive. Fear of air attack had taken hold in the meantime, and thousands of residents fled to the hills or sheltered in cellars. Zog chose this moment to return to the palace, where the Old Gang was waiting with the fleet of ministerial cars. He went straight to his study and emptied the safe. Then, sometime between six and seven o'clock, a heavily laden motorcade – the second in fifteen hours – sped out of the city in the direction of Elbasan.

'The Big Bird' had flown and the news quickly spread. There was no bombing, and the Italians later accused Zog of generating the panic in order to clear the streets for his departure. Tirana prison threw open its doors. By nightfall, several dozen cheerful looters were scurrying about the royal compound, brandishing such trophies as a velvet cushion, a box of handkerchiefs, or a carton of chocolate bars. One youth galloped around on Geraldine's white mare, firing volleys in the air. When the mob began to switch its attention from the palace to the Italian Legation, an admonishing burst of machine-gun fire put a damper on the party, however, and the city was more or less quiet from midnight until half past ten the following morning, when the first squad of *bersaglieri* roared into Skanderbeg Square on motorcycles. Nobody tried to stop them. Thirty minutes later, a triumphant Count Ciano touched down at the aerodrome, opened his cockpit, and tossed handfuls of lire notes to the hastily assembled claque. Chief among the passengers was Zef Sereqi, who had received assurances of his future seven months ago. Guzzoni, Jacomoni, the German Minister, and a cluster of second-rate beys formed the reception committee. Nearly a year after his previous visit, the Italian Foreign Minister drove once more through the Albanian capital, bowing and smiling. Black and red pennants, put up to mark Prince Leka's birth, had already been supplemented with posters of the Duce and a banner: 'We salute our Italian deliverers.'[7] To salute, however, was exactly what most of the onlookers would not do. 'There is a certain amount of coolness,' Ciano conceded. 'I see the eyes of some patriots flaming with anger and tears running down their faces.'[8]

At the Town Hall, he was introduced to Xhafer Bey Ypi, the mediocrity whom Zogu had shunted from the premiership in 1922. To that high office he now returned, having till yesterday held the Zogist sinecure of Chief Inspector of the Court. Though the serving cabinet had vanished overnight, Sereqi had to settle for the rank of an Italian divisional general. Toasted in champagne at the Italian Legation, Count Ciano explained to assorted local turncoats that he really could not accede to their wish that he take the throne himself. Even the embarrassing fact that the bulk of the fascist invasion force was still dragging itself up the road from Durrës failed to take the shine off his exultation. Did it not prove a crucial point? The tyrant had fled the wrath of his own unhappy people. Said Ciano, 'This is the end of Zog and all that he stood for in Albania.'[9]

CHAPTER THIRTY-EIGHT

A Reckoning

Red-eyed and unshaven, Zog stepped out of his mud-splashed car in the central square of Florina, a small market town in the far north of Greece, around 1.20 p.m. on Saturday 8 April. All contemporary sources give the same time within an hour or so. He asked the whereabouts of his wife and child and headed off to an unfurnished house on the outskirts without pausing to address a huddle of journalists. All they had collected so far were a few pathetic quotes from Geraldine relayed by her grandmother. They gained little more copy now, as an unnamed Zogist minister just said, 'It was impossible. We could not have made a stand against those millions and all their ships and airplanes.'[1]

This taciturnity is only one of the reasons why it is very difficult to compile an accurate outline of Zog's final eighteen hours in Albania. His movements were naturally veiled in secrecy and disinformation at the time. After his convoy had left Tirana early on Friday evening, word went round that the Government was withdrawing over the Krrabë Mountains to Elbasan, as the capital had few defences. It was widely assumed though that he would head north-east, since Mati lay in that direction, and a sizeable portion of the army was near Kruja. From this point on, precisely what happened was known only to him and his companions. Even an authorised account published in 1940 said no more than this:

Albania was occupied. A group of his officers forced King Zog to save himself and leave his country. He left to save himself, to save Albania, he left for he could not bear the knowledge of his ailing wife and baby being far from him. After five days [sic] Zog arrived in Florina with his retinue.[2]

Decades later, Colonel Selmani recounted that Zog stayed in Tirana till the Italian forces were only 7 kilometres away. He then went via Elbasan to Pogradec in the east with the aim of fighting in the mountains. However, the Yugoslav Government warned that, if there were any battle within 15 kilometres of the frontier, they would send in their own troops against the Zogists. Then the Greek Government advised that it would be closing its border at midnight sharp. Zog and retinue left Albania at Kapshtica at 11.50 p.m. and reached Florina at 1 a.m. – on 10 April, says the latest version.[3]

Thus have faithful Zogists striven, without much success, to soften the blow dealt to their hero's reputation by the speed of his departure. He never really lived down the imputation that, when the fateful hour struck, he chose to take the money and run, Italian radio having blazed the fact that he emptied the treasury of 550,000 gold francs before leaving. He also stood open to the charge of cowardice. Albania was not the first state to submit to Axis aggression without offering much resistance, but western newspapers, short of information, had initially served up stirring clichés about a heroic race of warriors. When the Italians reached the Greek frontier within four days and admitted to only twelve dead (though the figure must have been higher), this talk about legendary Albanian valiance should have been exposed as romanticism. Sooner than credit the hard-bitten pragmatism of real Gheg clansmen, however, many foreigners attributed their inactivity to the desertion of their ruler.

The day before the attack, Zog had told Hugh Grant that, while they could only manage a token protest, 'Albanians would not die without putting up a fight.'[4] He afterwards explained, 'Unfortunately, the forces of my country were neither large nor modern enough to resist successfully,' adding, 'We tried our chance, but we could only fight for a few days as we had no tanks, no planes, no mechanised units, and munitions sufficient only for three days.' This sounded persuasive to many people, but those with experience of Albania had never expected the King to mount a conventional defence. They envisaged him leading the clans in traditional guerrilla warfare. Zog's answer: 'But we had to leave when there was a danger of our retreat being cut off.'[5]

Thus attention turns to the attitude of neighbouring states. Three years later, hotly denying desertion, Zog recalled his predicament in a discussion with Sir Andrew Ryan:

He had wished to provide for the safety of his family and had successively asked the Greeks and Yugoslavs, but vainly, to provide a ship. He represented both powers as obsessed by their fear of Italy. His reports from his prefects in the frontier regions were discouraging as regards the attitude of both. The Yugoslav Minister had left Tirana and the report of the prefect at Dibra was to the effect that the Yugoslavs would carry submission to Italy to the extent of invading Albania, if necessary. Confronted with this possibility in the event of continued resistance to the Italian invasion, he had no alternative but to disband his forces at Elbasan and cross the frontier into Greece.[6]

Yugoslavia certainly acquiesced in Albania's downfall – passivity was its policy – but it had not colluded. Afraid about Kosovo and Croatia, Prince

Paul broke down and wept. Zog was right to assume that neither Yugoslavs nor Greeks would have risked supplying aid to Albanian resistance fighters. However, if he actually believed that Yugoslavia would have sent troops across the border against them, he was surely mistaken. The Yugoslavs dared not intervene without Italian agreement, and Italy had no desire to involve them at this late stage. It sounds rather as if King Zog was knowingly overstating his case to Ryan in 1942.

Apart from military weakness and alleged Yugoslav threats, there is a third explanation of why the King skedaddled – the obvious one that he could never admit. Very few Albanians showed any willingness to fight for him. The majority apparently accepted the Italian occupation in a spirit of resignation which verged upon indifference: proof, if it were needed, that two or three decades of independence had yet to produce a mature nation state. (Portraying himself as a tutor, Zog had recently observed that he had seen Albania 'grow to adolescence' over twenty years, and 'he only wanted twenty more almost to complete the task'.[7]) The loyalties of peasants and clansmen remained narrowly local, while educated youngsters felt ambivalent about their sovereign.

Italian propaganda, concentrating all its fire on the King, his sisters, and the Old Gang, said that the invasion was against a Government, not against a people; far from being conquered, the Albanians were simply gaining a new and better Head of State. Too many Tirana intellectuals spent Easter weekend not fighting for their country but debating whether Zog was worth having. Ciano strung them along with his 'personal union formula' (borrowed from the British Commonwealth), whereby Italy and Albania would supposedly continue as separate nations while sharing a Head of State (in the person of King Victor Emmanuel). Within six days, the Italians secured an endorsement of this from a constituent assembly of 159 invited Albanian notables. Among them were most of the parliamentary deputies; men who had voted for resistance on 6 April voted for collaboration on 12 April.

Whatever else may have changed in Albania during his reign, King Zog had absolutely failed to reform the political instincts of the beys and chieftains. By spoils and corruption he had kept them; by spoils and corruption he lost them, once Italy opted to cut out the middle-man and pay them their bounties direct. True, the gold disbursed by Giro and Jacomoni had not in fact brought the clans down from the hills in anti-Zogist rebellion, but, as soon as the invasion became a reality, almost all the big men defected at a stroke. Their only feeling for the King had been jealousy. When the new assembly 'elected' a puppet Government, several of the names were familiar: Fejzi Alizoti at Finance, Xhafer Ypi at Education, Xhemil Dino at Foreign Affairs. And the Prime Minister was none other than Shevqet Vërlaci, the bey whose daughter Zog had jilted.

Through him, Jacomoni reassured the ruling class: its clientele could carry on manning the civil service, army, and gendarmerie – with a 22 per cent pay rise.

Which is the more scathing critique? That Zog abandoned his people on Good Friday 1939, or that his people abandoned him? By the time he left Tirana, his isolation had already become clear. He still had the Old Gang with him – a liability rather than an asset – and he still had the clansmen of the Mati valley, whether Royal Guards or irregulars. His sole real alternative to flight was to lead them – and probably only them – in a final stand at Burreli. The Italians might have raised other clans (most likely the Roman Catholic ones) to oppose him. Jacomoni had assiduously courted Gjon Marka Gjoni, now called Prince of Mirdita. Zog may have wished to spare his fighters from defeat and reprisals. If circumstances ever allowed of a comeback attempt, he would need to have kept his power base intact. Italian forces entered Mati without difficulty on 15 April.

The brevity of the military campaign eased the task of the minority of western European commentators who wanted to carry on preaching appeasement. What marked them out was their inclination to scold Mussolini chiefly for desecrating a Holy day. Generally, however, international press opinion, outside the Axis bloc, did condemn the attack outright. To anti-appeasers, it confirmed the lesson of Prague: fascist dictators were hell-bent on expansion, and Mussolini was as bad as Hitler.

Nobody gave much credence to the reasons put forward by the Italians to justify their invasion. They made the classic mistake of having too many excuses. Italian radio had initially cited the need to save Italian lives from marauding bands. Then there was the claim that Italy intervened on humanitarian grounds to free the Albanians from (as Ciano put it) 'a selfish, narrow-minded, venal, treacherous, cruel ruler possessing all the despicable attributes of a feudal lord in the dark ages'.[8] Even those who accepted this estimate of Zog felt compelled to point out that the Italian Government had been funding him for years. In diplomatic interviews, Ciano concentrated on a different explanation: it had been necessary to drive Ahmed Zogu from power in order to preserve the peace of the Balkans. He 'had completely lost his senses' and initiated the crisis on 20 March by asking for Italian troops to take part in a joint invasion of Yugoslavia to redeem Kosovo. The Albanian had suddenly conceived of himself as the 'Hitler of the Balkans', said Ciano: a man with a mission to reorganise south-eastern Europe.[9] This was preposterous.

Strong condemnation of Italy, however, did not necessarily convert into sympathy for Zog. Everyone felt sorry for Geraldine, naturally, after her journey through the mountains (trembling on a mattress and deliriously chanting the rosary), but a number of journalists came close to blaming her husband for her plight. The diplomatic history of the previous fourteen years counted against him. Clement Attlee summed it up when, after voicing indignation at Italian treatment of Albania, he added, 'One always understood that its Ruler had been a most faithful follower of Signor Mussolini.'[10] Half the people who knew anything about the place thought that it had been a protectorate, sold to Italy by its King in 1926. In the western democracies, neither appeasers nor anti-appeasers, neither Left nor Right, wanted to identify with Zog. (In contrast, internationalists had flocked to Haile Selassie in 1936.)

A few experts were more understanding. 'The diplomatic game set before King Zog might have puzzled a Bismarck,' wrote Ronald Matthews.[11] Joseph Roucek even defended his domestic record: 'In his curious world, "Bird the First" did the work which Providence assigned to him with zest, urbanity, and serenity, combined with well-timed ruthlessness. His personal qualities stood him in good stead in a realm where the quickest trigger reigns over the quick trigger.'[12] More typical, however, was the foreign correspondent who informed his readers that Zog 'started as a creature of the Italians, regularly took ten million lire a year subsidy from them, and regularly failed to deliver the goods'.[13]

There was something of a contradiction here, which Zog would spend the rest of his life pointing out. Had he been a submissive fascist satrap, how was it that he had ended up where he was now? Even if he had 'sold' Albania to Mussolini in a sense, everybody acknowledged that he had tried to avoid delivery. The fact could not be plainer: Italy had just deposed him because he *refused* to sign away his country – unlike President Hácha, who had placed the Czech people in the hands of Hitler three weeks ago and kept his billet in Prague Castle as a Nazi puppet.

'I knew all along what the Italians were after,' Zog argued later, 'and I prevented them from getting control of the country by peaceful means.'[14] Looking back in September 1942, he stated, 'We tried – international politics left us no other choice – to come to an understanding with Italy. But the megalomania of the Fascist regime made us certain that one day we should have to fight to defend ourselves. The problem was to make our crisis coincide with the general crisis. We almost succeeded.'[15]

In April 1939, however, he presented no extensive public defence of his policies, and the mere fact of his overthrow did not prove his patriotism. Many analysts of international affairs doubted that the Italian attack had much connection to anything Zog had done or failed to do: Mussolini wanted an act of war to bolster his status relative to Hitler. In retrospect, though, it looks just possible that Zog could have kept his throne, had he instantly signed the shorter draft pact submitted to him on 3 April. Why did he not do so? On the face of it, the terms of the protectorate were not substantially different from those which he had endured from 1926 to 1931. That said, the international context had changed: the end of Yugoslav pretensions meant that similar treaty rights would have given Italy much more power in 1939. Determined anti-Zogists may suppose that he miscalculated and rejected the short draft in the hope of further concessions. Alternatively, he perhaps realised that his chances of lasting long as a pure puppet would have been slender. A more ignominious fate than exile might have befallen him: Emil Hácha died in prison in 1945 awaiting trial for high treason.

In his memoirs, Francesco Jacomoni went so far as to argue that Zog actually contrived to have himself driven from Albania because he foresaw the defeat of Italy in the Second World War and wanted to switch sides so as to be eligible for restoration by the British. This strains credulity, to put it mildly, given the reaction of the British Government to the aggression at the time. Chamberlain privately conceded 'that Mussolini has behaved to me like a sneak and a cad,' but he only wished that the Duce had troubled 'to make it look like an agreed arrangement'.[16] He refused to abandon the Anglo-Italian Agreement of 1938 (wherein Italy promised to respect the status quo in the Mediterranean), for, as Foreign Secretary Halifax told the cabinet, Albania had been an Italian satellite for a century. The French Government voiced sharper concern, as premier Daladier foresaw an Italo-German offensive from the North Sea to Egypt. He and Halifax pressed Chamberlain into widening the policy of guarantees to warn off Axis aggression. France and Britain guaranteed the independence of Greece and Romania on 13 April 1939.

Thus the fall of Albania did make an international impact. Ironically, a military operation conceived by Mussolini as a shot across the bows of German expansionism actually strengthened the British commitment against Italian ambitions, and made Rome still more dependent on Berlin. These ramifications cannot disguise the fact, however, that world leaders accepted the seizure of Albania itself as a *fait accompli*. They may not have rushed to recognise Victor Emmanuel's new title, but, in most eyes, a land which had been virtually Italian was now really Italian, and that was that. When Zog asked the moribund League of Nations to protest at 'a state of things accomplished by blood and iron', Avenol, the Secretary-General, remarked: 'The reading of the letter constitutes the action I intend to take.'[17]

By then, the Albanian story had all but vanished from the global press, displaced by Danzig, conscription in Britain, the Pact of Steel, and Anglo-Soviet alliance talks. Zog slipped from public view abroad, and the Italians effaced all overt reminders of him in Albania. The 'ZOG' on the mountain-side turned into 'REX', an eagle covered up his face on the banknotes, Boulevard Zog became Boulevard Victor Emmanuel, and Roman salutes replaced Zogist ones. After a mere eight months as Zogaj, Saranda had to change its name once again (to Porto Edda, after Ciano's wife). Jacomoni, raised to viceroy, moved into the Summer Palace, and it was to him that chieftains henceforth swore their besa when collecting their reserve-pay.

In June, a new fascist constitution finished off what Ciano called 'the operation of emasculating Albania without making the patient scream'.[18] It abolished the Foreign Ministry, merged the armed forces, and imposed a customs union. Wherever possible the Italians avoided the appearance of a military occupation. In the highlands, life went on as it had always done, while most towns experienced an economic boom, as public spending reached levels hitherto unknown. Whatever Albanians thought of it all, their Italian masters congratulated themselves.

Shevqet Bey Vërlaci came to Count Ciano with a predictable proposal. Did he have permission 'to take the initiative against King Zog who, when he is dead, will be less embarrassing than he is today'? Ciano replied, 'The matter does not interest us' – and his indifference may well have been genuine.[19] Even if Zog could convince the world that he was neither a fascist nor a deserter, he would now only have a political future if he could refute a more damaging assertion: namely, that he was an irrelevance.

CHAPTER THIRTY-NINE

Refugees

The first days of exile were chaotic. After a minute or two with Geraldine, Zog had hurried away to try and find quarters in Florina for the seventy-odd people who had accompanied him across the border that morning. Thirty or forty more had arrived the day before, and they typically expected him to take all the decisions for them – and he did, though operating like an automaton. Within hours, a Greek official appeared with orders that he should leave the country. General Metaxas, the Prime Minister, wanted to avoid giving Mussolini any pretext for an ultimatum to Greece. Rumours were flying of a second seizure of Corfu, perhaps in conjunction with a Bulgarian offensive in Thrace. Zog travelled straight to Salonika, taking Kostaq Kotta as interpreter, to negotiate with the authorities. They grudgingly allowed him to stay for a week, and he booked rooms for 115 people at Portaria, a summer resort on Mount Pelion, but before they could move in, Geraldine had a relapse and went into hospital at Larissa on 11 April. Large red blotches appeared all over her body, and doctors diagnosed puerperal fever. Zog and his sisters spent several days at her bedside, and Larissa became their temporary home. He took all the rooms of the main hotel, while the lesser Zogists lived in carriages on a railway siding. The Queen was patently too weak to travel, and King George lifted the threat of deportation on seeing the Italians halt at the frontier.

Hundreds more Albanians arrived in Greece in the meantime, including Prince Xhelal, who had escaped via Skopje. Most of the refugees were members of the Royal Guard and their families. Zog could do little more than thank them, pay their wages, and gently send them away. The majority returned to Mati, with his blessing, when they realised that the Italians were not in the business of reprisals. Others joined relations in Yugoslavia or Turkey.

The Greek Government demanded that Zog avoid publicity. He hardly ever left the hotel, especially after his wife joined him during convalescence. Frequently silent, as the adrenalin ebbed, he also tried to rest, but sound sleep had never come easily to him. Innumerable practical difficulties occupied his thoughts in a way that was almost therapeutic. His nephew Sherafedin needed rescuing from college in Italy, and Geraldine found herself with several fur coats and not one pair of shoes. A spokesman denied that she had any plans to divorce and start a film career.

The Zogists left Greece on 2 May by train for Istanbul, where the city governor greeted them with a guard of honour, a courtesy consonant with the anti-Italian tone of Turkish foreign policy. President Inönü even received Zog in a private audience, albeit six weeks later. In the interim, the King had started to recover his spirits. He ventured out of the Park Hotel, looking sombre but composed in a homburg hat and herringbone overcoat, to show Geraldine the Blue Mosque and St Sofia. He also sought out some classmates from 1911 (those holding public office) and considered buying one of Istanbul's many empty palaces. Turkey, an important neutral with a sizeable Albanian population, struck him as a suitable refuge. The immigration authorities judged otherwise. Zog's reputation for intrigue, and his link to the Ottomans (via Prince Abid), made him unwelcome as a permanent resident.

Geraldine still had her wedding-present estate near Oponice, but Slovakia was now a German satellite, and the Nazis might hand Zog over to Italy. Therefore the British and French Embassies in Ankara each received asylum applications from the thirty-two persons in 'King Zog's Circus': the royal family, plus Virginia Strale d'Ekna, Gyula Apponyi, Madam Rüling, three aides, four officers, and ten servants. (The King's four valets were really bodyguards.) Neither France nor Britain desired their presence, but how could they refuse after condemning Italian aggression?

Queries arose in London about the size of Zog's party. Could he afford to support so many? The Foreign Office ascertained that the King had at least £50,000 in gold and $2 million in the Chase Manhattan Bank, enough to yield a comfortable £12,000 per annum. Conspicuous consumption in exile, moreover, indicated before long that this was by no means the full extent of his wealth. With him in all his travels went nine or ten extraordinarily heavy coffers which were kept under constant guard. They contained gold bullion and became the stuff of legend, so much so that the popular press seldom mentioned Zog without some passing reference to 'suitcases said to contain fabulous treasures including the Crown jewels and royal regalia worth more than £1 million'.[1] Reports about French and Swiss bank accounts reinforced the common notion that he was a sterling millionaire. Some reckoned his fortune at £4 million or even £6 million. His comment: 'I wish I were as rich as some of my critics would have people believe.'[2]

King Zog admitted to taking £36,000 of public funds from the Albanian treasury in 1939, because it was 'better to have brought the money with him than to have allowed it to fall into the hands of Mussolini'.[3] But how had he obtained the rest? Zogists pointed to the sale of forests in Mati.

Practically everyone else assumed that, like other Zogist officials, he accepted Italian bribes and pocketed a percentage of monies passing through his hands. 'Here it's not about what should or can change tomorrow,' he once said of the Albanian political class; 'here one has quickly to secure an easily-lost sum today and wait for what the future brings.'[4] The limits to his self-enrichment may possibly be inferred from the scale of the opportunities. During his fourteen years in power, state revenue ranged between one and two million pounds per annum and Italian loans totalled about eight million. How big a cut would a King think appropriate in a land where money was so obviously power?

His affluence in exile more than satisfied the immigration authorities. He could bring his entourage to London or Paris on condition that he refrain from political activity – a ban which he reluctantly accepted. At the end of June, he said goodbye to the Old Gang. Krosi and Juka remained in Istanbul, where, with other Zogists of an oriental stamp, they formed the retinue of Prince Xhelal (till his death in 1944).

Zog arranged for his elder sisters, their children, and his favourite cars to be transported by sea to Marseilles, where they could be met by Senije and Salih (who had been in Paris when the invasion occurred). Fear of Italian piracy, however, led him to take Geraldine, Leka, and the younger Princesses to France by a most circuitous route. On 1 July, a steamer conveyed them to Constanta in Romania. As recipient of an Anglo-French guarantee, King Carol invited Zog to stay at Castle Pelesh. Paradoxically, dethronement made the Albanian a more admissible guest for some foreign Heads of State: he was now a symbolic victim of the Axis. He advised Carol that Hitler and Mussolini, not Stalin, posed the main threat to Romania. There were 'in Europe today two madmen' and 'two big fools who sleep': Chamberlain and Daladier.[5]

After four days, the grand detour continued. Arriving at Warsaw station, the Albanians puzzled a crowd of Polish well-wishers by closing ranks and shuffling in formation to their taxis; Zog had received a death threat. No attack occurred, however, so he felt able to stroll around the Old Town and visit museums. He then hired some cars and drove across Lithuania, Latvia, and Estonia, to satisfy his curiosity about three small states even newer than Albania.

On 17 July, the royal party left Riga by ferry for Sweden. There, in Stockholm, he gave his first press conference since his overthrow. Sitting at a desk behind a little Albanian flag, looking as well-groomed as ever, Zog vowed that every Albanian had a duty to strive for the liberty of his country. 'I will not give up the fight until it is ended or I am dead.'[6] Regarding his immediate plans, he said that, after a month or two in France, he would go to England and lease an estate – until they returned home, added Geraldine: 'We know that Albania is waiting for us.'[7]

The couple received a warm welcome in Sweden, maybe because newspapers wrongly reported that the Queen was of Nordic descent (Strale d'Ekna having been her step-grandfather). Stockholm made so favourable an impression on Zog that he fancied living there until reminded of the winter climate. He enjoyed a cruise of the fjords, before sailing from Copenhagen to Antwerp. His six cars were waiting on the dockside and the family reunion took place at Versailles on 8 August. Château de la Maye had housed the Duke of Windsor in 1938, till the Duchess deemed it too small. Not for the last time, Zog had to adjudicate the allocation of rooms among his household.

The King of the Albanians – for so he still styled himself – did not have a great many visitors at Versailles. His compatriots in France numbered only a few dozen. Of them, the most famous was Kosta Çekrezi, the republican who initiated the Fier revolt. Even Zog did not pretend that the Albanian diaspora gave him undivided support. Though a portion of the politicians exiled in 1924 chose to return and collaborate in 1939, the informal leadership of the émigré communities remained largely with men who had gone abroad to escape Zogist rule. They could bring themselves to appeal for unity against Italy but not for unity behind the monarchy. This was also true of a number of ex-diplomats. After their salaries dried up, Faik Konitza in Washington and Lec Kurti in London became open critics of their former sovereign.

Zog kept paying his envoys in Paris, though Prince Abid, the Albanian Minister, carried minimal weight in émigré politics. As a Turk, he viewed events with detachment, while his marriage with Princess Senije – never a great success – signified less and less now that she had her brother with her. Zog and Senije took a more western view of a wife's role than did Abid, whose playboy traits coexisted with a residue of Muslim conservatism.

The King relied far more on his Minister of the Court. Sotir Martini first worked with Zog in 1922, as chief of cabinet to the Interior Minister. Latterly, as Master of Ceremonies, he won the trust of the family, and exile transformed him from a major domo to the King's principal spokesman, the nearest he had to a political confidant. Whether Martini had ideas of his own, outsiders could never discern. By using an intermediary, Zog sustained an aura of royal aloofness. He especially needed to be able to negotiate with anti-Zogist exiles without conceding them an equal footing. Albanians in Paris could not agree on an anti-Italian platform. The King rejected any formula which cast doubt on his sovereign rights; Çekrezi rejected any which did not.

Zog, like most others in August 1939, realised that European war was imminent. The day before Germany invaded Poland, he sought permission for a private trip to London and, from 10 September, lodged incognito for a week at Brown's Hotel. His mission appears to have been purely financial:

to close his dollar account at the Westminster Bank, taking the $82,409 as a draft on New York, and to withdraw £50,000 in cash from Lloyds and bring it to France in defiance of exchange controls. Customs turned a blind eye (on Foreign Office advice), and his bodyguards liked to imagine that their menacing presence had silenced the bank manager. While Zog never showed much faith in financial institutions, there may have been a specific reason for his action. In Tirana, a Special Commission had confiscated royal property as a penalty for 'pillage, thefts, and outrages' and asked foreign governments to sequester his assets.[8] Perhaps it occurred to him that the British would now be more eager to appease Mussolini in order to keep Italy out of the war.

On his return, Zog found his womenfolk fearful that Paris would share the fate of Warsaw, so he moved to a hotel in the Breton resort of La Baule. Geraldine recalled decades later: 'That was the only time in our lives that by common consent we disregarded the presence of the Princesses and put our problems behind us. We made excursions alone from the early morning until late evening, on foot or by car. For me . . . this was my honeymoon.'[9] It did not last. When Princess Ruhije fell seriously ill, Zog led the family back to Versailles, where they stayed at the Hotel Palais Trianon. The 'Phoney War' posed no threat, and he preferred to be near the seat of power.

Most days, his chauffeur took him 'to work' in Paris. This work consisted of attempts at discreet lobbying and it was by no means easy. The French Government refused to lift its ban on his engaging in political activity, and Daladier told his ministers to avoid having anything to do with the 'appalling gangster who had been paid by Italy to clear out of Albania'.[10] Zog tried to meet influential deputies, civil servants, and army officers – either by turning up at *beau monde* charity functions or by working outwards from the few Frenchmen known to him: Marcel Ray, Louis Mercier, and other veterans of the Tirana Legation.

His tactic was to invite useful contacts to lunch at a top restaurant. There any who expected to see a broken man were soon disabused. He would arrive with Martini or Prince Abid (and three or four minders) and launch into blithe chatter: '*Monsieur*, how I love your country! It is the land of beautiful churches. It is also the land of beautiful handkerchiefs [drawing one from his breast pocket] . . . I bought a crate of them. *Monsieur*, the King of Italy never had such handkerchiefs.'[11] The guards, who pretended to follow the conversation, laughed scornfully at any mention of Italy. (These Mati warriors in suits and bow-ties attracted much comment wherever Zog went, on account of their appearance, their odour, and their spitting). The talk would turn to international politics and eventually the strategic importance of Albania. Zog spoke French with reasonable fluency, though he pronounced each word separately and amused his interlocutors by starting almost every sentence with *Monsieur* or *Madame*. Most guests would feign polite interest in his views, but few cared to impart their own, and even fewer returned the invitation. Frenchmen viewed Zog as a curiosity. The foremost Ruritanian novel in their literature, Daudet's *Les rois en exil*, concerned a deposed King of Illyria residing in a Paris hotel.

Britain recognised the Italian seizure of Albania when it appointed a Consul-General to Durrës in October 1939. Zog sent a protest to George VI and no more was heard about his moving to London. In Paris, Prince Abid still had diplomatic status, which was some consolation for the fact that Zog had not. Though riled by the illogicality of this, the King thought better of pressing the point. Egypt and Turkey were the only other countries where Albanian Legations stayed open.

To please Geraldine, who disliked hotel life, the Albanians moved in February 1940 to a fine old mansion at Le Mesnil-Saint-Denis in the Valley of Chevreuse. They found it far too cold. Zog then leased the Château de Méry-sur-Oise at Pontoise, north-west of Paris, but when the town was bombed on the first night of the Blitzkrieg, 10 May, some credulous locals attributed this to his presence. Zog promptly obliged them by shifting to the Hotel Plaza Athenée, just off the Champs Elysée. The Queen was unhappy about their fifth move in eight months. Would her baby ever know stability? Why stay in the capital now? The Germans broke through on 14 May and reached the Channel on 20 May. The Luftwaffe raided Paris after Dunkirk fell on 4 June. The Panzers turned south two days later. Still the King of the Albanians did not budge.

On 10 June, he lunched at Maxim's with Roger Peyrefitte, an employee of the Information Ministry who had formerly served in Athens. Peyrefitte loyally assured his host that the city was well defended. On returning to his office and finding it deserted, he felt honour-bound to send word to Prince Abid that the Government was abandoning Paris for Tours.

There was more momentous news that afternoon: the news for which Zog had been waiting. In Rome, Count Ciano told the French Ambassador that Italy would enter the war at midnight. With his heart set on hegemony in *Mare Nostrum*, Mussolini could not pass up the 'chance that comes only once in five thousand years'. At six o'clock, the Royal Albanian Legation in Paris declared that Albania, at war since 7 April 1939, was now allied to the democracies. Nobody took the slightest notice, but it meant that Zogists could later claim: 'This declaration, made at a moment when Fascism triumphed and when both friends and enemies believed that all was over, proves Albanian determination and also her confidence in the final victory of justice and liberty.'[12]

Next day, the royal family filled six cars and a lorry and joined the refugee exodus. It turned into a much more prolonged ordeal than their flight from Tirana the previous year. Over six million Frenchmen were on the move, and, as the traffic crawled westwards, bumper to bumper, food and petrol grew scarce. People slept in their cars or in fields beside the road. The diplomatic corps had swept through this turmoil with a motor-cycle escort, and King Zog tried to contact President Lebrun with appeals for recognition and aid. Forced from Tours to Bordeaux, the French Government was disintegrating, and offices still intact had better things to do than attend to exiled Albanians.

They suffered an air attack somewhere near Orléans. While others took cover, Zog stayed with his coffers in the back of the scarlet Mercedes given him by Hitler. No German pilot, he assured his wife, would strafe a car so like the Führer's. Exhaustion and hunger took their toll, especially on the invalid Ruhije. Finally reaching the Atlantic coast after a week on the road, they found that their pension at Royan had been requisitioned. A boarded-up convent became their temporary home.

By now, Pétain had taken the premiership and defeatism was rampant. The King went into Bordeaux the next morning, 18 June, to ask the ambassador if he could go to Britain. Permission came from London in hours: getting there was the problem. The Gironde teemed with tens of thousands of troops and refugees, all seeking berths on too few boats. The British and Poles took priority; Zog could only chase rumours of sailings and try to talk his way into the diplomatic corps. When Bordeaux was bombed, he went south to Bayonne on the advice of British naval intelligence (in the form of Lieutenant Ian Fleming, author of the James Bond books). Although loath to forsake the Allies himself, he thought that Spain might grant visas to his sisters. They flatly refused to leave him.

Pétain agreed terms with the Germans on 22 June and with the Italians on 24 June. That day, the Albanians learnt of merchant ships evacuating Polish troops and civilians from St-Jean-de-Luz. Seeing Bentleys and Rolls Royces abandoned at the roadside, they prayed they were not too late. It was dusk and the last boat was nearly full when British naval officers heard motor-horns in the distance. They decided that the SS *Ettrick* would somehow find room for royalty, but not for their hundred pieces of luggage. After crossing choppy seas in a tender to the liner, Zog learnt that his cases of gold remained stacked on the quayside. For once, he flew into a tremendous rage, at first to no avail. Luckily, the ship did not sail till dawn, because of the risk of mines. This allowed his Hungarian chauffeur to hire a speedboat and reunite the King with his treasure.

The armistice had been in effect for six hours by the time the *Ettrick* put to sea. For Zog, it had been a close-run thing, but now he was bound for a country at war with his enemies. The RAF had already bombed Milan. While other refugees despaired, this one looked forward to real possibilities.

CHAPTER FORTY

In London at War

When Zog received Sir Andrew Ryan at the Ritz Hotel on the morning of Wednesday, 3 July 1940, his intention was to unveil his plan for an anti-Italian uprising. First, however, he put the key question: did Britain support the restoration of independent Albania? His heart must have sunk when Ryan replied that he was not in any position to say, having retired after his recall last year. As an old friend, he had come only to pass on an official recommendation that the royal family leave for the United States.

The Albanians had arrived in London by train from Plymouth a week ago. There were still thirty-five people in the group, for although Zog had shed a few Hungarians, he had acquired a couple of secretaries (and their wives) from the Paris Legation. On 29 June, he had sent Martini to the Foreign Office to offer his help against Italy and enquire if he should call at Buckingham Palace.

The British Government remained unmoved by the argument that the Kingdom of Albania, embodied by Zog, automatically qualified as an ally. The Foreign Office actually thought it might be wise to leave the country under Italian rule after the war, given its seeming inability to stand alone. Laurence Grafftey-Smith, until recently Consul-General at Durrës, flatly informed his superiors that 'there was no pro-Zog party in Albania'.[1] Sooner than enter into direct communication, they had asked Ryan to send the exile on his way.

Without betraying the slightest annoyance, Zog dug in his heels. He reported that no ship would be available until the end of August, expressed anxiety about Ruhije's cancer, and said that he could not possibly leave without thanking Churchill in person for his rescue. His secretaries meanwhile orchestrated lobbying by émigrés, and General Percy put in a good word for him at the War Office. What persuaded the Foreign Secretary, however, was increasing American reluctance to accept troublesome refugees. On 23 July, Zog heard that he could stay, but as a private individual only. No one in authority would receive him (though informal contact might continue via Ryan), and he had to promise to abstain from political activity.

In London, as in Paris, Zog was confined to the diplomacy of the luncheon table. The Ritz offered tempting fare, and sandbags and taped window-panes failed to diminish the status of its clientele. Predictably, he found it easier to get onto speaking terms with other exiles, such as Sikorski and Beneš, than with influential British figures, but he did not want to stray from their proximity. When any Albanian complained about the Blitz, Zog would reply: 'The Londoners are our hosts! If they suffer, we must suffer!'[2]

The Zogu family lived at the Ritz for over ten months, with the King and Queen in a third-floor suite overlooking Green Park and half a dozen bodyguards on an upper level. Lesser members of the entourage lodged at the nearby Athenaeum Court. Although Zog himself rarely left his rooms, stories about him spread from the very first day, when, struggling to lift his heavy boxes, a hall porter asked if they contained anything of special value. 'Yes,' said the King, 'gold.'[3] Martini withdrew a £1,000 banknote every week, according to hotel gossip, which also spoke of wild nocturnal poker schools and 'blackish, dirty, greasy bandits' prowling the corridors with sawn-off shotguns.[4] The Princesses appeared odd and unapproachable; Zog did not allow them to visit theatres or nightclubs while their homeland was occupied. Occasionally, he walked down Piccadilly, and Dervish Duma, formerly of the Royal Legation, recalled him presenting a £50 note to a startled tobacconist to pay for a packet of cigarettes. The King's own favourite anecdote concerned a shopping trip to Harrods, where a pickpocket filched his wallet. In a crowded lift ten minutes later, Zog coolly snatched it back.

To anyone prepared to listen, the Albanian King reiterated his faith in a British victory. What about his past links with Mussolini? 'But I have never seen him in my life!' It was the Great Powers who had forced Albania under a sort of Italian protectorate with their wretched Paris Declaration. He had tried to join the Balkan Pact to block Italian expansion. 'After all, I was the first victim of Axis violence by arms,' he insisted – not that he ignored Ethiopia. The British Government had once shunned the ex-Emperor exiled in Bath, but, as soon as Italy entered the war, Churchill sent Haile Selassie back to Africa with guns for a Patriot Army. Zog asked only to help the Allies in the same way. The Albanians were keen to combat fascism, he asserted: 'I saw them fight the Italians . . . Mussolini will never gain friends in my country!'[5]

Intelligence from Albania, admittedly sketchy, indicated that there had been little resistance to Italian rule to date. Ciano treated 'my grand duchy' like a country estate, flying over for hunting weekends, and it pleased him to patronise the locals rather than terrorise them.[6] Apparently, Italian imperialism was establishing itself better in Albania, albeit at a high financial cost, than it had done in Ethiopia or Libya.

Then Italy invaded Greece from Albania on 28 October 1940. King Zog instantly offered the Greeks unconditional collaboration and requested an interview with Churchill. Failing to obtain one, he had to settle for

Ryan, but this did not dampen his enthusiasm 'to work for the common cause'. If the British agreed, he would raise an Albanian Legion in Istanbul, where the Albanian population numbered 14,000, and lead it across Greece to hold a small sector of the fighting front. His presence could spark a national revolt, starting in Mati and Dibra, which would sweep across Albania and wreck Italian communications. 'The King rattled off so many names of persons and places' that Ryan could not keep up, and the former diplomat might be forgiven a certain scepticism.[7] At their previous meeting, he had caught him citing Gjon Marka Gjoni among his supporters. For good measure, Zog now alleged that the Italians had in March 1939 offered him a palace in Rome or 30 million gold francs if he would only connive at an attack on Greece, and his refusal had cost him his throne.

The idea of the 'Sons of the Eagle' launching a guerrilla campaign appealed to the new Special Operations Executive (SOE), particularly after a Greek counter-offensive in November swept the war onto Albanian soil. *Picture Post* sent a photographer to the Ritz for a feature entitled 'Albania's Chance'. As for Zog, 'Twenty years had slipped from his shoulders.'[8]

On 22 November, Greek forces captured Korça. That evening, Philip Broad of SOE informed the King that there was a seat for him on a flight to Cairo next morning if he wanted it. From Egypt, he would be able to reach Turkey or Greece in time for Independence Day. Did Zog leap at the chance? He did not. He claimed to have a secret arsenal of 20,000 rifles hidden in the mountains and dismissed any doubts about the response of the clans. However, he 'made it quite clear that he did not desire to be rushed into anything'. More precisely, before departing, 'he felt it incumbent on him to see the Prime Minister and the Secretary of State in order to convey to them his thanks for the courtesy which he had received from this country'.[9]

The King had in mind (and so did the Foreign Office) major political complications which SOE overlooked. Zog saw himself as a Head of State; the British classed him as a private refugee – a distinction on which might rest his chances of regaining the throne. But the problems went beyond his own ambitions. Britain had yet to give any sign that it favoured Albanian independence. There was also the recrudescence of the frontier issue. Metaxas claimed to be fighting for Albania's liberation. To many Greeks, however, the liberation of Southern Albania meant the conquest of Northern Epirus. If Zog fought alongside the Greek army, his foes would accuse him of abetting the partition of his nation. Ideally, the British should prevail on Athens to affirm the borders of 1939. No wonder he wished to see Churchill.

Optimistically, Zog packed his uniform in a suitcase and sat up all night on 22 November (according to Geraldine) in the hope of a summons to Downing Street. No call came through, so the aeroplane went without him. Doubtless there would be another. His priority, now very urgent, was to mobilise the coterie of British Albanophils to put pressure on the Foreign Office, while he dealt with the Greek Legation in London. What, he asked, had the Greeks to lose? They could start him off where they liked, and, 'If they wanted to get rid of him later, they could easily do it, e.g. by flying him off and dumping him somewhere out of the way.'[10] This made no impression on Athens; Metaxas even retorted that Zog was so unpopular in Albania that his presence with Greek forces would aid the Italians. This assessment should be seen in the light of Greek refusal to rule out annexations. Greece had no interest in stimulating Albanian nationalist resistance. By mid-December, it held over a quarter of the country.

The possibility of partition only made Zog more desperate to gain a political hearing, and he was not to know that, after a brief interdepartmental spat, the Foreign Office had vetoed any SOE plans to utilise him. Even assuming that he could recruit an Albanian Legion, the British did not think it worth upsetting the Greeks, currently their only fighting allies. The Turks did not want him in Istanbul either, and General Wavell, commander-in-chief, Middle East, judged arming Albanian guerrillas a waste of resources. When Martini came to Whitehall for news, he was merely told 'nothing at present'.[11]

In early 1941, the King continued to present himself as the man who held the key to setting Albania ablaze. He insisted that he could gain support even from clans which had been against him in the past: 'If he did not believe this, he would not be willing to go back.'[12] Was the 45-year-old brave or foolhardy to volunteer to parachute into Mati? Or was he bluffing? It may not be too cynical to assume that his success or failure in raising a revolt would largely have depended on 'St George's cavalry': the quantity of gold sovereigns in his kitbag.

The British Government essentially ignored him while trying to avoid gratuitous offence. Its policy was to keep Zog in 'warm storage'[13] - for who could say for sure that he would never be of use? Ryan met him three times in 1941. The refusal to let him see any member of the Government, even for ten minutes of platitudes, angered him considerably, but, as Sargent of the Foreign Office bluntly observed: 'We need not become worried from what he might say. He is entirely dependent upon us and is not likely, even if he does feel he is being slighted, to cut off his nose to spite his face.'[14] SOE meanwhile looked elsewhere: former gendarmerie officer Oakley-Hill joined Gani Bey Kryeziu in leading several hundred Kosovars into Albania in the spring – just as *Blitzkrieg* hit the Balkans with a vengeance. Germany invaded Yugoslavia and Greece and crushed them in a fortnight. Soon afterwards,

Italian Albania gained half a million inhabitants when Hitler awarded it Chameria and the larger part of Kosovo.

The Balkan theatre of war closed down in April 1941, and Zog grasped that there would be nothing doing for some time. His wife and sisters were not entirely sorry. The King had been living in London to cultivate political influence; they craved a sanctuary from the nerve-wracking Blitz. Though the steel-framed hotel was really rather safe, the anti-aircraft battery in Green Park made the building shudder. Geraldine could not stop herself flinching at every bang and compulsively reaching for her child, who began to suffer convulsions due to the noise. Then Albanian mores made the Princesses unhappy about bedding down alongside other guests in the corridors during raids, so the management converted the underground ladies' lavatories into a private shelter. To reach it, they had to pass through the downstairs bar, whose raffish and blasé regulars took to mocking the ultra-cautious Albanians. Some people already scoffed whenever staff spoke of 'the royal party'. Zog felt compelled to explain that the shelter was for ladies: 'I stayed in my rooms with my officers.'[15]

His political preoccupations rendered him insensitive to the terrors gripping the rest of the family. Shrapnel might smash his windows; he hardly deigned to notice. After an enormous bomb-crater separated the Berkeley from the Ritz, however, Zog started to think about evacuating the women. Two of his sisters were ill, and his own health caused concern again after the haemorrhage of a stomach ulcer, but he lingered on in London until his presence became wholly nugatory. Geraldine's nerves could not have borne another night like 10 May 1941 (when the House of Commons was hit). 'King Zog's Circus' left the Ritz for Berkshire.

CHAPTER FORTY-ONE

A Lack of Recognition

There are no signs of any shortage of funds and the establishment is distinctly well-to-do, though in some ways simple. It runs for instance to an impeccable English butler, but the Swiss nurse had gone to London for the day and the Queen herself was looking after the Crown Prince, with the aid of a male attendant and all the adoring aunts. She seems to be a sensible housewife with a sense of the value of money and an over-anxious mother without probably much knowledge. The child looks delicate and rather over-grown for his age of not quite two and a half. The two sisters about whose health there was so much anxiety in the winter have both recovered. The King speaks most highly of the London surgeon who operated on the younger, Princess Ruhije. The other, Princess Senije, is still a grass widow, her husband Prince Abid of Turkey being still at Nice – she does not quite know why. The whole party seemed cheerful and pleasantly excited at having company which reminded them of Albania.[1]

Such were the impressions of Sir Andrew Ryan after an afternoon at Forest Ridge, Sunninghill, in September 1941. The Zogus had outwardly found peace amid the firs and rhododendrons of Bagshot Road, but, before long, Geraldine felt that, even after boarding out courtiers, the nine-bedroomed redbrick Victorian house was too small. Zog moved on after five months, leaving locals with only slight recollections of 'a very courteous and pleasant man always accompanied by two huge bodyguards', who suavely doffed his hat to passers-by.[2]

Parmoor House in south-west Buckinghamshire, five miles north of Henley-on-Thames, was a largely mid-nineteenth-century mansion in vaguely Queen Anne style. On the death of Alfred Cripps, First Baron Parmoor, it came up for rent at £1,300 per annum, and, with twenty-five rooms, it could accommodate the Zogist court. Parmoor itself was the merest hamlet, overlooking the beechclad Chiltern Hills. The Queen thought it would be lovely for Leka. At the same time, London was no more than 40 miles away, so the King could still host political luncheons once or twice a month and Princess Adile obtain in Soho such rarities as olive oil and pasta. Guests occasionally came down for the weekend (among them, Edvard Beneš and Sir Robert Hodgson), and Albanian hospitality could make its mark. Peter Kemp of SOE, taken to tea by Marygold Stirling, did not protest when 'instead of a cup of tea I was given a tumbler of neat Scotch'.[3] (Zog himself had no taste for alcohol.) Other visitors were less favourably impressed. Auberon Herbert, heir to the eminent Albanophil, reported that King Zog was 'frankly a cad' and his sisters not much better:

> The princesses were present and he overheard them openly speculating on his sexual potentialities. Auberon, who speaks Albanian, understood every word. Champagne flowed before and during every meal. The King enjoys diplomatic status, does nothing but nurse his majesty and take tiny Parisian walks.[4]

Of course, the King did *not* in fact enjoy diplomatic status, but his insistence that he should often verged on an assertion that he did (to the anxiety of his creditors left in doubt as to whether they could sue). In August 1941, he seized on the desire expressed by Churchill and Roosevelt in the Atlantic Charter 'to see sovereign rights . . . restored to those who have been forcibly deprived of them'.[5] His appeal to Allied Governments for Albanian representation at the St James's Palace Conference in September, however, elicited only brush-off letters – a refusal made more pointed by the admission of Czechoslovakia.

Zog's most outspoken opponents in the Allied camp remained the Greeks. He offered to hold a plebiscite on the frontier after the war, but Tsouderos, the Greek premier in exile, denounced him as a persecutor of the Greek minority, openly claimed Gjirokastra and Korça, and referred to Albanian 'semi-savages'.[6] His informal dealings with the Yugoslav Government-in-exile were comparatively civil, as its Foreign Minister was his old co-conspirator Nincic, yet Yugoslavia envisaged Albania becoming a joint Greek-Yugoslav protectorate. To outflank this disturbing proposal, Zog latched onto the fashionable idea of a postwar Balkan Federation. Like many others, he took the defeat of the Soviet Union by Germany to be a foregone conclusion. His advice to the British was to strike in southern Europe before the German armies could regroup. 'He would be willing to bear a share in operations in Italy or Greece,' he added.[7]

The self-made King never lost his penchant for talking big and considering the long shot. He seems to have assumed that he had nothing to lose by unblushing exaggeration. What price his own credibility? Rumours circulated in SOE about his trying to safeguard himself in the summer of 1942, when the Allies were faring badly, by contacting the Germans through Switzerland.

Conscious that they were turning down his every suggestion, the British humoured Zog in his personal affairs, chiefly by not raising the question of his paying tax. That said, he handled his finances very discreetly, holding cash and bankers' drafts, with the rest of his wealth invested overseas. (He remitted a sizeable sum to Argentina, breaking exchange controls with impunity). His family were exempted from restrictions on non-belligerent aliens, and the Foreign Office helped recover the luggage which they had abandoned in France. It reached Liverpool via Spain and Portugal in April 1941, when Zog, aiming to assert his status, challenged the right of customs officers to inspect 'diplomatic bags'. This delay cost him dear: on 5 May, incendiary bombs hit the bonded warehouse and destroyed the lot. Once again, though, the British indulged the King, who, after three years of haggling, extracted £51,500 in compensation. Princess Nafije alone had lost nine fur coats, and the Albanians went on trying to submit supplementary claims as late as 1948.

With sops like these, the British eased occasional twinges of bad conscience. Pierson Dixon of the Foreign Office admitted:

> Zog is, so to speak, a victim of the appeasement policy: had the Italians invaded Albania *after* they declared war on Great Britain, King Zog would no doubt have been received in this country as an honoured guest on a par with other Monarchs fleeing from countries overrun by the Axis.[8]

Haakon of Norway, Charlotte of Luxembourg, Peter of Yugoslavia, Wilhelmina of the Netherlands, and George of Greece all came to London, and the British never questioned their status (despite the Greek restoration of 1935 resting on a dubious referendum). King George VI did not want to see royalty insulted, but the Government asked him to draw the line at Albanians. Zog was the one European monarch not a blood relation of the Windsors (though Geraldine could claim a tenuous link via a seventeenth-century Prince of Anhalt-Dessau). Excluded from court circles, the King and Queen of Albania were confined in their public engagements to receptions at the Egyptian and Turkish Embassies.

Geraldine was much the best public relations asset that the Zogists possessed. 'The Queen,' observed Cecil Beaton, 'with her every-ready smile and bright popping eyes, is so pretty that she would make an ideal appendage to any chocolate shop.' He did not find the Crown Prince so photogenic: 'The child is two years old, yet looks four, with unhealthy pale skin, long pointed nose, and receding chin like a rodent.'[9] Though she charmed wherever she went, Geraldine's social success was somewhat held back by her companions. If not with Zog, she invariably had her grandmother in tow, and 'Chérie' Strale d'Ekna specialised in long recitals of the young Queen's woes.

The nearest thing to Zogist propaganda in print, meanwhile, was an English translation of *Ten Years, Ten Months, Ten Days* by Antoinette de

Szinyei-Merse. In her memoirs, the Hungarian lady-in-waiting depicted the King as 'a real philanthrope', who hated luxury, lies, and dictatorship. Albanians idolised him 'as if he were a hero – or a demigod'. His kingdom had been a 'cornerstone of democracy, of liberty, and of independence' in Europe.[10] Such stuff was unlikely to sway anyone who mattered.

Zog could still make an impression when given a chance to talk one-to-one. Julian Amery of SOE came away deeply struck by 'a man of Odyssean proportions, brave, without illusions and of many devices'.[11] His father, Leo Amery, then in the Government, raised his case with the Foreign Secretary, but Anthony Eden never had sympathy for the Zogist cause, and Sir Stafford Cripps, the Lord Privy Seal, avoided his brother's tenant.

Repeated rebuffs drove the King back to the usual band of Balkan enthusiasts. The doyenne of Anglo-Albania remained Edith Durham, almost eighty and too fond of Noli to doubt that Zog was 'too ignorant and uncultured to be capable of ruling rightly'.[12] With the Herberts also wary, the tiny Zogist 'Friends of Albania' included neither famous name. Beyond the core of old Albanophils, moreover, the more prominent personages to take an interest were left-leaning internationalists. Lord Noel-Buxton, F.W. Pethick-Lawrence, and Sylvia Pankhurst required some convincing that Zog was an asset to the national movement. By the time Mary Herbert revived the Anglo-Albanian Association in 1943, however, he had talked them into giving him the benefit of the doubt.

Outside Parmoor and environs, Albanians in Britain numbered under a score, yet the King could have wished for one fewer: former playboy-diplomat Çatin Saraçi made it his mission to inform British notables that Ahmed Zogu was a vicious pro-Nazi:

> Foreigners now know, like all we Albanians do, that your millions are stained with the blood of our nation's many best sons and that your wealth has been accumulated through crime, murder, treachery and theft.
>
> The Royal House of this Country and other Royalties residing here have ostentatiously ignored your presence.
>
> How low you have sunk . . . you are nothing but a living corpse. Less you struggle against the gripping iron-fingers which are closing around your throat less humiliating and less painful will be your miserable existence.
>
> ALBANIA IS FINDING HER VENGEANCE![13]

Soon Zog and Saraçi issued writs against each other, and it is not hard to guess who inspired the report which brought *Zog I, King of the Albanians* v. *Sunday Pictorial Newspapers (1920) Ltd.* before the King's Bench in 1943.

'He's dreaming of a white uniform,' said the headline: 'He came from nowhere. Now he has nowhere to go. Morose, sullen and bored he wanders along English country lanes with his bodyguard dreaming of pageantry and power. Because once this strange, pathetic individual was a king.'[14] The King's lawyers contested three specific points: that he was a 'commoner born in a pauper's mountain hut who smashed his way to the throne by violence', that he had taken two million pounds from the Albanian treasury, and that he 'had had a disappointed female shoot herself on the steps of the Cenotaph'.[15] This last accusation presumably related to the suicide of a woman outside the Albanian Legation in Pont Street some eight years earlier, but that involved the Minister, Xhemil Dino, not the King. The *Sunday Pictorial* paid £1,000 damages. Subscribing to a cuttings agency made Zog aware of the power of the press. He reportedly told Auberon Herbert that he intended to buy *The Times*, 'And I won't give a penny more than ten million for it.'[16]

More serious than the ravings of Saraçi was the scepticism of three English-speaking 'Young Men' – Tajar Zavalani, Dervish Duma, and Anton Logoreci – who read the news in Albanian for the BBC. The story spread in March 1942 that they had asked the King to hand over £75,000 to finance a Free Albania movement and give an assurance that he would not lead it. Nonsense, said Zog, their request had been for help in setting up an Albanian news bulletin (which the British disallowed). His position as Head of State was clear, he insisted, 'and could not be affected by the attitude of a few lads in London, even if they were opposed to him'.[17]

The idea of creating an Albanian national committee appealed to the British Albanophils, however, who desired more unity among their protégés. This presented him with a dilemma, for he did not relish the notion of an independent body usurping his role as the voice of Albania. He therefore responded with his own design for a government-in-exile, under his aegis but broadly based, as its members would not be obliged to commit themselves to restoration of the monarchy. The British Government reminded him (via Ryan) of his pledge to abstain from politics. 'He was not a prisoner,' he retorted. 'He was bound to work in the interests of Albania. Not to do so would be treason.'[18]

Zog claimed a significant following among the many Albanians of Egypt and Turkey. An Albanian Committee in Istanbul was indeed committed to the King: he had been funding it to the tune of £300 per month since January 1941, and its principal members were Musa Juka and Hiqmet Delvina. More important, however, were Albanians in Boston and Detroit. Here the King would have to come to terms with Fan Noli, Faik Konitza, and Kosta Çekrezi (now escaped from France). During 1942, Martini wooed them by letter on his behalf. Konitza, always in debt, consented to promote the government-in-exile after receiving $1,000 to cover his costs. Noli would also be favourable, he reported, and a 'gift of several thousands of dollars' would prevent him changing his mind, if accompanied by 'a letter from the King, which should say that this sum is for the bishop's private charities'.[19]

A deal was in the making. In November, King Zog published an announcement in Sylvia Pankhurst's anti-fascist weekly *New Times and Ethiopia News*:

> Let us all unite for an Albania, free, independent, democratic. After this war we shall have changes, political, economic and social, taking heed of the new conditions. Under the circumstances I believe that it is my duty before the nation, which has always accorded me its confidence, to render to it my account of the execution of the Mandate it has given me and to ask it freely again to express its will upon the political and social system it desires when once more it resumes its march on the path of its destiny. We all shall conform to its decision.[20]

This was taken to mean that Albanians would be given a free vote on the restoration of the monarchy. Zog had already assured Ryan that he was not out to maintain his personal position: 'He might think that he could manage things better than the next man,' yet 'If Albania seemed likely to succeed better as a republic, let it be a republic.'[21] A fortnight later, Noli and Konitza used the pages of the émigré paper *Dielli* to call for a united front: 'King Zog is the foremost living Albanian personality and his exclusion would rob the proposed movement of its strength.'[22] In private, the Bishop commented: 'At least we'll make him spend his stolen funds on a good cause.'[23]

This public reconciliation was timely. After British victory at El Alamein, the Allies were advancing in the Mediterranean and news emerging from Albania itself suggested the stirrings of real resistance there. On 17 December 1942, Eden declared that Great Britain wished to see Albania restored to independence. Frontiers would have to be considered at the peace conference, however, and 'the regime and government to be introduced . . . will be a matter for the Albanian people themselves to decide at the end of the war'.[24] The Americans and Russians issued similar statements. Zog was unimpressed. Albania did not need to be 'restored' to independence, he argued: its juridical sovereignty persisted in his person. As for the sentence about the future regime, could the Government perhaps oblige him by omitting it from *Hansard*?

The King now encountered a series of obstacles to his plans for a government-in-exile. Konitza died, Noli declined a cabinet place (though offered the premiership), and Çekrezi rejected his authority. In April

1943, Zog made a new proclamation: 'As soon as our territory is completely freed, a National Assembly, elected freely and democratically by the Albanian people, will at once be summoned to decide the political and social regime.' Even now, Çekrezi would only accept royal leadership of the Free Albanians if Zog promised that he would not set foot in Albania unless and until the postwar Assembly voted in his favour. The row dragged into 1944, while the King carried on sending $1100 per month to his 'friends' across the Atlantic. Supposing a government had come together, the Allies would still have been reluctant to recognise it. 'We have fought the invader, and we shall fight on still,' declared the King on the fourth anniversary of the invasion. 'But although our right to be included in the international family of the United Nations is in no way inferior to that of others, for reasons of political expediency, we are still left outside.'[25]

His own initiatives became even more improbable. In July 1943, Zog secretly met the Anglo-Jewish Association and offered 150,000 hectares of Albanian land for the postwar resettlement of 200,000 Jews. Sir Robert Waley Cohen and companions did not take him seriously. For all his doggedness, the King fell victim to bouts of gloom. Every day he put on his suit, sat at his desk in Lord Parmoor's library, and contrived to appear busy. He kept up to date with the progress of the war by listening to foreign-language radio broadcasts and summaries of the press read out by his aides – Nushi, Noçka, and Naçi – who lived separately nearby in Lane End. Heavily reliant on reading to occupy him during the afternoon (and late into the night), he found it hard to procure suitable books in Turkish or German, so, while gaining a passive knowledge of basic English, he concentrated on raising the level of his French. It was a multilingual household, as the King and Queen continued to speak primarily German to each other, but Zog refrained from using this language in public. Gjenco Naçi dealt with his English correspondence, while F.L. Kerran, a sometime Labour parliamentary candidate, acted as his agent.

The Albanians could not easily enter into the life of a community where only the English-educated Doshishti girls felt at all at home. Twenty-four-hour patrols of 'grim-faced bodyguards and Alsatian dogs famous for their ferocity' reinforced prejudice that the other residents of Parmoor (apart from the Queen) were a gang of uncouth aliens doing nothing for the war effort.[26] The Princesses were accustomed to isolation. Geraldine found life more trying. It was not that she regretted her marriage. Zog still liked to flirt – even with Teri's school-friends – but 'It was obvious that he and his Queen were very much in love.'[27] She doted on her son, and did his hair in ringlets till Zog put his foot down. He did not want another child; it would be 'unfair to bring any more babies into this turbulent world and our refugee situation.'[28] Geraldine accepted his view. In all their years together, they seem only to have had one major difference – but it never went away, however much they denied it. Geraldine was half-Hungarian and half-American. No matter how keenly she identified with her adopted country, she could not instinctively think like an Albanian.

To take one example, the Queen sometimes felt oppressed by her domestic duties. She was under thirty and the third youngest female in the family, yet, in the hierarchical scheme, hers alone was the responsibility for food and staff (both in short supply). Nobody else, except Adile, ever considered such mundanities. Zog did give her some chickens for Christmas; guess who had to clean out the coop. Few of the men at Parmoor would work in the garden or the house, and the King declined to insult them by suggesting that they should.

Even more sensitive was the relationship between the Queen and her six sisters-in-law. To westerners, it seems natural that she should have resented their constant presence. To Albanians, it appeared equally natural that the wife of Zog should be one of ten women in his home. Goodwill on both sides did not suffice to resolve this tension. The Princesses felt that they had done all they could to welcome Geraldine into the family (even going beyond duty and accepting her grandmother). The Queen harboured the grievance that they never left her husband alone. When not in his study, he sat reading in the drawing room, surrounded by them for hours on end. It actually required a doctor to explain to Zog the nervous strain that this placed on his wife. However, when somebody then raised the possibility of dividing his fortune among his dependants to enable them to lead separate lives, the result was an explosive confrontation. The Princesses accused the Queen of conspiring to break up a devoted family. Zog, who hated such quarrels, carefully avoided any recurrence, relying on the fact that his wife and sisters competed to please him. He generally seemed oblivious to the submerged jealousies festering around him, as he brooded on his political setbacks.

During 1943, the kings of Greece and Yugoslavia transferred to Cairo in the hope of an Allied offensive bringing them closer to their thrones. The Albanian had to bide his time in Buckinghamshire, with little to do but scour the war news, talk politics with Martini, play a few frames of billiards, and go to the pictures in High Wycombe.

CHAPTER FORTY-TWO

Twelve Hundred Miles Away

How much did Zog know about what was going on in occupied Albania? Next to nothing reached the foreign media. He claimed to receive information via agents in Istanbul, but this cannot have been very reliable. Communication was almost as difficult in the other direction: because of the Greeks and Zavalani, the BBC Albanian service did not let him broadcast. Zog languished as a redundant commentator on events only barely perceived.

The Italo-Greek War had brought hardship to Albania, yet sympathies were divided: once Greece and Yugoslavia joined the Allies, some Albanians leaned towards the Axis, especially when the Germans created Greater Albania. All the same, by late 1941, small resistance bands were operating in the mountains, and that autumn saw the emergence of a new force in Albanian politics. Tito, the Yugoslav communist boss, sent a couple of comrades to make something of Albania's eight heterodox Marxist factions. The result was an Albanian Communist Party, with 130 founder-members, led by Enver Hoxha. Most were urban Tosks, but they began to form peasants and deserters into Partisan units. Emulating Tito, Hoxha brought together various resistance groups in 1942 to create the National Liberation Movement – LNÇ in its Albanian acronym. This was ostensibly a broad united front, but his cadres quickly took control. LNÇ partisans wore red star badges, gave clenched fist salutes, and adulated Stalin.

In response, some anti-communist bands, concentrated in the Vlora region, started a loose rival grouping called the National Front (or *Balli Kombëtar*). The Ballist programme was nationalist, making much of Greater Albania. (The communists, by contrast, had to sideline the Kosovo issue, as it strained their relations with Tito.) The principal Ballists, mostly Tosk beys, had been enemies of Zog in 1924. Their resolve to prevent an LNÇ regime at the end of the war did not imply any wish to restore the King. Where then were the Zogists? Not yet greatly in evidence as such. Monarchism was most likely to be found among the Muslim Gheg clans, and they were not fully integrated into the LNÇ or BK.

By 1943, the assorted guerrilla units amounted to some six thousand men, and the Italians were plainly losing the wider war. When the Allies invaded Sicily in July, Mussolini soon fell from power. 'The natural result of the imperialist policy pursued by the Fascist regime', declared Zog.[1] His ardent hope was that the Allies would next land troops in Albania. Churchill was actually toying with the idea, though the USA opposed any operations that might divert resources from the invasion of France in 1944.

By the time the Italians surrendered in September 1943, the rival Albanian guerrilla groups had come down from the mountains and taken over the towns. Civil war might have broken out at once – if the Germans had not swept into Albania and driven them back into the highlands. One occupying army thus replaced another, and it therefore meant little to most Albanians when Italy completed its change of side. Zog, however, was appalled that the Allies accepted Italy as a co-belligerent without even requiring King Victor Emmanuel to drop his secondary Albanian title.

At Teheran in November, Churchill, Roosevelt, and Stalin ruled out any Anglo-American invasion of the Balkans. The only outside intervention would be further small SOE missions aimed at encouraging local resistance and raising false expectations of a major landing to distract the Germans in the run-up to D-Day. Between spring 1943 and autumn 1944, SOE sent over fifty British Liaison Officers (BLOs) into Albania. They soon realised that the divisive politics of the Albanian resistance replicated Partisans versus Chetniks in Yugoslavia and EAM/ELAS versus EDES in Greece. Their remit was to arrange supply-drops for all groups regularly active against the occupiers, yet many BLOs found their hosts infuriating. The guerrilla leaders presumed that an Allied victory was just a matter of time, so their chief concern was to prepare to seize power as soon as the Nazis withdrew. Each group demanded lots of arms for itself and none at all for its rivals.

The communists viewed the British with particular suspicion, and most BLOs found little to admire in Enver Hoxha, 'a tall, flabby creature in his early thirties, with a sulky, podgy face'.[2] The Ballist beys, if more courteous, were even less impressive, for they frankly wanted to avoid combat and save themselves for an uprising in the final stages of the German defeat. The BK also demanded that the Allies preserve Greater Albania. Differences over Kosovo wrecked a short-lived unity pact between Partisans and Ballists, and the Germans concentrated on fighting a major offensive against the former. Simultaneously, the German army channelled weapons to the *Balli Kombëtar* and promoted a civil war. Ballists began to resemble collaborators.

There was now a third guerrilla organisation in the running: the Legality Movement of Abas Kupi, who had broken his links with the LNÇ in September 1943. He chose the name *Legaliteti* to denote legitimacy and recall the 'Triumph of Legality' of 1924. This was the Zogist resistance, launched at the Congress of Herri on 23 November. Its manifesto promised not only democratic monarchy but also land reform, social insurance, and the retention of 'Ethnic Albania' (with Kosovo and Chameria).

This sounded like a big breakthrough for the King – and, relatively speaking, it was – but its significance needs to be qualified. On paper, Legality was a unified political movement. In truth, it was a fragile alliance of clans. Abas Kupi himself, a 'stocky, granite-faced illiterate Gheg', was a minor chieftain from Kruja, who had been no friend to Zogu in 1924 but latterly became a gendarmerie major as a means of keeping control of his district.[3] His reputation as a patriot stemmed from his command of the Durrës gendarmes in their battle against the Italians in 1939. Mati naturally supported Legality, as did various chiefs-cum-gendarmerie veterans, such as Xhemal Herri, Fiqri Dine, and Muharrem Bajraktari (who had conspired against Zog in the early 1930s). Even the Kryeziu brothers were involved on the margins. They all realised that Albania under an LNÇ regime (or even a BK one) would be dominated by Tosks. They associated communism with Russia, and Russia with Yugoslavia. And what role would there be for chieftains under Marxism-Leninism? The monarchy looked quite attractive by comparison. Zogism provided a unifying slogan for disparate local warlords.

Officially, at any rate, the political programme of Legality did not interest the BLOs, who were more troubled by its slowness to engage the Germans in a major way. Were the Zogists as passive as the Ballists? Gheg chieftains habitually hedged their bets and accepted guns from any source. More pointedly, the German command geared the political side of its occupation to winning over those who had not before collaborated. The Nazis claimed to have freed Albania from Italian rule. They classified its people as 'Aryans of Illyrian heritage' and promised to defend them from communism and partition, so long as they shunned the Allies and let Germany exploit the chrome mines. Despite the presence of German troops, Greater Albania was supposed to be independent and neutral from October 1943. To maintain this fiction, the Germans organised a constituent assembly to reinstate the 1928 constitution, which technically meant the restoration of the monarchy. Had King Zog not attached himself to the Allies, the Nazis might have placed him back on the throne. As it was, they made do with a regency, headed by the ex-premier Mehdi Frashëri (who had been interned by the Italians). Kostaq Kotta also accepted office in the new collaborationist regime. They imagined that they could install themselves in Tirana under German protection, declare Albanian neutrality, and then win Allied recognition as the war drew to a close. The Government had no authority beyond the towns and coastal plain, but there were secret contacts between the old Zogists with Frashëri in the capital and the old Zogists with Kupi in the mountains. To liaise with the Gheg chiefs, the German military even employed Zog's former adviser Myrdacz (till he was captured and shot by Partisans). There was not a simple dividing line between the lukewarm adherents of

Legality and the lukewarm adherents of the puppet Government. Certain Gheg clans wanted to balance between the Germans and British until the final possible moment. Why declare for the Allies too soon and risk a backlash? This thinking paralysed relations between Legality and SOE. The clansmen would not attack the Germans until the British supplied arms. The British refused to supply arms till the clans attacked the Germans. A step-by-step approach might have been the answer, but the longer SOE tolerated the equivocations of Zogists and Ballists, the closer it came to a breach with the Partisans.

The British had hoped to broker a degree of unity. Could not the LNÇ, mainly in the south, co-operate to a minimal extent with the Zogists in the north? Definitely not, said Hoxha, when asked by senior BLO Brigadier Davies:

> Zog was a murderer, a hangman, a thief, an adventurer and traitor. . . . This cruel feudal lord, agent of Austria–Hungary, agent of the Serbs and Wrangel's white Russians, agent of Mussolini, and executioner of the Albanian people, pretends to be King of the Albanians. . . . In our country the very stones of the road see Zog as an enemy, let alone the Albanians who will tear him to bits if they catch him. I find it regrettable, General, that you even mentioned the name of this bandit.[4]

In December 1943, shortly before he was captured, Davies advised the British Government to give exclusive backing to the Partisans (as in Yugoslavia), for the reason that the LNÇ was most inclined to fight the Germans. It appears that the threat of reprisals (at the rate of a hundred lives to one) deterred Hoxha less than it did the patriarchs. Paradoxically, moreover, the communists may have been more willing to play the SOE game – guns in return for dead Nazis – because they anticipated British hostility later on. The anti-communist resistance *hoped* for an Anglo-American landing in the Balkans in 1944; the communist-led resistance *feared* one, so Hoxha wanted to make his bid for power before it could occur.

The bulk of British aid was destined for the Partisans, yet SOE hesitated to sever links with the Ballists and Zogists. Some experienced BLOs, notably Julian Amery and Billy McLean, still wanted to send arms to Legality. Militarily, they argued that it would be folly to drive the anti-communists into the enemy camp. Personally, moreover, Amery and McLean hated the idea of helping to install Stalinism. In effect, a right-wing faction within SOE wanted to work with Kupi and Zog to save Albania from communism, while left-wingers favoured the Partisans, and other BLOs tried to see things from a purely military perspective. The result was confusion and ultimately bitterness, but Zogism at last had its advocates (however junior) in British official circles.

The King himself had carried on urging the Allies to set up a Balkan bridgehead from Italy. 'The alternative,' he told Amery, 'was to hand over the whole peninsula to the Soviets.'[5] Zog made light of the differences between the LNÇ, BK, and Legality. What was needed, he said, was a large-scale organisation to rise when the Allies landed. The Partisans were too closely connected with Yugoslavia to appeal to most Albanians. On the other hand, Abas Kupi was 'only one of several hundred small chiefs who could be mobilised' by a government-in-exile led by himself.[6]

McLean aimed to put Zog's influence to the test. In February 1944, he persuaded his superiors to let him try to bring Legality and the LNÇ together by getting Zog and Tito to write to Kupi and Hoxha respectively, each urging co-operation against the Germans. 'I didn't imagine that we would turn to Zog again,' minuted Eden, who feared that his involvement might enrage the Partisans.[7] The King was not to know that the young SOE man who presented himself at Parmoor had such weak political backing. Instead of supplying a straightforward message at once, he chose to haggle. His draft letter to Kupi referred, for example, to the futility of exposing Albanian villages to burning and destruction. This sounded like an endorsement of the passivity that the British condemned. He also wanted to tell supporters that 'The Fatherland is faced by a great danger: Korça and especially Kosovo and Gjirokastra are coveted by our neighbours who spare no effort to pluck them from us.'[8] Nationalist aspirations were strong in Legality, but Eden refused to let British officers convey a letter so offensive to Greek and Yugoslav opinion. Nor was a second draft satisfactory. McLean was on his way back to Albania by then, and no one else could be bothered to pursue the idea.

The BLOs on the ground tried again to persuade Legality to engage the Germans forthwith. Kupi replied that it would only do so when Britain recognised Zog as head of a government-in-exile. George Seymour, who received this ultimatum, dismissed it as a stalling device. Amery and McLean then undertook a mission to the Zogist heartland. His portrait adorned almost every home in Mati, though one old man frankly admitted, 'I am a monarchist in case the King should come back.'[9] Led by the Olomani family, Mati had risen against the Italians in 1943, and Burreli had been torched in retaliation. Once bitten, twice shy. The Gheg elders were in no hurry to fight. Duped by Allied disinformation, they believed that Anglo-American forces were going to intervene anyway.

Perhaps Kupi sensed that this sounded too complacent. The LNÇ was getting more British weapons all the time. In May 1944, he made a final offer: 'Let the King send me a message through your mission, and if he tells me to fight with my bare hands, I will.'[10] Amery and McLean at once contacted SOE headquarters in Bari, urging Eden to obtain the order from Zog right away. Their faith in Kupi stood in sharp contrast to reports from some BLOs, who almost despaired of the Ghegs. Others in SOE insisted on the primacy of the Partisans, whose numbers and morale were growing as they launched a full-scale offensive against the Germans. If it came out that the BLOs were acting as couriers for Legality, relations with Hoxha might suffer irreparable damage.

Eden felt that he could well do without all this. Albania, an insignificant backwater, threatened to become as vexatious as Greece or Yugoslavia. Churchill's support for the Greek monarchy was causing quite enough problems, and it could only suffer from association with Albanian royalists. Eden therefore did nothing about getting a letter to Kupi from Zog. Amery and McLean were simply urged to 'keep the pot boiling'.[11] In their view (later Zogist orthodoxy), this decision threw away the last chance of restoring the monarchy and consigned the country to communism. Others dispute that a telegram from the King would have made anything like the impact that Kupi claimed. Who can say with certainty? There is romance in the idea of faithful clansmen awaiting the royal word – a word that never came, because of Foreign Office fainthearts and closet Reds in SOE. Recriminations have never ceased.

In May 1944, Zog was still planning to send Colonel Selmani to Albania to 'turn' the gendarmerie in synchronisation with the Anglo-American invasion of the Balkans. After D-Day, he faced up to the probability, actually a fact, that this was never going to happen. His optimistic public utterances changed little in the final year of the war: Allied victory would bring liberty to his nation, Albania should join a Balkan Confederation, and so forth. Privately, he did not delude himself. 'You will see that for us there will be no joyful armistice,' he told Geraldine.[12]

By his own admission, King Zog received little news from his homeland during the fateful summer of 1944. What he did hear must have sounded as bad as he could ever have anticipated. Armed with British rifles, Hoxha's Partisans swept through Albania, battling all who opposed them: Germans, Ballists, and Zogists. Outnumbered and outgunned, anti-communist leaders increasingly sought the aid of the Germans. Fiqri Dine of Dibra, a founder of Legality, ended up as premier of the puppet Government. In June, the LNÇ overran Mati, laying waste homes and livestock and subjecting captives to the ultimate humiliation of arrest by women soldiers. Counter-attacks by Legality failed. Civil war turned to rout, and the old ruling families fled for their lives after the German withdrawal. Hoxha took Tirana on 28 November 1944 and formed a Provisional Government. Zog was barred from the country.

'Another King gone down the drain!' grumbled Churchill,[13] but, with communism sweeping all across eastern Europe, Albania in itself seemed hardly to matter. He had failed to mention it to Stalin when negotiating spheres of influence. The Americans cared even less.

The year 1945 was a bleak and empty one for King Zog, who appreciated the irony of congratulatory telegrams on VE Day from less astute supporters. Mussolini had gone before a firing squad ten days earlier, as had Ciano a year before, but this gave him no satisfaction. Italy had ceased to be a factor in Albanian politics in 1943. Tito and Stalin now exerted the leverage. While Geraldine and Leka spent the summer at Frinton, Zog went through the motions of protesting his rights. 'The King did not seem to despair of his eventual return to Albania.'[14]

The communist takeover had made more of the émigrés regard him as the lesser evil, but Fan Noli enraged the Zogists for the final time by pressing the United States Government to recognise the Hoxha regime, in the belief that recognition of an Albanian Government (regardless of ideology) would help preserve national integrity. Greece still coveted the south of Albania, and Tito wanted it to become a constituent republic of Yugoslavia.

When King Zog wrote to Allied Foreign Ministers in September 1945, only the Chinese even acknowledged his note. It was clearly time to close his overseas missions. The Big Three alone counted in international affairs, and two of them had all but surrendered the Balkans (save Greece) to the third, the USSR. The new Labour Government in London, he thought, was unlikely to be sympathetic. Of course, if only the Allies 'had taken advantage of his offers of service at an earlier stage', he might have saved the region. The more Zog learnt about British dealings with Hoxha and Kupi, the more indignant he grew. In November 1945, Britain recognised the Albanian Government. Had he not explained that there were no more than a hundred real communists in the country? Had he not alerted the Foreign Office to the fact that Hoxha was 'pursuing a drastic policy of trials and executions'?[15] The Reds accused their enemies of war crimes and collaboration. Meanwhile, land reform won over peasants (unaware that collectivisation would follow). A communist-run Democratic Front polled 93 per cent in single-party elections, and the People's Republic formally replaced the monarchy on 11 January 1946.

In his immediate response, Zog tried to sound statesmanlike:

The King cannot consider these elections as free. It would have been our desire, after this long and tragic period, that the people of the country should be free to re-establish the situation as they wanted, but for us Albanians there is a more important question than that of the regime, and that is the question of national and territorial integrity.[16]

Even so, for the rest of his life, he would deny that anyone else could be the legitimate Head of State of Albania. This contention did not depend on a rigid idea of monarchical rights, he avowed, but sprang from a genuine belief in popular sovereignty. 'I have always been Albania's first republican,' he informed a puzzled journalist (adding, 'When I was made King, I was the only one to protest').[17] His basic point was that the will of the people had not been properly ascertained: the elections were rigged, so the abolition of the monarchy was invalid. His status as King rested on legality – the word now a Zogist talisman – since he had never abdicated. This argument overlooked the fact that Prince Wilhelm of Albania (who died in 1945) had never abdicated either, and it was Zogu himself who had declared the first Albanian republic in 1925 with an equally dubious mandate. So much for constitutional casuistry. At the close of the war, as at its start, no foreign power had any use for Zog as a pretender.

'He will always be something of an embarrassment so long as he remains here,' noted a British official.[18] In fact, he did not require much pushing. His tenancy of Parmoor was about to expire, and, though he considered buying a house in Grosvenor Square, he objected to paying rates. The Albanians left Buckinghamshire by coach on 11 February 1946 and sailed from Liverpool next day. The press failed to print a 'message of appreciation and thanks to the British people' but reported parliamentary questions on the uneconomic use of shipping and secret supplies of clothing coupons. Salih Doshishti was stung to protest:

> The facts are that King Zog's party consisted of 19 people having between them only 136 pieces of luggage, and that these 136 pieces – and not 2,000 as reported in *The Times* of February 13 – include such items as a gramophone, two portable cases of gramophone records, two typewriters, a radio set, a few cases of books, some files, and a child's bicycle. These 136 pieces represent all their possessions accumulated through nearly six years of exile in this country, and which they had to take with them as they were leaving England for good. . . . The report of King Zog's 30 new suits is equally untrue . . . when he left this country the King possessed only five suits altogether.[19]

This final petty outburst of bad publicity can only have served to convince the King that he was making the right decision.

CHAPTER FORTY-THREE

At the Court of King Farouk

When King Zog and Queen Geraldine stepped on to the quayside at Port Said early on 23 February 1946, representatives of King Farouk and Queen Farida headed the reception committee. When they reached Cairo railway station, they found it decked with Albanian flags. At the Mena House Hotel, where their rooms looked onto the pyramids, Farouk called in person with an invitation to a banquet at the Koubbeh Palace. It was a far cry from British indifference and postwar austerity, and much farther still from the rigours of newly communist Albania (where Boulevard Zog became Boulevard Stalin). True, dysentery laid Leka and Geraldine low for a time, but the Egyptian Government made special efforts to supply them with penicillin. When the air of Giza became distressingly dry for unaccustomed lungs, a princess offered her villa in balmy Alexandria. In Egypt, King Zog had fallen on his feet.

The choice at first had seemed a strange one, but it made good sense. Egypt possessed a sizeable Albanian community dating back to the eighteenth century. More to the point, it had never ceased to recognise the Kingdom of Albania. In London, Zog had courted the Egyptian ambassador, Dr Hassan Nashaat Pasha, whose links with royal circles in Cairo expedited the formalities. It did no harm that the dynasty's founder was said to have been of Albanian origin. His great-great-grandson apparently warmed to King Zog. In 1946, they met once or twice a week. Farouk would turn up unannounced after dark and invite himself to dinner. It was easy to chat with the self-indulgent Egyptian, who insisted on playing cards till dawn. Luckily, Zog was now a nightbird himself, going to bed around three o'clock by choice.

As friends of the King, the Albanian royal family regularly attended his lavish palace parties. Whatever the truth about his own new suits, Zog had thoughtfully ordered a selection of gowns for his wife from Norman Hartnell before leaving England (exempt from rationing since for export). The ostentatious luxury of the Egyptian court was on a wholly different scale from his own past extravagances. The Koubbeh Palace had four hundred rooms and six miles of perimeter wall. At one reception there were five kings present (Egypt, Greece, Albania, Yugoslavia, and Bulgaria), with reigning and non-reigning shown equal courtesy. Egypt acted like a magnet for royal exiles from central and eastern Europe:

here Zogu-Mati finally rubbed shoulders with Romanov, Hohenzollern, and Coburg. Zog soon learnt that the aged Count Pollenzo, his next door neighbour in Alexandria, was actually ex-King Victor Emmanuel of Italy – and of Albania too. His son, King Umberto, expressed polite regret about the newer title.

In exile, people noticed, the House of Zogu seemed to live rather better than the House of Savoy. King Zog was reckoned one of the richer ex-monarchs, although he would have disputed this. The Czechoslovaks had just seized Geraldine's lands in a general confiscation of Hungarian property, despite her arguing that she was legally Albanian, and all his fruitless financing of overseas legations and émigré committees during the war left him eager to restore his capital. He invested in sundry import–export schemes and set up a small arms factory. Since diplomatic status exempted him from tax, his lifestyle matched that of the grandest pashas.

Rather as they had in Albania, the Zogus divided the year between the capital and the coast. Their only serious sightseeing was a cruise up the Nile in December 1947. By then, the King had finally acceded to Geraldine's wish that they should own a house. He bought a plot on the Ramleh corniche on the eastern outskirts of Alexandria, where cotton barons and colonial merchants built their opulent seaside villas. The dwelling needed to accommodate as full a retinue as ever, for, although Adile and her children remained in England and Mrs Strale d'Ekna went back to America, Zog engaged a fresh cohort of aides from the ranks of Legality refugees. Ruhije died of cancer early in 1948, to the intense grief of her siblings, who moved into their new abode in the summer. Leka, aged nine but as tall as a teenager, attended nearby Victoria College, always with two bodyguards. Apart from their egregious concern with security, Albanian royalty blended in with Alexandria's Levantine élite.

Every autumn, when the humidity rose, Zog joined the upper-class exodus to Cairo, renting a villa in Gezirah or Garden City or taking several suites at Shepheard's Hotel. Both King and Queen joined in the rituals of Cairene high life – shopping at Cicurel, gateaux at Groppi's, tennis on Zamalek, and cocktails in the Long Bar – but he (at least) was insufficiently pleasure-loving to be more than a marginal social figure. One of his favourite places was the Bektashi monastery on the Mukattam cliff, where, amid fountains and tame gazelles, he could sit and talk to Albanian-Egyptians. Most viewed him sympathetically, but few identified strongly with modern Albania. The national gala each 28 November brought together compatriots and friendly diplomats. Cairo had the last Royal Albanian Legation.

Usually, Zog avoided fashionable evening functions. He was slightly happier with the custom of private social calls in late afternoon. Egyptian pashas resembled the foremost Albanian beys: untaxed absentee landlords, flaunting their wealth, with courtly manners but little idea of genuine public service. Fascinated by their factional politics, the King, 'past master in the arts of insincere amiability', contrived to meet the men who mattered: Nokrashy, Nahas, and the rest.[1]

In coming to Egypt, Zog had in no sense scaled down his political activity. Quite the reverse: he immediately hosted a conference of monarchist politicians (twenty-two attended), and his sisters' first postwar holiday in Paris was described as a lobby of the peace conference. Knowing Albania, he did not doubt that Enver Hoxha could easily be overthrown. The dearth of news from the country allowed ample scope for wishful thinking, but maybe he was not far wrong in seeing the communists as a cabal of young Tosks kept in power by Yugoslavia in ways that sounded all too familiar (loans, customs union, Serbo-Croat in schools). How long would Albanians put up with increasing Slav influence? Although Hoxha had yet to construct the full Stalinist panoply of monolithic party, secret police, labour camps, and internal exile, enough reports of executions, torture, and starvation filtered out to keep anti-communism at fever pitch among the refugees in Italy. These would-be counter-revolutionaries, however, refused to make common cause. Legality veterans, Ballists, and 'Independents' (frequently a euphemism for collaborators) generally detested each other.

The continuance of the Balli Kombëtar as a republican party undermined Zog's claim to speak for all Albanian anti-communists. The Legality Movement stayed in being too, taking up some of his time and money. Although a great asset in many respects, its war-time commander Abas Kupi required delicate handling (as well as a pension). Then, outside the two main exile groups, old enemies like Vërlaci and Said Kryeziu remained unforgiving. Charged with having done nothing in the war, the King felt by 1946 that action was needed to win him the lead in the expanded émigré politics.

Turning east and donning the fez once more was thus for Zog a deliberate act of policy. The Anglo-Saxons had failed him. Did the Arabs have anything to offer? At fifty, the hitherto secular King of the Albanians suddenly became enthusiastic about Islamic unity. Did the leaders of the Muslim world not see the strategic potential of its lonely European outpost? How could the faithful of Cairo and Riyadh be indifferent to the fate of their brethren in Tirana and Elbasan? Muslims should awaken to the menace posed by atheistic communism. Not for the first time, the ignorance of his listeners about Albania could be turned to his advantage. In private life, meanwhile, his religion remained inconspicuous. At Shepheard's Hotel, indeed, he was quite disgruntled when waiters assumed that he would not want food before sunset during Ramadan.

His Pan-Islamist arguments usually culminated in a definite request: could he set up a training base for an Albanian national liberation army? Diligently pursued with the Egyptians, and taken up too with the Saudi Arabians, Jordanians, and Libyans, the plan gave the King some sense of purpose and boosted the morale of his staff. Secretary Gaqi Gogo recalled busy days – and late nights:

> It was hard work, but we did have time for games after dinner, bridge and poker. The King did not sleep easily, so Minister Martini and I were condemned to staying up with him. We played for symbolic money only, ten Egyptian pounds that the King put into the middle of the table every evening, but at least once a month King Farouk came to visit us and then we played for real money.[2]

The visits from Farouk, however, grew markedly less frequent, and only Geraldine dared tell her husband why: the younger King found his political talk a bore. Zog rated Farouk intelligent but lazy. None too secure on his own throne, the Egyptian told him: 'Soon, there will be only five kings left: Spades, Hearts, Diamonds, Clubs and the King of England.'[3] The idea of military training camps, in Egypt or elsewhere, came to nothing. After 1948, Zog accepted that Middle Eastern rulers were preoccupied with the Palestinian question.

He replaced Islamic appeals with Cold War rhetoric, as the Truman Doctrine and Berlin air-lift showed the West confronting the communist challenge. The civil war raging in Greece between communists and monarchists proved that the postwar politics of the Balkans were not yet set in stone. Zog wanted to meet King Paul of the Hellenes to fashion a common front against 'Bolshevik barbarism', in the hope that the fight could be taken across the frontier.[4] Equally interesting were the possibilities raised by the rift between Tito and Stalin in 1948. Any change in Belgrade might have huge repercussions in Tirana (where Yugoslav credits accounted for half the budget). Zog urged his European contacts, from Leo Amery to Ugo Sola, to spread word that the time was ripe for counter-revolution. No one could accuse him of under-playing his hand: 'He was sure that Albania was not communist at heart and was quite certain that he could return there. He was however refraining from doing so because he appreciated that the presence of a monarch in Albania would cause complications with Yugoslavia.'[5] The King liked to give a *tour d'horizon* of international affairs, ending in the Balkans, to any westerner who might have influence. American reporter Cyrus Sulzberger was not very impressed: 'Zog shot his trap at length about world strategy, accused America of stupidity in losing China, and suggested the only way to save Albania quickly was to land a "motorised brigade" by aeroplane.

Otherwise, Greece and Turkey would be cut off by the Russians and we could not "save them by an airlift".' Sulzberger, who had last seen Zog in Tirana in 1939, found him still 'silly-looking, but not unhandsome', despite his getting 'pasty faced, puffy, and slightly fat'.[6]

The Zogists derived encouragement from the fact that neither Britain nor the USA – contrary to their intentions in 1945 – had ever opened diplomatic relations with the communist Government in Albania. A dispute had arisen over whether foreign shipping could use the Corfu Channel. Hoxha wanted it closed; two British destroyers struck mines there in October 1946 and sank with the loss of over forty lives. The western powers also knew that Greek communist guerrillas were operating from Albania. Ernest Bevin, the British Foreign Secretary, told his American counterpart in 1949 of his unrelenting hostility to Hoxha, though they could identify no preferable alternative leader in Tirana. Bevin asked, 'Are there any kings around that could be put in?'[7] MI6 and the CIA already had the matter in hand.

CHAPTER FORTY-FOUR

Anglo-American Intrigues

On the morning of 14 July 1949, King Zog welcomed to his villa a couple of stalwart British supporters: Julian Amery and Billy McLean, formerly of SOE. Since 1944, they had never ceased to consider Albania a totally unnecessary sacrifice to communism and both thought well of the self-made king and his 'wonderfully liberal dictatorship'.[1] Accompanied by an American named Robert Low, they wished to meet the King in strict secrecy. Zog asked his wife to interpret.

The two ex-officers were now both Conservative prospective parliamentary candidates, but, in this context, they represented the Special Intelligence Service. MI6 had recently come round to their view that the smallest land in the communist bloc might be 'liberated' at no great cost. The escalation of the Cold War was giving rise to the idea of 'roll-back'. Albania was weak, prone to revolt, and already entangled in the Greek Civil War. Hoxha sided with Stalin, moreover, when Tito broke with Moscow. The USSR had instantly rewarded him with loans and started to send in military advisers. To the dismay of NATO, the Russians took over the old Italian naval base on the island of Sazan. On the other hand, the shift from Yugoslav to Soviet aid caused ructions in the politburo, and Albania was cut off from the rest of the Soviet bloc by 'deviationist' Yugoslavia. All these factors contributed to the British decision to try clandestine operations to overthrow Hoxha. They would train anti-communist exiles to return and lead an uprising. The Americans agreed to help, but only the British had experts on Albania – like Amery and McLean.

Zog had some idea of what was in the pipeline. Robert Low and another CIA man had sought his opinion on the weaknesses of the Hoxha regime in May, and since then British agents had been touring the Albanian refugee camps to recruit volunteers. Amery and McLean insisted on formal co-operation between Legality and the Balli Kombëtar to constitute the nucleus of a broadly-based post-liberation government. Moreover, they had finally obtained this – a minor miracle – by threatening to use the Independents if the two major factions would not work together. Amery opened the meeting with King Zog by proudly announcing the creation of an Albanian national committee to be chaired by Midhat Frashëri (leader of the Ballists), with a secret military council to be chaired by Abas Kupi (whom the westerners all too plainly rated a more important Zogist than Zog).

The King at once rose from his chair: 'It was I who made Albania. I left the country with the Parliament's authority and it is my duty to defend Albania. I cannot pass this duty on to anyone but my heir.'[2] Under whose legal authority, he demanded, had this 'government'-in-exile been created? By what right did the British and Americans make such appointments? Without even waiting for answers, he ordered the delegates to leave.

Such a display of indignation convinced the Anglo-American trio that the King might thwart the entire scheme if they failed to propitiate him. Even Amery, however, who thought Zog 'the most intelligent man I have ever met', accepted that he 'would not do' as a figure-head: 'the counter-revolution must have a leader who gave lip service to social democracy'.[3] Returning after luncheon, Amery insisted that a national committee was not at all the same thing as a government-in-exile and in no sense usurped the royal prerogative. Repeatedly assured that there would be a referendum on the restoration of the monarchy after the liberation, Zog allowed himself slowly to be talked round. This was, after all, the most promising development in years. Finally, he said that, while he could not support the committee publicly, neither would he work against it. The King wished 'Operation Valuable' every success at a much more friendly meeting three days later. The British thought better of telling him that they were already training thirty Ballists at a fortress on Malta.

The Committee for a Free Albania was officially launched in Paris on 26 August 'to guide and encourage our brave people in their resistance to cruel communist tyranny'.[4] A communiqué from the Royal Albanian Legation promptly denounced it and invited all Albanians to rally around their legitimate sovereign. The gesture left people guessing whether the Zogist members of the Committee represented him or not. The royalists and republicans predictably squabbled, especially when Frashëri suddenly died, and an obscure Ballist succeeded him as chairman in preference to Kupi. MI6 gave more weight to the Balli Kombëtar in the subversion operation for a practical reason: most Ballists had their origins in south-west Albania, which was far more accessible by sea and via Greece than the Legality heartlands further north.

The first nine infiltrators went ashore on the night of 3–4 October 1949. It was not an auspicious start: a group of four was ambushed within hours and killed. The next eleven had quickly to flee to Greece. They reported that villagers feared the secret police too much to risk any dealings with a rebel movement until it looked sure to succeed. After two missions in September 1950 produced similar findings – extraordinarily tight security and a sceptical populace – MI6 felt inclined to give up.

Not so the CIA. The Korean War and McCarthyism spurred the Americans to take over what they code-named 'Operation Fiend' and to expand it by enlisting 250 more Albanian anti-communists into a 'labour battalion' called Company 4000, ostensibly to perform auxiliary duties in the US occupation zone in southern Germany. So far, all the agents had been Ballists. The CIA thought that it was time to see if the Zogists could do any better among the Ghegs. Three missions were parachuted into northern Albania from low-flying aeroplanes between November 1950 and October 1951. The results remained discouraging: fourteen men lost without any sign of the genesis of organised insurgency. When Radio Tirana relayed the trial of four captured agents of Anglo-American-Italo-Graeco-Yugoslav imperialism, the western media dismissed the revelations as paranoid fantasy. The soldiers of Company 4000 knew otherwise. Morale slumped, and the constant quarrels between republicans and royalists began to get out of hand. When a Ballist platoon amused itself in the winter by building a snow structure like a tomb and writing Zog's name on it, Legality officers wanted them shot. In 1952, the Balli Kombëtar pulled out of active missions, leaving the CIA grateful to have a new Zogist initiative to pursue.

Sensing his growing leverage, the King (accompanied by Tati) had flown to New York in July 1951 and rented a suite at the Ritz Tower. 'My trip is strictly private and is only to see the United States,' he said[5] – something he would not have publicised had it been true. Zog paid a ceremonial visit to the US State Department on 8 August. His official host was no one more prestigious than the Deputy Assistant Secretary for European affairs, but his real interlocutor was secret-serviceman Gratian Yatsevich. Surveying the intelligence gathered over two years, Yatsevich remarked that all the spies told the same story. Locals in the remoter parts of Albania would not act against the regime unless they were first given explicit proof that the men who incited them to revolt really had the outside support which they claimed. But how could the United States confer this level of credibility on its agents without sacrificing the 'capacity for plausible denial'?

Zog at once replied 'that there was only one group with the necessary courage and authority' to convince the doubters: 'the men who had stayed with him throughout his exile and lived with him in Egypt now'.[6] The Royal Guard, still commanded by Colonel Selmani, currently consisted of just ten men. On his return to Alexandria in September, the King set about selecting three of them for the crucial mission. Six months on, when Zenel Shehu, Halil Branica, and Haxhi Gjyle escorted Myzejen and Maxhide to Paris, their ultimate destination was Mati.

Zog heard no more of them until the end of the summer (of 1952), when Yatsevich appeared at his villa to report excellent progress. Clearly, the name of King Zog still carried weight in his native valley. Since their arrival in Albania in late April, Shehu and Gjyle (with assistants from

Company 4000) had won the co-operation of their fellow clansmen, started making allies in neighbouring clans, and even 'turned' a few security policemen. Branica parachuted in to join them in August with gold, machine guns, and ammunition for the nascent guerrilla force. Now they wanted the CIA to drop Hamit Matjani, a brigand-cum-rebel, who regularly smuggled people over the Greek-Albanian frontier. He would know how to guide recruits into Greece for training.

The King could not fail to be excited at the possibilities. If the communists were overthrown by a rebellion spearheaded by Mati, the ensuing plebiscite on the monarchy would be held under ideal conditions. Yatsevich promised him regular reports, though the interval turned out be six months of tense expectation. When it came, the news was still favourable, but there were a couple of disconcerting details. Shortly after arrival, Captain Shehu's radio operator had broken his right arm, obliging him to tap his morse code with the left hand. A year had gone by and he had not reverted to his distinctive right-hand touch. Prearranged coded signals, however, continued to elicit the correct responses, and the CIA went ahead with parachuting Matjani and two other agents into Mati on 1 May 1953. The Americans started planning a full invasion, with ships, aircraft, and thousands of émigré soldiers. Zog did not wholly share their confidence. It had shocked him to learn how long Shehu and Gjyle had been in Albania, since he had made it a condition of their participation that no man should be there for more than five weeks at a time.

When the blow finally came, the King was unsurprised. Radio Tirana reported on New Year's Eve 1953 that five 'diversionists' and their contacts were being held in Tirana. The trial in April 1954 nonetheless appalled him (and everybody else involved). The secret police knew almost everything about the plot. It was with them, of course, and not the Royal Guards that the CIA had been in radio communication since 1952, yet they had more information than could have been extracted from Captain Shehu and the other captives (who were executed). Suspicion tore through the exile organisations and even touched Zog's staff. In retrospect, the role of Soviet spy Kim Philby has attracted more attention.

In Albania, Hoxha saw the conspiracy as justification of his police state. The communists were eliminating all those connected with the pre-war regime or with foreign countries, and interning their relatives and descendants, for, as in feuding, culpability for political crime was a family matter. No place faced a grimmer fate than Mati, where four hundred (more) men were executed after the Shehu trial and maybe thousands placed in camps. 'Dissenters must be exterminated like a weasel in a chicken coup,' explained Comrade Enver, who stayed in power until his death in 1985.[7] For Albanians, the pitiless totalitarianism of the Stalin era was to persist largely unmitigated for almost half a century. Even in 1954, it did not take clairvoyance to perceive the scale of the disaster, and the absence of Zenel Shehu, companion to the King since 1939, was a constant reminder to the residents of the royal villa in Alexandria, on which a pall of despondency descended.

Already, prior to the end of the CIA venture, Zog was beset by a series of problems, some of them grave. His exile in Egypt had latterly turned sour, and it was not as if he had failed to see the writing on the wall. A year after buying their home, Zog had told a despairing Geraldine: 'I do not think that we will be able to live here for long.' His premonitions of a third world war may have been unfounded, but he did not err in anticipating the downfall of Farouk. Even Zog had urged his brother sovereign to spend more time with Egyptians and shun 'the foreign riff-raff with whom he surrounded himself'.[8]

As political violence escalated in Egypt, King Zog obtained permission to migrate to America (thanks to his co-operation with the CIA) and, during his trip to New York in 1951, he purchased a property with at least 95 acres for $102,800 (or alternatively 'a bucket of diamonds and rubies').[9] Knollwood was palatial: a sixty-room granite mansion built by a Wall Street tycoon in the Muttontown district of Syosset, Long Island, in 1907, complete with Ionic columns, marble staircase, terraces, and fountains. On his return to Alexandria, he sold his villa in Ramleh to a Saudi Arabian prince and moved into a hotel pending departure. Then the US immigration department learnt that the King intended to bring, not just his family, but 115 people. His scheme was to turn Knollwood into an Albanian enclave, where Legality veterans could farm as his tenants. The Americans offered twenty entry visas, which Zog took to be the start of bargaining.

Time was against him. The Albanian party escaped suffering directly on 'Black Saturday', 26 January 1952, yet the burning of hundreds of foreign properties in Cairo by nationalistic mobs confirmed Zog's worst fears. They still had not left a few weeks later when a private disaster befell them: the King was found in his room, lying unconscious in a vast pool of blood. His stomach ulcer had haemorrhaged again and, for several months, he was too weak to travel. Having rented back their villa on the corniche, Zog and Geraldine were able to watch through binoculars as the royal yacht carried ex-King Farouk into exile after a military coup in July 1952. A week before, Zog had stayed up all night in the hope of seeing him, in the belief that his advice might 'possibly save the monarchy'.[10] Their intimacy with the old regime boded ill for the Albanians. While his wife and son took a precautionary 'holiday' in France, the King (with thirty-five US entry permits) intended to wind up his financial affairs and leave. Then he changed his mind. General

Neguib assured him that he could stay in Egypt on exactly the same terms as before, while the Americans were disputing his status, most plainly in respect of taxation. Two days before Nassau County's compulsory auction sale of Knollwood for property tax arrears, Zog did disburse the $2,914 demanded, but he complained of a breach of international law. To him, the issue was simple: 'A King pays no taxes.'[11]

Even with sovereign immunity, however, daily life for the exiles in Alexandria could no longer be what it had been. Pasha society was coming to an end, and, one by one, the mansions fell empty as the Levantine plutocracy dispersed. Geraldine suffered from a sense of isolation and monotony. Playing bridge with her husband's secretaries sustained her, she told Baroness Rüling in a letter: 'The rest of the family go into another salon and play rummy or poker. I cannot do so because the poor Princesses are so embittered with life on the whole that I just cannot swallow the atmosphere. Only I must say that everyone looks old.'[12] The suppressed tension grew more pronounced, as the Queen felt that Senije (divorced since 1948) tried to pass every waking hour in Zog's company.

Excitement of a most unwelcome kind disturbed the routine one day in August 1953. The Albanian Minister arrived from Cairo to announce that the Egyptian Government had closed his legation without warning, as a precursor to recognising the Hoxha regime. For the third time in as many years, the Zogu household prepared to depart – and this time in haste. The King booked them passage to Marseilles on the *Maréchal Joffre*, but he rightly anticipated the worst when the Egyptian Interior Ministry asked to see their pre-war diplomatic passports. They were retained.

The first police raid on 28 September ended with Egyptian officials seizing a number of documents after taking an inventory of the contents of the safe. The second on 1 November impounded two tommy-guns, three rifles, and nine revolvers. Zog was charged with fraudulent tax evasion and also questioned about hashish and currency smuggling. Rumours circulated that he had helped channel gold out of Egypt for Farouk and even sold arms to Israel. In the autumn of 1953, such allegations were widespread, as Nasser, the Interior Minister, conducted a purge of the old ruling class.

Brushing aside all his claims to majesty, the authorities maintained that the profits of Ahmed Zogu's commercial activities were taxable. Since he had avoided customs inspection on arrival, furthermore, he was unable to prove how many of the 9,000 gold coins in his safe had been brought into the country and how many had been subsequently acquired. All through the winter, the Albanians complained of surveillance and harassment by the local police and by communist agents. The King said that he was being used as a pawn – in the power struggles within the ruling junta and in Egyptian-Soviet relations – but his appeals for western diplomatic intervention struck most people (outside the secret services) as little short of ridiculous: 'I am kept a prisoner here while the free world needs me to free Communist Albania.'[13]

Eventually, once Nasser had installed himself as dictator, the tax inspectors consented to negotiate and Zog ended up paying an undisclosed amount in arrears and fines after selling the bulk of his gold. When at last free to leave, however, he was too sick to do so. He had suddenly lost over four stone in weight, and his doctors offered no clear explanation. A family which had seen the death agonies of Princess Ruhije now lived with the unspoken fear that his chronic gastritis had turned to gastric cancer. The King grew too weak to take decisions, and nobody else in the household knew how. The death of Nafije in March 1955 added to the distress of her helpless sisters. Prince Tati, now thirty-two and married, was entirely unused to responsibility. Sotir Martini, Zog's long-serving aide, had died in 1950, and his successor, Kemal Messare, did not impress outsiders. It fell to Queen Geraldine to try and make things happen. Troubled by contradictory medical advice, yet desperate to leave, she organised their departure in August 1955.

The invalid King could not face a long transatlantic voyage or a radical change of climate. In any case, his mansion on Long Island had been vandalised by people hunting for buried treasure. He sold Knollwood (demolished in 1959) when France agreed to let the Albanians convert their transit visas into residence permits. The doctors who examined him on arrival, however, did not expect that King Zog would be needing his for more than a few months.

CHAPTER FORTY-FIVE

Riviera Recluse

Queen Geraldine was to look back on her husband's final six years as one long nightmare. The combination of prolonged stress followed by prolonged frustration, physical inactivity, and heavy reliance on nicotine and caffeine had destroyed his health by the age of sixty. The problem of gastric erosion which intermittently afflicted him for decades was latterly compounded by a weak heart and liver ailments. Frequently confined to bed and always easily tired, he yet surprised the physicians by recovering some of his weight and most of his alertness within a short time of settling at Cannes. His condition then fluctuated from month to month. All he could ever do to take revenge on Nasser, though, was to place his knowledge of Egyptian politics at the disposal of MI6 during the Suez Crisis.

Rejoined by Adile and Salih, the royal family rented Villa Saint Blaise in La Californie, a district which was to Cannes as Ramleh had been to Alexandria, with splendid views of the Esterel massif and the Iles de Lérins. The French Riviera had for decades been the haunt of exiled royalty. The ex-wife of a King of Greece lived nearby, and the pathetic young King and Queen of Yugoslavia were also in Cannes, but Zog did not mix with the 'royal colony' to any great extent, still less with the fast set around Lady Docker and Ari Onassis. He did sometimes take his sisters to the Palm Beach Casino, which they loved, yet even when relatively well he preferred a drive in the country to the Hotel Carlton and its bevy of celebrities. For Zog, socialising outside the family had always been a political exercise. His next door neighbour, the American novelist David Dodge (author of *To Catch a Thief*) observed, 'King Zog was never a playboy, either, in fact wanted to be a writer more than anything else, God knows why.'[1]

The idea of writing memoirs may have sprung from a belated concern for posterity. In Albania, after all, every historian had to follow the leader and paint him as the 'pitiless feudal despot who sucked the blood of the people'.[2] His other motive was surely financial, as diminished capital meant a smaller income. His wife approached publishers with ambitious plans for a four-volume work (translated by herself), but nobody was interested – at any rate, not on the terms that Zog envisaged. Maybe this was just as well. After a lifetime of avoiding putting his thoughts down on paper, he found the task very difficult, and his modest archive had gone up in smoke in Liverpool in 1941. Despite his spending hours with pen in hand, nothing appeared in print. Geraldine did not earn a great deal from pseudonymous magazine stories either. She liked science fiction and romances of the Barbara Cartland type. A sale of her jewellery in 1958 made some money, but legal claims to war indemnities from Italy and a share of the reserves of the defunct National Bank of Albania were costly failures.

The House of Zogu tried to keep up standards. It retained its Minister of the Court and a couple of chamberlains. Perhaps the effort was misguided. Geoffrey Bocca, who interviewed many exiled monarchs, disparaged 'the ludicrous Zog':

> To the degree that he can make his presence felt King Zog leaves no one in doubt of his position. In the gardens of Zog's twenty-room kingdom, bodyguards patrol to safeguard him from invasion and a score of courtiers attend him to prevent him from feeling lonely. These address him as . . . 'Your Majesty' . . . and, on withdrawing, bow out backwards. . . . He keeps talking about coming to the United States but does nothing about it. All he does is wishfully think, and this he does on his customary extravagant level of philosophy. 'I believe,' he says, 'that Communism is on the retreat, and Albania can lead the way.'[3]

Occasionally, refugees who managed to escape from Albania (at enormous risk to themselves and their families) came to see the King, and they usually did assure him that communism was on the point of collapse and that the people wanted him back. They were a self-selecting sample: persecuted Legality veterans, who were often seeking his intercession with the French immigration authorities.

Zog continued to compose the odd memorandum in an attempt to bring his country, 'an advanced but isolated bastion of the Soviet menace', to the attention of western policy-makers. 'The prompt liberation of Albania,' he wanted Selwyn Lloyd to grasp, 'would complete the missing link in NATO's chain of defence in the Balkan sector.' Why had the 'indomitable' Albanians not yet risen against the 'tyranny which has martyred them'? Greece, a member of NATO since 1952, coveted 'Northern Epirus' still:

> . . . and there resides the poignant reason which obliges this valiant and fundamentally liberal little people . . . to bear the yoke of communist rulers who proclaim themselves the only vigilant guardians of the national frontiers, sustained in this endeavour by the total support of the USSR.[4]

Zog recommended that NATO guarantee the integrity and neutrality of Albania (just as he had wanted the British to do thirty years earlier). Ignorant of the exploits of MI6, the civil servant who read his paper merely minuted: 'King Zog does not explain how Albania is to be liberated without touching off a major war.'

Only the most hawkish of cold warriors still considered Zog to be of any possible significance, and that was not so much on account of 'legality' as due to the failure of anti-Zogist exiles to come up with any more credible figurehead. Fan Noli, once the obvious alternative, had latterly turned his back on Albania. By the late 1950s, the convolutions of émigré politics held no hint of promise. When Operation Fiend had fallen apart, so had the Committee for a Free Albania, leaving a 'National Committee for a Free Albania' pitted against a 'National Democratic Committee for a Free Albania'. The Legality Movement itself split in two, so the King could only make a virtue of standing above the fray.

With precious little in the way of politics to occupy him, life for Zog became bleak indeed. The court in Cannes had reached a stage when good news meant his gaining a pound or two in weight rather than his coming any closer to restoration. It was patently not going to happen – in *his* lifetime – yet he never betrayed the slightest doubt as to the ultimate return of the dynasty. Zogists could tell many striking stories to show the loyalty of Albanians to their chieftain (leaving foreigners to imagine that it carried over to their King). Zog, however, must have realised that, even if communism were to collapse, a reversion to monarchy would not be automatic (to put it mildly). The improbable can nevertheless occur, and pride did not allow him to admit defeat.

Prince Leka, proclaimed heir to the throne on his eighteenth birthday, had completed his schooling in Switzerland and attended Sandhurst (thanks to lobbying by Julian Amery MP). In 1959, Queen Geraldine wanted him to try for Oxford, but Zog said that his son must be with him, as there was not much time left for him to pass on his knowledge of Albanian politics. This he did, so far as his fragile health would permit. Late in 1960, however, he wanted the family to move to Paris, so that the Prince could study economics at the Sorbonne while continuing to live at home.

Geraldine hesitated, as the King was now severely ill again. He looked much older than his sixty-five years, although he still carefully arranged his thin hair and moustache. His face and neck had not wrinkles so much as deep vertical folds, and his body had once more grown skeletally thin. Above all, he felt terrible pain at the base of his spine. Nevertheless, as he willed it, the Zogu household forsook La Californie in the New Year and rented a home in Ablon-sur-Seine, south-east of Paris. Zog found the train ride excruciating, and, in their state of nerves, the women railed at the dirtiness and dilapidation of the house. The Queen could not get servants, and, as the King seemed to withdraw into a private hell, her tolerance of her sisters-in-law reached its limit when they objected to his being given morphine. After three weeks at Ablon, no one could cope any more.

Admitted to the Foch Hospital at Suresnes, Zog asked his wife for the miniature revolver which he had given her in Tirana. He had always placed his own gold-plated gun on his bedside table at night, but he no longer had the strength to lift it. Geraldine obediently substituted her little weapon. 'Open it,' Zog demanded and, seeing it empty, refused to rest until Leka had replaced the bullets which she had just removed. The King stated that, if he found out that he had cancer, he would shoot himself in the head. The Queen was appalled. After surviving fifty-five assassination plots, so people said, he had come to this. Needless to say, the diagnosis was never disclosed to him, but the onset of jaundice nine weeks later left no room for doubt.

On 5 April, recalled Leka, his father suddenly awakened to relate a vivid dream of his mature son and elderly wife arriving at Durrës in triumph at the head of a column of freedom fighters: 'All Albanians have a tendency to interpret dreams.'[5]

King Zog then fell into a restless coma. He died early in the afternoon of Sunday, 9 April 1961. Two days later, in the presence of hundreds of Albanian exiles, he was buried in Thiais cemetery, near Orly, with the grand mufti of Algiers officiating. Into the grave went a sachet of Albanian soil, gathered at the border in 1939. The grey marble tombstone bears the inscription, 'Fatherland Above All.'

CHAPTER FORTY-SIX

Epilogue

The Queen suffered a nervous breakdown after the death of her husband. Leka then split up the royal household. While Adile rejoined her children, the three other princesses were installed in a flat in Cannes. Lost without their brother, they pined away in seclusion. Myzejen and Senije suffered fatal heart attacks in the same week in April 1969. Maxhide died six months later (her age implausibly reported as fifty-four).

King Leka and his mother went to live in Spain, where Franco granted them extraterritorial rights. Geraldine, widowed at only forty-five, found herself welcome in royal exile circles, set up home with her sister, Virginia, and rediscovered a social life. The new King of the Albanians, aided by his contacts with Muslim dynasties, went into business selling tractors and cranes in the Middle East. He also toured Vietnam, Cambodia, Yemen, and Angola, in order to study guerrilla warfare. In the 1970s, he claimed to be conducting a campaign of sabotage against the Hoxha regime.

Some people questioned Leka's seriousness and alleged that his talk of military training camps was no more than a cover for arms trafficking. It was not difficult to deride a royal family that comprised a Queen Mother who had spent only fifteen months in her kingdom, a King who passed two and a half days there as a baby, and (from 1975) an Australian Queen. In fact, Leka felt a strong sense of duty to Albania and to the memory of King Zog, whose political subtlety he had not conspicuously inherited. 'I am primarily a military animal,' he once said, 'I would respond militarily rather than politically or diplomatically.'[1] Six feet eight inches tall, he made a habit of wearing combat dress with hand-grenades hooked to his belt. Leka settled in South Africa after Spain expelled him in 1979. Three years later, Queen Susan (or Suzani) gave birth to a Crown Prince named Leka Anwar Zog Reza Baudouin Msiziwe.

The end of communism in Albania came about in 1991–2, but it was not until central government had all but collapsed in 1997 that Leka won permission to return and take part in a referendum on the restoration of the monarchy. The official result recorded 66.7 per cent in favour of the republic. Leka branded it a fraud, and his protest rally ended in shooting. An Albanian court then sentenced him *in absentia* to three years in prison. Following an amnesty, however, the royal family in June 2002 took up residence in Tirana as private citizens. Queen Geraldine died there, aged eighty-seven, on 22 October 2002. Leka continued to 'pursue by all legitimate and pacific means the restoration of the Albanian monarchy in accordance with the wishes of the Albanian people'.[2]

* * *

Adventurer or patriot? Hero or scoundrel? There is in most people, however sophisticated, something which hankers after the good king/bad king classification of old-fashioned schoolbooks, but neither in international academic history (which strives to conceal it), nor in Albanian popular consciousness (which does not), has a broad enough consensus emerged about Zog to make a simple label stick.

Many foreign historians of the Balkans do have a few good words to say of him. Joseph Rothschild's view is not untypical:

On balance, to have in two short decades consolidated the new Albanian state against the pulls of regionalism and tribalism, against the pressure of the frondeur and brigand tradition, against the corrosions of mass poverty and illiteracy, and against the hazards of an international system that allowed predatory neighbours to deny the very legitimacy of an independent Albania was a creditable political achievement.[3]

Some place more emphasis on his ultimate failure. Other writers detect nothing worthy of praise and dismiss 'the appalling Zog' as 'an unsavoury tyrant'.[4] His personal wealth, sham elections, and political murder feature prominently here. The disagreement is not so much about facts as about motives and criteria. When argued with due qualifications, the pro-Zog and anti-Zog lines converge to a point where the choice essentially lies between a pragmatic patriot obliged by severe circumstances to adopt some very questionable expedients and an unscrupulous egotist whose self-glorification produced incidental benefits for his country. By what standard should a ruler like Zog be judged? A relativist approach might equally vindicate contemporary dictators in post-colonial nations with little cohesion, bad frontiers, and under-developed economies. Was the Zogist monarchy any more acceptable because Albania had never known democracy? The answer may depend on whether it is thought that Albania *could* have been much better governed in the 1920s and 1930s.

In evaluating a foreign leader, people may wish to take their cue from the nationality concerned. By origins, Zog was Albanian of the Albanians. Ekrem Bey Vlora, a lukewarm follower, went so far as to describe him as 'the archetype, the synthesis of all the merits and failings of the people of the new Albania. He possessed them altogether in the superlative; that is why he had such great success.'[5] The problem is that forty-seven years of neo-Stalinism badly distorted – where it did not halt – the processes whereby historical reputations develop. True, there were a few émigré intellectuals, whose liberalism turned them away from the King, while their nationalism forced them back towards him. Historian Stavro Skendi concluded, 'Whatever his flaws, he made a nation and a government where there had been a people and anarchy',[6] and more would agree that he at least made a start. Meanwhile, Albanians in Albania could admit to thinking only what Hoxha told them to think: that Zog was a traitor-despot who ruined the country. The communist period did bring material advances (funded by the Russians and Chinese), yet Albania was still by far the poorest nation in Europe and became the most brutally repressive.

The 1990s naturally saw the start of a reaction in favour of Zog. The novelist Ismail Kadare asserted that history would rehabilitate him: 'A monarch both archaic and modern, a man at once of his time and outside his time.'[7] Most Albanians in the decade after the end of totalitarianism, however, were too hard-pressed to survive amid social and economic breakdown to devote much time to historical reflection. What they thought about Zog often depended on what father or grandfather was doing in 1944 (just as much foreign opinion was based less on knowledge than on overriding attitudes to the Cold War). Praising Zog was one way of denigrating Hoxha; abusing him a way of defending Hoxha; hedgers pointed out similarities. In 2000, Tirana city council restored the name of Boulevard Zog.

Soon Albanians will be able to look more dispassionately at their history in the twentieth century: liberation, instability, occupation, instability, Zogist dictatorship, occupation, civil war, Stalinist dictatorship, and more instability. When they do, they may well count the reign of King Zog among the good times. It is a sobering thought.

Notes

PREFACE

1. *Time*, 21 April 1961 p. 60
2. *The Times*, 23 Feb. 1996

1. PROLOGUE: AN AUDIENCE

1. *New York Times*, 6 Sept. 1928
2. *Daily Express*, 2 July 1930
3. Robinson p. 56
4. *New York Times*, 6 Sept. 1928
5. Matthews (1937) p. 191
6. Ibid., p. 192
7. *Daily Express*, 2 July 1930
8. Matthews (1937) p. 192
9. *Daily Telegraph*, 12 Oct. 1928
10. Swire (1937) p. 123
11. *Daily Telegraph*, 12 Oct. 1928
12. *New York Times*, 2 Sept. 1928
13. Matthews (1935) p. 225
14. *Sunday Dispatch*, 28 Aug. 1938
15. *Daily Telegraph*, 12 Oct. 1928
16. Newman (1938) p. 35; Matthews
    (1935) p. 225
17. P. Brown p. 154
18. Robyns p. 66

2. THE STAR OF MATI

1. Redlich p. 33
2. Dako pp. v–vi

3. *Daily Express*, 7 Sept. 1928
4. Seeds to Chamberlain, 22 Jan.
   1927, FO 371/12064
5. Konitza (1957) pp. 46–8; Etherton
   & Allen p. 174
6. Interview with Teri Cooper
7. Matthews (1937) p. 182
8. Newman (1936) p. 239
9. Redlich p. 26

3. YOUNG AHMED

1. Dako p. 30
2. Robyns p. 63
3. Tocci p. 27
4. Robyns p. 64
5. Matthews (1937) pp. 183–4
6. Ibid., p. 184
7. Tocci p. 34
8. Dako p. 42
9. Vlora vol. II pp. 133, 173
10. Tocci p. 34
11. Amery (1948) p. 3

4. PRINCE WILHELM'S LOYAL
   SUBJECT

1. Herbert p. 252
2. Vlora vol. II p. 134
3. Amery (1948) p. 12
4. Swire (1929) p. 231

5. POWERS AND PUPPETS

1. Dako p. 65
2. Schmidt-Neke p. 42
3. Dako p. 72
4. Swire (1929) p. 262
5. Dako p. 78

6. COLONEL ZOGOLLI

1. Windischgraetz p. 97
2. Szinyei-Merse p. 70
3. Dako p. 75
4. Ibid., pp. 76–7
5. Barnes p. 48
6. Smiley p. 36
7. Veith p. 527
8. Glaise-Horstenau vol. 4 p. 246
9. Dako p. 77
10. Ibid., p. 79
11. Ibid., pp. 80–1

7. MINISTER OF THE INTERIOR

1. Fischer (1984) pp. 127–8
2. Xoxe p. 28
3. Dako p. 88
4. Robinson p. 37
5. Baerlein p. 62
6. Matthews (1937) p. 182
7. Cassels p. 242
8. Dako p. 100

8. HIS FIRST COUP

1. Tocci p. 97
2. Vlora vol. I p. 270
3. Annual Report 1921, FO 371/7332

9. SURVIVING

1. Barnes pp. 61–2
2. Eyres to Curzon, 16 Mar. 1922, FO371/7331
3. *Royalty Digest*, vol. 3 p. 341
4. Kontos pp. 192–3
5. Seeds to Chamberlain, 3 Dec. 1926, FO 371/11207
6. Parr to Curzon, 12 Nov. 1922, FO 371/7332
7. Dako p. 122

10. ZOGU, PM

1. Vlora vol. II p. 219
2. Letter by Shearme, 12 Dec. 1922, FO 371/8531
3. *Royalty Digest*, vol. 3 p. 341
4. Eyres to Curzon, 15 June 1922, FO 371/7331
5. Central European Summary, 11 May 1923, FO 371/8535
6. Eyres to Curzon, 27 Sept. 1923, FO 371/8534
7. Central European Summary, 11 May 1923, FO 371/8535
8. Barnes p. 121
9. Eyres to Curzon, 27 Oct. 1923, FO 371/8535
10. Ibid.
11. Ibid.

11. DOWN AND OUT

1. Parr to Curzon, 20 Nov. 1923 (enclosure), FO 371/8535
2. Eyres to Curzon, 27 Oct. 1923, FO 371/8535
3. Parr to Curzon, 1 Dec. 1923, FO 371/8535

4. Vlora vol. II p. 178
5. Ibid., p. 179; Szinyei-Merse p. 75
6. Szinyei-Merse p. 75
7. Tocci p. 87
8. Eyres to MacDonald, 24 April 1924, FO 371/9644
9. Notes by Harvey, 12 June 1924, FO 371/9639
10. Annual Report 1923, FO 371/9643; Eyres to MacDonald, 30 May 1924, FO 371/9644
11. *Near East*, 30 July 1924

12. FAN NOLI

1. Pipa p. 248
2. Parr to Nicolson, 15 July 1924, FO 371/9640
3. Pipa p. 245
4. Saraçi to Konitza, 7 Dec. 1942, FO 371/33111
5. Pipa pp. 247–8
6. Frashëri p. 227
7. League Assembly, 10 Sept. 1924, p. 7
8. Heathcote pp. 258–60
9. Swire (1929) p. 444
10. Macartney & Cremona p. 103

13. 'THE TRIUMPH OF LEGALITY'

1. McCulloch p. 134
2. Lessona p. 83
3. Graham to Chamberlain, 30 Dec. 1924, FO 371/10654
4. 29 Dec. 1925, FO 371/10654
5. Vlora vol. II p. 134
6. Dako pp. 134–5
7. Schmidt-Neke p. 140
8. Vlora vol. II p. 209
9. Eyres to Chamberlain, 27 Jan. 1925, FO 371/10656

10. Eyres to Chamberlain, 18 Feb. 1925, FO 371/10657
11. Eyres to Chamberlain, 17 Feb. 1925, FO 371/10656
12. Dako p. 136
13. Vlora vol. II p. 214
14. Parr to Chamberlain, 4 Jan. 1926, FO 371/11208
15. *Evening News* 16 Aug. 1923
16. Fry p. 296
17. Swire (1937) p. 16

14. LIRA IMPERIALISM

1. Seeds to Chamberlain, 16 Nov. 1927, FO 371/12069
2. Seton-Watson p. 678
3. Macartney & Cremona p. 334
4. Eyres to Foreign Office, 5 Feb. 1925, FO 371/10657
5. Graham to Foreign Office, 11 Feb. 1925, FO 371/10657
6. Swire (1929) p. 460
7. Seton-Watson p. 678
8. Konitza (1957) p. 155
9. Mack Smith p. 149
10. Seton-Watson p. 678
11. Cassels p. 317
12. Forbes (1949) p. 121

15. *AVANTI ITALIA!*

1. O'Reilly to Lampson, 9 May 1926, FO 371/11204
2. Seeds to Chamberlain, 2 Dec. 1926, FO 371/11207
3. Cassels p. 327
4. O'Reilly to Lampson, 27 June 1926, FO 371/11205
5. Eyres to Lampson, 25 Dec. 1924, FO 371/11204
6. O'Reilly to Tyrrell, 23 July 1926, FO 371/11205

7. Cassels pp. 312–13
8. Ibid., p. 327
9. Chamberlain to Toretta, 18 Aug. 1926, FO 371/11205
10. Chamberlain to Seeds, 20 Aug. 1926, FO 371/11205
11. Parr to Lampson, 28 Aug. 1926, FO 371/11210
12. Robinson p. 77
13. Seeds to Chamberlain, 30 Sept. 1926, FO 371/11208
14. Seeds to Chamberlain, 3 Dec. 1926, FO 371/11207; Seeds to Chamberlain, 25 Feb. 1927, FO 371/12068
15. Toynbee (1929) p. 169
16. Swire (1929) p. 483
17. Seeds to Chamberlain, 3 Dec. 1926, FO 371/11207

16. THE BREACH WITH BELGRADE

1. Jacomoni p. 56
2. Seeds to Chamberlain, 12 June 1927, FO 371/12072
3. Seeds to Chamberlain, 28 July 1927, FO 371/12073
4. Annual Report 1926, FO 371/12070
5. Zamboni p. 252
6. Seeds to Chamberlain, 16 Nov. 1927, FO 371/12069
7. Macleay to FO, 15 Oct. 1927, FO 371/12073
8. Seeds to Chamberlain, 23 Nov. 1927, FO 371/12066
9. Ibid.
10. Ibid.

17. ON THE STEPS OF THE THRONE

1. Dako pp. 142–3

2. Vaughan-Russell to Chamberlain, 16 Sept. 1927, FO 371/12069
3. Leeper to Chamberlain, 26 Aug. 1927, FO 371/12069
4. Etherton & Allen p. 194
5. Leeper to Chamberlain, 25 Aug. 1927, FO 371/12068
6. Parr to Chamberlain, 4 Jan. 1926, FO 371/11208
7. *Daily Express*, 7 Sept. 1928
8. Hodgson to Chamberlain, 15 Aug. 1928, FO 371/12845
9. Hodgson to Chamberlain, 8 Sept. 1928, FO 371/12846
10. Dako p. 152

18. HIS MAJESTY

1. Swire (1929) p. 520
2. Hodgson to Cushendun, 8 Sept. 1928, FO 371/12846
3. *New York Times*, 7 Sept. 1928
4. Hodgson to Balfour, 29 Aug. 1928, FO 371/12845
5. *New York Times*, 6 Sept. 1928
6. Dako pp. 154–5
7. Annual Report 1928, FO 371/13560
8. Béraud p. 118
9. Kinross pp. 479–80
10. Fenyvesi p. 233

19. KING AND CAPITAL

1. Powell (1931) p. 159
2. P. Brown p. 149
3. Dako p. 163
4. *Daily Mail*, 31 Mar. 1938
5. Dako p. 164
6. Heseltine p. 232

20. INSIDE THE COMPOUND

1. Quaroni p. 62
2. O'Doneven p. 175
3. Holtz p. 47
4. Annual Report 1926, FO 371/12070
5. Holtz p. 47
6. Powell (1938) p. 396
7. Ibid.
8. Xoxe p. 97
9. *New York Times*, 10 June 1929
10. Anderson p. 78
11. Matthews (1937) p. 13
12. ffoulkes p. 267
13. Diack & Mackenzie p. 162
14. ffoulkes p. 266
15. Powell (1938) p. 396

21. ZOG AND THE ZOGISTS

1. Luke p. 158
2. Hodgson to Chamberlain, 5 Dec. 1928, FO 371/12848
3. Quaroni p. 60
4. Holtz p. 59
5. Robinson p. 116
6. Konitza (1957) p. 155
7. Robinson pp. 110–11
8. Hodgson to Henderson, 29 July 1929, FO 371/13562
9. Annual Report 1927, FO 371/12847; Sulzberger p. 76
10. Konitza (1957) p. 150
11. Vlora vol. II p. 211
12. Ryan to Eden, 24 Feb. 1937, FO 371/21112
13. Quaroni p. 68
14. Ryan to Eden, 24 Feb. 1937, FO 371/21112
15. Hodgson to Henderson, 29 July 1929, FO 371/13562

16. Quaroni p. 69
17. Roucek (1939) p. 93

22. THE INSPECTORS-GENERAL

1. Stevens to Hodgson, 13 Nov. 1931, FO 371/15147
2. Stirling p. 157
3. Seeds to Chamberlain, 23 Jan. 1927, FO 371/12064
4. Annual Report 1927, FO 371/12847
5. Quaroni p. 62

23. ROYAL FAMILY

1. Szinyei-Merse p. 165
2. Ibid. p. 171
3. Hadwen to Henderson, 25 Aug. 1931, FO 371/15149
4. Robinson p. 30
5. Szinyei-Merse p. 155
6. Agolli p. 73
7. Memo by Watson, 28 Nov. 1927, FO 371/12066
8. *Daily Mail*, 31 Mar. 1938
9. Fenyvesi p. 233
10. Mitchell ch. 4
11. Robinson p. 61
12. Quaroni p. 65
13. Ibid.
14. Dedet p. 162
15. Interview with Teri Cooper
16. Ibid.
17. Backer pp. 58–9

24. THE PUBLIC FACE OF THE REGIME

1. Schmidt-Neke p. 211
2. Schmidt-Neke pp. 206, 219; Dako pp. 159, 164

3. Redlich p. 41
4. Ryan p. 340
5. Roucek (1939) p. 94
6. Hodgson to Sargent, 28 Jan. 1930, FO 371/14302
7. Holtz p. 60
8. Mitchell ch. 4
9. Jacques (1995) p. 393
10. *Daily Telegraph*, 12 Oct. 1928
11. Jacques (1995) p. 397
12. Ryan p. 323
13. Interview with Teri Cooper; Hodgson to Simon, 19 April 1933, FO 371/16625
14. Seeds to Chamberlain, 3 Feb. 1928, FO 371/12844
15. Seeds to Chamberlain, 27 Mar. 1928, FO 371/12847
16. Jacques (1995) p. 398

25. A FRAGILE STABILITY

1. Pollo & Puto p. 211
2. Vaughan-Russell to Chamberlain, 16 Sept. 1927, FO 371/12069
3. Amery (1948) p. 22
4. Hodgson to Henderson, 5 Aug. 1931, FO 371/15147
5. Roucek (1939) p. 88
6. *Daily Telegraph*, 23 Feb. 1931
7. Schmidt-Neke p. 233
8. Matthews (1937) p. 180
9. *Neue Freie Presse*, 12 Mar. 1931
10. Hodgson to Henderson, 11 June 1931, FO 371/15148
11. Hodgson to O'Malley, 2 Nov. 1931, FO 371/15147
12. Hodgson to Reading, 3 Nov. 1931, FO 371/15148
13. Hodgson to Sargent, 11 June 1931, FO 371/15146

26. SLOW PROGRESS

1. Hodgson to Chamberlain, 18 Dec. 1928 (enclosure), FO 371/12847
2. *Daily Express*, 2 July 1930
3. Monroe p. 153
4. Busch-Zantner p. 206
5. Redlich pp. 44–55
6. *Daily Telegraph*, 12 Oct. 1928; Yeats-Brown p. 237
7. Ryan to Eden, 9 Jan. 1937, FO 371/21112
8. Jacques (1995) p. 401
9. Leeper to Chamberlain, 26 Aug. 1927, FO 371/12069
10. Matthews (1937) p. 37; O'Doneven p. 163
11. Forbes (1940) pp. 243, 245

27. DEBTOR AND CREDITOR

1. Vanlande p. 106
2. *Daily Telegraph*, 12 Oct. 1928
3. Hodgson to Chamberlain, 15 Aug. 1928, FO 371/12845
4. Currey p. 251
5. Robinson p. 71
6. Quaroni p. 64
7. Leading personalities, 21 Feb. 1927, FO 371/12069
8. Quaroni pp. 59–60
9. Heseltine p. 186
10. Quaroni pp. 61–2
11. Hadwen to Henderson, 25 Aug. 1931, FO 371/15149
12. Robyns p. 67
13. Currey p. 209
14. Quaroni p. 62
15. Annual Report 1930, FO 371/15148
16. Knox p. 27
17. Hodgson to Simon, 17 Mar. 1933, FO 371/16623

18. Vaughan-Russell to Chamberlain, 16 Sept. 1927, FO 371/12069
19. Villari p. 259
20. Hodgson to Henderson, 3 Aug. 1931, FO 371/15148
21. Hodgson to Simon, 29 Dec. 1931, FO 371/15887
22. Annual Report 1932, FO 371/16623

28. HARD TIMES

1. Hodgson to Simon, 21 Mar. 1933, FO 371/16624
2. Ibid.
3. Ibid.
4. Annual Report 1934, FO 371/19478
5. Hodgson to Simon, 17 May 1933, FO 371/16624
6. Ibid.
7. Annual Report 1933, FO 371/18341
8. Kent p. 158
9. Hodgson to Simon, 18 Oct. 1933, FO 371/16623
10. Hodgson to Simon, 11 Dec. 1933, FO 371/16623
11. Montgomery p. 252
12. Hodgson to Simon, 25 April 1935, FO 371/19477

29. ILL WINDS

1. Montgomery p. 252
2. Mack Smith p. 181
3. Macartney & Cremona p. 117
4. Hodgson to Simon, 27 April 1935, FO 371/19477
5. Hodgson to Simon, 3 July 1935, FO 371/19477
6. Weld-Forester to Hoare, 21 Oct. 1935, FO 371/19476
7. Hodgson to Eden, 19 May 1936, FO 371/20357
8. Alastos p. 113
9. Toynbee (1935) p. 536
10. Slocombe p. 110
11. Hodgson to Eden, 21 April 1936, FO 371/20357
12. Monroe p. 151; Petrie p. 196
13. Ryan to Eden, 5 May 1937, FO 371/21112

30. YOUNG MEN AND OLD MEN

1. Annual Report 1932, FO 371/16623
2. Hodgson to Hoare, 2 Sept. 1935, FO 371/19476
3. Annual Report 1935, FO 371/20358
4. Weld-Forester to Hoare, 26 Sept. 1935, FO 371/19476
5. Hodgson to Hoare, 4 Nov. 1935, FO 371/19476
6. Weld-Forester to Hoare, 23 Oct. 1935, FO 371/19476
7. Busch-Zantner p. 134
8. Matthews (1937) p. 294
9. Schmidt-Neke pp. 254-5
10. Alastos p. 113
11. Ryan to Eden, 28 Nov. 1936, FO 371/20358
12. Hohler to Balfour, 8 April 1939, FO 371/23713
13. Ryan to Eden, 6 Feb. 1937, FO 371/21112
14. Ryan to Eden, 22 Feb. 1937, FO 371/21112
15. Jacques (1988) pp. 12-13
16. Schmidt-Neke p. 264
17. Lushaj (1995) vol. I p. 7

31. SEEKING A QUEEN

1. Bethell p. 12
2. Powell (1931) p. 159
3. Szinyei-Merse p. 162
4. Vanlande p. 35
5. Swire (1937) p. 201
6. O'Doneven p. 176
7. Hodgson to Sargant, 26 Mar. 1930, FO 371/14302
8. Hodgson to Cushendun, 15 Aug. 1928, FO 371/12845
9. Quaroni p. 74
10. Schmidt-Neke p. 229
11. *Daily Express*, 28 Aug. 1934
12. Unpublished memoir p. 15, Saraçi collection
13. Szinyei-Merse p. 165

32. GERALDINE

1. Robyns p. 22
2. Szinyei-Merse p. 55
3. Robyns p. 17
4. Szinyei-Merse pp. 95, 99–100
5. *Weekly Illustrated*, 12 Feb. 1938
6. Robyns p. 177
7. Szinyei-Merse pp. 104–5
8. Ibid. p. 108
9. Robyns p. 53
10. *Daily Telegraph*, 26 April 1938

33. A NATIONAL EVENT

1. *New York Times*, 1 Mar. 1938
2. Pipa p. 249
3. Szinyei-Merse p. 110
4. Robyns p. 59
5. Ciano (1952) p. 106
6. Moseley p. 51
7. *Picture Post*, 7 Oct. 1939
8. Ciano (1952) p. 106

9. Robyns p. 60
10. Ciano (1952) p. 107

34. BORROWED TIME

1. Report by Burrows, 13 Sept. 1938, FO 371/22307
2. Szinyei-Merse p. 140
3. Robyns p. 54
4. Szinyei-Merse pp. 164–7
5. Konitza (1957) p. 150
6. Lushaj (1995) vol. I p. 24
7. Robyns pp. 43, 66
8. Ryan to Eden, 11 Aug. 1936, FO 371/20358
9. Burgwyn p. 156
10. Ryan to Halifax, 2 April 1938, FO 371/22307
11. Ryan to Eden, 19 July 1937, FO 371/21111
12. Ciano (1952) p. 118
13. Ibid. pp. 176–7
14. Robyns p. 74
15. Ciano (1948) p. 203
16. Ciano (1952) p. 118
17. Ibid. p. 125
18. Ibid. p. 201
19. Ibid. p. 127
20. Sulzberger p. 72
21. Ciano (1952) p. 184; Moseley p. 52

35. INTO THE VORTEX

1. Hoptner pp. 125–6
2. Moseley p. 52; Robyns p. 81
3. Ciano (1952) p. 202
4. Szinyei-Merse p. 97
5. Ciano (1947) p. 48
6. Ibid. p. 29
7. Ibid. p. 54
8. Ryan p. 332

9. Hohler to Balfour, 8 April 1939, FO 371/23713
10. Ciano (1947) p. 55
11. *Daily Telegraph*, 26 Mar. 1939
12. Ciano (1947) p. 56

36. HOLY WEEK

1. Szinyei-Merse p. 229
2. *New York Times*, 5 April 1939
3. *Foreign Relations of the United States*, 1939 vol. 2 p. 368
4. Szinyei-Merse p. 235
5. Packard p. 60
6. *Foreign Relations of the United States*, 1939 vol. 2 p. 372
7. Macadam to Leeper, 13 April 1939, FO 371/23713
8. Ciano (1947) p. 64
9. *Foreign Relations of the United States*, 1939 vol. 2 p. 373
10. *Parliamentary Debates* vol. 345 c2995
11. Packard pp. 60-1
12. Robyns p. 91

37. GOOD FRIDAY

1. *New York Times*, 8 April 1939
2. Packard p. 61
3. Ibid. p. 62
4. *Evening Standard*, 8 April 1939
5. Broadcast by Kodeli, 7 April 1939, FO 371/23713
6. Kirkpatrick p. 375
7. Packard p. 66
8. Ciano (1947) pp. 64-5
9. Packard p. 66

38. A RECKONING

1. *New York Times*, 9 April 1939
2. Szinyei-Merse p. 249

3. Dedet p. 253; *Korrieri*, 29 Jan. 2003
4. *Foreign Relations of the United States*, 1939 vol. 2 p. 373
5. Madol pp. 118-19, 121
6. Memo by Ryan, 14 Mar. 1942, FO 371/33110
7. *Sunday Dispatch*, 28 Aug. 1938; Hohler to Balfour, 8 April 1939, FO 371/23713
8. *New York Times*, 16 April 1939
9. *Documents on German Foreign Policy* D:VI p208
10. *Parliamentary Debates* vol. 346 c16
11. *Daily Herald*, 8 April 1939
12. Roucek (1939) p. 97
13. *Evening Standard*, 13 April 1939
14. Robinson p. 73
15. *Manchester Guardian*, 12 Sept. 1942
16. Fischer (1999) p. 30; Charmley p. 178
17. League Council, 22 May 1939, FO 371/23711
18. Ciano (1947) p. 99
19. Ibid. p. 189

39. REFUGEES

1. *News Review*, 12 Mar. 1942
2. *Daily Sketch*, 17 Mar. 1942
3. *The Times*, 28 May 1943
4. Vlora vol. II p. 219
5. *New Times and Ethiopia News*, 27 May 1939
6. *New York Times*, 20 July 1939
7. *Daily Telegraph*, 20 July 1939
8. *New York Times*, 25 July 1939
9. Robyns p. 104
10. Phipps to FO, 4 July 1939, FO 371/23710
11. Peyrefitte p. 78
12. *The Albanian Question* FO 371/43558

40. IN LONDON AT WAR

1. Minute by Dixon, 2 July 1940, FO 371/24868
2. Interview with Teri Cooper
3. Montgomery-Massingberd p. 105
4. Beaton p. 41
5. Madol pp. 118–21
6. Moseley p. 55
7. Ryan to Dixon, 9 Nov. 1940, FO 371/24868
8. Robyns p. 122
9. Minute by Broad, 23 Nov. 1940, FO 371/24868
10. Ryan to Dixon, 22 Jan. 1941, FO 371/24868
11. Memo, 14 Dec. 1940, FO 371/24868
12. Toovey to Cazalet, 3 Feb. 1941, FO 371/29714
13. Minute by Dixon, 11 Feb. 1941, FO 371/29709
14. Puto p. 45
15. Madol p. 118

41. A LACK OF RECOGNITION

1. Memo by Ryan, 8 Sept. 1941, FO 371/29709
2. Morris p. 29
3. Kemp p. 248
4. Lees-Milne pp. 54–5
5. Jacques (1995) p. 419
6. Hibbert p. 33
7. Memo by Ryan, 23 Mar. 1942, FO 371/33110
8. Minute by Dixon, 10 July 1942, FO 371/33110
9. Beaton p. 41
10. Szinyei-Merse pp. 164–5, 145, 238
11. Amery (1973) p. 311
12. Vickers p. 124

13. Saraçi to Zog, 28 Nov. 1941, FO 371/33110
14. *Sunday Pictorial*, 3 Jan. 1943
15. *The Times*, 28 May 1943
16. Lees-Milne pp. 54–5
17. Memo by Ryan, 14 Mar. 1942, FO 371/33110
18. Memo by Ryan, 6 July 1942, FO 371/33110
19. Konitza to Martini, 24 July 1942, FO 371/33111; Puto p. 114
20. *New Times & Ethiopia News*, 14 Nov. 1942
21. Ryan to Dixon, 8 Sept. 1941, FO 371/29709
22. *Dielli*, 28 Nov. 1942
23. Fischer (1999) p. 244
24. *Parliamentary Debates* vol. 385 cc. 2114–15
25. Declaration by Zog, 7 April 1943, FO 371/37137
26. Kemp p. 248
27. Cripps p. 28
28. Robyns p. 128

42. TWELVE HUNDRED MILES AWAY

1. *News Chronicle*, 26 July 1943
2. Kemp p. 95
3. Ibid. p. 78
4. Hoxha pp. 99–100
5. Amery (1973) p. 312
6. Herbert to Cadogan, 20 Feb. 1944, FO 371/43562
7. Minute by Eden, 6 Feb. 1944, FO 371/43549
8. Hibbert pp. 134–5
9. Amery (1973) p. 339
10. Ibid. p. 345
11. Fielding p. 46
12. Robyns p. 136

13. Gilbert pp. 1000–1
14. Memo by Ryan, 4 Aug. 1945, FO 371/48100
15. Ibid.
16. *New York Times*, 12 Jan. 1946
17. *Daily Sketch*, 11 Dec. 1945
18. Minute by Lasky, 9 Oct. 1945, FO 371/48100
19. *The Times*, 19 Feb. 1946

43. AT THE COURT OF KING FAROUK

1. Ryan to Halifax, 14 Nov. 1938, FO 371/22305
2. Bethell p. 60
3. McLeave p. 214
4. Martini to Ryan, 1 July 1948, FO 371/72111
5. Cairo chancery to FO, 8 Oct. 1953, FO 371/107306
6. Sulzberger p. 442
7. Bethell p. 114

44. ANGLO-AMERICAN INTRIGUES

1. Bethell p. 12
2. Ibid. p. 61
3. Robyns p. 2; Dorril p. 379

4. Bethell p. 101
5. *New York Times*, 27 July 1951
6. Bethell p. 183
7. Jacques (1995) p. 455
8. Robyns pp. 156, 142
9. *New York Times*, 19 Sept. 1951
10. Robyns p. 159
11. Bocca p. 158
12. Robyns p. 144
13. Bocca p. 158

45. RIVIERA RECLUSE

1. Dodge pp. 121–2
2. Hoxha pp. 14, 263
3. Bocca pp. 12, 157, 162
4. Zog to Lloyd, 1 Aug. 1957, FO 371/130011
5. Robyns pp. 162, 11

46. EPILOGUE

1. Shakespeare p. 129
2. www.french-market.com/albania (7 Oct. 2002)
3. Rothschild p. 366
4. Glenny p. 149; Romero p. 212
5. Vlora vol. II p. 132
6. J. Brown p. 374
7. Dedet p. 376

Bibliography

Place of publication is London unless otherwise stated.

Agolli, D. *Mother Albania*, Tirana: 8 Nëntori Publishing House, 1985

Alastos, D. *The Balkans and Europe*, The Bodley Head, 1937

Alexandra, Queen of Yugoslavia, *For a King's Love*, Odhams, 1956

Amery, J. *Sons of the Eagle*, Macmillan, 1948

—— *Approach March*, Hutchinson, 1973

Anderson, I. *A Yacht in Mediterranean Seas*, Joiner & Steele, 1931

Backer, B. 'Mother, daughter, sister, wife – the Pillars of Traditional Albanian Patriarchal Society', in Bo Utas (ed.), *Women in Islamic Societies*, Curzon, 1983

Baerlein, H. *Under the Acroceraunian Mountains*, Leonard Parsons, 1922

Barnes, J.S. *Half a Life Left*, Eyre and Spottiswoode, 1937

Beaton, C. *The Years Between*, Weidenfeld & Nicolson, 1965

Benson, Hon. T. *The Unambitious Journey*, Chapman and Hall, 1935

Béraud, H. *Dictateurs d'Aujourdhui*, Paris: Flammarion 1933

Bernath, M. and Schroeder, F. *Biographisches Lexikon zur Geschichte Südosteuropas*, Munich: Oldenbourg, 1974–81

Bethell, N. *The Great Betrayal – The Untold Story of Kim Philby's Biggest Coup*, Hodder & Stoughton, 1984

Bocca, G. *The Uneasy Heads*, Weidenfeld & Nicolson, 1959

Bourcart, J. *L'Albanie et les Albanais*, Paris: Bossard, 1921

Brown, J.F. *Eastern Europe and Communist Rule*, Durham, North Carolina: Duke University Press, 1988

Brown, P. *Almost in Camera*, Hollis & Carter, 1944

Burgwyn, H.J. *Italian Foreign Policy in the Interwar Period 1918–1940*, Westport, Connecticut: Praeger, 1997

Burke's Royal Families of the World, Burke's Peerage, 1977

Busch-Zantner, R. *Albanien – Neues Land im Imperium*, Leipzig: Wilhelm Goldmann Verlag, 1939

Cassels, A. *Mussolini's Early Diplomacy*, Princeton, New Jersey: Princeton University Press, 1970

Charmley, J. *Chamberlain and the Lost Peace*, Hodder & Stoughton, 1989

Ciano, Count G. *Ciano's Diary 1939–1943*, Heinemann, 1947

—— *Ciano's Diplomatic Papers*, Odhams, 1948

—— *Ciano's Diary 1937–1938*, Methuen, 1952

Cripps, Hon. F.H. *Life's a Gamble*, Odhams, 1957

Currey, M. *Italian Foreign Policy 1918–1932*, Ivor Nicholson & Watson, 1932

Dako, C. *Zogu the First, King of the Albanians*, Tirana: Kristo Luarasi, 1937

Dedet, J. *Géraldine, Reine des Albanais*, Paris: Criterion, 1997

Diack, H. and Mackenzie, R.F. *Road Fortune*, Macmillan, 1935

Documents on German Foreign Policy Series D vol. VI, Her Majesty's Stationery Office, 1956

Dodge, D. *The Rich Man's Guide to the Riviera*, Cassell, 1963

Dorril, S. *MI6 – Fifty Years of Special Operations*, Fourth Estate, 2000

Durham, M.E. *Some Tribal Origins, Laws, and Customs of the Balkans*, George Allen & Unwin, 1928

Etherton, Lt.-Col. P.T. and Dunscombe Allen, A. *Through Europe and the Balkans – The Record of a Motor Tour*, Cassell, 1928

Fenyvesi, C. *Royalty in Exile*, Robson, 1981

ffoulkes, M. *All This Happened To Me*, Grayson, 1937

Fielding, X. *One Man in His Time: The Life of Lieutenant-Colonel N.L.D. ('Billy') McLean, DSO*, Macmillan, 1990

Fischer, B.J. *King Zog and the Struggle for Stability in Albania*, New York: Columbia University Press, 1984

——— *Albania at War 1939–1945*, Hurst, 1999

Forbes, R. *These Men I Knew*, The Right Book Club, 1940

——— *Appointment in the Sun*, Cassell, 1949

Foreign Relations of the United States 1939 vol. II, Washington: Government Printing Office, 1956

Frashëri, K. *The History of Albania*, Tirana, 1964

Fry, C.B. *Life Worth Living*, 2nd ed., Pavilion, 1986

Gárdos, M. *Magyar Királyné a Tiranai Trónon*, Budapest: Akadémiai Kiado, 1990

Gedye, G.E.R. *Heirs to the Habsburgs*, Arrowsmith, 1932

Gilbert, M. *Winston S. Churchill* vol.VII *The Road to Victory*, Heinemann, 1986

Glaise-Horstenau, E. (ed.) *Österreich-Ungarns Letzter Krieg 1914–18*, Vienna: Verlag der Militärwissenschaftlichen Mitteilungen, 1930–38

Glenny, M. *The Rebirth of History: Eastern Europe in the Age of Democracy*, Penguin, 1990

Grafftey-Smith, L. *Bright Levant*, John Murray, 1970

Gunther, J. *Inside Europe*, Hamish Hamilton, 1936

Hasluck, M. *The Unwritten Law in Albania*, Cambridge: Cambridge University Press, 1954

Heathcote, D. *My Wanderings in the Balkans*, Hutchinson, 1925

Herbert, A. *Ben Kendim*, Hutchinson, 1924

Heseltine, N. *Scarred Background*, Lovat Dickson, 1938

Hibbert, R. *Albania's National Liberation Struggle: The Bitter Victory*, Pinter, 1991

Holtz, W. (ed.) *Dorothy Thompson and Rose Wilder Lane – Forty Years of Friendship, Letters 1921–60*, Columbia: University of Missouri Press, 1991

Hoptner, J.B. *Yugoslavia in Crisis 1934–1941*, New York: Columbia University Press, 1962

Hoxha, E. *The Anglo-American Threat to Albania*, Tirana: 8 Nëntori Publishing House, 1982

Jacomoni, F. *La Politica dell'Italia in Albania*, Bologna: Capelli, 1965

Jacques, E.E. *The Furtherance and Afflictions of the Gospel: evangelism and intolerance in Albania 1935–40*, Wrexham: Albanian Evangelical Trust, 1988

—— *The Albanians: An Ethnic History from Prehistoric Times to the Present*, Jefferson, N. Carolina: McFarland, 1995

Kemp, P. *No Colours or Crest*, Cassell, 1958

Kent, P.C. *The Pope and the Duce – The International Impact of the Lateran Agreements*, Macmillan, 1981

Kinross, P. *Atatürk – The Rebirth of a Nation*, Weidenfeld, 1993

Kirkpatrick, Sir I. *Mussolini – Study of a Demagogue*, Odhams, 1964

Knox, M. *Mussolini Unleashed 1939–1941*, Cambridge: Cambridge University Press, 1982

Konitza, F. *Albania: The Rock Garden of Europe and Other Essays*, Boston: The Pan-Albanian Federation of America, 1957

—— *Selected Correspondence*, ed. by B. Destani, Centre for Albanian Studies, 2000

Kontos, J.F. *Red Cross, Black Eagle: A Biography of Albania's American School*, Boulder: Eastern European Monographs, 1981

Lauer, R. and Majer, H.G. (eds.) *Höfische Kultur in Südosteuropa*, Göttingen: Vandenhoeck & Ruprecht, 1994

League of Nations, *Verbatim Record of the Fifth Assembly*, Geneva 1924

Lees-Milne, J. *Diaries 1942–1945*, John Murray, 1995

Lessona, A. *Memorie* 2nd ed., Rome: Edizione Lessona, 1963

Luke, Sir H. *In the Margins of History*, Lovat Dickson, 1933

Lushaj, R. (ed.) *Oxhaku famëmadh Zogu* 2 vols., Tirana: Dardania, 1995

—— *Ahmet Zogu dhe Monarkia Shqiptare*, Tirana: Dardania, 1998

Lyall, A. *The Balkan Road*, Methuen, 1930

Macartney, M.H.H. and Cremona, P. *Italy's Foreign and Colonial Policy 1914–1937*, Oxford University Press, 1938

McCulloch, J.I.B. *Drums in the Balkan Night*, New York: Putnam's, 1936

McLeave, H. *The Last Pharaoh*, Michael Joseph, 1969

Mack Smith, D. *Mussolini*, Weidenfeld & Nicolson, 1981

Madol, H.R. *The League of London – A Book of Interviews with Allied Sovereigns and Statesmen*, Hutchinson, 1943

Matthews, R. 'Albania Faces the Future' *The Contemporary Review*, February 1935, vol. 147, pp. 218–26

—— *Sons of the Eagle*, Methuen, 1937

Mitchell, R. *The Serbs Choose War*, Garden City: Doubleday, 1943

Monroe, E. *The Mediterranean in Politics*, Oxford University Press, 1938

Montgomery, J.F. *Hungary – The Unwilling Satellite*, New York: Devin-Adair, 1947

Montgomery-Massingberd, H. and Watkin, D. *The London Ritz*, Aurum, 1980

Morris, R. *Distant Views from Sunninghill*, Ascot: The Durning Trust & Berkshire County Libraries, 1985

Bibliography

Moseley, R. *Mussolini's Shadow – The Double Life of Count Galeazzo Ciano*, New Haven: Yale University Press, 1999

Mousset, A. *L'Albanie devant l'Europe 1912–1929*, Paris: Librairie Delagrave, 1930

Najbor, P. *La dynastie des Zogu*, Paris: Textes & Prétextes, 2002

Newman, B. *Albanian Back-Door*, Herbert Jenkins, 1936

—— *Albanian Journey*, Pitman, 1938

Oakley-Hill, D.R. *An Englishman in Albania – Memoirs of a British Officer 1929–1955*, Centre for Albanian Studies, 2002

O'Doneven, E. *A Skillet of the Balkans*, Lymington: Charles King, 1932

Packard, R. and Packard, E. *Balcony Empire – Fascist Italy at War*, Chatto & Windus, 1943

Papel Hamsher, W. *The Balkans by Bicycle*, Witherby, 1937

Parliamentary Debates: House of Commons, Fifth Series.

Petrie, Sir C. *Lords of the Inland Sea: A Study of the Mediterranean Powers*, Lovat Dickson, 1937

Pettifer, J. *Albania – The Blue Guide*, A. & C. Black, 1994

Peyrefitte, R. *Diplomatic Conclusions*, Thames & Hudson, 1954

Pipa, A. 'Fan Noli as a National and International Figure' *Südost-Forschungen*, vol. 43, 1984, pp. 241–70

Pollo, S. and Puto, A. *The History of Albania*, Routledge & Kegan Paul, 1981

Powell, E.A. *Thunder over Europe*, New York: Ives Washburn, 1931

—— *Free-Lance*, Harrap, 1938

Puto, A. *From the Annals of British Diplomacy*, Tirana: 8 Nëntori Publishing House, 1981

Quaroni, P. *Diplomatic Bags – An Ambassador's Memoirs*, Weidenfeld & Nicolson, 1966

Redlich, Baron M.D.A.R. von *The Unconquered Albania*, Cincinnati: International Courier Publishing, 1935

Rey, L. *Guide de L'Albanie*, Paris, 1930

Robinson, V. *Albania's Road to Freedom*, Allen & Unwin, 1941

Robyns, G. *Geraldine of the Albanians*, Muller, Blond, and White, 1987

Romero, P. E. *Sylvia Pankhurst: Portrait of a Radical*, New York: Yale University Press, 1987

Roth, J. 'Beim Präsidenten Achmed Zogu', *Werke*, vol. 3, Cologne: Kiepenheuer & Witsch, 1976, pp. 1033–6

Rothschild, J. *East Central Europe between the Two World Wars*, Seattle: University of Washington Press, 1974

Roucek, J. 'Economic Conditions in Albania', *Economic Geography*, vol. 9, 1933, pp. 256–64

—— *The Politics of the Balkans*, New York: McGraw-Hill, 1939

Ryan, Sir A. *Last of the Dragomans*, Geoffrey Bles, 1951

Schmidt-Neke, M. *Entstehung und Ausbau der Königsdiktatur in Albanien 1912–1939*, Munich: Oldenbourg, 1987

Seton-Watson, C. *Italy from Liberalism to Fascism*, Methuen, 1967

Shakespeare, N. *The Men who would be King*, Sidgwick & Jackson, 1984

Slocombe, G. *The Dangerous Sea: The Mediterranean and its Future*, Hutchinson, 1936

Smiley, D. *Albanian Assignment*, Chatto & Windus, 1984

Stirling, Lt.-Col. W.F. *Safety Last*, Hollis & Carter, 1953

Sulzberger, C.L. *A Long Row of Candles – Memoirs and Diaries 1934–54*, Macdonald, 1969

Swire, J. *Albania – The Rise of a Kingdom*, Williams & Norgate, 1929

—— *King Zog's Albania*, Hale, 1937

Szinyei-Merse, A. de *Ten Years, Ten Months, Ten Days*, Hutchinson, 1940

Tocci, T. *Il Re degli Albanesi*, Milan: Mondadori, 1938

Toynbee, A. *Survey of International Affairs 1927*, Oxford: Oxford University Press, 1929

—— *Survey of International Affairs 1934*, Oxford: Oxford University Press, 1935

Traglia, G. *L'Albania di Re Zog*, Rome: Edizioni Tiber, 1930

Ushtelenca, I. *Diplomacia e Mbretit Zogu I-rë*, Tirana, 1995

Vanlande, R. *En Albanie sous l'oeil de Mussolini*, Paris: Peyronnet, 1933

Vickers, M. *The Albanians – A Modern History*, Taurus, 1995

Veith, G. 'Der Feldzug in Albanien', in M. Schwarte (ed.), *Der grosse Krieg 1914–1918*, vol. 4, Leipzig: Barth, 1922

Villari, L. *The Expansion of Italy*, Faber & Faber, 1930

Vlora, E. *Lebenserinnerungen*, 2 vols, Munich: Oldenbourg, 1968–73

Windischgraetz, Prince L. *My Memoirs*, Allen & Unwin, 1921

Xoxe, Z. (ed.) *10 vjet mbretni*, Tirana, 1938

Yeats-Brown, F. *European Jungle*, Eyre & Spottiswoode, 1939

Zamboni, G. *Mussolinis Expansionspolitik auf dem Balkan*, Hamburg: Helmut Buske Verlag, 1970

Ankara (Édition française)
La Bourse Égyptienne
Chicago Sun-Times
Daily Express
Daily Herald
Daily Mail
Daily Sketch
Daily Telegraph
Dielli
Evening News
Evening Standard
Il Giornale d'Italia
Illustrated London News
Korrieri

Bibliography

Manchester Guardian
Le Messager d'Athènes
Le Monde
The Near East and India
Neue Freie Presse
News Chronicle
News Review
New Times and Ethiopia News
New Yorker
New York Times
Picture Post
Royalty Digest
Sunday Dispatch
Sunday Pictorial
Time
The Times
Weekly Illustrated

Foreign Office general correspondence: Albania 1922–1957, Public Record Office, The National Archives, Kew
Gjenco Naçi collection, School of Slavonic and Eastern European Studies Library, University of London
Çatin P. Saraçi collection, Centre for Albanian Studies, London
www.french-market.com./albania/ – *Maison Royale d'Albanie* (7 October 2002)
Interview with Teri Cooper at Blandford St Mary, Dorset, 24 May 1997

Index

Index